W9-APH-491

Berkshire House's
Great Destinations™ travel guidebook series

Recommended by NATIONAL GEOGRAPHIC TRAVELER and TRAVEL & LEISURE magazines.

. . . a crisp and critical approach, for travelers who want to live like locals.

USA TODAY

Great Destinations™ guidebooks are known for their comprehensive, critical coverage of regions of extraordinary cultural interest and natural beauty. The authors in this series are professional travel writers who have lived for many years in the regions they describe. Each title in this series is continuously updated with each printing, in order to insure accurate and timely information. All of the books contain over 100 photographs and maps.

Neither the publisher, the authors, the reviewers, nor other contributors accept complimentary lodgings, meals, or any other consideration (such as advertising) while gathering information for any book in this series.

Current titles available:
The Adirondack Book
The Berkshire Book
The Charleston, Savannah & Coastal Islands Book
The Chesapeake Bay Book
The Coast of Maine Book
The Finger Lakes Book
The Hamptons Book
The Monterey Bay, Big Sur & Gold Coast Wine Country Book
The Nantucket Book
The Newport & Narragansett Bay Book
The Napa & Sonoma Book
The Santa Fe & Taos Book
The Sarasota, Sanibel Island & Naples Book
The Texas Hill Country Book
Touring East Coast Wine Country

If you are traveling to, moving to, residing in, or just interested in any (or all!) of these enchanting regions, a **Great Destinations**™ guidebook is a superior companion. Honest and painstakingly critical, full of information only a local can provide, **Great Destinations**™ guidebooks give you all the practical knowledge you need to enjoy the best of each region. Why not own them all?

To Gene and Theresa Koster,
who first instilled in me
a love for the road

THE SARASOTA, SANIBEL ISLAND & NAPLES BOOK

A Complete Guide

SECOND EDITION

Written by
CHELLE KOSTER WALTON

Photography by
KAREN T. BARTLETT

Berkshire House
Woodstock, Vermont

On the Cover and Frontispiece:
Front Cover: Naples Pier at twilight. Photo © Karen T. Bartlett.
Frontispiece: Palm trees on Marco Island. Photo © Karen T. Bartlett.
Back Cover: Author's photo by Karen T. Bartlett.

The Sarasota, Sanibel Island & Naples Book: A Complete Guide
Second Edition—2001
Copyright © 1993, 1998, 2001 by Berkshire House
Cover and interior photographs © 1993, 1998, 2001 by credited sources

Library of Congress Cataloging-in-Publication Data

Walton, Chelle Koster.
  The Sarasota, Sanibel Island & Naples book : a complete guide / written by Chelle Koster
  Walton ; photography by Karen T. Bartlett. – 2nd ed.
      p.   cm. — (Great destinations series, ISSN 1056-7968)
  Includes bibliographical references and indexes.
  ISBN 1-58157-051-1
  Includes bibliographical references and indexes.
  1. Gulf Coast (Fla.)—Guidebooks. 2. Sarasota Region (Fla.)—Guidebooks. 3. Sanibel Island
  (Fla.)—Guidebooks. 4. Naples Region (Fla.)—Guidebooks. 5. Charlotte Harbor Region
  (Fla.)—Guidebooks. I. Title: Sarasota, Sanibel Island, and Naples book. II. Title. III. Series.

  F317.G8 W36 2001
  917.59'4—dc21

                                                                                    2001025001

ISBN: 1-58157-051-1
ISSN: 1056-7968 (series)

Editor: Dale Evva Gelfand. Managing Editor: Philip Rich. Design and composition: Dianne Pinkowitz. Cover design and composition: Jane McWhorter. Index: Diane Brenner. Maps: Matt Paul/Yankee Doodles

Published by Berkshire House, an imprint of The Countryman Press,
P.O. Box 748, Woodstock, VT 05091
Distributed by W. W. Norton & Company, Inc., 500 Fifth Avenue, New York, NY 10110

Manufactured in the United States of America
10 9 8 7 6 5 4

No complimentary meals were accepted by the author/reviewer in gathering information for this work.

The
SARASOTA,
SANIBEL ISLAND
& NAPLES
Book
A Complete Guide

Karen T. Bartlett

Contents

CHAPTER ONE
Mangroves, Man, & Magnates
HISTORY
1

CHAPTER TWO
Blazing the Trail
TRANSPORTATION
26

CHAPTER THREE
Seashore Sophisticate
SARASOTA BAY COAST
38

CHAPTER FOUR
Wild and Watery
CHARLOTTE HARBOR COAST
118

CHAPTER FIVE
Sand, Shells, & Serenity
SANIBEL ISLAND & THE ISLAND COAST
154

CHAPTER SIX
Precious Commodities
NAPLES & THE SOUTH COAST
233

CHAPTER SEVEN
Practical Matters
INFORMATION
298

Acknowledgments

I can't list all of the people on whose patience and understanding I counted to see me through this project. First dibs on my gratitude must go to my husband, Rob, for not divorcing me, and my son, Aaron, who helped particularly with my beach and "kids' stuff" research. Thanks to Ron and Mindy Koster, who visited during my most intense stretch of writing-under-deadline, and helped out in many ways.

Special thanks to Prudy Taylor Board, who checked up on my historical facts and who will no doubt cringe at the pirate legends I couldn't bring myself to omit. Thanks to Amy Ligon, who spent hours on the phone doing the nitty-gritty final fact-checking.

Nancy Hamilton at the Lee County Visitor & Convention Bureau and Kelly Yatcko at the Sarasota Convention & Visitors Bureau have been particularly helpful. Beth Preddy, a personal friend and travel industry colleague, always provides me with insights and assistance when it comes to Naples research.

Thanks to photographer Karen Bartlett, who contributed creative energy to the project, and to my supportive editors at Berkshire House: Dale Gelfand and Philip Rich. You all helped me to extract the inherent agony of guidebook detail work and to make this book a joyful undertaking.

Introduction

Morning dawns like a boater's dream. The sky is clear except for a trace of last night's moon: wispy, like a wadded-up cloud. The water stretches like pulled-taut cellophane between Sanibel and Pine Islands. It is a morning to wonder why one ever does anything else on days off but return to the sea. On cue, a family of three dolphins pierces the surface with their fins and their smiles. The show has begun.

In the course of our leisurely, two-hour cruise between Sanibel Island and Boca Grande, we are entertained by leaping stingrays, a school of mackerel, and the usual dive-bomb squadron of brown pelicans.

At lights-out call — after lunch in a marina-side fish house, beach time on an unbridged island, and a duck-the-afternoon-rains cocktail at a historic island inn — nature's revue reaches its spectacular finale. In the moonless dark, the wake behind our boat sparkles like a watery fireworks display. The gulf has thrown an electric breaker switch. Liquid lightning strikes all around us as our 21-foot Mako powerboat parts the seas. White caps puff like nuclear popcorn.

Scientists call the phenomena *dinoflagellates*. Lay folks call the glowing organisms phosphorescence. Jamaicans call them sea-blinkies. The Ancient Mariner called them death-fires. I call their unpredictable visits to our summer waters magic: a topsy-turvy, ethereal feeling that someone — without warning — has transformed the sea into a starry sky.

Such a perfect day isn't required in order to appreciate fully this inimitable slice of Gulf Coast of Florida, but such days do help to remind me why I moved here from long-john land 20 years ago. Like so many who constitute our hodge-podge population, I escaped, I loved, I dug in. I stayed for the exotic, warm quality of tropical nature. I remain because of the miracles I discover — and watch my young son discover — every day.

Chelle Koster Walton
Sanibel Island, Florida

THE WAY THIS BOOK WORKS

ORGANIZATION

The area bounded on the north by the Braden River and on the south by Ten Thousand Islands is often lumped under the heading Southwest Florida. Sometimes the Bradenton-Sarasota area is omitted from the region this heading defines, and grouped otherwise with Tampa as Central West Florida. For the purpose of this guide, it is included. The book often refers to the region covered as Gulf Coast Florida, or West Coast Florida, although it, of course, does not cover the entire coast. It does cover in depth the cities, towns, and communities from Bradenton-Sarasota in the north to Naples-Marco Island and the Everglades in the south.

I have sliced this delectable pie into four geographical region chapters, north to south: Sarasota Bay Coast, Charlotte Harbor Coast, Island Coast, and South Coast. Within these chapters, I scan under separate headings each region's lodging, dining, culture, recreation, and shopping.

Other chapters deal with the coastline's history as a whole, transportation, and nitty-gritty information.

A series of indexes at the back of the book provides easy access to information. The first, a standard index, lists entries and subjects in alphabetical order. Next, hotels, inns, and resorts are categorized by price. Restaurants are organized in two separate indexes: one by price, one by type of cuisine.

LIST OF MAPS

The Gulf Coast of Florida
Gulf Coast Access Maps
Sarasota Bay Coast
Charlotte Harbor Coast
Island Coast
South Coast

PRICES

R ather than give specific prices, this guide rates dining and lodging options within a range.

Lodging prices normally are based on per person/double occupancy for hotel rooms; per unit for efficiencies, apartments, cottages, suites, and villas. Price ranges reflect the difference in off-season and high season (generally, Christmas through Easter). Generally, the colder the weather up north, the higher the cost of accommodations along the coast. Rates can double during the course of a year. Many resorts offer off-season packages at special rates.

Pricing does not include the 6 percent Florida sales tax. Many large resorts add gratuities or maid charges. Some counties impose a tourist tax as well, proceeds from which are applied to beach and environmental maintenance.

If rates seem high for rooms on the Gulf Coast, it's partially because many resorts cater to families by providing kitchen facilities. Take into consideration what this could save you on dining bills. A star after the pricing designation indicates that accommodations include at least continental breakfast with the cost of lodging; a few offer the American Plan of serving all meals, which is then explained within the description copy.

Dining costs are calculated upon a typical meal (at dinner, unless dinner is not served) that would include an appetizer or dessert, salad (if included with the meal), entrée, and coffee. To save money at the more expensive restaurants, look in this guide to see which ones offer "early bird specials." Restaurants at some large resorts add gratuities to the tab. This is also customary for large parties at most restaurants, so check your bill carefully before leaving a tip. Satisfied diners are expected to tip between 15 and 20 percent.

Heavy state taxes on liquor served in-house can mount up a drinking tab quickly. Paying as you drink is a wise measure to prevent sticker shock.

PRICE CODES

Lodging	Dining	
Inexpensive	Up to $75	Up to $15
Moderate	$75 to $150	$15 to $25
Expensive	$150 to $200	$25 to $35
Very Expensive	$200 and up	$35 or more

The following abbreviations are used for credit card information:

AE - American Express   DC - Diners Card
CB - Carte Blanche   MC - MasterCard
D - Discover Card   V - Visa

AREA CODE

The area code for the Sarasota Bay Coast and the Charlotte Harbor Coast (with the exception of Boca Grande and Placida) is **941**. The area code for Boca Grande and Placida, and for all points south — Sanibel Island and the Island Coast, Naples and the South Coast — is **239**.

Numbers prefixed with 800-, 888-, 866-, and 877- are toll free.

TOURIST INFORMATION

Local visitors' bureaus, tourism development councils, and chambers of commerce are adept at the dissemination of materials and information about their area. These are listed in Chapter Seven, *Information*.

For information on the entire region and other parts of Florida, contact Visit Florida, 661 E. Jefferson St., Suite 300, Tallahassee, FL 32301; 800-7FLA-USA; www.flausa.com.

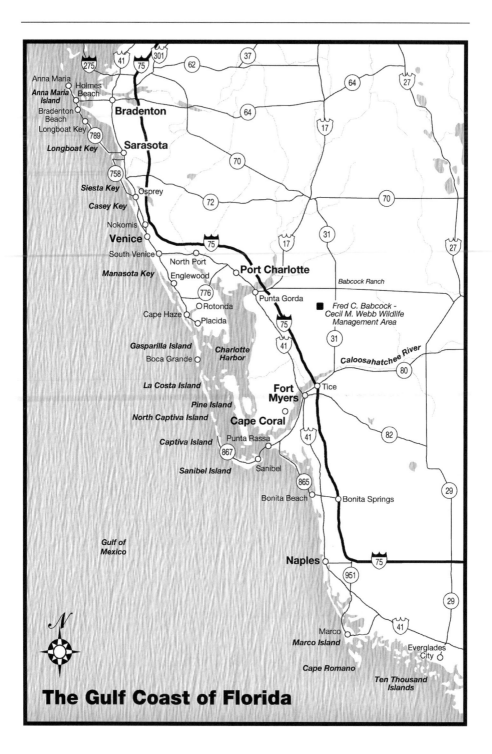

The Gulf Coast of Florida

CHAPTER ONE
Mangroves, Man, & Magnates
HISTORY

Karen T. Bartlett

Once an Indian trading post, Smallwood's Story today serves as a museum in the secluded Everlades outpost of Chokoloskee Island.

The essence of Gulf Coast Florida seems to be a balance of polar extremes: the ultimate in both natural wilderness and social civility. To understand the region and the richness of its heritage, culture, and environment, one must understand its roots, learn the names, and revel in the legends of its past — a past steeped in romance, adventure, and power.

The story begins with a single mangrove tree and evolves around man's need to conquer that tree's primeval world. Enter the characters: Ambition, Wealth, and Social Grace. How does the story end? Happily, we can hope, with the modern rediscovery of the coast's unique natural and historical heritage.

Islands continue to grow along Florida's fringes.

Karen T. Bartlett

NATURAL HISTORY

FROM GRAINS OF SAND

Each wave helps build a ridge of accumulating sand and shell that runs roughly parallel to the beach. Over a period of hundreds or thousands of years, a ridge may become a barrier island.

— Lynn Stone, Voyageurs Series,
Sanibel Island, 1991

On the floor is a straw mat. Under the mat is a layer of sand that has been tracked into the cottage and has sifted through the straw. I have thought some of taking the mat up and sweeping the sand into a pile and removing it, but have decided against it. This is the way keys form, apparently, and I have no particular reason to interfere.

— E. B. White, *On a Florida Key*, 1941

Billions of years ago, the Florida peninsula existed only as a scattering of volcanic keys, akin to the Caribbean islands. The passing years, silt, and the sea's power eventually buried all evidence of these volcanic origins. What is now Florida remained submerged until some 20 million years ago, when matter buildup brought land to the surface in the form of new islands.

Ice Age sea fluctuations molded Florida into solid land, and islands continued to grow along its fringes. From a single grain of sand or a lone mangrove sprout they stabilized into masses of sand and forests composed of leggy roots and finger shoots. As shells and marine encrustations accumulated, islands fell into formation along the Gulf Coast, protecting it from the battering of a storm-driven sea. In the gaps between the islands, the gulf's waters scoured the shore to forge inlets, estuaries, bayous, creeks, and rivers. The sea chiseled a mottled, labyrinthine shoreline that kept the southern Gulf Coast a secret while the rest of the state was being tamed.

Giant armadillos roamed prehistoric Florida. Their ancestors still scavenge for insects by night.

Karen T. Bartlett

During its infancy, the region hosted a slow parade of ever-changing creatures. In prehistoric graveyards modern archaeologists have found mummified remains of rhinoceroses, crocodiles, llamas, camels, pygmy horses, saber-toothed tigers, mastodons, and great woolly mammoths — Florida's first winter visitors at the advent of the Ice Age. Another era brought giant armadillos, tapirs, and other South American creatures. Fauna and flora from these ancient eras survive today: cabbage palms (the state tree), saw palmettos, garfish, seahorses, horseshoe crabs, alligators, manatees, armadillos, and loggerhead sea turtles.

The Miracle of the Mangrove

The mangrove forest is both a fertile incubator and a marine graveyard, the home of an island construction crew and a vegetative ballet troupe. It is a self-sustaining world marked by vivid contrasts. The Mangrove Coast (as one local historian terms it) is riddled with red, black, and white species of the tree. Red mangroves strut along mainland coastlines, canals, and the leeward sides of islands on graceful prop roots — or at least they look graceful until low tide reveals the oysters, barnacles, and tiny marine metropolises that weigh them down and keep them connected to the sea.

Farther inland, black and white mangroves create thick, impenetrable forests that buffer waves, filter pollutants, send out shoots, and always busily build. Encrustations of shellfish grab algae, silt, and sand, creating rich soil out of decaying material. Fish, crabs, and mollusks skitter among the roots, nibbling dinner, depositing eggs, and tending to their young. Birds rest and nest in the mangroves' scraggly branches, ready to dive for the fish on which they feed. Mother trees send their tubular offspring bobbing upon sea currents to find a foothold elsewhere and begin, perhaps, a new island.

The cycle is ancient and ongoing, threatened only by the chain saws of developers. A few decades ago these natural builders were leveled in favor of cement seawalls. Today, strict regulations prohibit mangrove destruction. The crucial role of the mangrove in the survival of Florida's sea life finally has been realized. And cherished.

AN EARLY PICTURE

*In the bay of Juan Ponce De Leon, in the west side of the land, we meet with innu-
merable small islands, and several fresh streams: the land in general is drowned mangrove swamp. . . . From this place [Cape Romano, latitude 25:43] to latitude 26:30 are
many inconsiderable inlets, all carefully laid down in the chart, here is Carlos Bay, and
the Coloosa Hatchee, or Coloosa river, with the island San Ybell, where we find the
southern entrance of Charlotte harbour. . . .*

— Bernard Romans, 1775

One of the earliest recorders of Florida native life and topography, Bernard
Romans is credited with naming Charlotte Harbor after the queen of his
adopted homeland, England, and Cape Romano after himself. Native
Americans and earlier Spanish explorers are responsible for other regional
place names.

The harbor was already the center of west coast life when the first explorers
discovered it. Its deep waters and barrier-island protection created a pocket of
unusually mild climate, attracting early aborigines and their descendants.

Romans and his contemporaries found the Gulf Coast alive with wild
turkeys, black bears, deer, golden panthers, bobcats, possums, raccoons, alligators, otters, lizards, and snakes. Wild boars and scrub cattle roamed freely,
descendants of stock brought by Spanish missionaries. Land birds and waterfowl of all varieties filled the skies and back bays, some permanent, some
migratory. Majestic ospreys and bald eagles swooped; kites soared effortlessly;
sandhill cranes dotted the countryside; wood storks nested; pelicans came in
colors of brown and white; gulls, terns, and sandpipers patrolled seashores;
cormorants, ducks, anhingas, ibises, egrets, roseate spoonbills, and herons fed
among the mangroves.

Marine life flourished. Manatees cleared waterways, dolphins frolicked in the
waves, and mullet burst from bay waters like cannon-shot. Tarpon, rays, snapper, snook, flounder, ladyfish, and mackerel churned the otherwise calm backwaters. Grouper, tripletail, tuna, and shark lurked in deep waters offshore.

On land a wide variety of vegetation abounded. Sea grapes, mahoes, sea
oats, nickerbeans, and railroad vines anchored sandy coasts. Thick, impenetrable jungles clogged inland areas. Cabbage palms and gumbo-limbo trees stood
tall. Native papayas flourished along with indigenous flowering shrubs. In
hardwood forests pines climbed skyward, and live oaks wore their eerie veils
of Spanish moss. Cedars fringed islands along the Sarasota Bay coast. Ferns
and grasses carpeted the marshes. Swamplands were home to great cypress
trees with bony knees and armfuls of parasitic mistletoe and epiphytic orchids
and bromeliads.

Primeval and teeming, Florida held an exotic and mysterious aura. The
swamp nurtured all of life, from the Everglades upward along the lowlands of
the Gulf Coast. It was a perfect ecosystem, designed by nature to withstand all
forces — except man.

The juicy mango was introduced into Florida by naturalists and growers.

Karen T. Bartlett

FACE-LIFTS AND IMPLANTS

With the arrival of the first settlers, the natural balance that existed along the Gulf Coast began to tilt. The Spanish brought citrus seedlings and livestock. Naturalists and growers introduced specimens from the north and south: mangoes, avocados, bougainvillea, hibiscus, frangipani, coconut palms, pineapples, sapodillas, tomatoes, and legumes. For the most part these exotics proved harmless to the fragile environment.

Three nonnative plants brought to the area in the past century have, however, harmed the ecosystem and changed the profile of the land. The prolific melaleuca tree (or cajeput), casuarina (Australian pine), and Brazilian pepper choke out the native vegetation upon which wildlife feed and harm both man and property. Many communities are attempting to eradicate these noxious plants, particularly the pepper tree.

The complexion of the west coast was further changed by dredging and plowing. In times when swampland was equated with slimy monsters and slick realtors, developers and governments thought nothing of filling it in to create more buildable land. This, too, threw the ecosystem off balance. Fortunately, such mistakes were recognized before their effects became irreversible. Today government strives to preserve, even restore, the delicate balance of the wetlands.

SOCIAL HISTORY

DATELINE: GULF COAST FLORIDA

The modern settlement of Florida's southwest coast can be traced like a dateline that begins on the shores of Sarasota Bay in 1841 and ends at

Naples in 1887. At first glance this time frame makes the region look young, without the gracious patina of age and the wrinkles of an interesting past. Common is the belief, in fact, that the Gulf Coast has no history because it lacks Williamsburg's colonial homes or Philadelphia's monuments.

True, the Gulf Coast's early pioneers left no standing architecture. Termites, flimsy building styles, erosion, and tropical storms saw to that. But earlier settlers did leave other proof of their existence, artifacts that date as far back as 10,000 years. If that isn't history, what is?

CALUSA KINGDOM

Archaeologists of this century have discovered remnants of early architecture and lifeways in the shell mounds of the Calusa and Timucua tribes, who settled the coastlines more than 2,500 years ago. The Timucua inhabited the Sarasota Bay coast for many years and then migrated northward and to the east; the Calusa later moved into the area around Sarasota and were centered around Charlotte Harbor.

Evidence of earlier even civilizations has been found, placing Florida's first immigrants, possibly from Asia, in the upper coast regions circa 8200 BC. Little is known about these early arrivals except that they used pointed spears.

Archaeological excavations and the writings of Spanish explorers give us a more complete picture of the Calusa and other tribes, who built shell mounds to bury their dead and debris. Learned consensus brings the Calusa and the Timucua to southern Florida from the Caribbean islands — evidence of similar lifestyles and sustained contact suggests a connection to the peaceful Arawak Indians of the West Indies. Similarities have also been found between the Calusa and South American tribes, leading some historians to consider Florida's tribes to be wayward relatives of the Mayans or Aztecs, given the indications of their great engineering skills. Others trace the connections to trade rather than origin.

The name Calusa, or Caloosa, was used first by Spanish conquerors, who understood the name of the tribe's chief to be Calos. They were said to be tall people with hip-length hair that men wore in a topknot. When clothed, men dressed in breeches of deerskin or woven palmetto fiber, and women fashioned garments out of Spanish moss. They cultivated corn, pumpkins, squash, and tobacco; fished for mullet and mackerel with harpoons and palmetto-fiber nets; hunted for turkey, deer, and bear with bow and arrow, deer-bone dirks, and Aztec-style weapons; and harvested wild sea grapes, fruit, yams, swamp cabbage (hearts of palm), and the coontie root, out of which they pounded flour for bread. Conch and whelk shells were crafted into tools for building and cooking. The natives spent their leisure time wrestling, celebrating the corn harvest, and worshiping the sun god.

Great men of the sea, the Calusa built canoes and traveled in them to Caribbean islands and the Yucatán. A different style of pirogue took them along riverways and bay waters to visit villages of their own tribe and those of other Nations.

Much of our information about the Calusa comes from the son of a Spanish official stationed in Cartagena, in what is now Colombia. The youngster, Hernando de Escalante Fontaneda, was shipwrecked along Calusa shores en route to Spain. He lived among the tribe for 17 years, learned its language, and, upon returning to Spain in 1574, recorded its customs. In 1895 Frank Hamilton Cushing explored Charlotte Harbor's Amerindian heritage. He surmised that the Calusa's religious structures and palmetto piling homes had perched on shell mounds along riverbanks and coastlines. Terraces and steps bit into the towering mounds where gardens and courts had been built. Manmade canals up to 30 feet wide connected neighboring villages. Pine Island, Mound Key, and Marco Island were important religious and governmental centers for the Calusa.

Excavations along the Gulf Coast continually provide new information about the region's native inhabitants and their symbiotic relationship with nature.

SPANISH IMPOSITION

Early Florida explorers encountered savage beauty on Gulf Coast shores.

Karen T. Bartlett

Greed and religious fervor eventually warped this idyllic picture, and peaceful fishermen became vicious warriors in order to preserve the life they knew. Juan Ponce de León first crashed the party in 1513. It's possible that early slavers from the Caribbean were responsible for the Calusa hostility he encountered, or perhaps the Amerindians' early hatred of the *conquistadores* was gained secondhand, from trading with island natives. Whatever the reason, Ponce was "blacklisted" by the Calusa shortly after he began his search, according to legend, for Bimini, a storied land of treasure and youth.

Ponce de León made his first landing on Florida's east coast. This celebrated Eastertime event went off without a hitch, and the conqueror named the land after the Spanish holiday Pascua Florida. However, his second landing, days later, was met by shell-tipped spears and bows and arrows. His three wounded sailors were the first Europeans known to shed blood in Florida. Ponce de León's ship continued to the west coast, where it stopped in the vicinity of Marco Island. Here one native astounded him by speaking to him in Spanish — learned, perhaps, from West Indies contacts. Impressed, Ponce de León allowed his party to be tricked by a marauding native army in canoes but escaped with the loss of only one man's life.

Still treasureless and now middle-aged, Ponce de León returned to Puerto Rico — after several trips to Florida and the Gulf Coast — to plot a new scheme. In 1521 he set out to establish a Gulf Coast colony as a base for treasure explorations. This time the party he crashed had been forewarned, possibly by smoke signals. Calusa arrows pierced the heavy armor of the Spaniards, killing and wounding many, including the great seeker of youth himself. Returned to Havana for medical attention, Ponce de León died there at the age of 60.

Lust for gold overcame common sense as more explorers and invaders followed in Ponce de León's tragic footsteps. In 1539 Hernando de Soto sailed from Havana and headed up the Gulf Coast, seeking, it would seem, a way to confuse future historians. Three different crewmen described the expedition three different ways. The Smithsonian Institution has published a report some locals still dispute, which claims that de Soto landed first on Longboat Key and then, looking for fresh water, headed toward Tampa Bay. Others are convinced that his first landfall was at Fort Myers Beach. De Soto set up his first mainland camp, according to the Smithsonian, at an abandoned native village at the mouth of the Manatee River, near modern-day Bradenton. Regardless of where the landing took place, we know that de Soto scoured the coast for gold, all the while torturing and killing native Americans who would not, or could not, lead him to it.

Sarasota and its environs embrace the Smithsonian study's findings. Some say the name of the town itself, initially written as "Sara Sota," comes from the conqueror. Others prefer a more romantic legend regarding his fictional daughter, Sara. Sarasota's first hotel, in any case, took its name from de Soto. Near Bradenton, a small national park marks the alleged spot of his first landing.

In 1565 Pedro Menendez de Aviles came to the Gulf Coast, searching for a son lost to shipwreck and a group of Spaniards being held captive by the Calusa. With the aid of one of Chief Calos's Spanish captives, he befriended Calos with flattery and gifts, then built a fort and a mission at a spot called San Anton, believed to have been on Pine Island. But Menendez insulted the great chieftain by rejecting his sister as a wife and allying himself with enemy tribes. Sensing Calos's anger, Menendez tricked the leader into captivity and had him beheaded. When Menendez later executed Calos's son and heir to the throne, along with 11 of his subchiefs, tribesmen burned their own villages, forcing the settlers to bail out in search of food.

The century that followed is considered the Golden Age of the Calusa. It was marked by freedom from European intrusion and great cultural advances, heightened by the contribution of Spanish captives who had refused to be saved by Menendez's rescue party and others who found Calusa ways preferable to "civilization."

Eventually, peaceful trading softened the hostility between Spanish settlers and the Calusa. Cuban immigrants began building a fishing industry around Charlotte Harbor. But although the Calusa had won the war against Spanish invaders, they were defenseless against the diseases the Europeans brought with them. By the turn of the 19th century, smallpox and other diseases had killed off most of them; the remainder were absorbed by inbreeding with the Cubans and newly arriving tribes. The most prominent of the latter were the Seminole — a name meaning "wanderer" — a mixture of Georgian Creek, African, and Spanish bloodlines.

THE VARMINT ERA

"A haunt of the picaroons of all nations," wrote explorer James Grant Forbes in 1772, referring to Charlotte Harbor — layover, if not home, for every scoundrel who sailed its island-clotted waters. The Gulf Coast's maze of forbidding bayous and barely navigable waterways made it a favorite hideout for escaped criminals, bootleggers, government refugees, smugglers, and — that most popular of all local folk characters — the buccaneer.

Pirate legends color the pages of regional history books in shades of blood red and doubloon gold. Besides willing to residents a certain cavalier spirit, these pirates have left, if one believes the tales, millions of dollars in buried treasure. "After researching the subject in 1950 . . . then State Attorney General Ralph E. Odum estimated that some $165 million is still buried beneath Florida's sands and waters," reported a 1978 issue of the *Miami Herald's Florida Almanac*, "$30 million of it originally the property of Jose Gaspar."

Besides the mostly mythical Gaspar, other picaresque names resound along the Gulf Coast: Jean La Fitte, of New Orleans fame; Bru Baker, Gaspar's Pine Island cohort; and a dark soul named Black Caesar. Henry Castor supposedly buried treasure on Egmont Key in the mid-1700s. Local legend places the notorious Calico Jack Rackham and his pirate lover, Anne Bonny, on the shores of Fort Myers Beach for a playful honeymoon. Black Augustus lived and died a hermit on Mound Key, to the south. On Panther Key, John Gomez, Gaspar's self-proclaimed cabin boy, lived to be 122 and sold maps purportedly leading to Gasparillan gold to many a gullible treasure hunter.

According to more reliable historical records, island pirate havens were replaced by, or coexisted with, crude Spanish fishing ranchos, which cropped up as early as the 1600s. The camps provided Cuban traders with salted mullet and roe to eat. They consisted of thatched shacks, some built on pilings in shallow waters, where families lived, according to customs inspector Henry B. Crews, "in a state of Savage Barbarism with no associate but the Seminole Indians and the lowest class of refugee Spaniards who from crime have most generally been compelled to abandon the haunts of civilized life."

Ice-making and railroads changed the direction of fish exportation from southern points to northern destinations. Punta Gorda, with the area's first railroad station, became the center for the transshipment of fresh fish. Major fish-shipping companies built stilt houses for the more than 200 men who harvested their mullet crops. These structures straddled shallows from Charlotte Harbor to Ten Thousand Islands, providing homes for the fishermen and their families until the late 1930s, when modern roads and the burning of Punta Gorda's Long

---

Kingdom of Gasparilla

Of all the rum-chugging and throat-slashing visitors to have set foot upon southwest Florida's tolerant shores, José Gaspar (known by the more properly pirate-sounding name "Gasparilla") is the one remembered most fondly. Gaspar set up headquarters, it is said, on Gasparilla Island, where Boca Grande now sits. In his time it was called High Town. He built a palmetto palace there and furnished it with the finest booty. Low Town he placed on a separate island, so as to distance himself from the crude lifestyles of his rowdy shipmates. On Cayo Costa stood Gasparilla's fort.

Legends say Gasparilla got his start as a pirate after some nasty business with the wife of a crown prince. He gave up his cushy position as admiral of the Spanish navy for the hardships of life at sea and in the jungles of late-18th-century Florida.

His address might have changed, but his love of beautiful women did not. He kidnapped the fairest and wealthiest of them from captured ships and whisked them off to another Gulf Coast island named for its inhabitants — Captiva — until ransom money arrived. Gasparilla took to High Town the most beautiful of his captives, to woo them with fine wines, jewels, and Spanish poetry. One object of his affection, a Mexican princess named Joséfa, would have nothing to do with such a barbarian. Finally, driven to madness by her insults, Gasparilla beheaded his beloved. He carried her body to another key in his island fiefdom, where he buried her with remorse and sand. He named the island Joséfa, which, through the years and the twistings of rum-swollen tongues, has been perverted to Useppa. And so the exclusive island is called today.

Nearby Sanibel Island, according to one legend, got its name from the abandoned lover of Gaspar's gunner. However, variations abound and improve with each telling. The legend began with the ramblings of old "Panther Key John" Gomez and was perpetuated by railroad press agents and optimistic treasure hunters.

Serious historians doubt the existence of a man named Gasparilla but concede that one of the many Gulf Coast pirates might have borrowed the island's name. Others hold tenaciously to the legend, plying coastal sands with shovels and dredges in search of his ill-gotten booty.

Dock brought the era to a close. Fewer than a dozen of the historic fish shacks have survived hurricanes, erosion, and the state's determination to tear them down as a public nuisance. They strut the shallows of Charlotte Harbor, in greatest concentration off the shore of Upper Captiva Island.

"It is highly important that no person should be permitted to settle on the Islands forming 'Charlotte Harbor' . . . which are of no value for the purpose of agriculture, being in general formed of sand and shells," advised Assistant Adjutant General Captain Lorenzo Thomas in 1844. Nonetheless, out of this era of varmints sprouted a tradition of farming. Coconuts, citrus, tomatoes, and other crops were raised, despite hardship and heartbreak, as plucky pioneers trickled in to coax their livelihood from a hostile environment.

YEARS OF DISCONTENT

The story of Chief Billy Bowlegs finds an audience along Venice's main thoroughfare.

Karen T. Bartlett

The bloody years of the Wars of Indian Removal began in 1821, when Andrew Jackson, then governor of the territory, decided to claim northern Florida from the Seminole tribes that were wreaking havoc on American settlers. By 1837 fighting had spread to the southern reaches of the peninsula, and two forts were built upriver from present-day Fort Myers. The following year the government reached an agreement with the Seminoles, restricting them to mainland areas along the Charlotte Harbor coast, the Caloosahatchee River, and southward.

News of imminent peace prompted Josiah Gates to build a hotel on the banks of the Manatee River, near modern-day Bradenton, in anticipation of the influx of settlers from Fort Brooke (Tampa) that the treaty would bring. A modest community rose up around this precursor of southwest Florida resorts. Families of soldiers and wealthy southern planters settled in the area. The latter brought their slaves and built sugarcane plantations on vast expanses of land that they bought for $1.25 an acre.

Sarasota got its first permanent settler in 1842 when William Whitaker, a fisherman, built his home on Yellow Bluff, overlooking Sarasota Bay. He and his new wife, daughter of one of the Manatee planters, had 10 children and later went into cattle ranching and farming. The year after the peace treaty was signed, a tribe of Seminoles attacked a settlement across the river from their village, on the same site as present-day Fort Myers. The Harney Point Massacre rekindled the war. Fort Harvie was built near the site of the violent attack. Chief Billy Bowlegs led his people in evasive tactics through the wild and mysterious Everglades, but by 1842 the government had captured 230 of his people and shipped them west. Further pursuit was abandoned. Only Fort Harvie and one other fortification remained operational. A new agreement contained the Seminoles along the Caloosahatchee and barred them from the islands, to protect the fishermen and their families. The treaty made no mention of the swampland, probably because the government considered it useless; the Seminoles assumed the territory was theirs.

By 1848, three years after Florida's admission to the Union as the 27th state, there was a surge of interest in the wetlands. The government, envisioning drainage projects to create more land, offered the Seminoles $250 each to relocate in the West. When they refused, a systematic plan to conquer them went into effect.

The plan included the repair of Fort Harvie, which was renamed Fort Myers after a U.S. colonel who had served for many years in Florida and was engaged to the commanding general's daughter. Manpower was increased there, and the fort was reinforced and enlarged. Scouting parties stalked the Seminoles but usually found only the remains of abandoned and burned villages when they arrived.

In December 1855, after soldiers destroyed Chief Billy Bowlegs's prize banana patch, the Seminole and his people retaliated. Fort Myers became the center of war activity. The government placed a bounty on the head of any Seminole brought to the fort and offered $1,000 to each Seminole warrior ($100 to each woman and child) who agreed to leave the area. Finally in 1858, after soldiers had captured his granddaughter and other women of the tribe, Billy Bowlegs capitulated, thus bringing an end to 37 years of killing and deception by the government and the military. Fort Myers was abandoned, and the remaining Seminole dispersed deep into the Everglades. Farmers, planters, fishermen, and cattlemen continued peacefully in their trades, although government vigilance against alliances with the Seminole forced some of the *ranchos* to close during the war's final years. Today the Seminole live on reservations, earning an income from tourism, fishing, and casinos.

In the late 1850s, Virginia planter Captain James Evans bought Fort Myers on the auction block. He brought in his slaves to work the crops he envisioned — tropical fruits, coconut palms, coffee, and other exotic plants. The Civil War interrupted this venture, sending him back to his home. Florida joined the Confederacy in 1861. West coast inhabitants generally remained uninvolved until a federal blockade at Key West cut off supplies, at which point they turned to the profitable business of blockade running.

CATTLE KINGS, CARPETBAGGERS, AND CRACKERS

Jacob Summerlin epitomized the Florida cattle king. He dressed in a floppy hat, leather boots, and trail dust. Having established a steady trade between Florida and ports south before the Civil War, Summerlin was in a good position to provide the Confederate Army with contraband beef. Working with his blockade-running partner, James McKay, Sr., he drove his cattle from inland Florida to Punta Rassa, where the causeway from Sanibel Island makes landfall today. There he sold his scrub cattle, descendants of livestock left by the early Spaniards. The U.S. Navy eventually learned of these illegal dealings and stationed boats at Sanibel and Punta Rassa. In spite of this attempt to thwart their trade, however, Summerlin and McKay sold 25,000 steers to the Confederates between 1861 and 1865.

Jake Summerlin lived by the seat of his pants, driving cattle to Punta Rassa and collecting big bags of Cuban gold, which he spent at the end of the line on drinking and gaming. In 1874 he built the Summerlin House at Punta Rassa, where he and his men could bunk and invest the profits of the business in frivolity.

The rough, free-and-easy lifestyle of the cow hunter attracted young post-Civil War drifters. In addition, Summerlin's success lured Civil War officers into the prosperous life of the cattle boss, including Captain F. A. Hendry, founder of an ongoing Fort Myers dynasty. Between 1870 and 1880 stockmen sold 165,000 head of cattle at Punta Rassa for over $2 million. Into the 1900s, the cow hunters drove their herds through the streets of downtown Fort Myers, past the homes of wealthy investors and bankers.

Reconstruction brought other settlers to Florida's west coast. Judah P. Benjamin, one notable rebel refugee who served as secretary of state in the Confederacy, ducked indictment as a war criminal by hiding out in Florida. His week-long refuge at the old Gamble plantation near Bradenton ensured the landmark's preservation by the United Daughters of the Confederacy.

The first postwar visitors to Fort Myers were the vultures who picked the fort clean of coveted building materials. Then came men who remembered the old fort in its heyday and hoped to settle with their families in this land of plenty. The first settler, Captain Manuel A. Gonzalez, had run a provisions boat from Tampa during the Seminole War. He and his family moved from Key West with another family named Vivas. Other war officers and refugees settled in and around the ruins of the old fort, planting gardens, opening stores, and living a blissful existence unknown elsewhere in the devastated South.

Captain James Evans returned to Fort Myers from Virginia to find his land comfortably occupied. After struggling in the courts to keep the land out of government hands, he split it with the squatters in exchange for a share of his legal fees. In 1872 the first school in Fort Myers was built. County government was centered 270 miles away, in Key West.

Some historians credit the cow hunters with contributing the name "Cracker" to early Florida settlers. They say it derives from the cracking of the long whips men used to drive their herds. Others say it originated with the Georgia settlers who cracked corn for their hush puppies, corn pone, and fritters. Though less romantic, the latter theory is likely the more accurate. Georgians did, in fact, drift down to southwest Florida, most notably the Knight clan, which founded a settlement at Horse and Chaise, named by seamen to describe a landmark clump of trees. (The name was changed to Venice in 1888 by developer Frank Higel, who was reminded of the Italian city by the area's many bayous and creeks.)

The Homestead Act, passed in 1862, entitled each settler in Florida to 160 acres of land, provided they built a home and tended the land for five years. As it was meant to, the act brought a flood of intrepid settlers into the area from all over the eastern seaboard and the Deep South. Traveling by foot or boat, they built rough palmetto huts, burned cow chips to ward off mosquitoes that carried yellow fever, ate raccoon purloo and turtle steaks. They stubbornly endured the heat, hurricanes, and freezes that stymied a number of enterprises: sugar refining, fish oil production, and pineapple and citrus shipping.

Florida's cow hunters proved detrimental to the agriculturally based enterprises associated with the Crackers of the Sarasota Bay region. They allied themselves with greedy land speculators who, by 1883, underhandedly nullified the beneficial effects of the Homestead Act. These speculators had discovered a loophole in Florida's land development legislation, namely the Swamp Land Act, which allowed them to purchase flooded land at rock-bottom prices while overriding homestead claims. They succeeded in declaring arable property swampland and ultimately bought up a good 90 percent of present-day Manatee County, much of which had been worked for years by hardy pioneers. Together the speculators and the cattlemen fought farmers' protests against "free ranging," the practice of letting herds roam and feed without restriction. A Sara Sota Vigilance Committee formed in opposition, and by the time the fighting ended, two men lay dead.

As thatch homes gave way to wooden farmhouses — the tin-roofed vernacular style today termed Cracker — Gulf Coast settlements entered a new era, an era that made "riffraff" out of Crackers, rich men out of schemers, and exclusive getaways out of crude frontier towns.

AT THE DROP OF A NAME

When your first guests are Juan Ponce de León and Hernando de Soto, whom do you invite next? The standard has been set, and it wouldn't do to host just anybody. So began west coast Florida's tradition of larger-than-life visitors with impressive names and pedigrees, all of whom just as impressively influenced the region's development. Thomas Edison, Henry Ford, Harvey Firestone, John and Charles Ringling, Charles Lindbergh, Teddy

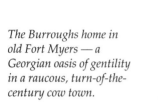
The Burroughs home in old Fort Myers — a Georgian oasis of gentility in a raucous, turn-of-the-century cow town.

Greg Wagner

Roosevelt, Henry Du Pont, Andrew Mellon, Rose Cleveland, and Shirley Temple were among the wide array of early southwest Florida winterers. Their fame and following quickly elevated the status of the lower Gulf Coast from crude and backward to avant-garde and exclusive, attracting the cutting-edge elite. They set national trends by declaring new hot spots — fresh, wild, unspoiled places about which no one else knew, especially the paparazzi. It was they who balanced the very wild coast with a very civilized clientele. The area's natural endowments of fish, fowl, and game attracted adventurers, fishermen, and hunters with the means to make the long, slow journey

The first and most influential name in any Gulf Coast retrospective is Thomas Edison. Disappointed by the cold winters of St. Augustine, the ailing inventor embarked on a scouting cruise along the Gulf Coast in 1885, the same year Fort Myers was incorporated. As Edison sailed along the Caloosahatchee River, he sighted a stand of bamboo trees. Then and there he decided to move to Fort Myers. And he wanted that property!

The bamboo worked well as filament in Edison's lightbulb experiments, and the climate bolstered his failing health, helping to add another 46 years to his life. On the banks of the Caloosahatchee the inventor fashioned his ideal winter home, Seminole Lodge, complete with laboratory and tropical gardens. Holder of more than a thousand patents, the genius experimented with rare plants in his quest to produce inexpensive rubber for his friend, tire mogul Harvey Firestone. So enamored with Fort Myers was Edison that he persuaded Firestone to spend his winters there. And he set up fellow visionary Henry

Ford on an estate next to his. A self-styled botanist, Edison planted the frequently photographed row of royal palms lining the street that eventually ran past his home, McGregor Boulevard, thereby earning the town its nickname, City of Palms.

Meanwhile, the Florida Mortgage and Investment Company — connected with such notables as the archbishop of Canterbury and estate owner Sir John Gillespie — lured a colony of politically disgruntled Scotsmen to Sara Sota, a paradise of genteel estates, bountiful orange groves, and cheap land. Or so the brochures promised. But instead of the Garden of Eden and the ready-made manor houses they had read about, these newcomers found shortages of food and building materials. Only through the kindness of the Whitakers and other pioneers did they survive their first month. Then the Gulf Coast's unpredictable winter weather dealt another cold blow, causing most of the colonists to return to their homeland. Those who stayed, however, brought life to the struggling village and sparked it with a determined spirit.

Most influential among the Scottish ranks was John Hamilton Gillespie, son of Sir John. He built the city's first hotel, the De Soto, became its first mayor in 1902, and introduced the game of golf to Florida. Gillespie transplanted the game from his homeland, first by building a two-hole links down Main Street in Sarasota, near his hotel. He later built the area's first real course and clubhouse nearby.

It was an American woman, however, who firmly and definitively upgraded Sarasota's image. At the turn of the 20th century the name Mrs. Potter (Berthe) Palmer stood for social elitism — not only in her hometown, Chicago, but also in London and Paris, where she kept homes and hobnobbed with royalty. When the widowed socialite decided to visit Sarasota in 1910, hearts palpitated: She could make or break the new town. Enchanted by the area's beauty and the town's quaintness, Mrs. Palmer immediately bought 13 acres that eventually grew to 140,000. She built her home, The Oaks, and a cattle ranch in a community south of Sarasota called Osprey, and from there proceeded to spread the word.

Mrs. Palmer's much-publicized love affair with the Gulf Coast drew the attention of John and Charles Ringling, the youngest of the illustrious circus family's seven sons. The two brothers, in a contest of one-upmanship, began buying property around town. They became active in civic affairs, built bridges to Sarasota's islands, and stoked the economy by making the town the winter home for the Ringling Circus. John Ringling, especially, and his wife, Mable, brought to Sarasota a new worldliness born of their extensive travels and love of European art.

The fate of the Charlotte Harbor coast lay mostly in the hands of one powerful man, Henry B. Plant. The west coast's counterpart to Henry Flagler — builder of the east coast's railroad and great hotels — Plant brought the railway to Tampa, where he built a fabulous resort of his own, always in competition with Flagler. At the same time, another railway company extended its tracks to some unknown, unsettled spot in the wilderness of Charlotte Harbor's shores and erected the Hotel Charlotte Harbor. It reigned briefly as the latest posh outpost for wealthy sportsmen and adventurers, counting Andrew Mellon and W. K. Vanderbilt among its patrons. But in 1897, after Plant had acquired the railway to Punta Gorda, he decided the town's deepwater port and resort posed too much competition for his Tampa enterprises. So he choked the life out of a thriving commercial and resort town by severing the rails to Punta Gorda's Long Dock.

Deepwater ports, railroads, and fabulous hotels went hand in hand in those days: Developers had to provide transportation before they could attract visitors. At the end of the line, the visitors needed a place to stay. In Boca Grande, where a railroad had been built in 1906, the deep waters of Boca Grande Pass attracted Rockefellers, Du Ponts, J. P. Morgan, and other industrialists, who used the port for shipping phosphate from central Florida. To accommodate them, the graciously refined Gasparilla Inn was built in 1913.

Another man who was to influence the discovery and development of the Gulf Coast came to town in 1911. John M. Roach, Chicago streetcar magnate and owner of Useppa Island, introduced Barron Collier to the area. Collier eventually bought Useppa from his friend and there established the Useppa Inn and the Izaak Walton Club. Both attracted tarpon fishing enthusiasts the likes of, according to local lore, Shirley Temple, Gloria Swanson, Mae West, Herbert Hoover, Zane Grey, and Mary Roberts Rinehart, who then bought nearby Cabbage Key for her son and his bride.

Collier went on to infuse life into the southwest coast by underwriting the completion of Tamiami Trail, stalled on its route from Tampa to Miami. He acquired land throughout the county that today bears his name, after earlier attempts by Louisville publisher Walter Haldeman had failed to put Naples on the map.

Along the lower Gulf Coast of Florida, Collier bought more than 1,000,000 acres, much of it under the infamous Swamp Act. Although he dreamed of development on the scale of Flagler and Plant, anticorporation outcry, hurricanes, the Depression, and war stymied his success. His sons inherited his kingdom, which they ruled with a heart for the unique environment their father so loved. Collier's influence increased the awareness of the Gulf Coast as a refuge for crowd-weary stars and illuminati. Its islands still are popular with the rich and famous who seek anonymity.

But what about the ordinary people — native Americans, fishermen, cattlemen, Crackers, pioneers, and common folk — who loved this land long before it became fashionable to do so? For the most part they lived side by side with this new brand of resident, called the "winterer" or "snowbird." (In Boca Grande they were termed "beachfronters" for their unusual — at the time — idiosyncrasy of building dangerously close to the shore.) The locals became their fishing guides, cooks, and innkeepers. In some cases their heads were turned by the brush with great wealth. In other instances heightened standards

Old fish houses around Charlotte Harbor survive from the 1930s, when fishermen's families lived in and worked out of the stilted structures.

Lee Island Coast Visitor & Convention Bureau

pulled the curtain on cruder lifestyles, especially that of the cow hunter, whose boisterousness and preference for free-running stock hastened his extinction.

Sometimes the common folk protested big-bucks development and were classified as riffraff. The "Cracker" label today, despite the culture's enriching influence on architecture and cuisine, is considered an insult by some native Floridians.

BOOMS, BURSTS, AND OTHER EXPLOSIONS

The Gulf Coast's resort reputation came of age at the turn of the 20th century. Sarasota's De Soto, the Hotel Charlotte Harbor, Boca Grande's Gasparilla Inn, the Useppa Inn, Fort Myers' Royal Palm Hotel, the Naples Hotel, and the Marco Inn pioneered in the hotel field, hosting visitors in styles ranging from bare bones to bend-over-backwards. They sparked an era touched with Gatsbian glamour, giddiness, and graciousness.

The Gulf Coast's halcyon days peaked in the early 1920s as the state entered a decade known as the Great Florida Land Boom. Growth came quickly to the young communities of Bradenton, Sarasota, Fort Myers, and Naples. In fact, the good people of the Gulf Coast grew dizzy with the whirl of growth and success.

According to the 1910 census, Sarasota's population was 840; before the 1920s drew to a close, almost 8,400 people called it home. In the meantime the city shaped itself with sidewalks, streets, schools, a newspaper, a pier, an airfield, and the establishment of its own county, having split from Bradenton's Manatee County. A bridge to Siesta Key added a whole new element to the town's personality by plugging it into the gulf and attracting a seaside resort trade.

World War I briefly interfered. Prohibition brought to the coast yet another roguish character: the rumrunner. Homes and hotels popped up like toadstools after a summer rain shower. Increased lodging options opened the Gulf

Coast to a wider range of vacationers. No longer just a socialites' haven, the average traveler could now afford Florida's Gulf Coast. A new class of winterer, known as the "tin-can tourist," arrived in force, pulling trailers and campers. Tourist camps sprang up overnight, and southwest Florida became an Everyman's paradise. Real estate profits added to the lure of tourism, and many visitors decided to remain permanently.

The 1920s created Charlotte County along the Charlotte Harbor coast. A bridge was built across the Peace River, connecting the pioneer towns of Charlotte Harbor and Punta Gorda, spurring growth, and spawning subdivisions by the score.

Fort Myers became the seat of a new county named for Confederate General Robert E. Lee. Between 1920 and 1930, the population grew from 3,600 to 9,000 boosted by the completion of Tamiami Trail in 1928. Fort Myers evolved from a raucous cattle town to a modern city with electricity (thanks to Edison), telephone lines, and a railroad. The Royal Palm Hotel treated guests to a regal departure from the cow trails that ran adjacent to the property. A country club put Fort Myers on the golfing map, and a bridge to Estero Island's beautiful beaches further boosted tourism. Real adventurers took the ferry to Sanibel Island, to be accommodated at Casa Ybel or the Palm Hotel.

South of Fort Myers, Survey, a farming community, was renamed Bonita Springs. In 1923 Naples (previously a well-kept secret among buyers from such faraway places as Kentucky and Ohio and distinguished vacationers from the upper echelons) became a city just in time to feel the effects of the tourism boom. The same year, Collier County seceded from Lee. Everglades City became the first county seat; later, growing, thriving Naples took the honors. The Naples Pier, which had served as a landing point for visitors and cargo since 1887, was replaced in importance by a railroad depot in 1927.

Gulf Coast skies had never been sunnier. Visitors spent lots of money. Residents prospered. Real estate prices soared. It seemed too good to be true. And indeed it was.

A 1926 hurricane hit Fort Myers, worsening a condition of already deepening debt. In Sarasota, John Ringling suffered severe financial losses from which he never recovered. On the southernmost coast, however, the national economy had little impact on the surge of interest sparked by the opening of Tamiami Trail.

The Depression blunted the momentum with which the Gulf Coast had developed during the 1920s but in many ways affected the region less drastically than it did other parts of the country. Since it most tragically affected the middle class, wealthy Gulf Coast residents were largely spared. Works Progress Administration (WPA) recovery projects built Fort Myers its waterfront park, yacht basin, and the city's first hospital. The WPA also funded the building of Bayfront Park, a municipal auditorium, and the Lido Beach Casino along the Sarasota Bay coast. And despite serious financial problems, Ringling kept his promises to build bridges and an art museum.

By the beginning of World War II, southwest Florida had firmly joined the 20th century, with modern conveniences that made it popular among retirees. New golf courses accommodated active seniors, who participated in the civic affairs of their adopted communities often more vigorously than they had in those of their hometowns. Professional golf tournaments were introduced, first in Naples and then along the coast, making the area golf's winter home. Later, spring baseball camps brought another spectator sport to this land of year-round recreation.

Heat seekers turned their attention to the Gulf Coast's islands and beach-fronts. Golfing communities and waterfront resorts swallowed up local farming and fishing industries. High-rise condominiums replaced Cracker houses, posh resorts toppled tourist fishing camps, and the Gulf Coast continued to grow — albeit not quite as loudly or erratically as in pre-Depression times.

Some areas learned to control their growth. Sanibel Island served as a model, taking control of its fate after a causeway connected it to the mainland in 1963. It incorporated and introduced measures to protect wilderness areas and limit takeover by developers. The southward expansion of Interstate 75 during the 1970s and 1980s changed the Gulf Coast from a series of towns connected by two-lane roads to communities keeping pace with the world. Communication and transportation systems improved. Commercial development spread to the freeway corridor, leaving downtown areas to fade in bygone glory. Light industry and winter-weary entrepreneurs relocated. Postsecondary schools worked to prepare local youth for the changing marketplace. The construction and tourism industries continued to prosper.

The Gulf Coast remained seemingly untouched by the fluctuations of the American economy. Urban blight was a distant reality. Northerners fled to the Gulf Coast to escape overcrowding, smog, and crime. In previous decades this had caused unnatural development in some of the metropolitan areas. The delicate balance of infrastructure, human services, nature, heritage preservation, and the arts spun out of kilter. The coast lived very much in the present, deaf to the demands of residents, both human and otherwise.

Finally, though, the new trends of eco-tourism and social responsibility amplified the voices of the few who had screamed over the decades for preservation of the environment against tourism and cultural sterility. While Sarasota and Naples served as cultural prototypes, Sanibel and Gasparilla Islands provided environmental models. The 1990s saw the dawn of an awareness of the fragility of the west coast's islands, wetlands, and shorelines. At the same time, interest in the area's history grew, and movements were launched to preserve architectural treasures that had so far been spared by the bulldozer. Eventually the dipping economic trends of the early 1990s affected the Gulf Coast. Construction slowed its racing pulse, and unemployment figures jumped as northerners continued to arrive, looking for jobs in this legendary land of treasure and youth.

All of these factors have contributed to the current perspective on the Gulf

Coast. Economic fluctuations give city planners occasion to pause and rethink. Future growth is being mapped out with more care than ever before. Dying downtown neighborhoods and abandoned Cracker homes are being revitalized, recognized as an important part of the area's heritage. Government is drawing into its blueprints the need for environmental preservation, cultural enrichment, and historic renovation. With the new millennium's economic boom comes a more enlightened attitude that promises to return the sunshine to Gulf Coast skies, free of the recent past's dimming clouds. The grain of sand and the mangrove pod from which this land was wrought will once again play a role in its future.

COASTAL CULTURE

Seminole Henry John Billie crafts canoes the traditional way.

Karen T. Bartlett

One of southwest Florida's great contradictions is that it lies more to the north than to the south on the cultural map. North of it, or inland, you will find Deep South cookery, clog dancing, bluegrass music, and traditional southern arts. In southwest Florida, however, midwestern and eastern U.S. influences are most noticeable. The only truly indigenous art forms have their origins in the Seminole Indian traditions of weaving, dancing, and festivals.

The arts have been heavily influenced through the years by the region's winter population. Many northern-based artists have relocated here, lured by the sea and tropical muses. Others bring with them their appetite for culture, sparking the finest in visual, performing, and culinary arts.

SOUTHWEST FLORIDA ARCHITECTURE

Years of simmering together Seminole, Cracker, "Yankee," and Caribbean traditions have yielded a unique southwest-Florida style, particularly in

A Seminole trademark, chickee (pronounced cheek-ee) huts have dotted the Everglades landscape since the Seminole Wars forced the Indians into hostile swamp-land.

Karen T. Bartlett

architecture and cuisine. But if one overall style could be said to represent local architecture, it would have to be Mediterranean — specifically Italian and Spanish-mission forms. Cracker vernacular runs a close second.

Southern European and North African influences are found primarily in public and commercial buildings constructed during the boom years of the Roaring Twenties, when they were lumped together under the label "Mediterranean Revival." It reveals itself in stucco finish, mission arches, red barrel-tile roofing, bell towers, and rounded step façades. Re-revived Mediterranean Postmodern — updated Mediterranean Revival blended with elements of tropical styles adopted from the Cracker era — serves as a popular style for upscale housing developments and commercial enterprises.

Pure Cracker style began as folk housing. From the vernacular, single-pen home — a wood-frame one-room house featuring a shady veranda, a high tin roof, an elevated floor, and wood siding — grew more sophisticated interpretations of the style. With Gothic touches, Victorian embellishments, Palladian accents, and New England influences, the humble Cracker house evolved into a trendy, modern-day version termed "Old Florida." Boxy and built on stilts, its most distinctive characteristics include a tin roof and wide wraparound porch.

The latest influence on the Cracker house comes from the Caribbean and the Bahamas via the Keys. Since indigenous West Indian styles are greatly similar to Cracker, especially in their suitability to tropical weather, the convergence was inevitable. The result: sherbet colors and hand-carved fretwork — used as much for ventilation as for decoration — that add charm and whimsy to the basic unit.

Like the Cracker home, the Seminole Indian's chickee (pronounced "cheek-ee") hut conformed to the tropical climate with its high-peaked roof, wide overhangs, and open sides. Today the thatched roofing that is the chickee's most distinctive feature has become an art form. Still a popular style of housing for the Seminoles and Miccosukees of the Everglades, the chickee has evolved as a trademark of the Gulf Coast watering-hole tradition known as chickee, or tiki, bars.

With the mid-1920s influx of "tin-can tourists," the mobile home replaced the Cracker house on the low end of the architectural totem pole. Mobile home parks still provide low-cost housing, mostly to part-time winter residents, homes that would "look a lot better as beer cans," according to an old Jimmy Buffett tune.

The concrete-block ranch, a popular residential style of the 1970s, was built to withstand hurricanes. The flood regulations of the 1980s raised these up on pilings; lattice and fretwork added interest. Art Deco returned later in the decade as Miami Beach's Art Deco District attracted attention.

Today's Gulf Coast towns are seasoned with period styles and spiced with contemporary looks that strive for compatibility with nature. Screened porches (often called lanais), windowed "Florida rooms," and lots of sliding doors let the outside in, to take full advantage of the unique, enviable climate and environment.

COASTAL CUISINE

Stone crab claws were "discovered" in the Everglades, and you don't find 'em any fresher than at local restaurants and fish markets.

Karen T. Bartlett

As for culinary richesse, southwest Florida has wowed hungry visitors since the first Europeans came ashore and discovered nature's abundantly stocked pantry. The seas were teeming with Neptune's bounty, and exotic fruits and vegetables flourished on land. In fact, one former Fort Myers newspaper columnist, Bob Morris, adheres to a theory that this was the original Paradise, and it was a sweet, luscious mango, not an apple, that caused Eve's downfall. Hence the fruit's name: Man! Go!

Mangoes, though, are not actually native to southwest Florida but grow bountifully along with other naturalized tropical fruit: bananas, coconuts, pineapples, avocados, sapodillas, carambola (star fruit), and lychees. Citrus fruit, particularly oranges, is of course the region's most visible and profitable crop. Key lime trees grow in profusion, as well. Practically year-round producers, they are a standard part of any good Florida cook's landscaping scheme. Here, as in the Florida Keys, where the tree got named and famed, key lime pie is a culinary paradigm, and each restaurant claims to make the best. In the finest restaurants with the most extravagant dessert menus, key lime pie inevitably outsells the rest. The classic recipe, created by Florida cooks before refrigeration, uses canned sweetened and condensed milk and is elegant in its simplicity. The most important factor is the freshness of the limes — sometimes a problem for restaurants since the fruit does not lend itself to commercial farming. One sure sign of an inauthentic version is the color green. Key limes turn yellow when ripe and, unless the cook adds food coloring, should impart a buttery hue to the pie.

Historically, crop farming has provided coastal residents with economic sustenance. Weather conditions bless farmers with two growing seasons for most ground crops. As land becomes too valuable to farm, agriculture has been pushed inland. Bonita Springs, where vast acreage remains devoted to tomatoes, and Pine Island, known for its tropical fruits, are the region's final bastions of the agricultural tradition.

Seafood is most commonly associated with Gulf Coast cuisine, including some delicacies unique to Florida. Our prize catch, the stone crab (Florida author Marjorie Kinnan Rawlings once described the taste as being "almost as rare as nightingales' tongues"), was discovered as a food source in the Everglades. They are in season from October 15 through May 15. Restaurants serve them hot, with drawn butter, or cold, with tangy mustard sauce. Their aptly named shells are usually precracked to facilitate diners' enjoyment.

The gulf shrimp is an emblem of local cuisine. Its poorer cousin, the rock shrimp, gets less publicity because of its hard-to-peel shell. More economical and with a flavor and texture akin to lobster, it's certainly worth tasting. Restaurants change their menus, or at least their daily specials, according to what's in season. Grouper, the most versatile food fish in the area, traditionally has been available year-round, but environmental pressure is limiting its availability. A large and meaty fish, its taste is so mild that you hardly know it's fish. Winter months bring red and yellowtail snapper — my favorite — to diners' plates. Warmer weather means pompano, cobia, shark, and dolphinfish (also known as mahimahi). Tuna and flounder are caught year-round but sporadically. Some restaurants serve less well-known species, such as triggerfish and catfish, to offset spiraling costs caused by dwindling supplies of the more popular varieties. Fish farming also addresses these shortages. Catfish and a Brazilian fish called tilapia (which tastes similar to snapper) are cultivated most commonly. Fresh fish from around the world supplement local bounty.

The best Gulf Coast restaurants buy their seafood directly from the docks of local commercial fishermen to ensure the utmost freshness. The traditional style of cooking seafood in Florida is deep-frying. Although constituting a mortal sin in this age of gourmet standards and cholesterol awareness, it is a true art when properly executed. There's a vast difference between what you find in the frozen food department at the supermarket and what comes hand-breaded, crunchy, and flavor-sealed on your plate at the local fish house.

New Florida style, at the other extreme, has evolved from so-called California, new American, new world, and eclectic styles of cuisine. This type also depends on freshness — of all its ingredients. For this reason it uses local produce, prepared in global culinary styles. Regional cookery, sometimes termed Gulfshore or Floribbean cuisine, prefers tropical foodways and ingredients, inspired by the cuisines of New Orleans, Mexico, Cuba, Puerto Rico, Haiti, the Bahamas, Jamaica, and Trinidad. Pacific Rim influences have become prominent in recent years. Depending on the cook, Deep South traditions take their place at the table, too. The outcome at its tamest merely twists the familiar; at its most adventurous, it can treat your taste buds to a veritable bungee jump.

Between the two extremes of old and new Florida styles, Continental cuisine survives in both classic and reinvented forms. Along with restaurants that serve the finest in French and Italian haute cuisine, you will find others that represent the Gulf Coast's melting pot, with authentic renditions or interpretations of a wide variety of cuisines: native American, Thai, Vietnamese, East Indian, Iranian, German, Irish, Greek, Cuban, Jamaican, Amish, Jewish, Mexican, and Puerto Rican.

In its cuisine and cultural makeup, as well as its history, the map of Gulf Coast Florida resembles a patchwork quilt. It blankets its people in warmth, checkers its past with colorful and contrasting patterns, and layers its character with intriguing, international textures.

CHAPTER TWO
Blazing the Trail
TRANSPORTATION

Karen T. Bartlett

Art shows and community functions give new life to the old Naples Depot, where celebrities disembarked during the Roaring Twenties.

The Gulf of Mexico and its great rivers and intracoastal waterways comprise the region's oldest and lowest-maintenance transportation system. From the days when the Calusa traveled the streams and estuaries in dugout canoes, through the romantic steamboat era, and until 1927, when the railroad to Naples was completed, boat travel was the most popular means of getting around. Early homes lined the waterways and today still face the water, not the roads that accommodate modern-day traffic. Even today the Caloosahatchee River, which empties into the sea along the Island Coast and connects to the east coast via Lake Okeechobee, constitutes part of a major intercoastal water route.

The railroad first came to Charlotte County's deepwater port in 1886 and created the town of Punta Gorda, much to the chagrin of Fort Myers's leaders, who had tried for years to persuade company officials to extend their Florida

Southern Railroad to the Caloosahatchee River. Instead, an unpopulated location was selected and a fabulous hotel built there, according to the custom of Florida's great railroad builders of the day. Besides transporting wealthy winterers to the nation's southernmost railroad stop, the trains hauled fresh fish, cattle, and produce.

A train nicknamed "Slow and Wobbly" ran between Bradenton and Sarasota from 1892 to 1894. The Seaboard Railroad built a more reliable version to Bradenton in 1902. In 1911 it was extended beyond Venice, under the influence of Chicago socialite and major landholder Berthe Palmer. When Palmer named the railway terminus Venice, infuriated residents of Venice changed their town's name to Nokomis. The Charlotte Harbor and Northern Railway laid track in 1906 to ship phosphate from inland mines to the deep waters of Boca Grande Pass, off Gasparilla Island. Another refined resort came with it.

Fort Myers finally got its first railroad station in 1904. In 1922 the trestles reached Bonita Springs and were later extended to Naples and Marco Island. Famous passengers such as Hedy Lamarr, Greta Garbo, and Gary Cooper rode the rails to vacation at the posh Naples Beach Hotel & Golf Club, one of Florida's first resorts to boast golf greens on the property.

The concept of a Tamiami Trail made headway when, in 1923, a group called the Trail Blazers traveled the proposed route that would connect Tampa and Miami. Mules, oxen, and tractors were used to complete that first motorized crossing of the Everglades. Progress was slowed by dense jungles, forbidding swampland, devastating heat, and mosquitoes so thick that they covered exposed skin like a buzzing body glove. Builders lived at the work site, and a whole body of legend grew up around the monumental task. The project was hampered by war and depletion of funds. A special new dredge had to be invented to build the section across the Everglades. Before the trail was paved, it had a sand surface. Summer rains caused flooding. Old-timers remember getting out of the car to catch fish in the road while their parents worked to get

Ed Frank (second from far right) invented the swamp buggy, an amphibious form of transportation engineered for travel in the Everglades. He poses here in 1947 with his brainchild and his hunting buddies.

Collier County Historical Society, Inc.

their vehicle unstuck. Even after the rains subsided, jarring, muck-crusted ruts made the trip less than comfortable.

As the trail's west coast leg inched toward its destination, it changed the communities it penetrated. Thirteen years in the building, the completion of Tamiami Trail in 1928 opened communities to land travel, trade, and tourism and was met with euphoria. Today the trail — also known as U.S. Highway 41 — strings together the region's oldest towns and cities, and newer communities have grown up around it.

With the extension of parallel Interstate 75, Tamiami Trail has lost its role as the sole intercoastal lifeline. Nonetheless, it remains the backbone of the lower west coast. Probing both metropolitan interiors and rural vistas, it provides glimpses of a cross-section of life — as it was and as it is — in southwest Florida.

Highway 41 runs through the middle of the area covered in this book. At the Gulf Coast's northern and southern extremes, the highway edges close to the shoreline. In midsections, it reaches inland to communities built along harbors and rivers.

Interstate 75 draws the eastern boundary for this guide's coverage. The freeway glimpses, at top speed, Gulf Coast life as it enters the 21st century. Although convenient and free of traffic lights, it misses the character that the more leisurely pace of Tamiami Trail reveals. However, it does extend the boundaries of Highway 41's family of communities and create new ones.

GETTING TO THE COAST

BY CAR

Southwest Florida is plugged into Florida's more highly charged areas by both major conduits and small feeders. Tampa/St. Petersburg lies at the Sarasota Bay coast's back door, along Highway 41 or I-75. Tamiami Trail ends here, but Highway 41 continues on. The interstate proceeds north and connects to Orlando and the east coast via Interstate 4. Highway 19 takes up the coastal route in St. Petersburg, heading toward Georgia. Highway 70 cuts across the state above Lake Okeechobee, to connect the east coast to the Sarasota Bay coast at Bradenton, and at Sarasota and Punta Gorda via Routes 72 and 17 respectively. These roads meander into Native American reservation territory, Arcadia's cowboy country, and the expansive Myakka River State Park. The route runs jaggedly between the Island Coast, the big lake, and West Palm Beach, following a series of lazy two- and four-lane roads, including Routes 80, 27, 441, and 98.

Alligator Alley (I-75) crosses the Everglades with a certain mystique. Once a two-lane toll road on which encounters with crossing gators and panthers were common (tragically, cars inevitably fared better in such encounters), today I-75 has been widened to four lanes, with underpasses for wildlife.

This namesake of Alligator Alley (I-75) enjoys the sun — as do many Florida inhabitants.

Karen T. Bartlett

Certain times of the year, it continues to earn its name, and a sharp eye can spot hundreds of gators sunning on water banks. But it's still a toll road and still less than user-friendly. Gas up before you approach — fuel station/restaurant exit breaks are few and far between on the two-hour drive until it reaches the east coast at Fort Lauderdale. Highway 41 takes you into Miami and branches off into Highway 1 to the Florida Keys.

BY PLANE

Two major airports service the lower Gulf Coast: Sarasota-Bradenton International Airport (SRQ) and Southwest Florida International (RSW) in Fort Myers. The Sarasota-Bradenton facility gives a proper introduction to the region, with shark tanks and tropical orchids from local attractions, a two-story waterfall, and works from its prolific artist community.

Welcome to paradise: Southwest Florida International Airport in Fort Myers.

Karen T. Bartlett

Smaller airports and fields service shuttle, charter, and private planes. The Charlotte County and Venice airports cater mainly to private craft. North Captiva Island and Everglades City have their own landing strips for private planes, and seaplane service is available to some islands.

Sarasota-Bradenton International Airport (SRQ), 941-359-2770 or 941-359-5200; www.srq-airport.com; 6000 Airport Circle, Sarasota 34243. American Eagle, American Trans-Air, Delta ComAir, Continental, Delta, Northwest, Trans-World Airlines, US Airways.

Charlotte County Airport, 941-639-1101; 28000 Airport Rd., Punta Gorda 33982.

Southwest Florida International Airport (RSW), 239-768-1000; swfia@swfia.com; www.swfia.com; 16000 Chamberlin Pkwy., Ft. Myers 33913. Air Canada, American, American Trans Air, Continental, Delta, Northwest, Spirit Airlines, Trans World Airlines, United, US Airways.

Naples Municipal Airport (APF), 239-643-0733, fax 239-684-4084; info@flynaples.com; www.flynaples.com; 160 Aviation Dr. N., Naples 34104. American Eagle, Cape Air, Delta ComAir, USAir Express.

Marco Island Executive Airport (MKY), 239-394-3355; info@collierairports; www.collierairports.com/mky; Collier County Airport Authority, 2003 Mainsail Dr., Naples 34114.

Venice Municipal Airport (VNC), 941-485-9293; www.venice-florida.com/community/government/airport; 150 Airport Ave. E., Venice 34285.

BY BUS

Greyhound Lines depots are found along the west coast at Sarasota (941-955-5735; 575 North Washington Blvd.), Fort Myers (941-334-1011; 2275 Cleveland Ave.), and Naples (941-774-5660; 2669 Davis Blvd.).

GETTING AROUND THE GULF COAST

BY CAR

BEST ROUTES

Tamiami Trail (Highway 41) forms the heart of the Gulf Coast's major metropolitan areas and provides north-south passage within and between them.

Sarasota Bay Coast

In Bradenton and Sarasota, Highway 41 runs along bay shores and converges with Highway 301, another major trunk road. Principal through streets for east-west traffic in this area generally are those with exits off I-75, north to

GULF COAST ACCESS

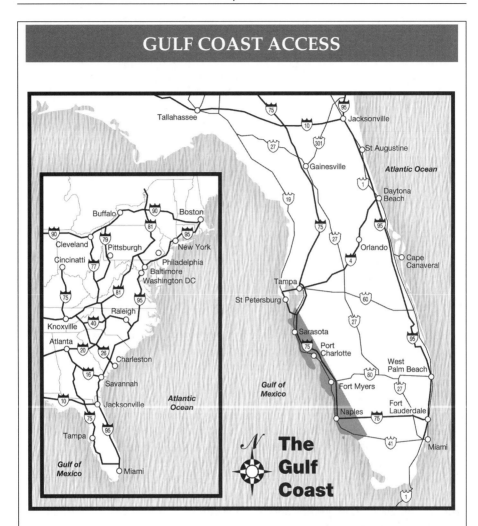

FROM FLORIDA CITIES

From	To Sarasota Bay	To Island Coast	To South Coast
Miami	212 mi./4.25 hr.	148 mi./2.5 hr.	110 mi./2 hr.
Orlando	132 mi./2.25 hr.	167 mi./3.5 hr.	187 mi./3.75 hr.
Daytona	185 mi./3.75 hr.	219 mi./4.25 hr.	241 mi./4.5 hr.
Jacksonville	239 mi./4.5 hr.	311 mi./6 hr.	325 mi./6.25 hr.

south: Manatee Avenue (Route 64), Carter Road (Route 70), University Parkway (closest to the Ringling Museums), Fruitville Road (closest to downtown), Bee Ridge Road, Clark Road (Route 72), and Venice Avenue.

Bradenton's 75th Street West (De Soto Memorial Highway) skims the town's western reaches close to the bay front. At exit 42, Route 64 travels straight into downtown and out to Anna Maria Island. From the south, take exit 41 and follow Route 70 to Highway 41. Head north on Highway 41, then turn west on Route 684 (Cortez Road/44th Avenue), which takes you across the south bridge. Both bridges lead to Gulf Drive (Route 789), the island's main road. Longboat Key lies to the south of Anna Maria Island, across a bridge, along Gulf of Mexico Drive. Lido Key is connected to Longboat Key by yet another bridge and also by bridge from the mainland in downtown Sarasota.

Streets hiccup through downtown Sarasota, starting and stopping without warning. Main Street runs north-south, crossed by Orange Avenue, one of the neighborhood's longest streets. Bayfront Drive arcs around the water and skirts a lot of the town's water-sports action. Bahia Vista intersects Orange at its southern extreme and constitutes a major route. To cross town from north to south between Highway 41 and I-75, take Tuttle Avenue, Beneva Road, McIntosh Road, or Cattlemen Road.

To get to St. Armands Key and Lido Key from downtown Sarasota, follow the signs on Tamiami Trail to cross Ringling Causeway. To reach Siesta Key from I-75, take exit 37 (Clark Road) or 38 (Bee Ridge Road). From Bee Ridge Road, turn north on Highway 41 and west on Siesta Drive, which leads to the north bridge. Clark Road (Route 72) crosses the south bridge and becomes Stickney Point Road. On Siesta's north end, Higel Avenue and Ocean Boulevard are the main routes into the shopping district. Beach Road runs gulfside and intersects with Midnight Pass Road, which travels to the island's south end, intersecting Stickney Point Road.

Take Venice Avenue off Interstate 75 to get to Venice's beaches and old, Mediterranean-influenced neighborhoods. Highway 41's business route splits from Tamiami Trail at Venice and takes you to the older part of town. Harbor Drive travels north-south along the beaches. The Esplanade and Tarpon Center Road reach into waterfront communities.

Charlotte Harbor Coast

Highway 41 heads inland, running within miles of I-75 at some points. In these parts getting to the gulf entails crossing several bodies of water. Most of the routes qualify as back roads and are listed under that heading.

Island Coast

Bonita Beach is touted as the closest sands to I-75 in this area. Highway 41 again distances itself from its modern counterpart to take you into downtown business districts and past upscale golfing communities. Pine Island Road, Route 78, diverges from the major arteries and crosses North Fort Myers and

Thomas Edison is credited with planting the royal palms flanking Fort Myers's prestigious McGregor Boulevard, thereby earning the city its nickname, City of Palms.

Karen T. Bartlett

Cape Coral to reach Pine Island. Del Prado Boulevard and Cape Coral Parkway, which intersect, are Cape Coral's main commercial routes. Stringfellow Road, which lies at the end of Pine Island Road, is Pine Island's principal north-south artery.

On the south side of the Caloosahatchee Bridge, Fort Myers's main east-west connectors are Martin Luther King Jr. Boulevard, Colonial Boulevard (which feeds into the Mid-Point Toll Bridge to Cape Coral), College Parkway (which also crosses the river between Fort Myers and Cape Coral at Cape Coral Parkway with a toll), and Daniels Parkway/Gladiolus Drive. Traveling roughly from north to south, historic and royal-palm-lined McGregor Boulevard (Route 867) follows the river past the old homes that line it. Summerlin Road (Route 869) and Metro Parkway run parallel, to the east. Tamiami Trail becomes Cleveland Avenue. Take McGregor or Summerlin west (they eventually merge) to get to Sanibel and Captiva Islands, land of no traffic lights. There's a $3 toll for crossing the bridge to Sanibel without a transponder gate-pass gizmo. Stay in the right lanes unless you have one. Periwinkle Way is the main drag and connects to Sanibel-Captiva Road via Tarpon Bay Road. Policemen with white gloves direct traffic at the main intersections during high-traffic hours. Sanibel-Captiva Road turns into Captiva Drive at the pass between the two islands. San Carlos Boulevard off of Summerlin Road takes you to Fort Myers Beach and the islands that lie to its south along Route 865 (Estero Boulevard in Fort Myers Beach, Hickory Boulevard in Bonita Beach).

South Coast

Here, Highway 41 (also known as Ninth Street) closes in on the sea once again as it travels through Naples. At Bonita Springs, Old Highway 41 branches off toward the town's business district. Bonita Beach road (exit 18) crosses Highway 41 to travel to Bonita Beach. I-75 exit 17 gets you to the Vanderbilt Beach/North Naples area via Route 846; exit 16 dumps you into

Pine Ridge Road, which leads to the north end of Naples. I-75 then swings east, so that Route 951 at exit 15 is closer to downtown Naples in a north-west direction but farther in an east-west direction. Depending upon the time of year, you are sometimes better off taking exit 16 to Highway 41when approaching from the north, then heading south to get downtown. When approaching from the south, take exit 16, and hook up with Highway 41.

Parallel to Highway 41 in Naples, major city dissectors include Goodlette-Frank Road (Route 851) and Airport-Pulling Road (Route 31). East-west trunks are, from north to south, the Naples-Immokalee Highway (Route 846) at the north edge of town, Pine Ridge Road (Route 896), Golden Gate Parkway (Route 886), Radio Road (Route 856), and Davis Boulevard (Route 84) in town, and Rattlesnake Hammock Road (Route 864) at the southern extreme.

To get to Marco Island from the north, take Route 951 (interstate exit 15), which will take you to the main high bridge at the island's north end. Route 951 becomes Collier Boulevard and continues through the island's commercial section and along the gulf front. Bald Eagle Drive (Route 953) heads north-south to Olde Marco and mid-island. It connects to San Marco Drive (Route 92), which crosses the south bridge. The south-end bridge is a better access if you're approaching from the east along Highway 41. Turn southwest off of Highway 41 onto Route 92 to cross the south bridge.

ALTERNATE BACK ROADS & SCENIC ROUTES

This section of Gulf Coast has many scenic back roads that bypass traffic and plunge the traveler into timeless scenes and unique neighborhoods. These routes are especially good to know when you tire of counting out-of-state license plates during rush hour in high season.

Sarasota Bay Coast

Follow the twisty road through a string of barrier islands, from Anna Maria in the north to Bird Key at the end. Route 789 adopts a different name on each island: John Ringling Parkway, Gulf of Mexico Drive, etc. To avoid Highway 41 traffic between downtown Sarasota and Siesta Key, turn west onto Orange Avenue and follow it through scenic neighborhoods along McClellan and Osprey avenues to Siesta Drive, and then turn west again. Route 758, along Siesta Key, makes a short, beachy bypass between Siesta Drive and Stickney Point Road. The loop through lovely Casey Key begins between Sarasota and Venice at Blackburn Point Road, off Highway 41, then proceeds south through Nokomis Beach and back to the mainland.

Charlotte Harbor Coast

To reach Englewood from Venice, cross quiet, out-of-the-way Manasota Key along Route 776 through Englewood Beach. Then follow Routes 775 and 771 back to Route 776 for a scenic drive through the peninsula, separated from the

Don't let winter-season traffic ruffle your feathers. Hit the scenic back roads.

Karen T. Bartlett

mainland by Charlotte Harbor, or to get to Gasparilla Island. (It costs $3.50 to cross the causeway onto the island.) Park Avenue is the shopper's route in Boca; Gulf Boulevard takes you to the beaches. Staying on 776 takes you more directly to Highway 41. To skirt Highway 41's chain-outlet anonymity in the Port Charlotte area, take Collingswood Boulevard off 776 to Edgewater Drive and back to 41.

Between Charlotte County and the Island Coast, Route 765, or Burnt Store Road, rambles through the county's Cracker era: scrub cattle, rusty tin roofs, and old fishermen bobbing cane poles. This connects to Highway 78, which leads to Pine Island when taken west, or Highway 41 and I-75 when followed east. To enter Cape Coral the back way, go east to Chiquita Boulevard and then south to Cape Coral Parkway.

Island Coast

The back roads along the Island Coast's shores plunge you briefly into the frenzied activity of Fort Myers Beach along Routes 968 (San Carlos Boulevard) and 865 (Estero Boulevard), then carry you along at a more mellow pace as you cross into Lovers Key and Big and Little Hickory Islands, where 865 becomes Hickory Boulevard. The road returns you via Bonita Beach Road to Highway 41 at Bonita Springs.

South Coast

Gulfshore Boulevard, which stops and starts to make way for Naples's waterways, is the town's most scenic route, skirting beaches and beautiful homes.

South of Naples, Routes 951, 952, and 953 carry you to Isles of Capri, Marco Island, Goodland, and back to Highway 41 just before the Everglades.

CAR RENTALS

R ental agencies with airport offices or shuttle service are listed below:

Alamo: 800-327-9633 (SRQ, 941-359-5540; RSW, 239-768-2424)
Avis: 800-331-1212 (SRQ, 941-359-5240; RSW, 239-768-2121; APF, 239-643-0900)
Budget: 800-527-0700 (SRQ, 941-359-5353; RSW, 239-768-1500; APF, 239-643-2212)
Dollar: 800-800-4000 (SRQ, 941-355-2996; RSW, 239-768-2223; APF, 239-793-2226)
Hertz: 800-654-3131 (SRQ, 941-355-8848; RSW, 239-768-3100; APF, 239-643-1515)
National: 800-328-4567 (SRQ, 941-355-7711; RSW, 239-768-2100; APF, 239-643-0200)
Thrifty: 800-367-2277 (SRQ, 941-355-8884; RSW, 239-768-2222; APF, 239-643-4550)

AIRPORT TAXIS/SHUTTLES

S ome hotels and resorts arrange pickup service to and from the airport. Taxi and limousine companies operate in most areas.

Taxi companies that provide transportation to and from the Bradenton-Sarasota airport include *Diplomat Taxi* (941-355-5155); *West Coast Executive Sedans* (941-355-9645, 941-359-8600); and *Longboat Limousine* (941-383-1235, 800-LB-LIMO-1; www.longboatlimousine.com). For more companies that service the Bradenton-Sarasota airport, call 941-359-5225.

Boca Grande Limo (239-964-0455, 800-771-7433) provides 24-hour connections to all Florida airports. For a more dramatic arrival or departure, call *Boca Grande Seaplane* (239-964-0234, 800-940-0234).

Charlotte Limousine Service (941-627-4494) will pick up from and deliver to all airports in the region.

Pine Island Taxi (239-283-7777) provides 24-hour service anywhere with advance notice.

Sanibel Island Taxi (239-472-4160) makes airport pickups and deliveries for Sanibel and Captiva visitors. Or call *Sanibel Island Limousine* (239-472-8888).

In the south coast area, call *Affordable Limousine Service* (239-455-6007, 800-245-6007) or *Naples Taxi* (239-643-2148).

BY BUS

T he Sarasota Bay coast boasts dependable public transportation, with discounts for schoolchildren and seniors. Buses run every day but Sunday, 6am to 6pm. A new downtown trolley runs around Sarasota and St. Armands Circle. For route information, call *Sarasota County Area Transit* (SCAT) (941-316-1234) or *Manatee County Transit* (MCAT) (941-747-8621).

On the Island Coast, city buses follow routes around Fort Myers, Cape Coral, and south Fort Myers. Call *Lee Tran* (239-275-8726) for schedules and information about trolley rides to and around Fort Myers Beach's beach accesses, including Lovers Key.

The *Naples Trolley* (239-262-7300) conducts sightseeing and shopping tours in the Naples area. The *Marco Island Trolley* (941-394-1600) visits 13 different historical sites.

BY CARRIAGE

The *Naples Horse and Carriage Company* (941-649-1210) provides evening tours of Old Naples, the beaches, and the fishing pier in season.

BY TRAIN

The *Seminole Gulf Railway* (239-275-8487, 800-SEM-GULF; www.sem gulf.com), stationed at the corner of Colonial Boulevard and Metro Parkway in Fort Myers, does dinner trips, Murder Mystery Tours, and other excursions throughout the area.

BY WATER

Water no longer provides functional transportation routes on the Gulf Coast, except to the unbridged islands, and today boat travel is purely recreational. The region boasts two trademark water vessels: The noisy, power-driven **airboat** is designed especially for the shallow waters of the Everglades. The **swamp buggy** is an all-terrain vehicle, built to carry 2 to 20 passengers, and travels on fat tire treads. In addition, **pontoon boats** offer a more conventional way to explore the Everglades and coastal shallows.

Numerous sightseeing tours and charters originate daily at marinas and resorts. Some specialize in fishing, others in shelling or birding. Many include lunch at an exotic island restaurant, while a few serve meals on board. All cater to the sightseer. Most tour operators are knowledgeable about sights and history on local waterways. These are all listed in the "Recreation" section of each chapter. Included here are shuttles designed purely to carry passengers to one or more island destinations where "by water" is still the only means of arrival.

The *Miss Cortez* (941-794-1223; 4330 127th St. W., Cortez 34215), an excursion boat out of the fishing village of Cortez near Anna Maria Island, takes visitors to Egmont Key every Tuesday and Thursday afternoon.

Island Charters (239-283-1113; 14113 Clubhouse Dr., Bokeelia 33922) offers shuttles from Pine Island's Pineland Marina to North Captiva and Cabbage Key.

CHAPTER THREE
Seashore Sophisticate
SARASOTA BAY COAST

The cities of **Braden-ton** and **Sarasota** dominate the Sarasota Bay coast, an expanse of metropolitan sprawl barricaded behind sybaritic, beach-centric islands. History and a heritage of high culture add dimension to this world of sand and city streets.

Bradenton draws much of its historical identity from the supposed landing of Hernando de Soto on local shores. Old Hernando, scoundrel and sadist though he turned out to be, gives the town a reason to celebrate its heritage each year when it re-enacts the momentous occasion. (A national park further recognizes the Indian-slaying conquis-

Karen T. Bartlett

Classical European statuary heralds the Renaissance pleasures inside the John and Mable Ringling Museum of Art.

tador.) Later in the history of Bradenton and the surrounding mainland communities, two pioneering influences dictated a low-key attitude and light development. The first, the wealthy plantation owners of the 1840s, ranked Manatee County as the largest area in the state for sugar and molasses production. Sugar's aristocratic families set the social standards of the town until the Civil War turned the lucrative sugar industry sour. The second, 19th-century land speculators, exploited Florida's Swamp Act, which had an opposite, stunting effect on the area's development. By having homestead property fraudulently declared wetlands, they prevented agricultural expansion and delayed its by-product, the building of railroads.

Most of Bradenton's modern growth has occurred since 1970, when tourism and shipping into deepwater Port Manatee became major income sources.

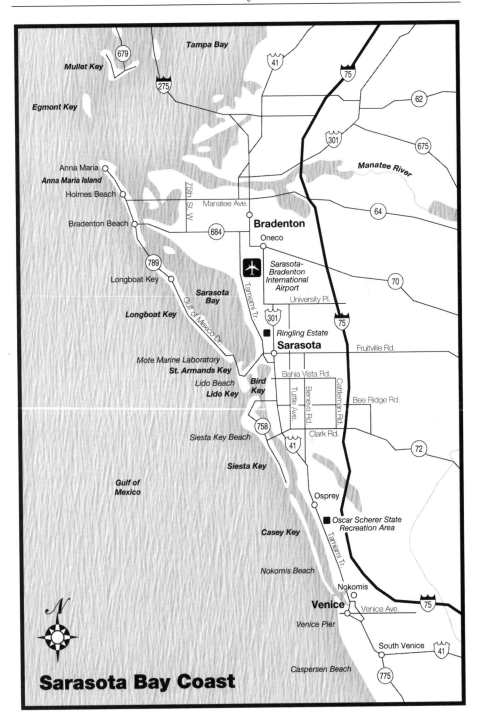

Sarasota Bay Coast

Today, preservation of the Gamble Plantation and original village structures, along with downtown waterfront restoration projects, make Bradenton a vital city textured with an interesting past.

Old fishing traditions endure in the village of Cortez.

The village of **Cortez** lies southwest of Bradenton and several eras to the past. Fishing made this peninsular community, and fishing remains its livelihood. Along its southern waterfront, a working fishing operation and its toilers reside in a time-stilled setting.

Fishing, resorts, and heterogeneous neighborhoods mark the three incorporated towns of **Anna Maria Island: Anna Maria, Holmes Beach,** and **Bradenton Beach**. The first Anna Maria Island settlers of record were George Emerson Bean and his family, circa 1890. He developed the island in the early 1900s for tourists, who arrived by boat at the Anna Maria City pier. In 1921 the first bridge to the island was built from Cortez.

Longboat Key was mentioned often on the maps and journals of early Spanish explorers. It supposedly got its name from the longboats that Hernando de Soto's scouting party used to come ashore. Aside from one tucked-away village with a salty, local flavor, Longboat Key is known for its prim-and-properness. It, along with Sarasota and its bracelet of other keys, proclaim John Ringling as godfather, for he is responsible for putting the area on the cultural map. His arrival in 1911 sparked Sarasota's first land boom.

Remote **Siesta Key** resisted settlement until the turn of the 20th century, when a hotel launched the island's reputation as a restful place. A bridge built in 1917 finally brought permanent residents to the island. Siesta Key has historically attracted creative types. One of its best-known citizens was prolific writer John D. Macdonald, most famous for his Travis McGee detective novels. While living on Siesta Key he is believed to have written more than 70 novels. Pulitzer Prize–winning author MacKinlay Kantor and late abstractionist Syd

Solomon also settled on the island, and Pulitzer Prize-winning cartoonist Mike Peters lives there today. Other cartoonists and artists have also found the area conducive to creativity. *Hagar the Horrible's* Dik Browne lived here while alive; now his son Chris has moved in. *Garfield's* Jim Davis winters on Longboat Key. Surrealist Jimmy Ernst, son of Dada master Max Ernst, spent much time on Casey Key during his life. Artist Thornton Utz and jazz notable Jerry Jerome still have homes in the area.

The Webb family first arrived in the Sarasota area in 1867 to plant the seed for a town they named **Osprey** 17 years later. Mrs. Palmer (Bertha) Potter, known as "queen of Chicago society," settled here in 1910. Though lesser known today, she exerted an influence equal to Ringling's in attracting attention to the area around Sarasota Bay.

The Town the Circus Built

The circus comes as close to being the world in microcosm as anything I know; in a way it puts all the rest of show business in the shade. Its magic is universal and complex.

— E. B. White, *Ring of Times*, March 22, 1956

Legend has it that Sarasota's barrier islands **Bird Key** and **St. Armands Key** became John Ringling's possessions in a poker game. Tales of the circus master's influence on the area's development have grown to mythic proportions: elephants that built bridges, midgets who built fortunes, and an eccentric who built himself an Italian palace. However true the legends, during the 20 years after he came to Sarasota to house his circus here in winter, John Ringling demonstrated a three-ring influence over the city and its barrier islands.

After falling in love with the fledgling mainland village and purchasing real estate offshore, Ringling erected his lavish Cà d'Zan ("House of John" in Italian, modeled after a Venetian palazzo). He also began the construction of a causeway to **Lido Key** by filling and dredging, and he dreamed of a city park and a shoppers' haven on **St. Armands**. For **Longboat Key** he envisioned a world-class hotel. With unbridled fervor he set out during his worldwide travels to acquire a fine collection of Baroque art for public display in a museum.

The dreams Ringling failed to realize before he died in 1936 were not abandoned. The causeway was completed and donated to the state. St. Armands Circle today is famed for its shops. The skeleton of what was to be the world's finest hotel sat rusting on Longboat Key for years until it was reborn as a modern resort. The John and Mable Ringling Museum of Art encompasses acres of bayside estate, and its collection and grounds include Baroque statuary, original Rubens masterpieces, a rose garden, Cà d'Zan, a circus museum, and an antique Italian theater.

Aside from John Ringling's concrete legacy to Sarasota, he bequeathed an undying commitment to beauty, fantasy, art, and showmanship. The circus remains an important industry in Sarasota — in fact, at the high school, circus is an extracurricular activity, like football. Theaters and galleries thrive, thanks to Ringling's patronage of the arts. Without his influence the entire coast might well have remained a cultural frontier for many more decades.

The original village of Venice sat where **Nokomis** does today. It moved south and seaward after the railroad bypassed it in 1922 toward a station in the middle of nowhere. Actually an island separated from the mainland by narrow waterways, the original Venice reflects the influence of Ringling and visionary urban planner John Nolen.

Casey Key was built on the principle that island real estate should be reserved for the well-to-do. This has kept it pristine and lightly developed, particularly at its north end. **Nokomis Beach**, at the southern end, contrasts as a more casual, beachy, fishing-oriented resort area.

LODGING

On Siesta Key you won't find a single chain hotel. However, you *will* find accommodations large and small by the score. Most vacationers on the Sarasota Bay coast gravitate toward the barrier islands. The others have their chains but more mom-and-pops, B&Bs, inns, destination resorts, and privately owned places. On the mainland, especially around the airport, business travelers find no-nonsense franchise and small motels, plus a couple of luxury options old and forthcoming. In 2001, two luxury condo resorts opened: a Ritz-Carlton and a Renaissance. With downtown's renewal, more and more vacationers are choosing mainland accommodations.

Privately owned second homes and condominiums provide another source of accommodations along the Sarasota Bay coast. Vacation brokers who match visitors with such properties are listed under "Home and Condo Rentals," at the end of this section.

I've listed here a well-rounded selection of Sarasota area accommodations, including a few of the better chain hotels. Toll-free 800, 888, 866, or 877 reservation numbers, where available, are listed after local numbers.

Pricing codes are explained below. They are normally per person/double occupancy for hotel rooms and per unit for efficiencies, apartments, cottages, suites, and villas. (An asterisk after the pricing designation indicates that the rate includes at least a continental breakfast in the cost of lodging and possibly more extensive meal service as noted in the listing.) The range spans low- and high-season rates. Many resorts offer off-season packages at special rates and free lodging for children. Pricing does not include the 6 percent Florida sales tax. Some large resorts add service gratuities or maid surcharges. Sarasota County also imposes a 3 percent tourist tax that is allotted to beach revitalization, arts funding, and tourism promotion.

Rate Categories

Inexpensive	Up to $75	Expensive	$150 to $200
Moderate	$75 to $150	Very Expensive	$200 and up

The following abbreviations are used for credit card information:

AE: American Express   MC: MasterCard
D: Discover Card   V: Visa
DC : Diners Club

Anna Maria

ROD & REEL MOTEL
Managers: Todd and Janet
  Test.
941-778-2780.
www.rodandreelmotel.com.
877 North Shore Dr., PO Box
  1939, Anna Maria Island
  34216.
Price: Inexpensive to
  Moderate.
Credit Cards: AE, D, MC, V.
Handicap Access: No.

This motel sits prettily on a narrow slab of bay-front beach with flowery landscaping, shuffle-board, picnic facilities, a sunning deck, and a tiki-roofed pavilion. Each of the 10 one-room efficiencies is fully furnished with a kitchenette (microwave, stovetop, and refrigerator), ironing board, couch, plastic dining room chairs, and spic-and-span housekeeping. The motel is next to the independently owned Rod & Reel Pier.

Bradenton

**HOLIDAY INN
  RIVERFRONT**
General Manager: Matt
  Coombs.
941-747-3727,
  800-HOLIDAY.
www.holiday-inn.com/
  bradentonfl.
100 Riverfront Dr. W.,
  Bradenton 34205.
Price: Moderate to
  Expensive.
Credit Cards: AE, D, DC,
  MC, V.

This is mainland Bradenton's loveliest property, perched riverside, pertly landscaped, and designed to mesh with Bradenton's Spanish colonial heritage. Dark, heavy wood and wrought iron embellish the striking atrium lobby, off of which lies a pleasant fountain courtyard dripping with hibiscus and oleander blossoms. Here you'll also find the pool and spa and the entrance to the hotel's various indoor and outdoor restaurants and bars. A few steps away flows the Manatee River, edged by Bradenton Waterfront Park. Other amenities include a fitness center, complimentary morning coffee and newspaper, and a gift shop. All 153 rooms and deluxe suites of the five-story hotel have private balconies that overlook the river or courtyard and are stocked with coffeemakers, wet bars, refrigerators, and hair dryers.

Bradenton Beach

DUNCAN HOUSE B&B
Innkeepers: Joe and Becky
  Garbus.
941-778-6858.
1703 Gulf Dr., Bradenton
  Beach 34217.
Price: Moderate.*

Scrunched between a breakfast joint and some condo tennis courts, across the street from the beach, resides an oasis of whimsy in tropical purple, pink, and blue, with carved balusters and scalloped edging — a vision amid ugliness when first restored but now looking a trifle shabby around the edges.

Duncan House made a ferry trip to come to rest at Bradenton Beach, where its current owners dressed it in gingerbread.

Karen T. Bartlett

Credit Cards: AE, MC, V.
Handicap Access: No.

Built in the 1800s, this home was moved from downtown Bradenton in 1946 to its present location. Ask the innkeepers to see pictures of the original building, its ferry trip, and their renovation project, which turned a decrepit triplex into a charming, six-unit facility. Public rooms are compact and lined with board-and-batten walls. Accommodations include two rooms, two apartments with living rooms and kitchens, and two cottages with shared living room and kitchen. All units have private baths and are dressed in extraordinary antique pieces, cheerful window treatments, lace coverlets, and floral wallpaper. A separate entrance leads to each apartment. A gourmet breakfast, pool, and beach access add to this B&B's special qualities.

SEASIDE MOTEL
Owners: Kevan and Fawn Ker.
941-778-5254, 800-447-7124.
www.seasideresort.com.
2200 Gulf Dr. N., Bradenton Beach 34217-2236.
Price: Moderate to Expensive.
Credit Cards: D, MC, V.
Handicap Access: No.

Like the rest of Bradenton Beach, things are constantly looking better here. The spotless seven efficiencies and three rooms have all-new kitchen counters, toasters, refrigerators, and microwaves, with stovetops in the efficiencies, plus remodeled tiled bathrooms. Fawn, one of the owners, is adding lovely trompe l'oeil touches to the white walls. The penthouse (expensive to very expensive) has a separate bedroom and luxury appointments. Each room looks out on the gulf with a patio or deck balcony, and the motel has its own private beach, segregated behind an eyesore concrete wall. Here guests can use the chaise lounges or walk the steps down to the beach and water. It's a good value for beachside lodging with pleasant amenities.

Holmes Beach

HARRINGTON HOUSE B&B

Innkeepers: JoAdele and Frank Davis.
941-778-5444, 888-828-5566.
5626 Gulf Dr., Holmes Beach 34217.
www.harringtonhouse.com.
Price: Moderate to Very Expensive.* (Two-night minimum weekends and holidays.)
Credit Cards: MC, V.
Handicap Access: Living area and one downstairs room in the main house is accessible, as are some of the beach-house rooms, but they are not outfitted otherwise for physically impaired guests.

One of Florida's loveliest and best-maintained bed-and-breakfasts, Harrington adds to its homey, historic allure with a beachfront. Built in 1925 of local coquina rock and pecky cypress, with Mediterranean flourishes, the home was refurbished with casual elegance and magical touches. Each of the seven rooms is labeled — Renaissance, Birdsong, Sunset, etc. — with a needlepoint door sign. Room sizes vary from spacious, with a king-sized bed, to comfortably cozy. Each guestroom has its own bathroom, refrigerator, and TV. An eclectic collection of handpicked antique furniture enhances guests' comfort. A dramatic cut-stone fireplace dominates the sitting room, where taped classical music is interrupted only by an occasional piano solo, and homemade chocolate chip cookies are always on hand. Guests enjoy full home-cooked breakfasts at individual tables amid Victorian pieces and filmy white curtains. Outdoor areas include sun decks, a pool, a wide beach, and charmingly colorful landscaping around picket fences and arched alcoves. Eight more rooms, some with Jacuzzi-style tubs and fireplaces, occupy two beach houses down the beach. Bikes and kayaks are available for guests' use.

Lido Key

HALF MOON BEACH CLUB

General Manager: Charles Parmelee.
914-388-3694, 800-358-3245.
www.halfmoon-lidokey.com
2050 Ben Franklin Dr., Sarasota 34236.
Price: Moderate to Very Expensive.
Credit Cards: AE, D, DC, MC, V.

Half Moon's stretch of beach is so romantic that people come here to get married and shoot commercials. During the winter months, repeat business, comfortable social areas, and the sheer intimacy of the property lend it a community feeling. Two neo Art Deco buildings roughly form a half-moon and hold 86 guestrooms, efficiencies, and suites, all with refrigerators, coffeemakers, and hair dryers. Contemporary light wood, glass blocks, and Deco appointments grace the rooms and public areas, but the beach is this British-owned resort's best feature. Everything draws you outdoors, including a beach sun deck with thatch cabanas, well-tended grounds, volleyball, bike rentals, a curiously wild-feeling dunes-edged beach, dramatic sunsets, and an indoor restaurant that overlooks the pool.

RADISSON LIDO BEACH RESORT
General Manager: Tim Hunter.
941-388-2161, 800-441-2113.
www.radisson.com/ sarasotafl.
700 Ben Franklin Dr., Sarasota 34236.
Price: Moderate to Very Expensive.
Credit Cards: AE, D, MC, V.

Located next to Lido Key's public beach, the 116-unit Radisson provides attractive, pleasant accommodations and a full range of water sports in the thick of beach activity. The tiled pool sits on the shell-scattered beach and has its own beach bar. The color scheme indoors and out and in the alfresco restaurant is tropical greens and pinks. Modern, nicely furnished rooms come with or without full kitchens. Some have a small refrigerator and microwave instead; all have coffeemakers.

Longboat Key

COLONY BEACH AND TENNIS RESORT
General Manager: Katherine Klauber Moulton.
941-383-6464, 800-282-1138.
info@colonyfl.com.
www.colonybeachresort. com.
1620 Gulf of Mexico Dr., Longboat Key 34228.
Price: Very Expensive.
Credit Cards: AE, D, DC, MC, V.

The Colony ranks among Florida's finest resorts, a place where you could hide indefinitely behind security gates without ever having to face the real world. It stakes its reputation on top-notch tennis and dining: The 21 tennis courts are state-of-the-art soft surface, including 10 that use a revolutionary underground watering system known as Hydro-Court. *Tennis* magazine has named it the top U.S. tennis resort for six consecutive years. The Colony Dining Room, one of the property's two dining spots, also consistently wins awards. The 18-acre resort occupies a stretch of private beach that was recently rejuvenated. Complimentary kids' recreational programs take young guests to the courts, beach, pool, and off-property attractions. The Colony's 235 privately owned units range from a high-rise penthouse to tony beach houses, but most are one- or two-bedroom suites. All units contain modern kitchen facilities; designer lamps, art, and furnishings; and marble master baths. Guests have free use of tennis facilities as well as a spa and a health club with an aerobic studio. Golf is available at 10 local private and semiprivate clubs.

HOLIDAY INN HOTEL & SUITES
General Manager: Gary Dorschel.
941-383-3771, 800-465-4436.
www.hilongboat.com.
4949 Gulf of Mexico Drive, Longboat Key 34228.
Price: Expensive to Very Expensive.
Credit Cards: AE, DC, D, MC, V.

There's less starch in the attitude of Longboat Key's northern end. The Holiday Inn here is classier than the average hotel chain standard but still more easygoing than the island's secured southern properties. The lobby makes an elegant introduction, with marble floors and potted plants. One of two swimming pools is contained inside the Holidome, an indoor, climate-controlled recreation center complete with whirlpool bath and exercise room. Other recreation possibilities center around a wide and luxurious beach with a cabana, sailboat rentals, and a beach bar and café. There's also an outdoor swimming pool, sauna, four lit tennis courts, a bar, a restaurant, and a convenience food court. Rooms and suites — 146 in all, 13 of them kitchen suites — provide comfortable accommodations with above-standard furnishings and a view of either the indoor or the outdoor pool. Thirteen of the rooms and two of the suites have recently been renovated as "Kidsuites," perfectly structured for families with a separate room within a room where kids have their own bunk beds, television, video games, and radio. A convenience food court is also new.

ROLLING WAVES COTTAGES
General Manager: Vince LaPorta.
941-383-1323.
www.rollingwaves.com.
6351 Gulf of Mexico Dr., Longboat Key 34228.
Price: Moderate to Expensive. (Minimum week-long stay at peak times.)
Credit Cards: MC, V.
Handicap Access: No.

What more could you ask of a beach vacation: a cute little 1940s cottage furnished modernly in bright colors, containing a remodeled full kitchen and bath and provided with picnic table, grill, sea grapes, huge pink hibiscus blossoms, and a quiet beach outside the door? Rolling Waves's eight cottages are kept meticulous and decorated with touches of character: clay tile kitchen floor, a rag rug over wood floors in a couple of the cottages, full-sized futons in the living room, VCRs, and an exterior paint job that evokes the chattel houses of the Caribbean. Located in Longboat Key's old, historic section, it escapes the glitz and the throngs with classic class.

Nokomis Beach

A BEACH RETREAT
Owner: Gregory Snyder.
941-485-8771, 866-232-2480.
www.venice-fla.com/ beachretreat.
105 Casey Key Rd., Nokomis 34275.
Price: Moderate to Expensive.
Credit Cards: MC, V.
Handicap Access: Yes.

Having taken over the fishing-oriented Sea Grape, A Beach Retreat now has efficiencies and apartments on both the beach and the bay. The new owner has substantially fancied up the place with a jaunty yellow paint job and lattice trim. There's a swimming pool on the bay side, where six boat docks and five units accommodate guests and their vessels. The gulf rooms, mostly ground level, are steps from a lovely, natural beach, but because of the wonderful tall sea oats, they have no view of the gulf. The 27 units all have their own look and layout — largely modern but with some imperfections that lend beach character. All but two have a full kitchen.

Sarasota

THE CYPRESS
Innkeepers: Vicki Hadley and Robert and Nina Belott.

Details make a bed-and-breakfast inn, and the Cypress's attention to special touches, flourishes, and minutiae place it among the top in its genre. Notice the antique ice cream table with

941-955-4683.
www.bbonline.com/fl/
  cypress/
621 Gulfstream Ave. S.,
  Sarasota 34236.
Price: Expensive to Very
  Expensive.*
Credit Cards: AE, D, MC, V.
Handicap Access: No.

swivel-out stools in the sunny breakfast room, Robert's masterful photographs on the walls, the exquisite crown molding throughout, the vintage Edison phonograph in the Martha Rose room, the fresh flowers in every room, the multicourse gourmet breakfasts, the happy-hour hors d'oeuvres, the complimentary top-shelf cordials before bedtime, and the cookie-turndown service. In short, the innkeepers spoil their guests. This young trio of talent took a 1940s home that the original owner's daughter refused to sell out to encroaching condos. That leaves the Cypress — named for its sturdy building material — a flower in the shadow of high-rises. Still, the location is quite enviable. From the front deck guests can watch the sun set over the masts of yachts in the marina across the way. Downtown's burgeoning Palm Avenue district of galleries, sidewalk cafés, and specialty shops, meanwhile, is a short stroll away — a quieter, gentler place than Main Street to shop.

HYATT SARASOTA
General Manager: Steve
  Mehas.
941-953-1234, 800-233-1234.
www.hyatt.com.
1000 Boulevard of the Arts,
  Sarasota 34236.
Price: Moderate to Very
  Expensive.
Credit Cards: AE, D, DC,
  MC, V.

Inside the Hyatt, a pinnacle of mainland lodging in Sarasota, unfolds a world of modern decor, contemporary comfort, and bayside splendor. A soaring atrium makes way for a clubby lounge and formal Italian restaurant Scalini, with windows overlooking the water. At the front desk, staff in crisp uniforms are efficient. Spaciousness and good taste characterize the 12-story hotel's 297 rooms and 12 suites, newly renovated in regal gold and blue tones and dark wood — businesslike and complete with deluxe amenities. Some have balconies overlooking the bay. Boat slips, a marina, and a waterfront restaurant highlight the bay. A full fitness center, a swimming pool, and close proximity to the Sarasota Quay, Van Wezel Performing Arts Hall, and downtown attractions make this long-standing landmark a favorite with business and leisure travelers.

Siesta Key

Most of Siesta Key's accommodations require a minimum stay (usually one week) during season.

**CRESCENT HOUSE B&B
  RESORT**
Innkeepers: Matthew and
  Cathy Ellis.
941-346-0857.
www.crescenthouse.com.
459 Beach Rd., Siesta Key
  34242.

The Crescent House was the first B&B in the Sarasota-Bradenton region. A classic 1908 Florida bungalow, it was moved to Siesta Key by barge in the 1930s. When opened as a B&B, it was popular for its location right across the street from access to the world's whitest beach, but it later fell

Karen T. Bartlett

Martha Stewart meets the beach at Siesta Key's newly renovated Crescent House B&B.

Price: Moderate to Very
  Expensive.*
Credit Cards: AE, MC, V.

into demise. The Ellises rescued the historic property in 1997, effected a stunning renovation, and have since been buying up homes and spreading their charm up and down one city block. The original Main House holds four rooms (two with private baths, two with shared), a glassed-in porch, a dining area, and a high-ceilinged sitting room with fireplace. All are furnished with antiques and decorated in a homey, light-bright fashion — "Martha Stewart meets the beach," owner Matt describes it. The guesthouse out back contains one suite, and a new addition next door offers another six in the same style, with original wood floors and special touches such as a Jacuzzi tub in the living area of one. On the other side of Main House, five more suites were added in 2001, fully outfitted apartments done up in a clean, classy, Art Deco style. Guests in all units have access to a small sequestered pool with spa plus another hot tub. The Ellises or one of two staff chefs prepare a glorious breakfast for all guests, served indoors or out. This modern-day B&B has all the amenities — laundry, television, ice — while maintaining an intimate, personal feel. Children are welcome in the suites with full kitchens. Nightly rentals are allowed whenever rooms are available.

TURTLE BEACH RESORT
Innkeepers: David and Gail
  Rubinfeld.
941-349-4554.
www.turtlebeachresort.com.
9049 Midnight Pass Rd.,
  Siesta Key 34242.
Price: Expensive to Very
  Expensive. (Minimum
  stay required in season.)
Credit Cards: MC, V.

One of Sarasota's Small Superior Lodgings, this one's a real find at the southern, quiet end, of the island, steps away from Turtle Beach. Ten cottages on the bay contain studio, one-bedroom, or two-bedroom accommodations, plus a private hot tub. Each cottage has its own personality, reflected in names such as Rain Forest, Montego Bay, and Southwestern. Modern designer furniture and lamps, objects d'art, and other decorative pieces

A touch of the Old World at Banyan House, a venerable bed-and-breakfast in Venice.

Courtesy of Banyan House

carry out the themes. Most have sleeper sofas; all come with complete kitchen facilities. Bathrobes, TV, VCR, and sherry are provided each of the cottages, which spread along a lushly landscaped strip well-planned with private nooks along waterside docks, poolside, or tucked into courtyard foliage. Use of washers and dryers is free after 4 pm, and bicycles, canoes, kayaks, rowboats, and boat docks are available complimentary for guest enjoyment. Very romantic, this resort is nonetheless conducive to families as well, and pets are permitted.

Venice

BANYAN HOUSE
Innkeepers: Chuck and
  Susan McCormick.
941-484-1385.
www.banyanhouse.com.
relax@banyanhouse.com.
519 S. Harbor Dr., Venice
  34285.
Price: Moderate to
  Expensive.*
Credit Cards: MC, V.
Handicap Access: No.

In the mid-1920s architects designed Venice in accordance with its Italian name. Homes and buildings are modeled after northern Mediterranean styles. The town's first community swimming pool was located in the backyard of one of the original homes, next to a fledgling banyan tree. Today that small pool, with its now-sprawling tree, resides at the same home, a red-tile-roofed B&B inn known as the Banyan House. Classic statuary, fountains, multihued blossoms, a courtyard, a sun deck, and a hot tub share the property. Five rooms, each with a private bath, exert their individual personalities but with less panache than the public rooms. The Palm Room has a fireplace; the Laurel Room, an outdoor balcony; the Tree House, a sunny sitting room overlooking the pool; the Sun Deck, a separate entrance; the Palmetto Room, hardwood floors and lavender hues. All units contain at least a small refrigerator; three are efficiencies. Two rooms and one apartment are also available in the carriage house. Deluxe touches include bathrobes in the closet and wine in the fridge. Susan serves homemade gourmet breakfast in a solarium off the formal sitting room, the latter furnished with an antique Italian fireplace, a circa 1890 hoopskirt bench, and other Victorian period pieces. Pecky cypress, wood-beam ceilings, terra-cotta slate tiling, and wrought-iron banisters are all original. Free use of bicycles allows guests to explore old Venice's nearby shopping mecca and beach.

INN AT THE BEACH
General Manager: Pam Orr.
941-484-8471, 800-255-8471.
www.inn-at-the-
  beach.com.
725 W. Venice Ave., Venice
  34285
Price: Moderate to Very
  Expensive.*
Credit Cards: AE, D, DC,
  MC, V.

This modern resort was built to include Mediterranean architectural overtones and contemporary Florida comfort and décor. Located across the street from the public access to Venice Beach, many of the two-floor hotel's 49 units overlook the gulf. Its newly renovated rooms have a clean white, light-wood, understated-floral motif. Plantation shutters and tile floors add designer touches. All contain at least a microwave, coffeemaker, and minifridge; efficiencies and one- and two-bedroom suites add full refrigerators, stovetops, dishware, and pans. A small pool with spa and sundeck is tucked away behind the hotel in the parking lot — not high on atmosphere. I'd opt for the beach. Continental breakfast is included in the rate.

HOME & CONDO RENTALS

Florida Vacation Accommodations (941-383-9505; www.vacationinfl.com; 4030 Gulf of Mexico Dr., Longboat Key 34228; or 941-346-9505; 5218 Ocean Blvd, Siesta Key 34242; or 941-364-9505; 3800 S. Tamiami Trail, Ste. 14, Sarasota 34239.) Call or write for a catalog of more than 2,000 waterfront properties throughout the region.

Hartmann Accommodations (941-346-2525; www.hartmannaccommodations .com; 523 Beach Rd., PO Box 35174, Siesta Key 34278;) They own several small properties on Siesta Key, from efficiencies to three-bedroom apartments. Each property site has access to a swimming pool and all units are clean, modern, and equipped with kitchens.

A Paradise Rental Management (941-778-4800, 800-237-2252; www.aparadise rentals.com; 5201 Gulf Dr., Holmes Beach 34217) Rental condos and homes on Anna Maria Island for short and long term.

RV RESORTS

Horseshoe Cove (941-758-5335; 5100 60th St. E., Bradenton 34203) A 60-acre oak-grove riverfront site, including a 12-acre island with a pavilion and nature and biking trails. Resort has a heated pool and spa, a postal facility, hookup to phone and cable, lighted fishing docks on the Braden River, shuffleboard courts, and other recreational facilities.

Linger Lodge (941-755-2757; 7205 Linger Lodge Rd., Bradenton 34202) By dint of its old Florida style character and slightly bizarre restaurant, this place has gained a reputation for funky. RV sites lie along or near the Braden River. Amenities include a boat ramp, fishing, and laundry.

Sarasota Bay Travel Trailer Park (941-794-1200, 800-247-8361; 10777 44th Ave. W., Bradenton 34210; at Cortez Rd.) Located on the bay with full hookups, a boat ramp and dock, fishing, horseshoes, exercise room, recreation hall, and entertainment, it caters mostly to permanent abodes, with some spots for transients. This is an exceptionally well-kept and scenic facility.

Venice Campground (941-488-0850; 4085 E. Venice Ave., Venice 34292; at exit 34 off Interstate 75) Full hookups and waterfront sites. Amenities include security gates, heated swimming pool, shuffleboard, horseshoe, nature trail, fishing, boat and canoe rentals, laundry room, and supply store.

DINING

For Sarasotans, eating out is as much a cultural event as attending the opera. It is often an inextricable part of an evening at the theater or a gallery opening. Sarasotans take dining out quite seriously and keep restaurants full, even off-season. Their enthusiasm for newness makes kitchens more innovative than those of their neighbors to the south. (Out of 20 Golden Spoon winners awarded in 2001 by *Florida Trend* magazine, 4 — Beach Bistro, Euphemia Haye, Michael's on East, and Summerhouse — are found in this region.) Sarasota slides along the cutting edge of New World cuisine while maintaining classic favorites that range from rickety oyster bars to French cafés.

The following listings span the diversity of Sarasota Bay coast cuisine in these price categories:

Inexpensive	Up to $15
Moderate	$15 to $25
Expensive	$25 to $35
Very Expensive	$35 or more

Cost is figured on a typical meal (at dinner, unless dinner is not served) that would include an appetizer or dessert, salad (if included with the meal), entrée, and coffee. Many restaurants offer early-dining discounts, often called early-bird specials. These rarely are listed on the regular menu and sometimes are not publicized by tip-conscious servers. I have noted restaurants that offer them. Certain restrictions apply, such as time constraints, a specific menu, or number of people first in the door. Call the restaurant and ask about its policy. Those restaurants listed with "Healthy Selections" usually mark such on their menu.

The following abbreviations are used for credit card information and meals:

AE: American Express
D: Discover Card
DC: Diners Club
MC: MasterCard
V: Visa

B: Breakfast
L: Lunch
D: Dinner
SB: Sunday Brunch

Anna Maria

ROTTEN RALPH'S
941-778-3953.
902 Bay Blvd. S., Anna
Maria 34216.
At the Galati Yacht Basin.
Price: Inexpensive to
Moderate.
Early-Dining Menu: Yes.
Children's Menu: No (kid-
suitable items on regular
menu)
Cuisine: Old Florida.
Liquor: Full.
Serving: L, D.
Credit Cards: DC, MC, V.
Handicap Access: Yes.
Reservations: No.
Special Features: Dock seat-
ing on the marina.

The atmosphere here is due entirely to the setting. It's a place that locals frequent, full of
character and characters. The laminated placemat
menu describes many finger food selections
(steamed shellfish, Buffalo shrimp, oysters Rocke-
feller, onion rings, chicken wings, nachos), Old
Florida fried seafood standards, steamed seafood
pots, and other, more esoteric concessions such as
shrimp linguine Alfredo, Danish baby back ribs,
and Cajun shrimp. The blackened grouper in my
sandwich obviously had been swimming not long
before and was well seasoned. We've always found
the food fresh and tasty, but truthfully we enjoy
the view more.

Bradenton

LEE'S CRAB TRAP II
941-729-7777.
4815 17th St. E., PO Box
450, Ellenton 34222.
Right off I-75 exit 43.
Price: Moderate to
Expensive.
Cuisine: Seafood.
Children's Menu: Yes
Liquor: Full.
Serving: L, D.
Credit Cards: D, MC, V.
Handicap Access: Yes.
Reservations: No.
Special Features: View of
the river.

If you're visiting Gamble Mansion, or happen to
be passing by this interstate exit with a hunger on,
this is a must-stop and has been as long as I can
remember. The menu is given largely to, of course,
crab. Try it steamed (stone or king), provincial, deviled, or a variety of other treatments. The crab cakes
are excellent, as is the three-crab soup with asparagus. All of their soups have a distinct from-scratch,
long-mulled flavor. The soup-of-the-day vegetable
chowder I had there recently was the best soup I can
remember. The menu doesn't limit itself to seafood.
It flexes to include fine Angus beef, lobster, frog
legs, catfish, chicken, ostrich, kangaroo, wild pig,
alligator, and pasta. The large, wood-encased dining
rooms have a view of the river out back. Expect a
wait for lunch or dinner in season.

NADINE'S 10th STREET BISTRO

941-748-0434.
309 10th Street W.,
  Bradenton 32405.
In the Riverpark Hotel.
Price: Inexpensive.
Cuisine: American.
Liquor: Full.
Serving: L.
Closed: Sat., Sun.
Credit Cards: AE, MC, V.
Handicap Access: Yes.
Reservations: No.
Special Features: Historic
  setting.

In historic, pink, neo-Mediterranean Riverpark Hotel, built in the 1920s as Manatee River Hotel, Nadine's is the latest popular lunch spot downtown Bradenton. The setting is bright and cheerful, with high ceilings and windows, market umbrellas, a stone fountain, and occasional music from a player piano. Diners are greeted with a helping of skinny breadsticks for dipping into a tasty cheese concoction. Classic and imaginative salads (chicken pita and seafood with shrimp, langostino, and real crab on pasta and greens) and sandwiches come in generous portions. Choose one of the River Park Favorites sandwiches for a complex meal with lots of nutritional variety. I had fun with the Bruchetta, done up with pesto, muenster cheese, roma tomatoes, fresh mozzarella with a lovely orange-vinai-grette-dressed salad. Others include the New Yorker with beef, black pepper, and slaw; and the Fresh Italian, dauntingly ample with portobello mushroom, roma tomatoes, mozzarella, prosciutto, and garlic-basil mayonnaise. The comprehensive menu offers more traditional fare as well. The hamburger boasts Angus beef and other sandwiches demonstrate great variety.

TWIN DOLPHIN MARINA GRILL

941-748-8087.
1200 First Ave. W.,
  Bradenton 34205
At Memorial Pier.
Price: Moderate to
  Expensive.
Children's Menu: Yes.
Cuisine: Floribbean.
Liquor: Full.
Serving: L, D.
Credit Cards: AE, D, DC,
  MC, V.
Handicap Access: Yes.
Reservations: Yes, for lunch
  and dinner.
Special Features: Riverfront
  view and alfresco dining.

This pleasant bistro replaces the Pier Restaurant, waterside on the Manatee River, and it's still the only waterfront restaurant downtown. I would go there just for the view — calming water, yacht masts saluting the sunshine — which can be enjoyed outdoors at Flipper's Dockside Patio or inside through large half-moon windows. Remodeling has turned the inside dining room quite handsome, with dark-wood chairs and bar, sumptuous booths, open kitchen, and clay tile floors. Outside is casual, with plastic chairs, glass tables, and a bar beneath coconut palms. The food provides another good reason to dine here, with its worthy interpretation of Floribbean and affinity for grilling. Start with Bahamian seafood gumbo, tuna sashimi, or Jamaican jerk chicken skewers. The latter were tasty morsels crisply grilled but a bit dry and served with an unspectacular (perhaps bottled?) barbecue sauce and a mango sauce with an unpleasant off flavor. However, its presentation and pineapple salsa, added up in the plus column. For lunch you can order a salad, Cuban sandwich, burger, grouper sandwich, crab-cake sandwich, or other sandwiches and pasta selections. Dinner concentrates on seafood, tropical drinks, and martinis. I sampled the crab cakes, whose heavy thyme seasoning and spicy mustard drizzle gave them a Caribbean flair. The day's fresh catches come blackened, bronzed, grilled, or broiled. (If you crave deep-fried seafood, order the platter.) Grilled vegetable linguine, Mediterranean stuffed (with Italian sausage and seasonings) roasted pork loin, and grilled chicken penne pasta are among the options offered non-seafood eaters. A showcase tempts you with luring desserts that I was afraid to even ask about.

Bradenton Beach

HISTORIC BRIDGE STREET CAFÉ
941-779-1706.
200 Bridge St., Bradenton Beach 34217.
Price: Inexpensive.
Children's Menu: Yes.
Cuisine: American/Seafood.
Liquor: No.
Serving: B, L, D.
Credit Cards: MC, V.
Handicap Access: Yes.
Reservations: No.
Special Features: Outdoor seating at the city pier.

Come awake to the slosh of bay waters against pier pilings and the hum of early morning traffic crossing the Cortez Bridge. Breakfast is an event here — not a grand event but one steeped in local color and history; nothing fancier than French toast and patio furniture. The servers have a soft southern accent and a no-nonsense friendliness and sense of humor. The humble, shacklike café straddles the city pier, a truncated former bridge. You can take one of the few tables inside, but you'd be foolish to pass up the outdoor view in any weather short of a downpour. Lunch and dinner demonstrate classic Old Florida fish-house style with seafood selections from the deep fryer plunked into a basket: oysters, grouper, shrimp, crab cakes.

For a sampler, order one of the two seafood platters. The café also serves great burgers, the signature one being the Pier Burger, with onions, mushrooms, and Swiss cheese. Three days a week (Monday, Wednesday, and Friday 11:30am to 9pm), come for all-you-can-eat grouper, only $11.95.

Holmes Beach

BEACH BISTRO
941-778-6444.
6600 Gulf Dr., Holmes Beach 34217.
Price: Very Expensive.
Early Dining Menu: No.
Children's Menu: No.
Cuisine: New American.
Liquor: Full.
Serving: D.
Credit Cards: AE, D, DC, MC, V.
Handicap Access: Close quarters and no bathroom

The talk of connoisseurs for many years, this little bit of gourmet heaven has fewer than twenty tables in a two-room cottage. Most of them cluster around picture windows in a room with one of the best local dining views of sunset. The other room is tinier and back by the bar with four tables. The exacting menu showcases the chefs' quirky talents that are difficult to define but easy to enjoy. The lobstercargots appetizers, for instance, replaces those "chewy little slugs" with succulent morsels of Florida lobster in bubbling garlic butter and spinach. We had a hard time letting them cool

wheelchair access.
Reservations: Yes.
Special Features: Front room
   view of gulf.

before we ate them, they were that tantalizing. A signature "kicker" sauce keeps the jumbo shrimp from drying on the grill and adds a spark nicely complemented by its Grand Marnier ginger beurre blanc. Tournedos comes with portabellas or peppered. We tried the latter, a wonderfully fiery demiglace of black, green, and pink peppercorns and cognac. Each dish was executed to perfection, but we came to understand what all the hubbub is about as the meal progressed, and our server attended us with skilled timing and pleasant surprises. Before our appetizer came herbed bread with a marvelous dip of tomatoes and basil, then two entwined shrimp with red pepper coulis. The vegetable accompaniments to our main courses were delicious enough to fight them for attention. And our wine-by-the-glass was poured from the bottle, a touch I always appreciate. In short, if you hear critics and regular folks raving about Beach Bistro, it's all true.

CHAPTERS CAFÉ
941-779-2665.
5904 Marina Dr., Holmes
   Beach 34217.
Price: Inexpensive to
   Moderate.
Children's Menu: Yes.
Cuisine: American.
Liquor: Beer and wine.
Serving: L, D.
Credit Cards: AE, D, DC,
   MC, V.
Handicap Access: Yes.
Reservations: No.
Special Features: Setting of
   a bookshop.

Gustatorily and intellectually satisfying, Chapters is a clever little café with walls of books and patio seating. It feels inviting, and the menu, while as "gourmet" as it says, is equally user-friendly. Sandwiches, salads, quiches, and pizzas on the all-day menu contain worldly ingredients but ones we recognize. My sun-dried tomato wrap, for instance, swaddled hummus, carmelized onions, tomatoes, sautééd mushrooms, and greens, with a tasty pasta salad on the side. There's a curry chicken salad, pretzel-bread smoky club, croissant crab cake, barbecue chicken pizza, brie-and-bacon quiche, apple brie and tomato-basil chutney appetizer, vermicelli pesto, and luscious desserts. The shop sells mostly used and collector books to go with your meal.

Lido Key

OLD SALTY DOG
941-388-4311.
1601 Ken Thompson Pkwy.,
   Sarasota 34236.
On City Island.
Price: Inexpensive.
Children's Menu: No, but
   the menu offers child-
   appropriate selections.
Cuisine: American/
   Seafood.
Liquor: Beer, wine.
Serving: L, D.

A spin-off of the Siesta Key original, this one has a more properly salty setting: a tin-roofed red stucco building tucked into a marina in the shadow of the Longboat Key bridge. If you sit outside on the patios, you'll be entertained by boaters, waverunners, and water skiers. The menu, painted on signs over the boat-shaped outside bar plus handed out on paper, lists fine casual eats such as City Island wings, New England clam chowder, deep-fried clams on a bed of fries, peel-and-eat shrimp, burgers, fish 'n chips, and the trademark

You're shipshape at the bar of Old Salty Dog, overlooking the waters between Longboat Key and City Island.

Karen T. Bartlett

Credit Cards: V, MC.
Handicap Access: Yes.
Reservations: No.
Special Features: Outdoor,
    waterfront seating.

Salty Dog (beer-battered and deep-fried, and not for the faint of heart). I ordered the grouper sandwich blackened and was pleased to have a choice of hot, medium, or mild. (Too many places assume palate sensitivity and water down the heat of a properly executed blackening.) I ordered hot and got it just right, not so fiery as to overpower the full-flavored freshness of the fish. This is a great place to stop after a visit to Mote Marine and its nearby attractions. We liked the wide selection of beers it offers on tap as well as bottled. My son liked that we didn't have to wait long for our food.

Longboat Key

EUPHEMIA HAYE
941-383-3633.
www.euphemiahaye.com.
5540 Gulf of Mexico Dr.,
    Longboat Key 34228
Price: Very Expensive.
Early Dining Menu: No.
Children's Menu: No.
Cuisine: Continental.
Healthy Selections: No.
Liquor: Full.
Serving: D.
Credit Cards: DC, D, MC, V.
Handicap Access:
    Downstairs, yes.
Reservations: Yes.
Special Features:
    Appetizer/dessert parlor;
    entertainment nightly.

A cross between a dollhouse and an art gallery, Euphemia Haye exudes the sort of whimsy and distinction at which its unusual name hints. The appellation actually comes from the founder's grandmother. There's nothing grandmotherly about the concept and cuisine, however. Dishes get their inspiration from around the world: a beef empanada appetizer from Argentina, lamb shank from Greece, fettucine pesto arugula from Italy, Shrimp Taj Mahal from India, grouper Jamaica, and so on. The signature roast duckling is a fine example of the perfected details that make a meal at Euphemia Haye surpass mere meal status. With bread stuffing and tangy sweet fruity sauce, it blends elements of Old World and new. Filet mignon Fritzie is another Euphemia specialty on the seasonally changing menu. It sits atop a potato pancake with caramelized shallots and bourbon demi-glace. To top off the experience, a trip upstairs to the Haye Loft for dessert is de rigueur. The selection is mind-boggling (not to mention diet-blowing, but let that thought go in this atmosphere). Besides sinful desserts, you can order coffee and after-dinner drinks. The peanut butter mousse with chocolate rum topping was much heavier than its name suggests, enough to go around a table of four; the coconut cream pie, extraordinary.

MAR-VISTA DOCKSIDE RESTAURANT & PUB
941-383-2391.
760 Broadway St.,
  Longboat Key 34228.
In the Village.
Price: Moderate.
Early Dining Menu: No.
Children's Menu: Yes.
Cuisine: Seafood.
Liquor: Full.
Serving: L, D.
Credit Cards: AE, D, MC,
  V.
Handicap Access:
  Restaurant yes, rest
  rooms no.
Reservations: Preferred
  seating.
Special Features: Boat
  access.

Locals refer to it simply as The Pub. Casual at its best, it has that lovely, lived-in, borderline ramshackle look on the outside, crowned by an appropriately rusting tin roof. Inside, tables don't match, mounted fish and sailors' dollar bills adorn the wall, boaters hoist beers at the bar, and a view of the harbor dominates the decorator's scheme. There's also seating on the patio, on plastic chairs with heaters when it's cool (and where you may occasionally get an earful of cooks' disagreements in the kitchen). Seafood is fresh and prepared with signature twists: oysters Longboat (topped with crabmeat, horseradish, and hazelnut dressing) and shrimp and conch fritters for appetizers; grilled grouper reuben, garlic-fried shrimp, and Caribbean chicken sandwich for lunch; Longbeach Bouillabaise, sesame tuna, and chicken Colombo stuffed with chutney-flavored cream cheese with coconut-curry cream sauce for dinner. Steamer pots in two sizes brim with shellfish and vegetables, large enough to be shared by two. We've enjoyed the cuisine and casual atmosphere here many times. On a recent visit I ordered off the specials menu. My chicken soup with wild rice and rosemary was flavorful and warming on the patio. My salad was slightly freezer-burn wilted but varied and rescued by its parmesan-pepper dressing. My entrée clearly raised this old-island eatery above fish-house status, preparing swordfish au poivre style, with a brandy cream peppercorn sauce atop a mound of horseradish mashed potatoes. I could have kissed the cook (had I not feared re-incurring his earlier ire).

Nokomis

CAPT. EDDIE'S SEAFOOD BAR
941-484-4623.
107 Colonia Ln. E.,
  Nokomis 34275
Price: Inexpensive.
Children's Menu: Yes.

Ask anyone around the Venice-Nokomis-Osprey area where to get seafood, and nine out of ten will recommend, without pause, Capt. Eddie's. I was told by more than one that it sells the freshest. The restaurant began as a fish market that took over a convenience store and set up a few pic-

Cuisine: Seafood/Florida.
Liquor: Beer and wine.
Serving: L, D.
Closed: In summer, Sun.
  and Mon. and Sat. L.
Credit Cards: D, MC, V.
Handicap Access:
  Restaurant yes, rest
  rooms no.
Reservations: No.

nic tables to fill the space. Those picnic tables came to be in such great demand that the market eventually grew into a restaurant where the locals know they can get their money's worth in fresh fish. The picnic tables remain; if you're a small party, you may be sharing with others. Or you can sit at the counter. This is a true Florida fish house, my favorite brand of dining. Don't expect tableware that won't get tossed at the end of the meal. Expect a roll of paper towels for linen and neighborly service. The hostess calls most of the patrons by name. The menu carries a lot of fried fish items typical of this genre (but fried right and in canola oil) as well as broiled options. I tried, after an appetizer of alligator bites, a broiled grouper sandwich that was the best I've tasted since my husband came home from a deep-sea fishing trip. Broiled grouper can be bland, but this was tastefully prepared, served on a yummy hoagie in a plastic basket. The only dessert, key lime pie, is the real thing, though with a discernible off-flavor that sometimes comes from bottled lime juice. (But, then, I have my own tree and am something of a snob!)

St. Armands Circle

**COLUMBIA
  RESTAURANT**
941-388-3987.
www.columbiarestaurant.
  com.
411 St. Armands Circle,
  Sarasota 34236.
Price: Moderate to
  Expensive.
Children's Menu: No.
Cuisine: Spanish/Cuban.
Liquor: Full.
Serving: L, D.
Credit Cards: AE, D, DC,
  MC, V.
Handicap Access: Yes.
Reservations: Yes, for lunch
  and dinner.

A spin-off of an almost hundred-year-old bastion of Spanish cuisine in Tampa, this one pales in comparison and is more yuppified to fit its posh setting. Seating is indoors or out, under umbrellas along the busy sidewalks of the Circle. The menu lists all the classics — *ropa vieja, palomilla, boliche,* pork *mojo,* and *paella* — plus some Florida seafood adaptations such as Florida grouper (breaded with toasted Cuban bread crumbs, grilled and topped with lemon butter, chopped parsley, and egg), pompano en papillot, and stone crab claws in season (October 15–May 15). Columbia is famous for its Spanish-bean-and-black-bean soup, its "1905" salad with garlic dressing, and its Cuban sandwich on the lunch menu. Recently I unwisely strayed from the traditionals and ordered *empanada de cangrejo,* a deviled blue-crab tart that consisted mostly of dry breading served with black-bean salsa and *moros y cristianos*: black beans and white rice studded with chunks of sausage. I requested a side of mojo to rescue the dryness of the beans, which were full-flavored nonetheless. The guava cheesecake smeared guava paste atop plain cheesecake, which was disappointing. Moral of the story: Stick with the tapas and Cuban dishes for a taste of what makes this place so popular.

Sarasota

BIJOU CAFÉ
941-366-8111.
www.bijoucafe.net.
1287 First St., Sarasota
  34236.
Price: Expensive to Very
  Expensive.
Early Dining Menu: No.
Children's Menu: No.
Cuisine: New American.
Healthy Selections: Yes.
Liquor: Full.
Serving: L, D.
Closed: Sun. in summer;
  Sat. and Sun. for lunch
  year-round.
Credit Cards: AE, DC, MC,
  V.
Handicap Access: Yes.
Reservations:
  Recommended.

Situated in the midst of the Theater and Arts District, the Bijou is the pick of the pre- and post-theater crowd and the upper-echelon business community of Sarasota. Small and simply decorated, only lacy curtains, some heavily framed paintings, and a few stylish vases (here you'd pronounce that *vah-zes*) embellish. Linen and fresh flowers dress the tables, even at lunch, when the clientele is equally dressed up. The eclectic menu offers choices from continental, New Orleans, and American cuisine, from fruit soup to duck. On a recent chilly-day visit, I ordered the hot soup du jour: Hungarian goulash, folk-food flavorful. We also sampled the ham Parisienne sandwich — with brie on a croissant — and the pasta du jour — bowties swaddled in cream sauce with spinach, artichoke hearts, tomatoes, and prosciutto. All were outstanding. One of my favorite dishes, shrimp Piri-Piri, makes a classic example of how chef/owner Jean-Pierre Knaggs perfectly balances flavors to create entirely fresh taste sensations. It is mildly spicy with citrusy tones and appears on both the lunch and dinner menus. Other dinner specialties include roast duckling, crab cakes Remoulade; veal Louisville with pecans, bourbon, and pears; and rack of lamb with roasted shallots and minted demiglace. The pommes gratinées Dauphinoise with Gruyere is a signature side dish, available à la carte. Desserts, made in-house, have an excellent reputation.

CAFÉ BACI
941-921-4848.
4001 S. Tamiami Trail,
  Sarasota 34231.
Price: Moderate to
  Expensive.
Early Dining Menu: Yes.
Children's Menu: Yes.
Cuisine: Northern Italian.
Liquor: Full.
Serving: L, D.
Closed: Lunch Sat. and Sun.
Credit Cards: AE, D, DC,
  MC, V.
Handicap Access: Restaurant
  yes, rest room no.
Reservations: For dinner.

I describe this place as " affordably dressy." It has, after all, a porte cochere out front and linens on the tables (even at lunch) inside, the business clientele and older crowd wear nice clothes, and the northern Italian specialties dwell in the realm of fine cuisine. Yet its location on plebeian South Tamiami Trail, away from Sarasota's centers of chichi, allows for a reasonably priced menu. Lunch is especially popular with locals, who squeeze the parking lot full to capacity. I enjoy lunch there, too; it imparts a bit of affordable elegance in the middle of a hectic day alongside a road-rage street. Many of the dinner entrées are available in smaller portions and prices. I recently ordered, for example, the ravioli di funghi, an exquisite plate of homemade half-moon pasta pockets filled with delicately creamed wild mushrooms and topped with a buttery tomato cream sauce. It cost only $6.25 and was, with its rich sauce, the most I could eat for lunch — thanks also to the bread basket, which was filled with marvelous focaccia squares baked with onions, garlic, sun-dried tomatoes, and parmesan cheese. Both lunch and dinner menus touch on the four major Italian food groups: pasta, veal, chicken, and seafood. These and the salads and soups beforehand are tended with a creative hand. Here's a taste: corkscrew pasta with mushrooms, peas, prosciutto, and cream; lasagna verde (made with spinach noodles); grilled breast of chicken stuffed with cheese and prosciutto with a pancetta, mushroom, and onion sauce; breaded veal scaloppine with arugula, onion, tomatoes, and basil; pan-seared salmon with white wine, leeks, pine nuts, and sun-dried-tomato sauce; and polenta-crusted sea bass. The dinner menu also features broiled meats and the fresh catch of the day. The extensive wine list has received the Wine Spectator Award of Excellence.

MICHAEL'S ON EAST

941-366-0007.
www.bestfood.com.
1212 East Ave. S., Sarasota 34239.
In Midtown Plaza at Bahia Vista St. and Tamiami Trail.
Price: Expensive to Very Expensive.
Early Dining Menu: Yes.
Children's Menu: No, but will halve portions.
Cuisine: New American.
Liquor: Full.
Serving: L, D.
Closed: Saturday and Sunday for lunch.
Credit Cards: AE, DC, MC, V.
Handicap Access: Yes.
Reservations: Recommended for lunch or dinner.
Special Features: Piano bar with late-night menu.

Michael Klauber is a well-respected name in Sarasota culinary circles. He learned successful restauranteuring early in life as a member of Longboat Key's Colony Beach Resort family and is responsible for Sarasota's annual wine festival. He created an immediate sensation when he opened his own place back in 1987 and has since opened another fine restaurant at the Quay with partners. Michael's on East remains the pinnacle of cutting-edge cuisine and atmosphere. Oh so Art Deco, you won't find a square corner in the wavy motif. You can dine around the circular bar or in two other rooms separated by scrims and glass (wavy, of course, and très chic). The lunch menu (with its wavy margin sets) is a pricey proposition. The best bet is to order an $8.50 combination, where you have your choice of two: duck spring rolls, Caesar salad, angel hair onion rings, chef's soup, seasonal salad, sweet and spicy calamari, half turkey wrap. If your idea of calamari has anything to do with rubber bands, try Michael's cornmeal-battered, hand-breaded version — tender to a T, and complemented with a wonderful sauce and corn-pancetta relish. Such are the touches that makes Michael's a consistent winner. Specialties on the dinner menu include pan-seared Chilean sea bass with vegetable couscous, artichoke hearts, and thyme-tomato coulis; marinated lamb chops with goat cheese Yukon gold potatoes gratin; and crab cakes with remoulade. For dessert, why not a key lime martini or roasted apple croustade? The menus change bimonthly as chefs come up with ever more creative dishes. Michael's is also known, naturally, for its extensive wine list, featuring 20 wines by the glass, including sparkling. In the same shopping center, you can buy take-home bottles at Michael's Wine Cellar.

MÌ PUEBLO
941-379-2880.
4436 Bee Ridge Rd.,
  Sarasota 34233.
In Palm Plaza.
Price: Inexpensive to
  Moderate.
Children's Menu: Yes.
Cuisine: Mexican.
Liquor: Full.
Serving: L, D.
Credit Cards: AE, MC, V.
Handicap Access: Yes.
Reservations: No.

Tucked into a nondescript shopping center (look for the most stand-out, colorful storefront) far from Sarasota's trendy dining districts, Mì Pueblo serves authentic Mexican (from the Chihuahua region) and Tex-Mex specialties from a simple menu in a modest but gaily decorated cantina. Airbrushed paintings of beer and hot sauce labels brighten pueblo-style walls. Painted tiles inlay heavy wooden tables, and saltillo floor tiles complete the south-of-the-border look. The owners, servers, and chefs chatter in Spanish. Typical dishes such as fajitas, burritos, tamales, and enchiladas (three varieties: ropa, verde, and suiza) comprise the menu. Specialties include pollo con mole, chili relleno, pollo Zargoza (marinated and grilled chicken), and carne asada — grilled sirloin nicely seasoned Chihuahua style with grilled bell peppers, onions, and homemade tortillas. Everything has just that extra ounce of flavor more than the chain restaurants purveying their versions of the same. The salsa was boldly spicy, served with homemade multicolored nacho chips for a kick of trendy. More than typical side dishes to fill a plate, the refried beans and rice were worthwhile companions. The Mexican toothpicks appetizer — batter-fried strips of onion and jalapeno — come recommended. The flan had character, coarser than you find in the assembly-line chains but flavored with that inimitable something that smacks of someplace warm, exotic, and folksy.

PHILLIPPI CREEK
  VILLAGE OYSTER
  BAR
941-925-4444.
5353 S. Tamiami Trail,
  Sarasota 34231.
Price: Moderate.
Early Dining Menu: No.
Children's Menu: Yes.
Cuisine: Seafood/Old
  Florida.
Healthy Selections: Yes.
Liquor: Full.
Serving: L, D.
Credit Cards: AE, MC, V.
Handicap Access: Yes.
Reservations: No.

In Sarasota they call their fish houses "oyster bars," and Phillippi Creek sets the gold standard. Combo pots for two are the specialty of the house: pans full of steamed oysters, shrimp, corn on the cob, and a selection of specialty items (clams, lobster, crab, or scallops). The seafood is so fresh, it ought to be slapped. We've eaten here on several occasions; it's my husband's first choice when we're in town. He loves the gooey-thick clam chowder and fried oyster sandwich. I typically pick the blackened grouper sandwich, which comes with a mustardy tartar sauce, a dill pickle, and sliced pickled banana peppers for relish. You have your choice of settings here, either indoors, glassed-in with a

THE BANGKOK RESTAURANT
941-922-0703.
4791 Swift Rd., Sarasota 34231.
Price: Inexpensive to Moderate.
Children's Menu: check
Cuisine: Thai.
Liquor: Beer and wine.
Serving: L, D.
Closed: Fri.–Sun. for lunch.
Credit Cards: check
Handicap Access: Yes.
Reservations: check

Special Features: Patio and floating dock seating creekside.

boathouse motif, or out in the breeze on dry dock. Either way you get a backwater view and the kind of service that puts you at ease.

With its intricately sculpted wood tables and Thai art, the Bangkok feels like a cultural refuge from the anonymity of old suburban Sarasota. Sink into long booths, whose benches are padded with gaily colored pillows as you peruse a menu that takes a virtual tour of Thailand's regional cooking styles and pan-Asian influences. Popular for lunch, the Bangkok's strip mall parking lot often is jammed. Both lunch and dinner are incredibly reasonable and offer many of the same dishes with a choice of beef, chicken, pork, shrimp, scallops, squid, and vegetarian preparations. Curry dishes are slathered in rich, thick coconut milk sauce, and although indicated as native hot with a chile icon, they are actually fairly temperate. Fortunately, for us fire-eaters, a vessel of hot sauce is provided each table. The massaman, with its peanut crunch, was tasty, but a bit short on the beef I had selected. The extensive menu covers the traditional fried rice, sweet and sour, pepper steak, stir-fries, noodle dishes, satay, and soups that are standard Thai fare. Specialties include crispy duckling, barbecue chicken, grilled prawns, and whole fish. I skipped on dessert but was intrigued nonetheless by the honey banana wrapped in rice paper and Thai custard over soft Thai sweet purple rice.

SUGAR & SPICE
941-342-1649.
4000 Cattlemen Rd., Sarasota 34233.
Price: Inexpensive to Moderate.
Early Dining Menu: No.
Children's Menu: Yes.
Cuisine: Mennonite/ Home-Style.
Healthy Selections: Yes, vegetarian.
Liquor: No.
Serving: L, D.
Closed: Sun.
Credit Cards: D, MC, V.
Handicap Access: Yes.
Reservations: No.

Ahappy outgrowth of the Amish/Mennonite community in Sarasota is the home cooking found in family restaurants throughout the area. These folks are principally farmers, so you can expect farmhouse-style freshness at their table. Most of their eateries occupy large dining rooms with all the ambiance of a fast-food chain. This one displays some nice homey touches, such as lacy curtains and stenciled walls. Daily specials showcase typical old-fashioned goodness: baked chicken, chicken pot pie, Swiss steak, and barbecued pork ribs. Under the "Just Downright Good Eat'n'" heading you can choose from meat loaf, liver and onions, fried catfish, and breaded chopped veal — good old Midwestern comfort foods, all enhanced by home-baked bread and your choice of side dishes. There are also sandwiches, salads, and vegetarian items on the menu. Don't dare forget to leave room for dessert — Sugar & Spice tempts you with close to two dozen choices — especially the famous Amish forte: pie. My favorite is the rhubarb pie, crusted with sugar and topped with rich, ivory-colored vanilla ice cream. The specialty is shoofly pie, with a cake-like texture, wet bottom, and molasses flavor.

Siesta Key

THE BROKEN EGG
941-346-2750.
www.the brokenegg.com.
210 Avenida Madera, Siesta Key 34242.
Price: Inexpensive.
Children's Menu: No.
Cuisine: American.
Healthy Selections: No.
Liquor: Beer and wine.
Serving: B, L daily.
Credit Cards: AE, D, DC, MC, V.
Handicap Access: Restaurant yes, rest rooms no.
Reservations: No.
Special Features: Sidewalk seating, attached deli, bakery, and art gallery.

If you're wondering where all the islanders are at breakfast time, turn the corner at Coldwell Banker on Beach Avenue, and take a seat indoors or out at the Broken Egg. I was warned that this was cholesterol overload, and it's true: How could a restaurant with "egg" in its name not be? Besides breakfast omelets, 12 types of fluffy platter-sized pancakes, banana nut bread French toast, deep-dish quiches, muffins, coffee cake, and other fresh bakery items, the café serves lunch, which consists of soup, salad, and sandwiches. From the bakery, I recommend a cinnamon swirl, topped with cream cheesy frosting. The portobello benedict takes a semihealthy departure, adding mushrooms and tomatoes while subtracting meat. Try the Sheep-herder: poached eggs over hash browns with ched-dar and Swiss. Lunchtime, Brad's Fave is a grilled, seasoned chicken breast with onion, tomatoes, cheddar, and pineapple pepper jelly between slices of sourdough bread. If you do feel the compulsion to offset the richness of the menu, do as I did: Order a carrot-apple juice cocktail. Then ask for dessert.

THE SUMMERHOUSE
941-349-1100.
www.sarasotarestaurants. com.
6101 Midnight Pass Rd., Sarasota 34242.
Price: Expensive to Very Expensive.
Early Dining Menu: No.
Children's Menu: No, but a light menu from upstairs has appropriate items.
Cuisine: Continental.
Healthy Selections: Yes.
Liquor: Full.

Summerhouse: The name connotes an upscale informality. I love the name, always have. And I love the setting. The Summerhouse is acclaimed for its design, a prime example of the so-called Sarasota School of Architecture, which brings the outdoors inside via walls of glass and junglelike grounds. You feel like you're dining in a garden, surrounded by bamboo, palms, and wild coffee plants. It's a totally pleasant experience. The servers are unpretentious; mine went out of his way to make my meal all that it could be. The menu is a study in continental gone off on a nouvelle tangent, with the accent more on flavor than lightness. Take the Tournedos Rossini: Fork-tender beef medallions

Siesta Key's Summerhouse restaurant lets the outdoors in.

Karen T. Bartlett

Serving: D.
Credit Cards: AE, DC, D, MC, V.
Handicap Access: Yes.
Reservations: Yes.
Special Features: Glass walls surrounded by gardens and outdoor seating; piano and other live entertainment.

topped with seared foie gras and the most elegant port and sage sauce. Entrées favor meat and seafood: grilled pork tenderloin with honey mustard, roast duckling, veal Oscar, venison chop, grouper piccata, and lightly pan-blackened yellowfin tuna (delicious with a lemon-lime beurre blanc), as a sampling. I recommend the Caesar salad (heavy on the parmesan cheese) and macadamia-nut shrimp with a light vinegary honey-mustard dip to start and the crème brûlée for the perfect finish. The latter had the most delicate custard I've tasted beneath an ever-so-thin caramel veneer.

Venice

KEY WEST GRILL
941-488-0583
900 Venetia Bay Blvd, Venice 34292.
Off Hwy. 41 north of Hwy. 41 Bypass.
Price: Moderate.
Children's Menu: No.
Cuisine: Floribbean.
Liquor: Full.
Serving: L, D.
Credit Cards: AE, D, DC, MC, V.
Handicap Access: Yes.
Reservations: No.

Fresh and pretty, overlooking a fountained pond, Key West Grill promises to be a lot of fun, both in its Hemingwayesque oak barroom and its airy and light multi-roomed restaurant. The theme is obvious — yet another copycat of that inimitable Key West *je ne sais quoi*. How does *this* impersonator fare? I was excited and hopeful when a miniature loaf of banana bread with strawberry butter arrived as I perused the coconut- and fruit-saturated menu. The restaurant's perception of Key West cuisine was well described on the back but didn't translate well to the dishes —a disappointment. The ubiquitous conch fritters are there, but most everything else only effects island style with bits of fruit or fruity sauces. The Paradise dinner salad, for instance, contained strawberries and canned mandarin oranges. Not exactly tropical, though I did enjoy its sweet and cream coconut-mango dressing. The Sanibel blackened scallops (Sanibel, by the way, is not a Florida Key), were recommended, but I found the seasoning off, even with the addition of the side of pineapple-ginger sauce — though easily helped by a dosage from the bottle of Hot Lava pepper sauce on the table (next to a bottle of Pickapeppa Sauce, score one more). It came on a nice bed of orzo. Hemingway's BBQ Ribs were tender enough, and the sauce spicy-tasty, but the latter was applied much too heavily and I suspect came from a jar. Other offerings include grilled and blackened fish, steak, and combinations thereof, also cheeseburgers, salads, and sandwiches. The key lime pie, made from real key lime juice says the menu, was good, though the crust tasted a bit overbaked. In short, Key West Grill is a fun, congenial place to dine. The price is right and the food satisfying to someone not looking for a true Key West-Caribbean experience.

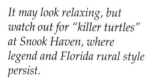

It may look relaxing, but watch out for "killer turtles" at Snook Haven, where legend and Florida rural style persist.

Karen T. Bartlett

SNOOK HAVEN
941-485-7221.
www.venice-fla.com/
  snookhaven/.
5000 E. Venice Ave., Venice
  34292.
Exit 34 off Interstate 75.
Price: Inexpensive to
  moderate.
Children's Menu: No, but
  kid-appropriate items on
  regular menu.
Cuisine: Old Florida/
  Barbecue.
Liquor: Full bar.

For a poignant taste of rural Old Florida close to the freeway, visit Snook Haven on a Sunday for live country music and barbecue. Make a day of it and go for a boat ride. Hear the legend of the killer turtles (a leftover from the 1940s on-site filming of *Revenge of the Killer Turtles*). Or visit any day and enjoy ultracasual dining — burgers, fried fish and okra, chicken gizzards, barbecue specialties, etc. — on the banks of the wild and scenic Myakka River. A rare taste treat, snook — a mild-tasting game fish that can't be sold commercially, but this is farmed — appears on the menu either grilled, fried, or

Serving: L, D.
Credit Cards: MC, V.
Handicap Access:
  Restaurant yes, rest
  rooms no.
Reservations: No.
Special Features: Barbecue
  bashes Sundays; live
  music nightly; view of
  the Myakka River with
  canoeing available.

blackened. The baked beans are among the best I've ever tasted, liberally flavored with bacon. Sit at the stretch tables and plastic chairs inside or at a picnic table on the screened porch or riverside deck. Afterward, work off your meal with a leisurely canoe paddle down the lazy river. It's truly a "y'all come" kind of place.

FOOD PURVEYORS

BAKERIES

The Broken Egg (941-346-2750; www.thebrokenegg.com; 210 Avenida Madera, Siesta Key 34242) Yummy cinnamon swirls, muffins, coffee cakes, pies, and gourmet items including an impressive collection of hot sauces, some their own brand.

La Fille du Boulanger (941-955-8871; 1960 Hillview St., Sarasota 34239) French bread and pastries in a bistro setting.

Pastry Art Bakery (941-795-1719; 6753 Manatee Ave. W., Bradenton 34209; and 1508 Main St., Sarasota 34236) A true bakery, with luscious cakes, cookies, desserts, European pastries, breads, rolls, and fragrant coffees.

Sarasota Bread Company (941-957-3200; 208 Southgate Plaza, Sarasota 34239; www.sarasotarestaurants.com) From Chef Paul of Siesta Key's Summerhouse fame (see above), this bakery-café sells "artisan breads," cakes, and pastries along with wine and gourmet "to go" items.

CANDY & ICE CREAM

Big Olaf Creamery (941-349-9392; 5208 Ocean Blvd., Siesta Key 34242) A vintage purveyor of fresh fudge, hand-made waffle cones, homemade ice cream, skinny dips (low-fat frozen dessert), espresso, and cappuccino.

Kilwin's Chocolates & Ice Cream (941-388-3200; 312 John Ringling Blvd., Sarasota 34236; at St. Armands Circle) Homemade ice cream, specialty sundaes, Mackinac Island fudge, and handmade chocolates.

Joe's Eats & Sweets (941-778-0007; joesweets@juno.com; 219 Gulf Dr. S., Bradenton Beach 34217) Forty gourmet flavors of ice cream (pumpkin, cotton candy, pineapple coconut, etc.) made on the premises, including sugar-free and fat-free varieties, plus low-fat yogurt. Homemade fudge in dozens of unusual flavors, sodas, creative sundaes (black forest, Hawaiian delight, apple picker, and wet walnut, for instance), shakes, espresso, and cappuccino.

Martha's Candy & Clutter (941-485-4904; 237 W. Venice Ave., Venice 34285) Homemade bonbons, chocolates in all shapes and foils, old-fashioned hard candies, plus candles and gifts.

Simply Chocolate (941-906-8848; 1907 S. Osprey Ave., Sarasota 34239; at Southside Village) Just walk in and take a whiff; you're bound to buy something. Featuring various flavors of homemade chocolate bark, truffles, dipped chocolates, and ice cream.

The Soda Fountain (941-412-9860; 349 W. Venice Ave., Venice 34285) An old-fashioned place with counter seating, chrome swizzle stools, and marble-table booths. The extensive menu includes sandwiches, 18 types of hot dogs, phosphates, sundaes, floats, freezes, malts, and ice cream sodas (peanut butter, pineapple, mocha, etc.).

COFFEE

Anna Maria Island Coffee Co. (941-779-0341, 877-779-0341; www.amicoffee.com; 314 Pine Ave., Anna Maria 34216) House-roasted coffee, espresso, cappuccino, latte, frappé, teas, pastries, biscotti, and desserts.

Smokin Joe's Cigars & Coffee (941-365-3556; smokinjoescigars@cs.com; 1448 Main St., Sarasota 34236) A succinct statement of how downtown Sarasota meshes cutting-edge with old-fashioned, this counter gourmet coffee shop shares space with an old-fashioned smoke shop made au courant with a number of fancy walk-in humidors.

Venice Wine & Coffee/Island Gourmet (941-484-3667; 201 Venice Ave. W., Venice 34285) Buy gourmet coffee by the bag or cup at the espresso bar. Also teas, wine, spices, and hard-to-find gourmet food items.

DELI & SPECIALTY FOODS

The Broken Egg (941-346-2750; www.thebrokenegg.com; 210 Avenida Madera, Siesta Key, 34242) Bakery and gourmet items including an impressive collection of hot sauces, some the house brand.

Columbia Restaurant Cigar and Gift Store (941-388-1026, 800-426-5862; www.columbiarestaurant.com; 421 St. Armands Circle, Sarasota 34236) Dressings, black beans mix, sangria jelly, cookbook, coffee, and other items sold in the renowned Spanish restaurant.

The Chop Shop (941-794-MEAT; 5906 Manatee Ave. W. Bradenton 34209) Prime meats, fresh seafood, deli items, oven-ready entrées, wine, and beer.

Geier's Sausage Kitchen (941-923-3004; 7447 Tamiami Trail, Sarasota 34231) European-style sausage and smoked meats, prime fresh meats.

The Gourmet Market (941-953-9101, 888-953-9101; www.thegourmetmarket. com; 1469 Main St., Sarasota 34236) A delightful place full of good smells, cheeses, Godiva chocolate, pastas, oils, vinegars, coffees, wine, and hot sauces.

Morton's Market (941-955-9856; www.epicureanlife.com; 1924 S. Osprey Ave., Sarasota 34239; Southside Village) The ultimate gourmet's delight, it sells hot and cold prepared items for take-out, fresh produce, deli and fresh meats, seafood, coffees, shelves of gourmet products, you name it.

St. Armands Deli (941-388-3187; 7 S. Blvd. of Presidents, Sarasota 34236; at St. Armands Circle) Meats, cheeses, pre-made salads, hot and cold sandwiches, fresh bagels, baguettes, croissants, fruit cobblers, cookies.

FRUIT & VEGETABLE STANDS

Albritton Fruit (941-365-3855, 800-237-3682; 1825 S. Tamiami Trail, Sarasota 34239) With five locations throughout the area, Albritton is a well-known name in citrus. Grove and packing house trolley tours available in the growing season.

Bradenton Farmers' Market (941-748-7949; 500 15th St. W., Bradenton 34205; at the Bradenton City Hall parking lot,) Runs 8 to noon on Saturday, October through April. Fresh local produce, plants, flowers, and baked goods.

Mixon Fruit Farms (941-748-5829, 800-608-2525; www.mixon.com; 2712 26th Ave. E., PO Box 25200, Bradenton 34206) Large, old, family-owned business specializing in citrus. Tours of the grove and processing plant, free samples, shipping, and a gift shop selling fruit, fudge, ice cream, and jellies. Open Nov.–Apr.

Sarasota Farmers' Market (941-951-2656; Lemon Ave. between First St. and Main St., downtown Sarasota) Florida fruits, vegetables, flowers, plants, and honey. Every Saturday 7 to noon.

NATURAL FOODS

Here's to Your Health (941-778-4322; 5340 Gulf Dr., Holmes Beach 34217) Juice bar, teas, produce, vitamins, homeopathic treatments, organic beer and wine. Delivery available.

Kristine's Coffee House & Juice Bar (941-486-8797; 200 Miami Ave. W., Venice 34285) Organic vegetable juice blends such as beet, carrot, cucumber, celery, spinach, and parsley; fruit and fruit-vegetable blends, wheatgrass juice.

PIZZA & TAKEOUT

Circle Deli-Diner at the Pharmacy (941-388-2110; 19 N. Blvd. of Presidents, Sarasota 34236; at St. Armands Circle) Breakfast items (all day), sandwiches, soups, and salads to go or eat in.

Crusty Louie's Pizza (941-366-3100; 3800 Tamiami Trail S. #29, Sarasota 34239; at Paradise Plaza) Stuffed, pan, Chicago-style, or thin-crust pizza made with whole-wheat crust and low-fat, low-salt cheeses.

Lonni's Sandwiches, Etc. (941-363-9222; www.lonnissandwiches.com; 1535 Main St., Sarasota 34236) Pick up homemade gourmet hot and cold sandwiches, salads, soups, and healthy selections here amid Main Street's activity. Call ahead for fastest service. Free delivery to local businesses.

Morton's Market (941-955-9856; www.epicureanlife.com; 1924 S. Osprey Ave., Sarasota 34239; at Southside Village) Wildly popular (practically legendary), Morton's sells hot prepared items, pizza, deli sandwiches, salads, bakery goods, and homemade desserts for take-out, plus fresh produce, deli and fresh meats, seafood, coffees, and gourmet products.

Steve's Super Subs & Sandwiches (941-484-7151; 339 W. Venice Ave., Venice 34285) Deli and veggie sandwiches, breakfast, homemade soups.

SEAFOOD

Star Fish Company (941-794-1243; 12306 46th Ave. W., PO Box 1, Cortez 34215) To get any closer to the source, you'd have to get wet. This longstanding tradition is the anchor of Cortez village's working waterfront, where crusty old fishing boats pull up and murals and plaques deliver lessons on history and heritage. Buy fresh, fresh fish in the market to take home or eat it there dockside on picnic tables.

CULTURE

Culture arrived on the Sarasota Bay coast with the early settlers of wealth and means. Eager at first to escape metropolitan ways for the simplicity of life on the beach, they eventually craved access to theater and fine arts, and so ensured their existence.

Sarasota benefited most from the generous cultural endowment of the Ringling brothers. Not only did the Ringlings bring circus magic to a quiet frontier town, but they also exposed the pioneers to the wonders of European art and architecture. In their wake they left a spirit still palpable and entirely unique to the Gulf Coast. Art schools and theater groups in Sarasota breed a freshness, vitality, daring, and avant-garde spirit unusual for a town its size. Siesta Key, especially, has an atmosphere that has attracted writers, artists, actors, and cartoonists since folks began settling there.

Sarasota's cultural heritage began with an influx of Scottish settlers at the turn of the century. Now widely varied, its population includes a colony of Amish/Mennonite residents in a district known as Pinecraft, around Bahia Vista Street and Beneva Road. Here you'll see long-bearded men driving tractors down the streets, a Mennonite Church, simple homes, a neighborhood park, and an Amish restaurant or two. The African-American district is known as Newtown and lies between Highways 41 and 301 between 10th Street and Myrtle Road.

Cà D'Zan, a salute to Gilded Age prosperity on the Ringling Estate.

Karen T. Bartlett

ARCHITECTURE

In the Bradenton area, the Greek Revival style of plantation house has left its mark. The best example of it survives grandly at Gamble Plantation (see "Historic Sites"). Pioneer styles are preserved at the Manatee Historical Village, including a Cracker Gothic farmhouse, a one-room schoolhouse, and an early brick store. In downtown Bradenton you'll find primo Mediterranean influence at the pink Riverpark Residence Hotel (rumored to have hosted Al Capone in a former life) and in later-generation buildings such as the South Florida Museum. Old Florida-Victorian style survives in the homes of neighborhoods around downtown.

On Longboat Key, resorts and mansions are modern and ostentatious. In the village once known as Longbeach, one finds a return to comfortable, older styles with a bit of New England charm.

Sarasota's downtown and bay areas hold a smorgasbord of old-European styles, from the lavish Italian-inspired Cà d'Zan at the Ringling Estate to the Spanish Opera House downtown. Fine examples of old residential architecture are found on the fringes of the downtown area. In contrast, the Frank Lloyd Wright Foundation's Van Wezel Performing Hall makes a big purple shell statement on the bay shoreline.

In the 1950s Sarasota revolutionized local architecture by developing a contemporary style suitable to the environment. Examples of the "Sarasota School of Architecture" are spread throughout the area, notably at Summerhouse Restaurant on Siesta Key. Often overlooked, Venice houses many architectural treasures created in the 1920s, when the Brotherhood of Locomotive Engineers selected it as a retirement center and subsequently built a model city in northern-Italian style. Two shining examples are the Park Place Nursing Home at Tampa Avenue and Nassau Street — originally the Hotel Venice — and the nearby Venice Centre Mall, once the San Marco Hotel, later the Kentucky Military

Institute. The length of West Venice Avenue reveals stunning shops and homes in the prevailing Mediterranean Revival style as does the Venezia Park neighborhood along nearby Nassau Street. You'll find architectural treasures throughout the city, which strives to preserve its treasures. To help in your search, look for a copy of *Venice Historical Walking/Driving Tour,* available at Venice Archives and Area Historical Collection (see Museums) or other locations.

CINEMA

FILM

Sarasota is a hotbed for film, with its celebrated film festivals, alternative film cinema, and ideal location for filming.

Sarasota Film Society (941-364-8662, box office 955-FILM; www.filmsociety .org; Burns Court Cinema, 506 Burns Ln., Sarasota 34236; downtown) This group is devoted to screening quality international films year-round, both first-run and classic. It sponsor the Cine-World Film Festival (see "Calendar of Events" at the end of this chapter).

MOVIES

Bradenton Cinema 8 (941-954-5768; www.regalcinemas.com; 7150 Cortez Rd. W., Bradenton 34210)

Burns Court Cinema (941-364-8662; 506 Burns Ln., Sarasota 34236) Bright-pink movie theater showing art and other out-of-the-mainstream films.

Hollywood 20 (941-954-5768; www.regalcinemas.com; 1993 Main St. at Hwy. 301, Sarasota 34236; downtown) New state-of-the-art theaters with stadium seating and surround-sound stereo.

Venetian 6 Theatres (941-493-0522; 1733 Tamiami Trail S., Venice 34293; Venetian Plaza)

AMC 12 Theatres at Sarasota Square Mall (941-924-1383; 8027 Beneva Rd., Sarasota 34238; at Tamiami Trail S. and Beneva Rd.)

DANCE

American International Dance Centre (941-955-8363; 556 S. Pineapple Ave., Sarasota 34236) Ballroom dancing instruction and competition for adults and children.

Grapevine Folk Dance Group (941-927-7548; Adult Recreation Center, 801 Tamiami Trail, Sarasota; mailing address: 3880 El Poinier, Sarasota 34243) Authentic international folk dances.

Sarasota Ballet (941-359-0099, box office 351-8000; www.sarasotaballet.org; 5555 N. Tamiami Trail, Sarasota 34243) Classic and interpretative dance performances are staged by professionals at the FSU Center for the Performing Arts and Van Wezel Performing Arts Center, from September to April.

Sarasota Scottish Country Dancers (941-485-7488, 755-6212; 194 Sunrae Terrace, Nokomis 34275) Evidence of the town's Scottish heritage, the group meets regularly and participates at special events.

GARDENS

HISTORIC SPANISH POINT
941-966-5214.
www.historicspanishpoint.org.
337 N. Tamiami Trail, PO Box 846, Osprey 34229.
Open: 9am–5pm Mon.–Sat.; 12–5pm Sun.
Admission: $7 adults, $3 children 6–12.

This multi-era historic attraction (see "Historic Homes & Sites," below) features the ornamental and native gardens built by Sarasota matriarch Bertha Honore Palmer in the 1910s. The Duchene Lawn, the most dramatic, is lined with towering palms and holds a Greek-column portal that once framed a view of the sea. To create the lovely jungle walk, Mrs. Palmer built a miniature aqueduct system. A sunken garden, fern walk, and ornamental pond also provide oases of lush respite along the path at this 30-acre site.

MARIE SELBY BOTANICAL GARDENS
941-366-5731.
www.selby.org.
811 S. Palm Ave., Sarasota 34236.
Admission: $8 adults, $4 children ages 6–11, free for children 5 and under.
Open: 10am–5pm daily.
Closed: Christmas Day.

This 1920s residence on Sarasota Bay occupies 10 acres planted in gardens that wow plant lovers with plots of palm, bamboo, hibiscus, tropical food plants, herbs, and other exotic flora. Selby is world-renowned for its collection of more than 6,000 orchids in a lush rainforest setting among bromeliads and rare tropical plants.

RINGLING ESTATE ROSE GARDEN AND GROUNDS
941-359-5725.
www.ringling.org.
5401 Bay Shore Rd., Sarasota 34243.
On the Ringling Estate.
Open: Daily 10am–5:30pm.
Admission: Free.

Mammoth banyan trees (gifts from Thomas Edison, who had an estate in Fort Myers), a showy poinciana, statuesque royal palms, and a rose garden planted in 1913 are the centerpieces of the lovely bayfront Ringling Estate. Family graves are situated in the Secret Garden near Cà d'Zan, and the Dwarf Garden lies between the art museum and Asolo Theater.

SARASOTA JUNGLE GARDENS
941-355-5305.
www.sarasotajunglegardens.com
3701 Bayshore Rd., Sarasota 34234.

Although this is largely a kiddy attraction, plant lovers will enjoy the botanical gardens and cool, tropical jungle. Winding paved paths lead easily through the grounds' 16 acres, a hundred varieties of palms, and countless species of indigenous

Open: Daily 9am–5pm.
Admission: $10 adults; $9
   seniors; $6 children 3–12.

and exotic flora, all identified. Private nooks and bubbling brooks make this a lovely spot for quiet reflection, especially in the early morning before the throngs arrive. Exotic birds and other attractions are gravy for the connoisseur of nature. (See "Kids' Stuff" in this section.) Snack bar and gift shop.

HISTORIC HOMES & SITES

BRADEN CASTLE RUINS
27th St. E. and Rte. 64,
   Bradenton, FL.
Open: Sunrise to sunset.

At the juncture of the Manatee and Braden Rivers, antebellum memories crumble gracefully in a setting recognized by the National Register of Historic Sites. Just short of spectacular, the plantation house ruins are chain-linked and posted with KEEP OUT DANGER signs. They hide at the center of a retirement trailer community in a riverside park that's not easy to find. A marker tells the story of Dr. Joseph Addison Braden from Virginia and his ill-fated Braden Plantation.

CÀ D'ZAN
941-359-7500.
www.ringling.org.
5401 Bay Shore Rd.,
   Sarasota 34243.
On the Ringling Estate.
Open: Daily 10am–5:30pm.
Closed: Major holidays.
Admission: $9 adults, $8
   seniors 55 and over;
   covers entry to all
   Ringling attractions.
   Children 12 and under
   accompanied by an
   adult, free; Florida
   students and teachers
   free with proper ID.

Two years of restoration, completed in December 2001, have brought this showpiece back to its Gilded Age glory. Using the Doges Palace in Venice as a model, circus king John Ringling spared no expense building a monument to success and overindulgence in the 1920s. He imported styles, materials, and pieces from Italy, France, and elsewhere around the world to embellish his so-called (in Italian) House of John. Baroque, Gothic, and Renaissance elements, marble, colored tiles, and multicolor tinted jesterlike leaded windows contribute to a breathtaking and ornate look of Roaring Twenties opulence in the 30-room, $1.5 million mansion on the bay at the John and Mable Ringling Museum of Art (see "Visual Arts Centers & Resources," below).

CORTEZ VILLAGE
Cortez Rd. and 123rd St.,
   Bradenton, FL.

Remnants of an 1880s fishing village include old tin-roofed fish houses, boat works, and a waterfront store. Exhibits and painted murals throughout the ramshackle district describe local culture and environmental practices.

Karen T. Bartlett

Walking in history's footsteps at De Soto National Memorial Park in Bradenton.

DE SOTO NATIONAL MEMORIAL PARK
941-792-0458, ext. 14.
www.nps.gov.deso.index. htm.
75th St. NW, PO Box 15390, Bradenton 34280.
Open: Visitors center 9am–5pm daily, park sunrise to sunset.
Admission: Free.

Somewhat off the beaten path, this is a place where you can imagine yourself back in the 16th century among *conquistadores* in heavy armor trying to survive among irate Native Americans, mosquitoes, and sweltering heat. Engraved plaques, a recreated Amerindian village, and a half-mile-long trail tell the story of Hernando de Soto's life and adventures here, where supposedly he first breached the shores of the Florida mainland to begin his heroic trek to the Mississippi River. A visitors center holds artifacts and shells, and a 22-minute video presentation is available. In the winter, rangers dress and play the part of 16th-century inhabitants, demonstrating weaponry and methods of food preparation.

DOWNTOWN BRADENTON
Main Street and Manatee Avenue (Route 64).

Old Main Street and the city yacht basin are the historic downtown district's backbone. Compact, it's easy to walk and experience the old architecture, a fine museum, an intimate theater, park benches, shiny-silver hot dog stands at corners, and brick-paved crosswalks. Locals are trying hard to pump new life into a river town that died with the advent of the automobile. A walking plaza is in the works. Signs announce new antique marts, restaurants, and shops "coming soon." The future looks bright. In the meantime, visit the shops on Main Street and have lunch at a sidewalk café, Nadine's, or Twin Dolphin Marina, then stroll around nearby Point Pleasant for a taste of Bradenton's oak-studded homeyness and heritage.

Karen T. Bartlett

Sugar built the antebellum plantations along Bradenton's Manatee River — perhaps literally in some cases. It is rumored that molasses was mixed into the Gamble Mansion columns' tabby (seashell) mortar.

GAMBLE PLANTATION STATE HISTORICAL SITE

941-723-4536.
3708 Patten Ave., Ellenton 34222.
Route 301 near I-75.
Open: Visitors' Center 8am–4:30pm (closed 11:45am–12:45pm); tours depart at 9:30, 10:30, 1, 2, 3, and 4.
Closed: Tues., Weds.
Admission: Mansion tour, $4 adults, $2 children 6–12. Free admission to visitors center museum.

Major Robert Gamble, originally from Scotland, learned about sugar planting in Virginia and Tallahassee before he moved to the Manatee River. He eventually cleared 1,500 acres of jungle using slave labor and built a home in Greek Revival style. The mansion's crowning touch — eighteen Greek columns — he constructed with a mortar known as "tabby," made of crushed and burned seashells. The spacious (by local standards) palace was inhabited by bachelor Gamble alone but served as the area's social hub until the major was forced to sell it in 1856 because of hurricane, frosts, and market losses. In 1925 the United Daughters of the Confederacy rescued the mansion from decades of neglect. The site was declared a Confederate shrine for its role in sheltering Confederate Secretary of State Judah P. Benjamin, when he fled for his life after the Civil War. The United Daughters donated the monument to the state a couple of years later. Visitors can see the inside of the home by tour only, which takes less than an hour. The two floors contain period furnishings and housewares, which the ranger explains in lively, interesting dialogue. You'll learn, for example, how such expressions as "hush puppy," "sleep tight," and "pop goes the weasel" came to be, and about the lives of 19th-century plantation owners and slaves. The museum in the visitors center tells the plantation's story through the eras. A picnic shelter accommodates lunchers.

HISTORIC SPANISH POINT
941-966-5214.
www.historicspanishpoint.org.
337 N. Tamiami Trail, PO Box 846, Osprey 34229.
Open: 9am–5pm Mon.–Sat.; 12–5pm Sun.
Admission: $7 adults, $3 children 6–12.

This historic site spans multiple eras of the region's past — 2150 B.C. through 1918. Its importance lies not only in its historical aspects but also in its environmental and archaeological significance. Assembled on the 30-acre Little Sarasota Bay estate, once owned by socialite Mrs. Bertha Palmer, are prehistoric Indian burial grounds, a cutaway of a shell midden mound, the relocated homestead and family chapel of the pioneering Webb dynasty, Mrs. Palmer's restored gardens, a late Victorian pioneer home, and lovely gardens (see "Gardens" in this section). Local actors give living-history performances Saturdays and Sundays in the winter. Guided tours and tram rides are available; reserve ahead. Another tip: Bring mosquito repellent in warm weather.

MANATEE VILLAGE HISTORICAL PARK
941-741-4075.
604 15th St. E., Bradenton 34208.
At Manatee Ave.
Open: 9am–4:30pm weekdays, 1:30–4:30pm Sun. Closed Sat. year-round and Sun. July–Aug.
Admission: Free.

Several buildings with local historical significance have been restored and moved to a pleasant, oak-shaded park strongly representative of Bradenton's old wooded and winding neighborhoods. The County Courthouse is the oldest of the structures, completed in 1860. Others include a circa-1889 church, a Cracker farmhouse, a one-room schoolhouse, a smokehouse, and a general store from the early 19th century. A museum of artifacts, photographs, and hands-on exhibits for children is located in the general store. The Stephens House is stocked with preserves, period kitchen items, furniture, and farm implements. Fogarty Boat Works reflects Bradenton's boat-building heritage. The staff wears historically accurate dress. Across the street the Manatee Burying Ground, which dates from 1850, is appropriately eerie, with garlands of Spanish moss swathing craggy oaks. All in all, the park is a romantic site, grossly underrated and lightly visited.

KIDS' STUFF

BISHOP PLANETARIUM
941-746-4131.
www.sfmbp.org.
201 10th St. W., Bradenton
   34205.
Admission: $7.50 adults, $6
   seniors, $5 students, $4
   children 5–12.

Changing Saturday morning family programs at 10:30 for students K-3, including star show and hands-on program in adjacent South Florida Museum. In summer the facility hosts the Junior Space Camp.

G. WIZ is even more fun on the inside!

Karen T. Bartlett

G. WIZ
941-906-1851.
www.gwiz.org.
1001 Boulevard of the Arts,
   Sarasota 34236.
Selby Library Bldg.
Open: Tues.–Sat. 10am–
   5pm, Sun. 1pm–5pm.
Admission: $6 for adults, $5
   for seniors, $4 for ages
   2–18. Free admission the
   first Wed. of the month
   5pm–8pm.

G. WIZ stands for Gulfcoast Wonder & Imagination Zone. But G. Wiz about sums it up. And wow! Recently opened at its new home near the Van Wezel Hall and other cultural attractions, this hands-on affair has been completely reinvented. All shiny and high-tech, it brings hours worth of enrichment entertainment in an uncrowded, gallery-like, glass geodesic setting. The state-of-the-art playground outside is free and far beyond mere swings and slides. Inside on two levels, theme areas explore various scientific and artistic phenomena. The overall theme downstairs is using your senses to find your way. Navigational instruments, a maze, and a map exhibit contribute. Kids love the timed dash against one another and the jump measurer. Kids Lab is geared toward toddlers with a table for fossil digging, a bubble table, and fun-house mirrors. Upstairs, we like the animation workstations best. Here kids can pose and click action figures and other toys one frame at a time to create a short film. For constructive play, this is the best place around to take the kids. Still in progress, more exhibits are being added all the time. Don't forget to stop in the gift shop (as though the kids would let you) for educational playthings.

SARASOTA JUNGLE GARDENS
941-355-5305.
www.sarasotajungle
gardens.com.
3701 Bayshore Rd., Sarasota 34243.
Open: Daily 9am–5pm.
Admission: $10 adults, $9 adults, $6 children 3–12.

Anew birds of prey exhibit and show, reptile and rainforest bird shows, a Meet the Keeper program, free-strolling peacocks and other feathered friends, a playground with a jungle theme, a bird posing area, black leopards, monkeys, flamingos, swans, wallabies, and other live animals make this the area's favorite children's attraction. Peaceful, junglelike gardens appeal to others. (See "Gardens" in this section.)

VAN WEZEL SATURDAY MORNINGS FOR KIDS
941-953-3366, 953-3368.
www.vanwezel.org.
777 N. Tamiami Trail, Sarasota 34236.

Puss *in Books, Wind in the Willows,* other kiddy classics, and contemporary favorites take the stage one Saturday morning each month at 10:30, November through May.

VENICE LITTLE THEATRE FOR YOUNG PEOPLE
941-488-1115.
140 W. Tampa Ave., Venice 34285.

One of the most successful nonprofit community theaters in the U.S., the Little Theatre hosts off-season summer theatrical instruction and three musical performances for youngsters November through May.

MUSEUMS

ANNA MARIA ISLAND HISTORICAL MUSEUM
941-778-0492.
norwoodgc@aol.com.
402 Pine Ave., Anna Maria 34216.
Open: 10am–3pm Sept.–May; 10am–1pm other months.
Closed: Mon., Fri., Sun.
Admission: Donations accepted.

Ahomey little museum inside an icehouse of the 1920s holds a wealth of photos, maps, records, books, a shell collection, a loggerhead turtle display, and vintage movies on video. Next door sits the old jail, its humorous graffiti worth a chuckle.

SARASOTA CLASSIC CAR MUSEUM
941-355-6228.

Displays of more than 100 antique and celebrity cars and 1,200 musical instruments combine under one roof. A half-hour tour explains the his-

www.sarasotacarmuseum.
org.
5500 N. Tamiami Trail,
Sarasota 34239
Open: 9am–6pm daily.
Admission: $8.50 adults; $4
children 6–12.

tory of the player piano, phonographs, music boxes, hurdy-gurdies, and record albums. On tour through the car collection you'll see John Lennon's Mercedes Benz roadster, "Christine" from the eponymous Stephen King movie, John Ringling's Rolls Royces and Pierce Arrows, and vintage motorized vehicles dating from 1903. While waiting for the tours, you can spend nickels, dimes, and quarters in the vintage game arcade. Make Peppy the Musical Clown dance, get your fortune told by the Great Swami, and motor cross-country on the Drive Mobile. It's lots more fun than modern-day arcades.

RINGLING MUSEUM OF THE CIRCUS
941-355-5101.
www.ringling.org.
5401 Bay Shore Rd.,
Sarasota 34243.
On the Ringling Estate.
Open: Daily 10am–5:30pm.
Closed: Holidays.
Admission: $9 adults, $8
seniors 55 and over;
covers admission to all
Ringling attractions.
Children 12 and under
free. Florida students and
teachers free with proper
ID.

The Circus Museum was Florida's way of saying thank you back in 1948. Its re-creation of Big Top magic paid tribute to a man many believed invented the circus, a man who bequeathed to the city — along with the giddy world of the Big Top — a legacy of exotica, sophistication, and art appreciation. The museum reflects Ringling's seemingly contradictory interests. Fine-arts displays counterbalance high-wire exhibits. Black-and-white photography is juxtaposed with gilded fantasy. Tasteful cloth mannequins model plumed and sequined costumes. My favorite parts are the animated scale model of the circus grounds and a narrated behind-the-scenes look at circus lifestyles. In recent years, interactive aspects have been added, such as the "create a circus costume" exhibit, where kids can Velcro props and clothing onto the forms of clowns and an acrobat. The museum is located on the grounds of the John and Mable Ringling Museum of Art (see "Visual Arts Centers & Resources," below).

SOUTH FLORIDA MUSEUM
941-746-4131.
www.sfmbp.org.
201 10th St. W., Bradenton
32405.
Open: 10am–5pm
Mon.–Sat., 12–5pm Sun.
Closed: Mon. May-Dec.
(except July).
Admission: $7.50 adults, $6
seniors, $5 students, $4
children 5–12.

This two-story museum, undergoing renovation but remaining open, scans Florida history with a focus on Native American life and Civil War days. The star of the museum is Snooty, the oldest manatee born in captivity (1948) in the United States. You can watch him and his playmate, Mo, underwater from aquarium windows or from above at the Parker Aquarium, where interactive exhibits explain the plight of the endangered manatee and educational presentations take place throughout the day. The museum walks you through the region's historical eras with realistic, life-size Native American dioramas, replicated early Spanish buildings, a log cabin, Victorian furniture, and a host of other displays. One of the museum's most prized exhibits, the Tallant Collection, displays artifacts excavated mostly from Manatee County. A portion of it has been placed in the Smithsonian Institution. The Bishop Planetarium adjoins the handsome neo-Mediterranean museum with a 50-foot hemispherical dome, laser shows, and other special effects. The museum's $5 million renovation is expected to be complete sometime in 2002. It focuses on a new entryway, which introduces visitors to the region's first people, and other exhibit upgrades.

VENICE ARCHIVES AND AREA HISTORICAL COLLECTION
941-486-2487.
www.venice-florida.com/
community/archive.
351 S. Nassau St., Venice 34285.
Open: Mon. and Wed. 10am–4pm.
Admission: Free or by donation.

The most interesting relic here is the building that houses the facility. A 1927 Italianiate structure with a triangular base and a Renaissance tower, it once was called the Triangular Inn. Stop for a peek at whatever exhibit is showing, a room full of local fossils, and another honoring city father Dr. Fred Albee, whose operating table you'll find, among other memorabilia. A city park lies across the street.

MUSIC & NIGHTLIFE

Sarasota dances with action throughout the week and especially on weekends. Besides local bands, both well-known and up-and-coming stars appear in theaters, cabarets, and nightclubs. Cores of activity include downtown, the neon-bright Sarasota Quay, and posh St. Armands Circle. Check the *Sarasota Herald-Tribune*'s Ticket and *Bradenton Herald*'s Weekend every Friday to learn what's happening in the clubs throughout the area.

Bradenton

Speak Easy Grill (941-747-2729; 1012 Manatee Ave. W., Bradenton 34205) Drinking and dining with live entertainment Thursday through Saturday.

Bradenton Beach

Dockside Bar (941-778-3886; 135 Bridge St., Bradenton Beach 34217) Rock to live music with a view of the bay.

Sarasota

Down Under Jazz Club (941-951-2467; 214 Sarasota Quay, Sarasota 34236; Fruitville Road at Tamiami Trail) The Gulf Coast's top jazz performers, cigars, and casual dockside meals.

Florida West Coast Symphony (941-953-4252, box office 941-953-3434; www
.fwcs.org; 709 Tamiami Trail N., Sarasota 34236) Besides classical symphony
concerts in season September to May, this group sponsors various related
ensembles, including a string quartet, wind quintet, brass quintet, new artists'
quartet, youth orchestra, and pops series.

The Gator Club (941-366-5969; 1490 Main St., Sarasota 34236; downtown) One of
the hottest places downtown in historic digs, with pressed-tin ceiling and
straw ceiling fans. Live music weekends.

In Extremis (941-954-2008; 204 Sarasota Quay, Sarasota 32346) It parties with
laser, light, sound, video, and live shows. Next door, Zanzibar is a mellower
scene.

Jazz Club of Sarasota (941-316-9207; 330 S. Pineapple Ave., Suite 11, Sarasota
34236) This organization dedicates itself to the perpetuation and encourage-
ment of jazz performance by presenting various monthly and annual events,
Saturday jazz jams, members concerts, special presentations, and youth programs, with a musical instrument lending library. It sponsors a week-long Jazz
Festival in March, featuring top musicians (see "Calendar of Events" at the end
of this chapter).

King Creole (941-365-7474; 1991 Main St., Sarasota 34236) Creole fare with
weekly shows featuring blues, zydeco, world beat, Afro-Cuban, and New
Orleans-rhythm artists.

La Musica (941-364-8802; PO Box 5442, Sarasota 34277) International chamber
musicians in concert at Sarasota Opera House in April.

Sarasota Concert Band (941-364-2263; 1345 Main St., Sarasota 34236) This ensemble's fifty-some members perform at Van Wezel Performing Arts Hall and other
venues from October through May and at outdoor concerts throughout the area.

Sarasota Friends of Folk Music (941-377-9256; www.foff.org; 3874 Wolverine St.,
Sarasota 34232) Musical group specializing in Florida folk music performs free
monthly concerts on City Island at the Sarasota Sailing Squadron.

Sarasota Pops Orchestra (941-795-7677; 8003 Twelfth Ave. NW, Bradenton
34209) Presents a series of concerts each year November through April.

Venice Symphony (941-488-1010; www.thevenicesymphony.org; PO Box 1561,
Venice 34284) Classical and pops concerts January through April at Church of
the Nazarene (1535 E. Venice Ave.), with a free outdoor pops concert in March.

Siesta Key

Beach Club (941-349-6311; 5151 Ocean Blvd., Siesta Key 34242) Amid the
atmosphere of a rowdy college bar, it hosts local rock, jazz, and reggae
groups nightly.

St. Armands Key

ChaCha Coconuts (941-388-3300; 417 St. Armands Circle, Sarasota 34236)
Contemporary music and dancing Thursday-Sunday, some Wednesdays.

Venice

Crow's Nest (941-484-9551; 1968 Tarpon Center Dr., Venice 34285) Features live jazz musicians and singers on a changing calendar, every night but Sunday.

SPECIALTY LIBRARIES

Arthur Vining Davis Library (941-388-4441; 1600 Ken Thompson Pkwy., Sarasota 34236; on City Island at the Mote Marine Laboratory) Gathers research for lab scientists. Open to the public for reference, preferably by advance appointment.

Family Heritage House (941-752-5319; Manatee Community College, 5840 26th St. W., Bradenton 34207) Part of Florida's Black Heritage Trail, it contains children's books, videotapes, audiotapes, books, magazines, and other materials relevant to black heritage, arts, and culture.

John and Mable Ringling Museum of Art Research Library (941-359-5743; www.ringling.org; 5401 Bay Shore Rd., Sarasota 34243) Specializes in 17th-century Dutch, Flemish, and Italian paintings.

Manatee County Central Library (941-748-5555; 1301 Barcarrotta Blvd. W., Bradenton 34205) The Eaton Room contains a collection of Florida and county historical photographs, newspapers, books, census records, and articles.

Selby Public Library (941-316-1181; 1331 First St., Sarasota 34236) The region's central library, it schedules cultural events throughout the year.

Verman Kimbrough Memorial Library (941-359-7587; Ringling School of Art and Design, 2700 N. Tamiami Trail, Sarasota 34234) Art history and instruction.

THEATER

Anna Maria Island Players (941-778-5755; 10009 Gulf Dr. at Pine Ave., Anna Maria 34216) Year-round community theater in an Old Florida-style building.

Asolo Center for the Performing Arts/Florida State University Acting Conservatory (Box office 941-351-8000, 800-361-8388; www.asolo.org; 5555 N. Tamiami Trail, Sarasota 34243) The Asolo tradition began in Italy in 1798, in a theater built in the queen's castle. It ended up on the Ringling Estate in the 1940s, where it was reconstructed and, in 1965, designated State Theater of Florida. In the early 1980s a new center was built, incorporating into the interior of one of its theaters another dismantled, historic European theater — a Scottish opera house circa 1900. Carved box fronts, friezes, and ornate cornice work from the old theater decorate the new, lending an aura of Old World heritage. Opened in 1989, the 500-seat Harold E. and Esther M. Mertz Theatre hosts the excellent, 40-plus-year-old **Asolo Theatre Company**

The sculpture Applause *greets visitors to the Van Wezel Performing Arts Center.*

Karen T. Bartlett

November through May. Free tours are available Wednesday-Saturday at 10 and 11am, November through June. A separate, more intimate, 161-seat theater called the **Jane B. Cook Theatre** is the home of Florida State University's graduate actor training program.

Circus Sarasota (941-355-7054; www.circussarasota.org; PO Box 18638, Sarasota 34276) This new troupe resurrects Sarasota's deeply entrenched Big Top tradition with a fluctuating schedule of in-town and on-the-road performances. Conceived by Sarasota native Dolly Jacobs (daughter of the late, great circus clown Lou Jacobs), it is a not-for-profit, educational organization.

Florida Studio Theatre and Cabaret Club (941-366-9000; www.fst2000.org; 1241 N. Palm Ave., Sarasota 34236; downtown) A major testing ground for budding playwrights and new works, Florida Studio Theatre's professional troupe presents seven productions during its November–August season and a summertime Florida Playwrights Festival at its intimate main stage (see "Calendar of Events" at the end of this chapter). Musical revues and other light entertainment December-June in the Parisian-style Cabaret Club, with full-service dining.

Golden Apple Dinner Theatre (941-366-5454, 800-652-0920; 25 N. Pineapple Ave., Sarasota 34236; downtown) Year-round Broadway dinner entertainment.

Manatee Players Riverfront Theater (941-748-0111, box office 748-5875; 102 Old Main St., Bradenton 34205) Community theater in an intimate, historic setting. Family and children's theater.

The Players (941-365-2494; www.sarasota-online.com/players; 838 N. Tamiami Trail, Sarasota 34236) Stages musicals, live music, and other programs, plus operates a performing arts school.

Sarasota Opera House (941-366-8450; www.sarasotaopera.org; 61 N. Pineapple Ave., Sarasota 34346; downtown) Don't even try to park or dine downtown on opera opening nights during the February-March season.

Southwest Florida's oldest opera company's opening galas are popular events that require ticket purchase months in advance. In operation for more than 30 years, the Sarasota Opera Association stages all the classics. Its beautifully restored Spanish-mission-style structure in the Theater and Arts District was built in 1926. You can tour the facility (and see the chandelier from the set of *Gone With the Wind*) for $2. Advance arrangements required.

Theatre Works (941-952-9170; 1247 First St., Sarasota 34236; downtown) Professional performances of musicals, comedies, and contemporary plays October through May in an historic, intimate setting.

Van Wezel Performing Arts Hall (941-953-3366, 800-826-9303; www.van wezel.org; 777 N. Tamiami Trail, Sarasota 34236) If a performance is worth seeing, it's at the Van Wezel — that purple eye-catcher that radiates outward like a scallop shell on the shores of Sarasota Bay, designed by the Frank Lloyd Wright Foundation. Tickets should be purchased at least a month in advance. Newly renovated and expanded, the Van Wezel hosts name comedians, musicians, and dance groups; Broadway shows; major orchestras; ethnic music and dance groups; chamber and choral music; and Saturday children's shows.

Venice Little Theatre (941-488-1115; www.venicestage.com; 140 W. Tampa Ave., Venice 34285; downtown) A community-theater company performs seven Mainstage shows in a Mediterranean Revival structure, October through May, and contemporary plays at Stage II, November through April.

VISUAL ARTS CENTERS & RESOURCES

The canvas of Sarasota Bay arts reveals a complex masterpiece, layered with the diverse patterns and local color of its many communities. With its backdrop of artistic types dating back to avid collector John Ringling, Sarasota leads the region to avant-garde heights.

The following entries introduce you to opportunities for experiencing art as either an appreciator or a practicing artist. A listing of commercial galleries is included under "Shopping" in this chapter. Read the *Sarasota Arts Review* for openings and changing exhibitions.

Art Center Sarasota (941-365-2032; www.artsarasota.org; 707 N. Tamiami Trail, Sarasota 34236) Exhibition and sales galleries feature the paintings, jewelry, sculpture, pottery, and enamelware of local and national artists. Art instruction and demonstrations are available. The gallery features an outdoor sculpture garden.

Artists Guild Gallery of Anna Maria Island (941-778-6694; 5414 Marina Dr., Holmes Beach 34217) Features changing exhibitions by local artists.

Art League of Manatee County (941-746-2862; www.almc.org; 209 Ninth St. W., Bradenton 34205) Classes and demonstrations in all media for all ages; sales gallery.

The Fine Arts Society of Sarasota (941-953-3366; Van Wezel Performing Arts Hall, 777 N. Tamiami Trail, Sarasota 34236) Van Wezel houses a permanent collection of Florida artists' works on loan from the Society, which conducts tours weekdays November through April.

The John and Mable Ringling Museum of Art, one of the circus' most enduring legacies to Florida.

Karen T. Bartlett

The John and Mable Ringling Museum of Art (941-359-5700; www.ringling .org; 5401 Bay Shore Rd., Sarasota 34243) Sarasota's pride and joy, this is not only an art museum but also the nucleus of tourism activity and the heart of the local art community. It shares its sixty-six-acre bay front estate with Ringling's extravagant Cà d'Zan Palace, a circus museum (see "Museums"), a rose garden (see "Gardens"), and a Big Top-shaped restaurant. Designated the State Art Museum of Florida, the collection specializes in late medieval and Renaissance Italian works, covering 500 years of European art, most of which was purchased by Ringling. The Old Masters collection contains five original Rubens tapestries as well as Spanish Baroque, French, Dutch, and northern European works, mostly portraits of a religious nature. A hands-on gallery deals with conserving art works, including an exhibit on X-radiography. The museum continually adds to its collection of American and contemporary works. The lushly landscaped courtyards feature reproduction classic statues and Italian decorative columns, which Ringling originally purchased for the hotel he hoped to build on Longboat Key. Admission is charged every day but Saturday and covers all property attractions: $9 for adults, $8 for seniors, free for children 12 and under and Florida students and teachers with ID.

Longboat Key Art Center (941-383-2345; www.longboatkeyartcenter.org; 6860 Longboat Dr. S., Longboat Key 34228) Hidden from mainstream traffic, here is a find for the buyer and would-be artisan. A gallery sells works mostly by Florida artists. Changing exhibits feature local, emerging, and experimental artists. A crafts shop sells wares made at the center's surrounding workshops, where classes are taught in basketry, watercolor, jewelry making, metal craft, pottery, and more.

Manatee Community College Fine Art Gallery (941-755-1511 ext. 65251; 5840 26th St. W., Bradenton 34207) Features works of major artists.

Museum of Asian Art (941-954-7117; www.museumasianart.org; 640 S. Washington Blvd. at Sarasota Art & Antique Center, Sarasota 34236) This newest addition to Sarasota's Art and Theater District displays works dating back to the Han Dynasty (206 B.C.–220 A.D.) originating in China, Thailand, Cambodia, Nepal, and Burma. It is known for its exquisite Yangtze River Collection of Chinese jades, which was previously a traveling exhibit. This and other intricate Chinese jade carvings are the most impressive part of the exhibit, aside from the sheer age of other pieces. Many of the stone and bronze sculptures depict Buddha, Vishnu, and other spiritual figures. Most of the exhibit is permanent, but some rotation is expected to take place in years to come. Admission is $5 for adults, free for students with ID and children. Open Wednesday, Thursday, and Friday 11am–5pm.

Selby Gallery (941-359-7563; 2700 N. Tamiami Trail, Sarasota 34234; at the Ringling School of Art and Design) An intimate, modern space exhibits the works of contemporary student, local, national, and international artists and designers. Free admission. Open 10am–4pm Mon.–Sat., 10am–7pm Tues.

Towles Court Art Association (941-330-9817; www.towlescourt.com; 1945 Morrill St., Sarasota 34236) A charming, blossomy district of restored and brightly painted tin-roofed bungalows turned art colony. Art schools, showings, studios, and galleries. Third Friday "Art By the Light of the Moon" gallery walks, 6–10pm. Guided studio tours available.

Venice Art Center (941-485-7136; 390 S. Nokomis Ave., Venice 34285) Local artists' exhibitions, gift shop, and art instruction.

Village of the Arts (18-block radius around 12th Street and 11th Avenue West, Bradenton) Officially welcomed in January 2001, this new artist colony revitalized an old drug neighborhood, turning it into a work of pride for the community. Artisans from all disciplines — visual arts, healing arts, culinary arts, and performing arts — have moved into the neighborhood to work and sell their art and services.

RECREATION

Known both for its superlative white sand beaches and as the birthplace of Florida golfing, Sarasota and its environs draw outdoors lovers to its year-round playgrounds.

BEACHES

The Sarasota area claims more than 35 miles of sandy seashore. Island beaches are, for the most part, highly developed, with lots of facilities and concessions. Recent years have seen a concession of another sort — to nature

For a change, try making sand angels— in Siesta Key's heavenly white sand.

Chelle Koster Walton

— as boardwalks and sea oat plantings restore the dunes. On the islands, erosion takes its toll, and beaches must be periodically renourished. This stretch of the Gulf Coast boasts some of the whitest beaches this side of the Florida Panhandle, and some of the darkest. Parking is free at all area beaches. Pets and glass containers are prohibited. So is walking across dune vegetation any way but on the boardwalk crossovers.

ANNA MARIA BAYFRONT PARK
Northeast end of Anna Maria Island.
Facilities: Picnic areas, rest rooms, showers, playground, recreational facilities, fishing pier.

One of the region's more secluded beach parks, this one is narrower than the rest of the island's beaches. You get a magnificent view of St. Petersburg's Sunshine Skyway Bridge from the bay. A historical marker tells about the islands' early settlers. Heed danger signs that mark where heavy tidal currents make swimming perilous.

BROHARD BEACH
941-316-1172.
1600 S. Harbor Dr., Venice 34285.
Facilities: Picnic areas, rest rooms, showers, fitness trail, fishing pier, restaurant.

This narrow, dark-flecked sand beach threads under the Venice Fishing Pier and around covered picnic tables. Folks come here to fish, hang out at the pier tiki bar, and hunt for sharks' teeth.

CASPERSEN BEACH
941-316-1172.
South end of Harbor Dr., Venice.
Facilities: Picnic areas, rest rooms, showers.

At the end of the road lies natural, lightly developed Caspersen Beach, where a series of boardwalks cross scrub-vegetated dunes onto diminishing dark sands. It's popular with sharktooth hunters and young beachgoers. From here you can walk to Manasota Key Beach, to the south.

COQUINA BEACH
Southern end of Gulf Dr.,
  Bradenton Beach, Anna
  Maria Island.
Facilities: Picnic areas, rest
  rooms, showers, life-
  guard, café, concessions,
  boat ramps.

Recently renourished, this large and popular park boasts plump wide sands edged in Australian pines. Waters at the south end provide good snorkeling. The park continues on the bay, where swimming should be avoided because of currents and boat traffic. The Coquina BayWalk takes you to environmentally restored Leffis Key, with its towering mound and newly replaced mangrove habitat, a $321 million restoration project.

CORTEZ BEACH
North end of Gulf Dr.,
  Bradenton Beach, Anna
  Maria Island.

Here's a long stretch of revamped sands that meets up with Coquina, its more popular cousin. Surfers like it here. It's convenient for the heavily laden beachgoer because you park right along the sand's edge.

LIDO BEACH
941-346-3310.
400 Benjamin Franklin Dr.,
  Lido Key 34236.
Facilities: Picnic areas, rest
  rooms, showers,
  lifeguards, swimming
  pool, snack bar, swings,
  volleyball.

This is the main beach on Lido Key, heavily developed and popular. Canvas cabanas and stylish, umbrella-shaded lounge chairs may be rented along the stretch of shelly sand. Shellers look for best finds among the piles of boulders and sea rubble. It's a great beach for tiki-bar hopping along the hotel strip. South of the pavilion you'll find water-sports equipment rentals.

LONGBOAT KEY
Public accesses at
  Broadway St. on the
  north end of island.

Longboat Key has beautiful beaches, mostly enjoyed by resort guests and waterfront residents. Public accesses are marked subtly and have no facilities or lifeguards. Parking is limited. The beach stretches wide as well as long, with fluffy white sand and dramatic sunset views.

MANATEE COUNTY PARK
Gulf Blvd., Holmes Beach.
Facilities: Picnic area, rest
  rooms, showers,
  lifeguard, playground,
  restaurant, beach rentals,
  volleyball.

The hot spot of Anna Maria Island beachgoing, this park appeals to families because of its full complement of facilities. The beach is wide enough to accommodate rows and rows of beach towels. Australian pines shade picnic areas.

NOKOMIS BEACH/ NORTH JETTY
914-316-1172.
South end Casey Key Rd.,
  Casey Key.

Remote and exclusive Casey Key gives way to beachy abandon at its south end. The town of Nokomis Beach is a fisherman's haven, and North Jetty, at its south end, lures anglers. A bait shop keeps them supplied. The beach's wide sands, fes-

Facilities: Picnic area, rest rooms, showers, lifeguards, concessions.

NORTH LIDO BEACH
941-316-1172.
North end of Ben Franklin Dr., Lido Key.

PALMA SOLA CAUSEWAY BEACH
Anna Maria Bridge, Route 64.
Facilities: Picnic area, rest rooms, restaurant, watersports rentals.

POINT OF ROCKS BEACH
941-316-1172.
Access #12, south of Siesta Public Beach on Midnight Pass Rd. near Stickney Point Rd. intersection, Siesta Key.

SERVICE CLUB PARK
941-316-1172.
S. Harbor Dr., Venice
Facilities: Rest rooms, showers, sheltered picnic tables, grills, tot play area, volleyball court.

SIESTA KEY COUNTY BEACH
941-346-3310.
Midnight Pass Rd. at Beach Way Dr., Siesta Key.
Facilities: Picnic areas, rest rooms, showers, lifeguard, snack bar, playground, volleyball courts, tennis courts, ball fields, soccer field, fitness trail, sun decks.

tooned with Australian pines and sea grape trees, are well loved by serious local beachgoers.

The beach less traveled on Lido, this one extends from the main beach up to New Pass. Lack of facilities and limited parking keep the throngs away. Wide with fine, spic-and-span sand.

Fairly narrow sands edge the causeway between mainland and Anna Maria Island. They gain some character from Australian pines and are popular with windsurfers and jet skiers. Most beachgoers congregate around the restaurant and rental concession at the west end.

Part of Crescent Beach — named for its shape — this beach is popular with snorkelers and fishermen because of an accumulation of rocks that attracts marine life. Like the main public beach (see below), it boasts sands whiter than white but has neither the facilities nor the ease of parking.

An extensive system of boardwalks cross scrub pinelands (watch for rare scrub jays and gopher tortoises) and provide picnic nooks off the beach. This is quieter than neighboring Brohard Park and its fishing pier but within walking distance.

Siesta Key's Crescent Beach sand was once judged "the finest, whitest beach in the world" by the Woods Hole Oceanographic Institute. (Anna Maria Island's placed third.) The blinding whiteness comes from its quartz origins (99 percent quartz); the fineness, from Mother Nature's efficient pulverizer, the sea. Unfortunately, these facts have not been kept secret. The park averages about 20,000 visitors a day. Arrive early to find a parking space. Condos and motels line the edge of the wide beach. Swimming is wonderful, with gradually sloping sands and usually clear waters. Public accesses along Beach Road to the north provide more seclusion, but parking is on the street and limited.

SOUTH BROHARD PARK
941-316-1172.
S. Harbor Dr., Venice.

South of Brohard Park, parking and boardwalks over mangrove wetlands provide access to the beach away from noise, fishing hooks, and crowds. The undeveloped, natural beach appeals to escapists, who are nonetheless within walking distance of facilities at Brohard.

SOUTH JETTY
941-316-1172.
End of Tarpon Center Dr., Venice.
Facilities: Rest rooms, picnic tables, food concession.

Also known as Humphris Park, the jetty at Casey's Pass — a favorite of fishing types — is shored with huge boulders. Past them stretches a span of condo-lined beach that's popular with surfers and sailboarders. Across the pass lies North Jetty. Here, people while away time eating lunch and watching boat traffic through the pass.

SOUTH LIDO BEACH
941-316-1172.
South end of Benjamin Franklin Dr., Lido Key.
Facilities: Picnic areas, rest rooms, showers, playground, volleyball, ball fields, soccer field, fitness trail, nature trail, sun decks.

A wide sugar beach wraps around the tip of the island from the gulf to the bay, facing Siesta Key. Picnic areas are overhung with Australian pines and carpeted by their needles. Within its 130 acres several brands of Florida ecology thrive on different waterfronts. Squirrels are the most evident wildlife throughout the park. Hiking trails lead you to an observation tower and along the mangrove worlds of Little Grassy and Big Grassy lagoons. Brushy Bayou is a good place to canoe.

TURTLE BEACH
941-346-3310.
South end of Blind Pass Rd., Siesta Key.
Facilities: Picnic areas, rest rooms, showers, playground, volleyball, boat ramp, horseshoes; restaurants and bars across the street.

The sands become coarser and more shell studded at Siesta's lower extremes as the high-rise buildings become scarcer. Along here and Midnight Pass Road the island's upper echelon resides behind iron gates. Less crowded than the other Siesta beaches, it's sports- and family-oriented but without lifeguards. If you walk southward, you'll reach Palmer Point Beach (otherwise only reachable by boat), where Midnight Pass has filled in, and shark's teeth are easy to find.

VENICE BEACH
941-316-1172.
100 The Esplanade, Venice.
Facilities: Picnic area, rest rooms, showers, food concession, lifeguards, volleyball.

This beach feels cramped and more urban to me compared to the spaciousness of Venice's south-end beaches. High rises border the sands, which spread wide here. Wooden benches provide places to gaze at the normally calm sea. Alcohol is prohibited here.

BICYCLING

Sarasota's best bikeways lie on barrier islands, in parks, and in rural areas to the east. Most biking elsewhere is on the sides of roads or sidewalks.

By state law, bicyclists must conduct themselves as pedestrians when using sidewalks. Where they share the road with other vehicles, they must follow all the rules of the road. Children under age 16 must wear a helmet.

BEST BIKING

Longboat Key's 12 miles of bike path and lane parallel Gulf of Mexico Drive's vista of good taste and wealth on both sides of the road. Bike paths travel through parts of Lido Key and Siesta Key. Oscar Scherer State Recreation Area provides a more nature venue backdrop for biking.

RENTAL SHOPS

Resorts and parks often rent bikes or provide free use of them.

Bicycle Center (941-377-4505; 4084 Bee Ridge Rd., Sarasota 34233) Offers pickup and delivery on mountain bike and beach cruiser rentals.

Siesta Sports Rentals (941-346-1797; 6551 Midnight Pass Rd., Southbridge Mall, Siesta Key 34242) Has beach cruisers, speed bikes, kid bikes, tandems, surreys, jogger strollers, and in-line skates.

BOATS & BOATING

CANOEING AND KAYAKING

In addition to the outlets listed below, many resorts and parks rent canoes.

By the Bay Outfitters (941-966-3937; 520 Blackburn Point Rd., Osprey 34229) Kayak classes, top quality rentals, and tours conducted by the owner, a long-time resident knowledgeable about local lore. Classes include a three-hour introductory course and a rolling and rescue class. Tours last two to four hours, taking in the sunset, wildlife preserves, Midnight Pass beach (accessible only by boat and known for its shark's teeth), Casey Key's fine homes, and fishing hot spots.

Kayak Tours (941-778-7757; 5336 Gulf Dr., Holmes Beach 34217) Quality rentals and self-guided tours through bay waters and bird islands.

Oscar Scherer State Recreation Area (941-483-5956; 1843 S. Tamiami Trail, Osprey 34229) Canoe rentals and tidal creek canoeing along scrubby and pine flatwoods. River otters and alligators inhabit the waters; scrub jays, bobcats, and bald eagles, the land.

Silent Sports (941-966-5477; 2301 Tamiami Trail, Nokomis 34275) Rents kayaks and canoes and leads three-hour tours.

Snook Haven (941-485-7221; 5000 E. Venice Ave., Venice 34292) Canoe and kayak rentals on the Myakka River.

Walk on the Wild Side (941-351-6500; www.walkwild.com; 3434 N. Tamiami Trail, Suite 817, PO Box 817, Sarasota 34234) Guided nature hikes, kayaking, and canoeing.

How do you start this thing?

Karen T. Bartlett

PERSONAL WATERCRAFT RENTALS/TOURS

Cortez Watercraft Rentals (941-792-5263; 4328 127th St. W., Cortez 34215; at the Cortez bridge) Waverunner and pontoon boat rentals.

Don & Mike's Boat Rental (941-966-4000, 800-550-2007; 482 Blackburn Point Rd., Casey Key, Osprey 34229; at the Casey Key Marina) Rents jet skis and waverunners.

O'Leary's Sarasota Sailing School (941-953-7505; 5 Bayfront Dr. Sarasota 34236; at Bayfront Park) Rents jet skis by the half-hour and hour; instruction available.

POWERBOAT RENTALS

Bradenton Beach Marina (941-778-2288; 402 Church Ave., Bradenton Beach 34217) Runabouts and pontoons.

Cannons Marina (941-383-1311, 800-566-1955; 6040 Gulf of Mexico Dr., Longboat Key 34228) Rentals by half day, day, and week; runabouts, deck boats, and open skiffs. Also fishing tackle and water skis.

CB's (941-349-4400; cbsoutfitters@aol.com; 1249 Stickney Point Rd., Siesta Key 34242) Runabouts, center console boats, pontoons, and deck boats, also rod and reel rentals, fishing licenses, and fishing guides.

Don & Mike's Boat Rental (941-966-4000, 800-550-2007; 482 Blackburn Point Rd., Casey Key, Osprey 34229; at Casey Key Marina,) Power- and sailboats, pontoons, and waterskiing equipment.

Palma Sola Boat Rentals (941-778-4083; 9915 Manatee Ave. W., Bradenton 34209; on Anna Maria Island causeway) Powerboat and pontoon rentals.

Snook Haven (5000 E. Venice Ave., Venice 34292) Rents pontoon boats and 12- to 14-foot motorboats with 6 HP engines for use on the Myakka River. Also sells bait and fishing licenses.

PUBLIC BOAT RAMPS

City Island (Ken Thompson Pkwy.) Three ramps.
Coquina Beach Bayside Park (Gulf Blvd., Bradenton Beach) Picnic and recreational facilities; rest rooms nearby.
Higel Park (Tarpon Center Dr., Venice Beach, Venice Inlet)
Kingfish Ramp (Hwy. 64 on causeway to Anna Maria Island) Picnic facilities.
Marina Boat Ramp Park (215 E. Venice Ave., Venice)
Nokomis Beach (Venice Inlet)
Palma Sola Causeway (Palma Sola Bay and Route 64) Rest rooms and picnicking.
Turtle Beach (Blind Pass Rd., Siesta Key) Two ramps.

SAILBOAT CHARTERS

The Enterprise Sailing Charters (941-951-1833; 2 Marina Plaza, Sarasota 34236; in Bayfront Park) Morning, afternoon, sunset, and full-moon sails on a tall-masted Morgan 41 footer.
Key Sailing (941-346-7245, 888-539-7245; 1219 Southport Dr., Sarasota 34242; at Marina Jack) Sail-away adventures that last one, two, or however many days you decide, aboard a 41-foot Morgan Classic.
Spice Sailing Charters (941-778-3240; 902 Bay Blvd. S., Anna Maria 34216; at the Galati Yacht Basin) Sails to Egmont Key and for sunset aboard a 27-foot vessel. Sailing lessons available.
Spindrift Yacht Services (941-383-7781; 410 Gulf of Mexico Dr., Longboat Key 34228) Sailing ventures for up to six.

SAILBOAT RENTALS & INSTRUCTION

Many resorts have concessions that rent Hobie Cats and other small sailboats. Instruction is often available with the rental. For something more sophisticated, try these.
Bradenton Beach Sailboat Rentals (941-778-4969; 1301 Gulf Dr., Bradenton Beach 34217) Free sailing lessons with G-Cat rentals.
Don & Mike's Boat Rental (941-966-4000, 800-550-2007; 482 Blackburn Point Rd., Casey Key, Osprey 34229; at Casey Key Marina) Rental and instruction.
O'Leary's Sarasota Sailing School (941-953-7505; Bayfront Park, 5 Bayfront Dr. Sarasota 34236) Rents sailing crafts 19- to 27-feet long; rates by the hour, half day, full day, and week. Instruction and captained boats available.

SIGHTSEEING & ENTERTAINMENT CRUISES

Bay Lady (941-485-6366; 480 Blackburn Point Rd., Osprey 34229; Osprey

Marine Center) Two-hour cruises along the Intracoastal Waterway to see bird sanctuaries, manatees, and the lovely homes of Sarasota and Venice.

LeBarge Tropical Cruises (941-366-6116; 2 Marine Plaza, Sarasota 34236; at Marina Jack in Bayfront Park) Island-style crooning, an aquarium bar, and live on-board coconut palms put the tropical in this excursion. Sightseeing, nature, and sunset party cruises depart daily. Dolphin tours guarantee a sighting or another trip free. Light snacks and drinks available.

Myakka Queen Tours (941-485-7221; Snook Haven, 5000 E. Venice Ave., Venice 34292) One-hour trips on the Myakka River Thursday through Sunday.

FISHING

Nonresidents age 16 and older must obtain a license unless fishing from a vessel or pier covered by its own license. You can buy inexpensive, temporary nonresident licenses at county tax collectors' offices and most Kmarts, hardware stores, marinas, and bait shops. Bradenton waters are known to avid fishermen and divers as "Jewfish Country" for the profusion of the gigantic sea creatures. In the Intracoastal Waterway between Sarasota and Venice, snook are so plentiful, it's been dubbed "Snook Alley." Other fine catches include mangrove snapper, sheepshead, and pompano in backwaters, and grouper, amberjack, and mackerel in deep seas. Check local regulations for season, size, and catch restrictions.

DEEP-SEA PARTY BOATS

Flying Fish Fleet (941-366-3373; www.flyingfishfleet.com; 627 Avenida del Norte, Sarasota 34242; at Marina Jack in Bayfront Park) Half-day, six-hour, and all-day deep-sea trips aboard an 85-foot boat.

Miss Cortez Fleet (941-794-1223; 4330 127th St. W., Cortez 34215) Long-established and well-respected, these charters out of the region's fishing hub last four hours to a day.

Spindrift Yacht Services (941-383-7781; 410 Gulf of Mexico Dr., Longboat Key 34228) Half-day offshore and bay-fishing excursions.

FISHING CHARTERS/OUTFITTERS

To find fishing guides, check with major marinas, such as Marina Jack's in downtown Sarasota. Capacity is smaller and prices higher than for party boat excursions.

Big Catch (941-366-3373; 627 Avenida del Norte, Sarasota 34242; at Marina Jack's in Bayfront Park) Four- to eight-hour charters.

CB's (941-349-4400; cbsoutfitters@aol.com; 1249 Stickney Point Rd., Siesta Key, FL34242) Light tackle sportfishing charters in Sarasota Bay, the gulf, "Snook Alley," and Charlotte Harbor, four to eight hours. Orvis endorsed.

Catch a fishing charter from the Cortez docks—and don't forget to bring along a bone.

Karen T. Bartlett

Compleat Angler (941-778-9712; PO Box 314, Anna Maria 34216) Inshore fishing for a maximum of four; half and full day trips.

Gypsy Guide Service (941-923-6095; www.floridaflyfishing.com; 2416 Parson Ln., Sarasota 34239) Light tackle and fly fishing, bay and backwater fishing, half- or full-day trips.

FISHING PIERS

Anna Maria City Pier (Anna Maria Island) Unrailed and low to the water, it juts 700 feet into Anna Maria Sound at the south end of Bayshore Park.

Bradenton Beach City Pier (Bridge St., Bradenton Beach) Reaching into intracoastal waters; it was part of the first bridge from the island to the mainland. Restaurant and bait concession. Admission for fishing.

Green Bridge Pier (Business Hwy. 41 over the Manatee River) A popular spot with bait and tackle at the north end in Palmetto.

Ken Thompson Pier (941-316-1172; 1700 Ken Thompson Pkwy., City Island) Three small piers into New Pass.

Nokomis Beach North Jetty (941-316-1172; south end Casey Key Rd., Nokomis Beach) Manmade rock projection into the gulf, with beach and picnic area.

Osprey Fishing Pier (west end of Main St., Osprey)

Rod & Reel Pier (941-778-1885; www.rodandreel.net; 875 North Shore Dr., Anna Maria 34216) A privately owned fishermen's complex 350 feet into Tampa Bay with café and bait shop. The world's record hammerhead shark reportedly was caught here. Admission for fishing only.

Tony Saprito Fishing Pier (941-316-1172; Hart's Landing, Ringling Causeway Park en route to St. Armands Key) Bait store across the road.

Turtle Beach (941-346-3310; south end Blind Pass Rd., Siesta Key) Fishing pier, recreational facilities and boat ramps available.

Venice Fishing Pier (1600 S. Harbor Dr., Venice 34285; at Brohard Park) 740 feet long, complete with rest rooms, showers, bait shop, rod and reel rentals, and restaurant. Admission.

Venice's South Jetty (941-316-1172; Tarpon Center Dr., Venice) A stretch of boulder buffer with a paved walkway at Venice's north end.

GOLF

In 1902 Sarasota's founder and first mayor, a Scotsman, built a two-hole golf course in the middle of town. This is believed to have been Florida's first golf course. Through the years the sport has grown in Sarasota, and today there are more courses than you can swing a club at, the majority of which are private or semiprivate. Many large resorts have their own greens or arrange golf-around programs at local links. In winter season, rates are highest and greens most crowded. Carts are often required. Make tee times well in advance.

PUBLIC GOLF COURSES

Bobby Jones Golf Complex (941-365-4653; 1000 Circus Blvd., Sarasota 34232) Sarasota's only municipal course, it has 36 holes plus a 9-hole executive course. Restaurant and lounge.

Foxfire Golf Course (941-921-7757; www.golf-foxfire.com; 7200 Proctor Rd., Sarasota 34241) Highly rated public course with wildlife, 27 holes, par 72. Full service restaurant, instructions.

Manatee County Golf Course (941-792-6773; 6415 53rd Ave. W., Bradenton 34210) One of the county's most popular courses, 18 holes, par 72. Clubhouse and restaurant. Reasonable rates; twilight rate applies.

Sarasota Golf Club (941-371-2431; 7280 N. Leewynn Dr., Sarasota 34240) Public course with 18 holes, par 72. Restaurant and bar. Reasonable rates, especially in summer.

GOLF CENTERS

David Leadbetter Junior Golf Academy (941-753-0177; IMG Academies, 1414 69th Ave. W., Bradenton 34207) A highly respected full-time boarding school that also offers summer and week-long lesson programs.

Evie's Eagle Golf Center (941-377-2399; 4735 Bee Ridge Rd., Sarasota 34233) Practice sand traps, chipping and putting greens, lessons with PGA pros, miniature golf.

HEALTH & FITNESS CLUBS

Arlington Park & Aquatic Complex (941-316-1346; 2650 Waldemere St., Sarasota 34239) City-owned, county-operated facility with swimming pool, fitness center, tennis, racquetball, and basketball.

Earth Spa (941-365-6581; 330 S. Pineapple Ave., Suite 202, Sarasota 34236) A combination fitness gym and day spa with fitness equipment and personal trainers. Yoga, massage, cardio training, and nutrition counseling in a fashionable setting.

Evalyn Sadlier Jones YMCA (941-922-9622; 8301 Potter Park, Sarasota 34238) With its Olympic-sized pool and kid's water park, this Y goes beyond fitness to fun. For workouts, there is a weight room, locker room, 50-meter pool, diving boards, and Jacuzzi area. At the water park, families will enjoy the activity pool, slides, water cannons, fountains, and other cool stuff.

Lifestyle Family Fitness (941-921-4400; 8383 S. Tamiami Trail, Sarasota 34238) Exercise equipment, sauna, whirlpool, lap pool, child care.

Sarasota Family YMCA (941-366-6778; 1991 Main St., Ste. 200, Sarasota 34236) Weight machines, sauna and steam room, classes.

HIKING

Oscar Scherer State Recreation Area (941-483-5956; 1843 S. Tamiami Trail, Osprey 34229) More than 15 miles of level-ground nature trails, including a trail for disabled persons.

Sarasota Bay Walk (1550 Ken Thompson Pkwy., City Island, next to Mote Marine) Self-guided nature hike.

South Lido Park (941-316-1172; south end of Benjamin Franklin Dr., Lido Key) Nature trails into the wetlands of Brushy Bayou.

HUNTING

Knight Trail Park (941-486-2350; 3445 Rustic Road, Nokomis 34275; east of Interstate 75 at exit 35A, Laurel Rd.) Public facility maintained by the Sarasota Parks and Recreation Department. Trap and skeet, pistol and rifle range, archery range, picnic areas, shooting supplies.

KIDS' STUFF

J.P. Igloo (941-723-3663; www.jpigloo.com; 5309 29th St. E., Ellenton 34222; at Interstate 75 exit 43) Ice skating is getting hot in Florida. Of course, it's a totally indoor sport here. Keep your cool at this ice and in-line sports complex. Besides regulation hockey ice and in-line skating rinks, you'll find a restaurant, snack stand, pro shop, fitness center, and video games. Public skating is scheduled daily; times vary. Admission is $5.50 for sessions lasting two hours and 15 minutes. Skate rentals are $2 each. The rinks host ice and in-line hockey leagues, schools, and clinics for all ages.

Pirates Cove (941-755-4608; 5410 14th St. W., Bradenton 34207) Baseball/ softball cages, go-carts for all ages, minigolf, bumper boats, kiddie rides, laser tag, game rooms, and snack bar entertain families at this older but well-maintained indoor-outdoor facility. Admission is free; charges per activity.

Planet Fun (941-792-0555; 7250 Cortez Rd. W., Bradenton 34210) A perfect place for toddlers and kids under age 10 on a hot day, this new and fully inside and air-conditioned playground has a complex jungle gym, a smaller one for toddlers, kiddy rides (choo-choo, spaceships, etc), fun games, and a pizza and sandwich stand. You can buy packages or pay for individual rides with tokens. Don't forget to wear socks because shoes are taboo on the jungle gym.

Smuggler's Cove Adventure Golf (941-756-0043; 2000 Cortez Rd. W., Bradenton 34207) 18 holes and live gators with a pirate's motif. Admission is per player per game.

RACQUET SPORTS

Anna Maria Youth Center (Magnolia Ave., Anna Maria) Two lit courts.

Bayfront Park (Longboat Key)

Gillespie Park (941-316-1172; 710 N. Osprey Ave., Sarasota 34236) Three courts.

Glazier Gates Park (Manatee Ave. E., Bradenton) Two unlit cement public tennis courts.

G. T. Bray Recreation Center (5502 33rd Ave. Dr. W., Bradenton 34209) Eight each of cement, clay, and racquetball courts.

Hecksher Park (941-316-1172; 450 W. Venice Ave., Venice 34285) Six courts with lights.

Holmes Beach Courts (near City Hall, Holmes Beach) Three lit courts.

Jessie P. Miller (9th Ave. and 43rd St. W., Bradenton) Four lit cement courts and one handball court.

New World International Tennis Academy (941-756-9417; 4905 Cortez Rd. W, Bradenton 34210) One month to full-year training programs.

Nick Bollettieri Tennis at IMG Academies (941-755-1000, 800-872-6425; www.bollettieri.com; 5500 34th St. W., Bradenton 34210) Training camp for adults and juniors, with state-of-the-art tennis, 78 courts (8 of them indoors), swimming pools, a sports-therapy care center, and high-tech sports center. Andre Agassi and other pros have trained here.

Siesta Key County Beach (941-346-3310; Midnight Pass Rd. at Beach Way Dr., Siesta Key) Four courts with lights.

SHELLING

Though not comparable to the coast's southern beaches for shelling, the islands of Bradenton and Sarasota do yield some unusual finds. Venice Beach, for instance, is known for its shark's teeth, which come in all sizes and various shades from black to rare white. Manasota Beach and the south end of Siesta Key also boast toothy waters, but Venice's northern beaches have the best pickings.

Toothsome finds on Venice Beach, hailed as the Shark's Tooth Capital of the World.

Karen T. Bartlett

Sharks continually shed teeth and grow new ones. Most of what you find is prehistoric. The white ones are recent sheddings. Teeth range in size from one-eighth of an inch to a rare three inches. Some resorts provide "Florida snow shovels" — screen baskets fastened to broomsticks. You can also buy them in local hardware stores. Digging for specimens is taboo.

SPAS

Hollywood Salon & Spa (941-953-3523; 1812 Hillview St., Sarasota 34239) Performing a complete menu of Phytomer facials, and massages, scrubs, polishes, and body masks as well as manicures, pedicures, waxing, and other salon services.

Body & Spirit (941-921-1388; www.bodayandspirit.net; 8590 Potter Park Dr., Sarasota 34238) A luxury day spa with alternative medical practice: chiropractic, yoga, personal training, massage, facials, beauty services.

Earth Spa (941-365-6581; 330 S. Pineapple Ave., Suite 202, Sarasota 34236) A day spa with fitness gyms and personal trainers. Yoga, massage, cardio training, and nutrition counseling in a fashionable setting.

The Met (941-388-1772; 35 S. Blvd. of Presidents, St. Armands Circle, Sarasota 34236) Upstairs from a posh clothing store in an elegant setting, the Met offers full spa and beauty facilities and treatments, including hydrotherapy, packages, and spa lunch.

Warm Mineral Springs (941-426-1692; San Servando Ave., Warm Mineral Springs 34287; south of Venice near North Port) Water of a rare quality attracts health seekers to a 2.5-acre lake fed by nine million gallons of water each day. If you know your spas, you will appreciate the springs' chemical analysis of 17,439 parts per million, way above that of the world's most renowned mineral waters. The lake, which maintains a year-round temperature of 87 degrees, has soothing and, some believe, healing powers that attract people from around the world. Folks bathe at a roped-off beach area and sun on a grassy lawn. A thatched chickee pavilion provides shade and a picnic area is provided. Opened in 1940, the facilities are undergoing a major renovation under new ownership. The old historic cyclorama will become a $3-million-plus archaeological museum dedicated to the ancient finds from the springs. Archaeologists have discovered artifacts suggesting that Native Americans came here for a bit of mineral-washed R&R 10,000 years ago. Some claim this was the Fountain of Youth about which they told Ponce de León. Massages are now available at the springs facility; a wellness center, acupuncture, and additional holistic procedures are planned, along with an on-site café. There is a motel down the street for the spa enthusiast. For the casual visitor, I suggest staying in one of the area's resorts instead. Admission is $10.00 per visit per person or $70 for 10 visits. Students pay $5 with ID, children 12 and under pay $2. Beachwear, chairs, and towels are available for rent.

SPECTATOR SPORTS

PRO BASEBALL

Ed Smith Stadium (941-954-SOXX; 2700 12th St., Sarasota 34237) Spring training home of the Chicago White Sox (March and early April) and off-season home of the Sarasox (941-365-4460).

McKechnie Field (941-748-4610; Ninth St. and 17th Ave. W., Bradenton 34205) Site of the Pittsburgh Pirates' exhibition games during March and into April; a small but fun park.

Pirate City (941-747-3031; 1701 27th St. E., Bradenton 34208) Spring practice field for the Pittsburgh Pirates's major and minor leagues. Catch the major-leaguers during spring season working out from 10am to 1:30pm. The minor leaguers play their games here March–May.

POLO

Sarasota Polo Club (941-907-0000; poloclub@gte.net; 8201 Polo Club Ln., Sarasota 34240) Watch from the grandstands, or bring a tailgate picnic. Game time is 1pm every Sunday, mid-December through March. Admission.

RACING

Sarasota Kennel Club (941-355-7744; 5400 Bradenton Rd., Sarasota 34234) Greyhound racing January to mid-April. Pari-mutuel betting, matinee (except Tuesdays) and evening shows year-round. Simulcasts thoroughbred horse racing from Miami and other tracks year-round. Admission. Closed Sunday. Must be 18 or older to enter.

WATERSKIING

Sarasota Ski-A-Rees Show (941-388-1666; www.skiarees.com; PO Box 1493, Sarasota 34230; at Ken Thompson Park, adjacent to Mote Marine Laboratory) Free amateur performances in the bay every Sunday at 2pm.

WATER SPORTS

PARASAILING & WATERSKIING

Adventure Parasail (941-926-1300; 504 S. Tamiami Trail, Nokomis 34275; at Dona Bay Marina) Serving Casey Key, Nokomis, Manasota Key, Englewood, and Charlotte County.

Cortez Parasail (941-795-2700; 12507 Cortez Rd., Bradenton 34210; at the bridge) Rides up to 1,200 feet, with an option to free fall.

Don & Mike's Boat & Ski Rental (941-966-4000; 520 Blackburn Point Rd., Casey Key, Osprey 34229; at Casey Key Marina) Ski rides and lessons.

Longboat Pass Parasail (941-792-1900; 4330 127th St. W., PO Box 729, Cortez 34215) Rides up to 1,400 feet and free falls.

Aquarius Parasail (941-346-3532; cbsoutfitters@aol.com; CB's, 1249 Stickney Point Rd., Siesta Key 34242) Rides up to 1,000 feet, with optional free fall.

SAILBOATING & SURFING

Gulf Coast waters are generally too tame to inspire awe in surfers, except in inclement weather. Sailboarders, however, find fine conditions all along the coast. Look in the "Beaches" section for surfing and windsurfing venues. Listed below are resources for lessons and rentals.

The Board Room (941-955-4093; 3800 S. Tamiami Trail, Sarasota 34236) Sells surfboards and skateboards and equipment.

Palma Sola Causeway Beach (941-778-4083; Route 64 to Anna Maria Island) Good windsurfing.

SNORKELING & SCUBA

Of all the southern Gulf Coast, this region generally boasts the best visibility, especially in spring. Manmade reefs make up for the lack of natural reefs on Florida's west coast.

DIVE SHOPS & CHARTERS

Dolphin Dive Center (941-924-2785; www.floridakayak.com; 6018 S. Tamiami Trail, Sarasota 34242) Local charters, instruction, snorkel and scuba rentals.

SeaTrek Divers (941-779-1506; www.seatrekdivers.com; 105 Seventh St. N., Bradenton Beach 34217) Two-tank, offshore dives and snorkel trips to Egmont Key. Scuba certification courses.

SHORE SNORKELING & DIVING

Bradenton Beach (Anna Maria Island) An old sugar barge sank here many years ago and houses various forms of marine life.

Point of Rocks (Siesta Key) South of Crescent Beach at the island's central zone; rocks, underwater caves, and coral formations make good submerged sightseeing.

WILDERNESS CAMPING

Oscar Scherer State Recreation Area (941-483-5956; 1843 S. Tamiami Trail, Osprey 34229) Nearly 1,400 acres in size, this natural oasis provides full facilities for the camper in a wooded, creek-side setting of palmettos, pines, and venerable, moss-draped oaks. The threatened Florida scrub jay seeks refuge here, along with bald eagles, bobcats, river otters, gopher tortoises, and alligators. There's swimming in a freshwater lake plus a bird walk, nature and canoe trails, picnicking, and fishing.

WILDLIFE SPOTTING

BIRDS

The Sarasota coast is the least natural of the Gulf Coast's four regions. Determined bird spotters can find feathered friends at parks and refuges such as the Passage Key sanctuary, north of Anna Maria Island (bring binoculars — landing ashore is forbidden); Rookery Islands, north of Siesta Key (approachable by boat only); and Oscar Scherer State Recreation Area in Osprey, home of the endangered scrub jay. Look for the wild peacocks that roam the streets of the village on Longboat Key and, I'm told, Holmes Beach.

DOLPHINS

Dolphins often follow in the wake of tour boats, but they're unpredictable. You can't plan on them; you can only be thrilled and charmed when they do appear. If you learn their feeding schedules, you have a better chance of catching their act.

Holy Sea Cows!

We know them today as Florida manatees: 1,300-pound blimps with skin like burlap and a face only a nature buff could love. They also go by the name sea cow, although they are more closely related to the elephant. In days of yore, many a sea-weary sailor mistook them for mermaids.

Well, Ariel they're not, but bewitching they can be. Gentle and herbivorous — consuming up to 100 pounds of aquatic plants daily — they make no enemies and have only one stumbling block to survival: man. Being mammals, manatees must surface for air, like whales and dolphins. Their girth makes them a prime target for boaters speeding through their habitat. Warning signs designate popular manatee areas. Instead of zipping through these waters and further threatening the seriously endangered manatee population, boaters can better benefit by slowing down and trying to spot the reclusive creatures as they take a breath. It requires a sharp eye, patience, and experience. Watch channels during low tides, when the manatees take to deeper water. Concentric circles, known as "manatee footprints," signal surfacing animals. They usually travel in a line and appear as drifting coconuts or fronds.

To report manatee deaths, injuries, harassment, or orphans, call 941-332-6972.

MANATEES

Named after the lovable creatures, Bradenton's Manatee County has erected "Manatee Watch" signs at manatee-frequented areas — on the bridges and city pier of the Manatee River, on the Palma Sola Causeway, and on Anna Maria Island at Bayfront Park, Coquina Beach and Boat Ramp, and Kingfish Boat Ramp.

NATURE PRESERVES & ECO-ATTRACTIONS

Mote Marine Aquarium invites you to pet a ray.

Karen T. Bartlett

MOTE MARINE LABORATORY
941-388-2451,
800-691-MOTE.
www.mote.org.
1600 Ken Thompson Pkwy.,
Sarasota 34236.
On City Island, northeast of
Lido Key.
Open: 10am–5pm daily.
Admission: $10 for adults;
$7 for children 4–17.

Mote Marine is known around the world for its research on sharks, marine mammals, and environmental pollutants. Its visitors centers educate the public on projects and marine life. A 135,000-gallon shark tank centerpieces the original facility and is kept stocked with sharks and fish typical of the area: grouper, snook, pompano, and snapper. Twenty-some smaller aquariums, one touch tank, and one no-touch tank hold more than 200 varieties of common and unusual species. Newly renovated, the original visitors center has expanded its shark focus with a Sea Cinema and cool interactive shark film. Another new addition, the 1,500-gallon Remarkable Rays touch tank, sits outside in a chickee hut. In spring 2001 a new mollusk tank opened, featuring a preserved 25-foot giant squid from New Zealand. In the Marine Mammal Visitors' Center, the main attraction is a floor-to-ceiling glass tank that holds manatees Hugh and Buffett. It also features a marine mammal rehabilitation tank and a sea turtle exhibit, which host some of the world's most fascinating sea creatures.

OSCAR SCHERER STATE RECREATION AREA
941-483-5956.
1843 S. Tamiami Trail, Osprey 34229.
Admission: $3.25 per car, $1 per pedestrian or cyclist.

Home of the threatened Florida scrub jay plus bald eagles, bobcats, river otters, gopher tortoises, and alligators. Experience wildlife in a canoe along a saltwater tidal creek or by hiking an extensive system of nature trails. Take heed: If you swim in the freshwater lake, you may become more closely acquainted with an alligator than you care to be. The 1,284-acre park offers camping, swimming, fishing, and picnicking.

PELICAN MAN'S BIRD SANCTUARY
941-388-4444.
www.pelicanman.com.
1708 Ken Thompson Pkwy., Sarasota 34236.
Next to Mote Marine Laboratory on City Island.
Open: 10am–5pm daily.
Admission: Suggested donation $3 adults, $1 children.

One man, Dale Shields, laid the foundation for this two-acre refuge for injured pelicans and other birds — 39 species in all. It's a must if you're visiting Mote Marine Lab and also for nature lovers. Don't expect exotic birds, just on-the-mend local varieties.

QUICK POINT NATURE PRESERVE
South end of Longboat Key.
Open: Daily.
Admission: Free.

The town of Longboat Key worked to restore the natural environment of this 34-acre plot, once covered over and nearly destroyed by sand dredged from New Pass. Park on the west side of the road and follow a boardwalk under the pass bridge to get to the trails through beach, uplands, mangrove, and lagoon habitat. It's a popular spot for ospreys, egrets, ibises, and other shore birds.

SARASOTA BAY WALK
1550 Ken Thompson Pkwy., Sarasota 34236
On City Island, next to Mote Marine Laboratory.
Admission: Free.

Take a quiet, self-guided walk along the bay, estuaries, lagoons, and uplands to learn more about coastland ecology. Boardwalk and shell paths lead you past mangroves, old fishing boats bobbing on the bay, egrets, and illustrated signs detailing nature's wonders.

WILDLIFE TOURS & CHARTERS

Around the Bend Nature Tours (941-794-8773; www.aroundbend.com; 1815 Palma Sola Blvd., Bradenton 34209) A local naturalist leads short guided walks and boat tours to area natural and cultural heritage sites.

Sarasota Bay Explorers (941-388-4200; Mote Marine Laboratory, 1600 Ken Thompson Pkwy., Sarasota 34236; on City Island) A pontoon tour of intracoastal waters between City Island and Siesta Key. Features include trawl net toss, binocular study of rookery islands, and naturalist narration. It also offers custom and kayak tours. Packages with Mote Marine are available.

SHOPPING

In season you may well be tempted, like everyone else, to save shopping and sightseeing for rainy, cold, off-beach days. Don't. You'll lose your diligently attained good beach attitude by the time you've found your first parking spot. Go in the morning for best results and the most relaxing experience.

Sarasota's St. Armands Circle is known far and wide for its arena of posh shops, galleries, and restaurants. Downtown Sarasota is steadily improving its shopping outlook, especially for art and antiques lovers. Nearby Southside Village, at Hillview St. and Osprey Ave., has grown into an intriguing little shopping and dining destination. On the islands you'll find fun shops and beach boutiques that blend with the sand and sun.

Folks shop till they dine in the blossomy setting of St. Armands Circle.

Karen T. Bartlett

SHOPPING CENTERS & MALLS

De Soto Square Mall (941-747-5868; 303 Hwy. 301, Bradenton 34205) Some 700,000 feet of shop-till-you-drop opportunities in over 100 stores, including Sears, Burdines, and Dillards.

Downtown Sarasota One of the Gulf Coast's most successful downtown restoration projects has returned Sarasota's vitality to Main Street and environs. The area is also known as the Sarasota Theater and Arts District. It encompasses approximately 1.5 square miles, centered at Five Points, where Main Street intersects with four other streets. Old, renovated buildings house galleries (particularly along South Palm Avenue, where it's less rushed than Main Street), bookstores, clothing boutiques, antique shops, restaurants, sidewalk cafés, cabarets, clubs, and gift shops. Palm Avenue Association hosts gallery walks the first Friday of each month, with music, refreshments, and gallery openings, beginning at 6pm. At Burns Court (Pineapple and Palm Avenues) lies a unique shopping enclave of historic bungalows and unusual finds.

Longboat Key You'll find a smattering of interesting shops and galleries at The Centre Shops (5370 Gulf of Mexico Dr.) and Avenue of Flowers (off Gulf of Mexico Dr.).

St. Armands Circle (941-388-1554; www.starmandscircleassoc.com; 300 Madison Dr., Sarasota 34236; on St. Armands Key) John Ringling envisioned a world-class shopping center on one of the Sarasota barrier islands he owned, complete with park-lined walkways and baroque statuary. He would be gratified by St. Armands Circle. On a scale with Beverly Hills's Rodeo Drive and Palm Beach's Worth Avenue, it was named for developer Charles St. Amand [sic]. Its spin-off formation is suited geographically to the pancake shape of the island. Four sections arc off the circular center drive. "The Circle," as it is known in local shorthand, encompasses shops of the most upscale nature, galleries, restaurants, clubs, and specialty boutiques. International style is well represented. The Circle is a hub of activity for the entire region. Horse-drawn carriages offer sunset rides. The Circus Ring of Fame honors distinguished Big Top entertainers. People dress in finery just to shop here, but don't feel obligated. Once monthly, it hosts Fourth Friday Walks from 6–9 pm. Parking is free on the street and in the garage nearby.

Sarasota Quay (941-957-0120; 603 Sarasota Quay, Sarasota 34236; at Rte. 41 and Fruitville Rd.) An exclusive venue to shop, dine, and party, on the shores of Sarasota Bay near downtown.

Sarasota Square Mall (941-922-9609; 8201 S. Tamiami Trail, Sarasota 34238; at Beneva Rd.) Your choice of four major department stores, movie theaters, and more than 140 specialty shops and eateries.

Siesta Key In the village along Ocean Blvd., Siesta Key's shopping style is refreshingly barefoot with a touch of beach bawdiness, mixed in with a generous dose of casual eateries. You'll find a more upscale collection of shops around Stickney Point Road.

Southgate Plaza (941-955-0900; 3501 S. Tamiami Trail Sarasota 34239; at Bee Ridge Rd.) A major shopping mall, this one houses Burdines, Dillards, and Saks Fifth Avenue.

Venice Main Street (941-484-6722; PO Box 602, Venice 34248; at Venice Ave. W. and Tamiami Trail) Down a Mediterranean-type, date-palm-lined boulevard, you'll find shops and restaurants to fit every budget.

Venice Centre Mall (226 Tampa Ave. W., Venice 34285) Occupying the erstwhile winter quarters of the Kentucky Military Institute, the mall is listed on the National Register of Historic Buildings. It includes shops that specialize in unique gifts and clothing that fall into formation along a spit-and-polish hall.

ANTIQUES & COLLECTIBLES

Antiques shops are plentiful and easy to find in and around Sarasota. You'll find a row of them on Pineapple Street, downtown. Many specialize in fine art and rare, high-end pieces. Pick up a copy of the *Sarasota Antique Guide & Locator Map* from the Sarasota Visitors Center.

Apple & Carpenter Antique Gallery (941-951-2314; 64 S. Palm Ave., Sarasota 34236; downtown) One of the most deluxe antiquarians, this shop specializes in American and European paintings of the 19th and 20th centuries as well as bronze and marble sculptures, fine furniture, French cameo glass, silver, bronze, porcelain, and other objets d'art.

Islander Market Antiques and Art (941-779-2501; 9807 Gulf Dr., Anna Maria 34216) Formerly an island grocer, this shop now sells predominantly country-style antiques, including lots of furniture.

Old Feed Store Antique Mall (941-729-1379; 4407 Hwy. 301, Ellenton 34222) Around Gamble Plantation Historic Site you'll find a few interesting antiques markets, including this one.

Sarasota Art & Antique Center (640 S. Washington Ave., Sarasota 34236) This huge pink building holds a number of fine antiques galleries including **Crissy Galleries** (941-957-1110), selling quality furniture, jewelry, and art; **Sarasota Rare Coin Gallery** (941-366-2191, 800-447-8778); **Yellow Bird Antiques** (941-388-1823), specializing in decorative items; **Sarasota Jewelry, Watch & Clock** (941-951-1962); **Ashland Coin** (941-957-3760), dealing in timepieces, coins, and jewelry; and **R.A. Blekicki Antiques** (941-365-4990), period American furniture and paintings.

Shadow Box (941-957-3896; 1520 Fruitville Rd., Sarasota 34236) Along Fruitville Road's western end, which runs on the edge of downtown, you can find a few more antiques shops, generally more affordable than mainstream downtown's. This one carries a nice collection of 18th century, Victorian, Art Deco, and modern home furnishings and decoratives.

Treasures in Time (941-486-1700; 251 W. Venice Ave., Venice 34285) Vintage knickknacks, Oriental pieces, and new collectibles and objets d'art.

BOOKS

Chapters Café and Bookshop (941-779-2665; 5904 Marina Dr., Holmes Beach 34217) Munch on gourmet salads, sandwiches, pizza, and pasta (see "Dining" in this chapter) while you dig in to your newly purchased used book. Vintage mysteries, hardcover and paperbacks, collector's editions, some new books.

Circle Books (941-388-2850; 478 John Ringling Blvd., Sarasota 34236; at St. Armands Circle) Features author signings.

Bookshop (941-488-1307; 241 W. Venice Ave., Venice 34285) Small but complete store with several books on sharks and other local nature plus an extensive kids collection.

Main Bookshop (941-366-7653; www.mainbookshop.com; 1962 Main St., Sarasota 34236; downtown) A landmark store with four floors full of discounted (30 to 90 percent off) and used books on all subjects.

Sarasota News & Books (941-365-6332; 1341 Main St., Sarasota 34236; downtown) Specializes in art, architecture, and interior design. Beyond books and periodicals, Sarasota News sells cards, gifts, coffee, and lunch.

Venice Newsstand (941-488-6969; 329 W. Venice Ave., Venice 34285) Old-fashioned newsstand selling cigars, greeting cards, magazines, out-of-town newspapers, and paperbacks.

CLOTHING

Bridgewear (941-778-4299; 121 Bridge St., Bradenton Beach 34217) Breezy, fun women's casual clothes among shops and cafés at the approach to the historic pier.

Cravats' (941-366-7780; 222 Sarasota Quay, Sarasota 34236) Custom hand-tailored shirts and fine clothing for men.

Dream Weaver (941-388-1974; 364 St. Armands Circle, Sarasota 34236) Fine woven wear that crosses the line to fabric art, in silk, suede, and other extravagant materials.

Global Navigator (941-388-4515; 357 St. Armands Circle, Sarasota 34236) Men's explorer fashions.

Ivory Coast (941-388-1999; 15 N. Blvd. of Presidents, Sarasota 34236; at St. Armands Circle) Outstanding imported women's fashions, jewelry, and decorative items inspired by Africa.

LaCheape Boutique (941-488-6388; 530 Highway 41 Bypass S., Venice 34292) Liquidated stock from expensive boutiques sold at greatly reduced cost.

Little Bo-Tique (941-388-1737; 19 Fillmore Dr., Sarasota 34236; at St. Armands Circle) Adorable and stylish children's wear for boys and girls.

The Met (941-388-1772; 35 S. Blvd. of Presidents, Sarasota 34236; at St. Armands Circle) Expensive dressy and casual fashions for men and women in a divine setting.

Nana's (941-488-4108; 223 W. Venice Ave., Venice 34285) Quality kids' clothes and toys.

Peggy's (941-365-4485; 218 Sarasota Quay, Sarasota 34236) Ladies' formal and evening wear and accessories.

Sun Bug (941-485-7946; 141 W. Venice Ave., Venice 34285) The most fun in women's fashions, from dressy to casual. Great cotton styles, swimsuits, and unusual, comfortable dresses.

Three Crowns Dress Shop (941-488-6882; 323 W. Venice Ave., Venice 34285) Elegant women's fashions featuring personal assistance.

Tropics (941-346-2950; 5251 Ocean Blvd., Siesta Key Village 34242) Cool, tropical fashions and T-shirts for women and kids, including Jams World and Fresh Produce labels.

CONSIGNMENT

In Sarasota it's not the embarrassment that it is in some places to buy second-hand. Because of the wealth and transient nature of its residents, the area offers the possibility of great discoveries in its consignment shops. In Sarasota, especially, recycled apparel is the "in" thing among the young and artistic.

Claire's Closet (941-954-3334; 1648 Main St., Sarasota 34236) Women's clothing.

Designer Consigner (941-953-5995; 3639 Bahia Vista St., Sarasota 34232) Wedding gowns, evening wear, sports and career fashions.

The Green Butterfly (941-485-6223; 211 W. Miami Ave., Venice 34285) Antique, old, and new furniture.

Kids Care-O-Sell Consignments (941-761-8405; 6600 Manatee Ave. W., Bradenton 34209) Maternity wear, kids' clothes, and furniture.

Laura Jean's (941-378-9002; 4214 Bee Ridge Rd., Sarasota 34233) Women's business, sports, and cocktail attire. Two other locations in Sarasota.

St. George's Fine Consignments (941-952-1849; 1849 Hillview St., Sarasota 34239; at Southside Village) Designer and other women's clothing, furs, and jewelry.

Woman's Exchange (941-955-7873; 539 S. Orange Ave., Sarasota 34236; downtown) Furniture, family clothing, antiques, housewares, and china. Profits support local arts.

FACTORY OUTLET CENTERS

Prime Outlets (941-729-8615, 888-260-7608; www.primeoutlets.com; 5461 Factory Shops Blvd., Ellenton 34222; at I-75 exit 43) As far as the factory outlet malls covered in this book go, this is the most comprehensive, with more than 135 shops, a nice food court, and a children's playground in a Caribbean setting. Besides the typical kitchen and clothing stores, it boasts some top designer names, such as Off 5th (outlet for Saks Fifth Avenue, Donna Karan, Liz Claiborne, and others. Plans are to expand.

Sarasota Outlet Center (941-359-2050; 8303 Cooper Creek Blvd., Sarasota 34201; I-75 exit 40 at University Parkway) More than 40 factory outlets and discount stores.

FLEA MARKETS & BAZAARS

Bradenton Farmers' Market (941-748-7949; Bradenton City Hall parking lot, 500 15th St. W., Bradenton) Runs 8am to noon every Saturday, October through April. Fresh local produce, baked goods, and crafts.

The Dome (941-493-6773; 5115 Rte. 775, Venice) A small indoor market open Friday, Saturday, and Sunday 9am–4pm.

Red Barn Flea Market (941-747-3794, 800-274-FLEA; www.redbarnfleamar ket.net; 1707 First St. E., Bradenton 34205) More than 600 stores and booths selling baseball cards to car parts. Fully open 8 to 4 Wednesday, Saturday, and Sunday; mall area stores open Tuesday through Sunday 10-4.

Sarasota Farmers Market (941-951-2656; Lemon Ave. and Main St., downtown Sarasota) Fresh fruits, vegetables, baked goods, plants, arts and crafts. Open 7am–noon Saturday, year-round.

GALLERIES

Chasen Galleries (941-366-4278; 16 S. Palm Ave., Sarasota 34236; downtown) Contemporary sculpture, unique oversized jug pottery, artistic clocks, fig- ures, paintings, and glass.

Corbino Galleries (941-387-0822; www.corbino.com; The Centre Shops, 5350 Gulf of Mexico Dr., Longboat Key 34228) A serious, sophisticated gallery and sculpture garden showcasing the highly stylized work of namesake artist, Italian Jon Corbino, and other world-renowned modern artists.

Galleria Silecchia (941-365-7414; 888-366-7414; www.galleriasilecchia.com; 12 & 20 S. Palm Ave., Sarasota 34236) These two storefronts contain some of the most interesting art we've seen in all of Sarasota. The larger, corner gallery contains large bronze sculptures and other pieces. The smaller one showcases the exquisite glass lamp works of Ulla Darni, whimsical cut-metal wall sculp- tures, colorful painted sculptures, and a select collection of decorative art.

L'Attitude (941-779-1600; 9908 Gulf Dr., Anna Maria 34216) Anna Maria vil- lage is developing quite the artistic attitude. This gallery, with its contempo- rary sculpture and crafts, says it all. You'll find metal, ceramic, glass, textile, stone, and wood media in the gallery and its garden.

Towles Court Artist Colony (941-330-9817; www.towlescourt.com; 1945 Morrill St. Sarasota 34230 off Hwy. 301) A charming district of restored and

Downtown Sarasota's Towles Court, a working artists' colony, colorfully took over an old bungalow neighborhood

Karen T. Bartlett

brightly painted bungalows turned art colony, featuring the galleries and working art studios of artists in all media. The Towles Court Art Center (1838 Adams Ln.) contains several galleries and a café. It is the colony's headquarters, with other studio-galleries scattered around it. We enjoy the work of Marge Bennett (941-955-0050), whose vibrant watercolors are displayed at the Art Center. Third Friday "Art By the Light of the Moon Stroll at Towles" gallery walks, 6 to 10pm., with live music.

Tropical Scenes & Things (941-485-9869; 317 W. Venice Ave., Venice 34285) Affordable metal sculptures and other unusual wall hangings, framed originals, decorative items with an emphasis on the sea and tropics.

Wyland Galleries (941-388-5331, 888-588-5331; 465 John Ringling Blvd., Sarasota 34236; at St. Armands Circle) The work of artist Wyland (of worldwide Whaling Walls fame) as well as other renowned marine and wildlife artists.

Ziegenfuss Gallery of Fine Art (941-365-3266; 76 S. Palm Ave., Sarasota 34236; downtown) One of my favorites along Palm Avenue, this gallery features pop art, tasteful Sarasota-theme and other city paintings, sculptures by Jack Dowd, and the work of other whimsical local artists.

GIFTS

Some of the best gifts and souvenirs are found in attraction gift shops, especially those at the Ringling museums, Sarasota Jungle Gardens, G. WIZ, and South Florida Museum.

The Artful Dodger (941-925-8266; 1522 Stickney Point Rd., Sarasota 34231; at Boatyard Shopping Village, near Siesta Key) Artist-quality table and decorative ware: pottery, glass, jewelry, and other fun and colorful gifts.

Exit Art Gallery (941-383-4099 or 800-833-0894; www.exit-art.com; 5380 Gulf of Mexico Dr., Longboat Key 34228; at the Centre Shops) Artistically designed home and office tools, pop art, colorful tableware, jewelry, and clothes.

Giving Tree Wood Gallery (941-388-1353; 5 N. Boulevard of Presidents, Sarasota 34236) Beautiful inset and sculpted wood art, unique jewelry, Oriental pottery, and other find and unusual gifts.

Hurricane Rita's (941-346-7712; 5212 Ocean Blvd., Siesta Key Village, Siesta Key 34242. Also 941-388-2766; 319 John Ringling Blvd., Sarasota 34236; at St. Armands Circle) Unique and colorful home decorations with a tropical theme, toys for kids, and imported clothing.

Love from Florida (941-388-2656; 362 John Ringling Blvd., Sarasota 34236; at St. Armands Circle) Not just your usual tacky Florida souvenirs (but some of that): small fountains, Florida-appropriate plastic tableware, metal sculptures, adorable glass and metal palm trees, and more.

Moonflowers (941-316-9888; 1924 S. Osprey Ave., Sarasota 34239; at Morton's Plaza, Southside Village) Fairies, teddy bears, and things equally whimsical inspire the gift collection here.

JEWELRY

Bari Jewelers (941-484-9197; 315 W. Venice Ave., Venice 34285) Buy your shark's teeth necklaces and large fossil specimens here; also sea-motif charms, gold, diamonds, and other fine pieces.

Coffrin Jewelers (941-366-6871; 1829 S. Osprey Ave., Sarasota 34239; at Southside Village) Fine creations in gold, silver, and platinum, specializing in original designs. Also vendor of hand-painted French Quimper tableware.

Fawn Custom Jewelers (941-349-2748; 5221 Ocean Blvd., Siesta Key 34242) Specializing in Florida seashore-motif pieces, mostly for women.

Jewelry by Cole (941-388-3323, 800-572-9375; 7 N. Blvd. of Presidents, Sarasota 34236; at St. Armands Circle) Lovely set gems, a wide variety of the usual to the unusual in sea-themed pieces, custom work.

Jess Jewelers (941-756-5019; 401 Cortez Rd. W., Ste. 110, Bradenton 34205) Estate diamonds, beach-theme pieces, master goldsmiths.

June Simmons Designs (941-388-4535; 68 S. Palm Ave., Sarasota 34236) Artistic exclusive edition jewelry and custom work.

Sarasota Silver Co. (941-388-5564; 9 N. Blvd. of Presidents, Sarasota 34236; at St. Armands Circle) The most unusual jewelry in the Circle, if you like silver. These are stunning, stand-out creations.

Zodiac Jewelry & Fine Gifts (941-383-9460; 5350 Gulf of Mexico Dr., Longboat Key 34228; at the Centre Shops,) Small, select collection of island-flavor jewelry; unusual gold, silver, and set gem pieces; and fine gifts and collectibles such as Lladro, Hummel, and Swarovski.

KITCHENWARE & HOME DECOR

Atizana Imports (941-955-8184; 1472 Main St., Sarasota 34236) A step above most Haitian-ware shops, this one sells wood furnishings, fine bowls, and sculptures of wood and stone.

Basketville (941-493-0007; 4411 S. Tamiami Trail, Venice 34293) Region's widest selection of basketry, pottery, wicker furniture, silk flowers, and other household items.

Garden Argosy (941-388-6402; www.gardenargosy.com; 361 St. Armands Circle, Sarasota 34236) Gifts for the home and garden: extensive selection of candles, frames, painted wood bowls, garden statues, fountains.

Lee's of St. Armands (941-388-1336; 27 N. Blvd. of Presidents, Sarasota 34236; at St. Armands Circle) Truly distinctive tableware, trays, glass, and pewter for the kitchen and for decorating throughout the home.

The Lofty Lion (941-485-2588; 203 W. Venice Ave., Venice 34285) A select collection of whimsical home-decor items: hand-painted furniture, indoor fountains, cat lovers' dishware, and other country-style delights.

Rolling Pin Kitchen Emporium (941-925-2434; 8201 S. Tamiami Trail, Sarasota 34238; Sarasota Square Mall) German cutlery and fine kitchenware.

Siam Heritage (941-363-0032; www.siamheritage.net; 1453 Main St., Sarasota 34236) Truly unusual and authentic Thai imports, including classic Thai instruments, functional and decorative pottery, large teak carvings, pillows, and silk shawls.

Whit's End (941-953-9448; 51 S. Palm Ave., Sarasota 34236) European antique pine and other furnishings, a wide variety of deluxe candles, framed art, and other unusual finds.

SHELL SHOPS

Beach Bazaar (941-346-2995; 5211 Ocean Blvd., Siesta Key 34242) A one-stop mart for seashells, toys, beach clothes, and other vacation must haves.

Sea Pleasures and Treasures (941-488-3510; 255 Venice Ave. W., Venice 34285) Quantity, not necessarily quality: sea-theme gifts, shells, and shell craft supplies.

SPORTS STORES

Note: This listing includes general sports outlets only. For supplies and equipment for specific sports, please refer to "Recreation" in this chapter.

CB's Saltwater Outfitters (941-349-4400; 1249 Stickney Point Rd., Siesta Key 34242) Fishing gear and sportswear.

Cook's Sportland (941-493-0025; 4419 Tamiami Trail, Venice 34293; next to Basketville) Equipment for archery, golf, camping, and fishing; also fishing licenses, tackle repair, sportswear, shoes, and western clothing.

CALENDAR OF EVENTS

For a complete listing of local cultural events, visit www.sarasota-arts.org or call 941-365-5118.

JANUARY

Arts Day Festival (941-365-5118; downtown Sarasota) A gala confluence of Sarasota's visual and performing arts that spills from the galleries and theaters onto outdoor stages and sidewalks.

Sarasota Film Festival (941-364-9514; www.sarasotafilmfestival.com; Courtyard of the Stars next to Regal Cinemas on Main St., downtown Sarasota) Five days of films, celebrities, outdoor screenings, and live entertainment.

FEBRUARY

Cortez Commercial Fishing Festival (941-794-0280; village of Cortez) Food vendors, music, net-mending demonstrations, arts and crafts, and educational exhibits describing the community of Cortez's hundred-year-old fishing industry. One weekend late in the month.

Greek Glendi Festival (941-355-2616; St. Barbara's Greek Orthodox Church, 7671 Lockwood Ridge Rd., Sarasota 34243) Greek food, dancing, arts, and crafts on one weekend near Valentine's Day.

Scottish Highland Games & Heritage Festival (941-953-6707) held at the Sarasota Fair Grounds, Fruitville Ave.

MARCH

Anna Maria Island Springfest (941-778-2099) A celebration of island arts: artist and crafts booths, local entertainment, and food concessions. Two days early in the month.

Manatee Arts Fest (941-721-0405; Old Main St., downtown Bradenton) One weekend late in the month devoted to all the arts, with fine arts and crafts, music, dance, food, poetry reading, and children's art activities.

Manatee Heritage Month (941-741-4070) The entire month is devoted to the celebration of local history and traditions throughout Bradenton and Manatee County. Special tours are arranged by local attractions, and demonstrators weave, quilt, and make baskets and doilies.

Medieval Fair (941-359-5700; Ringling Museum of Arts grounds, Sarasota) The event of the year, this fair is the culmination of Sarasota's love for art, theater, food, and circus, all within the atmosphere of a 15th-century flashback. Four days at the turn of March.

Run For the Turtles (941-388-4441; Siesta Beach Pavilion, Siesta Key) 5K race to benefit Mote Marine Laboratory.

Sailor Circus (941-361-6350; 2075 Bahia Vista St., Sarasota 34239) Proof that the circus is still in the blood of many Sarasota families. Students from grades 3 to 12 perform professional circus feats during a two-week season. Also Christmastime performances.

Seafood by the mound at Siesta Fiesta

Karen T. Bartlett

Sarasota Jazz Festival (941-366-1552; throughout Sarasota) Big-name jazz players lead a slate of big bands and jazz combos. One week.

APRIL

Florida Heritage Festival (941-747-1998; Bradenton) Commemorates Hernando de Soto's discovery of the region. A reenactment of the 1539 landing highlights the schedule of month-long events, which include a children's parade, Easter egg hunt, seafood festival, and plastic bottle boat regatta.

Florida Playwrights Festival (941-366-9000; Florida Studio Theatre, 1241 N. Palm Ave., Sarasota 34236; downtown) Premieres the works of emerging playwrights from Florida and around the nation, launching almost 70 main stage productions. April through May.

Florida Winefest and Auction (941-952-1109; The Resort at Longboat Key Club, 3-1 gulf of Mexico Dr., Longboat Key 34228) A prestigious event featuring food and wine seminars, tastes from the area's finest restaurants, top entertainment, black-tie dinner, and fine wine auction. Four days.

La Musica International Chamber Music Festival (941-364-8802; 1741 Main St., Sarasota 34236) Concerts held at the Sarasota Opera House, 61 N. Pineapple Ave., downtown Sarasota, during two weekends in April.

Sharks' Tooth and Seafood Festival (941-412-0402; Sharky's Restaurant at the Venice Pier, Venice) A bacchanal of seafood bounty, the festival gets its name also from its reputation among shark-tooth collectors. One weekend.

Siesta Fiesta (941-349-3800; Siesta Key) A weekend of crafts shows, food fest, live musical and kids' entertainment.

JUNE

Sarasota Music Festival (941-953-4252, 941-953-3434; Florida West Coast Symphony, 709 N. Tamiami Trail, Sarasota 34236) Presents classical and chamber music by promising musicians from around the world. Sponsored by the Florida West Coast Symphony, the program includes lectures for participants. The public is welcome at the performances. Three weeks.

Suncoast Offshore Grand Prix (941-371-2827; Sarasota Bay) A national attraction, with powerboat racers from around the world. Eleven days at month's end.

AUGUST

DeSoto Fishing Tournament (941-747-1998; Twin Dolphin Marina Grill, 1200 1st Ave. W., Bradenton 34205; downtown) Inshore and offshore divisions. Entry fee. Takes place one weekend midmonth. Entrance fee.

OCTOBER

St. Armands Circle Art Festival (941-388-1554; St. Armands Circle) Features more than 200 national artists.

Stone Crab, Seafood & Wine Festival (941-383-6464, 800-4-COLONY; Colony Beach & Tennis Resort, 1620 Gulf of Mexico Dr., Longboat Key 34228) Celebrates the opening of stone crab season with dinners, cooking demonstrations, and wine tastings.

NOVEMBER

Blues Fest (941-377-3279; Sarasota Fairgrounds) Blues musicians of world renown. One day early in the month.

Cine-World Film Festival (941-955-FILM ; Burns Court Cinema, 506 Burns Ln., Sarasota 34236; downtown) Screens 20 to 30 films from around the world for one week early in the month.

Sarasota Comedy Festival (941-954-2006; various locations in Sarasota) A result of Sarasota's large population of cartoonists, the festival takes place for a week midmonth and includes a comedy film festival, comedy dinner shows with name comedians, a "cartoon walk," a mainstage show, golf events, and gala dinners.

Sarasota School of Architecture Tour and Symposia (941-388-1400) Tours by foot, trolley, and boat; exhibits and lectures on Sarasota's namesake architectural style.

Taste of Manatee (941-729-7777; Barcarrota Blvd., downtown Bradenton) Restaurant samplings one day early in the month.

A Taste of Sarasota (941-377-0064; Phillipi Estate, Sarasota) The best from Sarasota restaurants, live entertainment, a kids' park and petting zoo.

Venice Art Festival (941-484-6722; downtown Venice) Artisans from around the U.S. for one weekend.

CHAPTER FOUR
Wild and Watery
CHARLOTTE HARBOR COAST

As one of Florida's largest bays, Charlotte Harbor supplies a huge gulp of nature and a place to play on many waterfronts. The region has remained the most isolated and undeveloped of any in southwest Florida, primarily because its beaches — glorious though they might be — are so far removed from main highways. The Charlotte coast retains a quiet, natural temperament and still holds on to fishing as a way of life and livelihood.

This chapter begins where the last left off, on twisty, out-of-the-way **Manasota Key**, a refuge for wealthy isolationists at its north end and the site of the unpretentious, underappreciated resort community of **Englewood Beach** at its south.

Lee Island Coast Visitor and Convention Bureau

Angler's silver: A hooked tarpon fights for freedom in Boca Grande Pass.

On the mainland Cape Haze peninsula, bounded by the Myakka River and Charlotte Harbor, small residential communities such as **Englewood**, **Grove City**, **Cape Haze**, **Placida**, and **Rotonda West** hold Amerindian mounds, fishermen, retirees, golf course communities, and families. Placida is the jump-off point for **Gasparilla Island**, which has built its reputation and character on one fish in particular: tarpon. Phosphate shipping and legends of bygone buccaneers first attracted attention to the area. Later the Silver King, prize of the fishing world, drew millionaires to the island community of **Boca Grande**. They're still around; the town reportedly has a median household income of more than $85,000. Privately owned **Little Gasparilla** and **Palm Islands** and

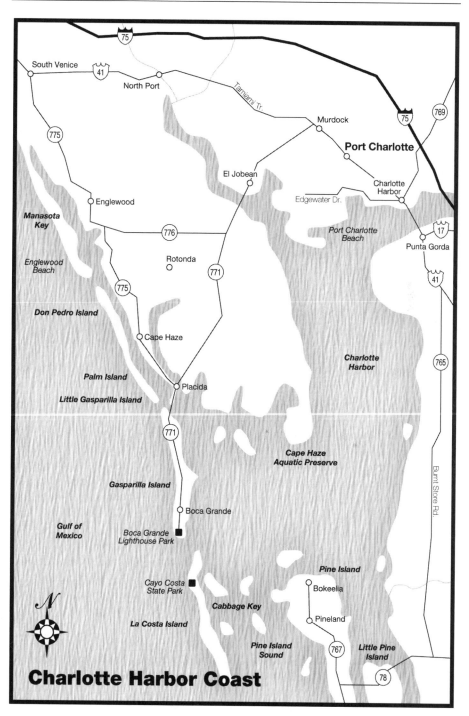

Charlotte Harbor Coast

mostly state-owned **Don Pedro Island** have run together with shifts of tides and time. They remain three of Florida's most pristine barrier islands.

Inland, across the harbor, **Port Charlotte** is a new city that was built around Tamiami Trail, principally as a retirement community. The town of **Charlotte Harbor** was settled shortly after the Civil War by farmers and cattle ranchers. Facing it across the Peace River's widest point, **Punta Gorda** boasts a past as deep as its harbor. The southernmost station for the Florida Southern Railroad in 1886, this deepwater port town enjoyed a bustling era of commerce and tourism before railroad builder Henry Plant decided to shut it down in favor of further developing Tampa Bay. Ice making, turpentine stilling, pineapple growing, and especially commercial fishing continued to earn local citizens a living for some time. Today Punta Gorda is working to recover its past glories through downtown and riverfront restoration. *Money* magazine regularly declares it one of America's most desirable places to live. Home of Ponce de León Park, where the explorer is believed to have met his death, it hosts subdivisions of modern-day youth seekers.

LODGING

A ccommodations along the Charlotte Harbor coast tend to exude personality. Sure, you have your Days Inn and Econo Lodge, but the remainder are either old-money polished, new-money luxurious, or money's-not-the-issue sporting. From beach cottages to the grand old Gasparilla Inn, the Charlotte Harbor coast promises something special in the way of lodging.

During high season, which begins shortly before Christmas and ends after Easter, rates may rise anywhere from 10 to 100 percent above those charged during the off-season. Some resorts schedule their rates based on as many as six different seasons, with the highest rates applying from mid-February through Easter. Reservations are recommended during these months. Some resorts and rental services require a minimum stay, especially during the peak season.

The following selection includes some of the coast's greatest lodging characters. Toll-free 800, 888, 866, or 877 reservation numbers, where available, are listed after local numbers. A star after the pricing designation indicates that the rate includes at least continental breakfast in the cost of lodging; one follows the American Plan, pricing all meals into the rate charged.

Pricing codes are explained below. They are normally per person/double occupancy for hotel rooms and per unit for efficiencies, apartments, and cottages. Many resorts offer off-season packages at special rates. Pricing does not include the 7 percent Florida sales tax. Charlotte County also charges a 3 percent bed tax. Some large resorts add service gratuities or maid charges.

Rate Categories

Inexpensive	Up to $75
Moderate	$75 to $150
Expensive	$150 to $200
Very Expensive	$200 and up

The following abbreviations are used for credit card information:

AE: American Express	MC: MasterCard
D: Discover Card	V: Visa
DC : Diners Club	

Federal law mandates that properties with 50 rooms or more provide accommodations for physically handicapped persons. I have indicated only those small places that do not make such allowances.

Boca Grande

The Gasparilla Inn, doyenne of the Gulf Coast.

Karen T. Bartlett

GASPARILLA INN
General Manager: Steve
  Seidensticker.
239-964-2201.
500 Palm Ave., Boca
  Grande 33921.
At 5th St. and Palm Ave.
Closed: Mid- June–mid-
  Dec.
Price: Expensive to Very
  Expensive.*
Credit Cards: No.

With subtle grandeur the Gasparilla Inn sits on her throne of lush greenery. Dressed in pale-yellow clapboard with white columns, Georgian porticos, and Victorian sensibilities, it has been a town anchor and social emblem since 1912. The region's oldest surviving resort, the Gasparilla first opened its doors as a retreat for such families as the Vanderbilts and Du Ponts, whose descendants still winter there. Not that accommodations are ultrael-egant. The 140 rooms and cottages reflect the era of their construction, with understated furnishings. A more elegant wood-and-wicker dining room, a beauty salon, an 18-hole golf course, a croquet lawn, tennis courts, and a beach club with fitness facilities and two pools provide amenities. It's said that the Gasparilla Inn, in quiet Boca Grande, was where Palm Beach socialites used to come to escape charity balls and the perpetual fashion show of their glittery hometown.

THE INNLET
General Manager: Steve Seidensticker.
239-964-2294.
1251 Twelfth St. E., PO Box 248, Boca Grande 33921.
At 11th St. and East Ave.
Price: Moderate.
Credit Cards: AE, MC, V.

Little stepsister to the Gasparilla Inn, the Innlet has been yellowed to fit in with the family. Fancy lattice touches and new renovations pretty up a motel remake. The name is a double entendre on its sub-inn status and its bayou location with a ramp and docking, handy for boating and fishing types. It has a nice little pool, playground, and restaurant with 25 rooms and efficiencies (with stovetop, microwave, and fridge) in modern, tasteful attire. Guests share communal porches and balconies.

Cape Haze

Palm Island Resort: the ultimate island steal-away.

Palm Island Resort

PALM ISLAND RESORT
President: Dean L. Beckstead.
941-697-4800, 800-824-5412, in Fla. 800-282-6142.
www.palmisland.com.
7092 Placida Rd., Cape Haze 33946.
Price: Expensive to Very Expensive.
Credit Cards: AE, MC, V.

A true island getaway in grand style, Palm Island is a slab of sand above Gasparilla Island devoted mostly to a private resort with villa lodging. One must boat in; an hourly ferry runs from the resort's mainland marina and its two-level suite accommodations. On Palm Island, Old-Florida-style villas front a wide, isolated apron of beach and come with fully equipped kitchens, laundries, one to three bedrooms, exquisite appointments, and screened porches overlooking more than 2 miles of deserted beach. The 160-unit (counting the mainland accommodations) property has 5 pools and 11 tennis courts, plus restaurants and bars, an island store, a full-service marina, boat rentals, charter services, a nature trail, kids programs, summer turtle walks, bicycle and water-sports equipment rentals — all the makings for an I'm-never-leaving-this-island vacation. What it doesn't have is roads, cars, stress, and rigorous time schedules.

Englewood Beach

WESTON'S RESORT
Owner: Deborah L. Weston.
941-474-3431.
www.sunstate.com/
  westons.
985 Gulf Blvd., Englewood
  34223.
Price: Inexpensive to
  Expensive.
Credit Cards: D, MC, V.

Taking up a good block at Englewood Beach's southern end, Weston's spreads from bay to beach to please both fishermen and sand-loving types. For the former it rents boats, motors, and paraphernalia and provides boat slips, fishing docks, and freezer storage. Free for the use of all guests are two swimming pools, tennis courts, barbecue grills, and shuffleboard. Accommodations on the 83-unit property range from studio efficiencies (inexpensive) to three-bedroom apartments (expensive) in cement-block buildings, all modernly outfitted. The rooms are clean and well kept, with the exception of some carpeting that looked as though it needed replacing. In some rooms the Murphy-style beds flip up into closets for more room. Kitchens are large and modern. Beach rooms look out on seawalled sand and eroding beach beyond that. One pool sits in the middle of an asphalt parking lot. There's nothing luxurious about the resort, but its reasonable rates and beach location at the quiet end of the island make it a good choice for people who love water and water sports.

Manasota Key

**MANASOTA BEACH
  CLUB**
Owners: Robert and
  Sydney Buffum.
Manager: Warren Francis.
941-474-2614.
www.manasotabeachclub.
  com.
7660 Manasota Key Rd.,
  Englewood 34223.
Closed: Mid-May through
  mid-Nov.
Price: Very Expensive.*
Credit Cards: MC, V.
Handicap Access: Yes.

A tiny, low-impact sign whispers MANASOTA BEACH CLUB. And although it occupies 25 acres of Manasota Key, the resort itself is just as unobtrusive. The unadvertised property preserves the island's natural attributes with a low-key attitude, wooded paths, and a deserted beach. I saw a pileated woodpecker while there, and guests have reported seeing 92 other species about the grounds. Fifteen cottages, from rustic to designer in style, the dining room, the bottle club (no alcohol is sold on the premises), and a library display Old Florida charm. The resort appeals to the "sink into oblivion" type of vacationer who wishes to hide out amongst natural, gnarly vegetation. (There are no televisions in the units, unless requested.) The property, which has a summer-camp feel to it, also appeals to the sportsperson, with three tennis courts, a swimming pool, bocci ball, shuffleboard, basketball, horseshoes, playground, croquet, bicycling, sailing, windsurfing, a children's program, and charter fishing. A private 18-hole golf course nearby is available to guests. During social season (late November through April), cottage-room guests receive meals on the American Plan (three meals) or Modified American Plan (two meals). May through mid-November, the resort rents out entire cottages with kitchens and provides no meals.

Port Charlotte

**BANANA BAY
WATERFRONT
MOTEL**
Owner: Richard Michno.
941-743-4441.
www.bananabaymotel.
com.
32385 Bayshore Rd.,
Charlotte Harbor 33980.
At Hwy. 41.
Price: Inexpensive.
Credit Cards: AE, D, DC,
MC, V.
Handicap Access: No.

Along Bayshore Drive in Charlotte Harbor, the feeling is Old Florida, relaxed, and fishy. Across the wide mouth of the Peace River lies Punta Gorda. Down the way, a free fishing pier juts into waters flush with fish. A few inexpensive motels in this neighborhood serve the stay-away-from-the-crowds crowd, and Banana Bay is one of the prettiest, with its mammoth potted staghorn ferns in front and banana tree murals on its one-story stucco rooms and efficiencies (one and two bedroom) — 13 in all. The rooms have a tropical look — maybe a bit faded and floored in old-fashioned linoleum but clean and perky. Even the motel rooms have small fridges. Along the bay, shuffleboard, grills, and picnic tables put the focus outdoors on the fetching water view.

Punta Gorda

**FISHERMEN'S VILLAGE
VILLAS**
Manager: Diane Smith.
941-639-8721, 800-639-0020.
www.fishville.com.
1200 W. Retta Esplanade
#58, Punta Gorda 33950.
Price: Moderate.
Credit Cards: D, MC, V.
Handicap Access: Yes.

One of the Gulf Coast's best lodging bargains, these spacious time-share units— all decorated in modern taste and all with a view of the water — each contain two bedrooms, a loft, a living area, a big, full kitchen with counter bar and stools, and one bath. They're situated above the shops, restaurants, and courtyard hubbub of Fishermen's Village, but the rooms are well soundproofed. Guests have free use of a swimming pool, clay tennis courts, and bicycles. They are close to all the action there is to find in Punta Gorda, on land and on water. Convenient for boat-in guests, Fishermen's Village fronts a yacht harbor and a 98-slip full-service marina.

**GILCHRIST BED &
BREAKFAST**
Innkeepers: Betty and
  Johnny Surles.
941-575-4129.
www.all-florida.com/
  gilchrist.
115 Gilchrist St., Punta
  Gorda 33950.
Price: Moderate.
Credit Cards: MC, V.
Handicap Access: No.

In a charming old neighborhood lined with royal palms and Cuban laurels, and within walking distance of Punta Gorda's historic district and waterfront Gilchrist Park, this B&B fits right in. Green-shakes siding, a tin roof, lattice trim, flowery grounds, and a serene, fountained backyard give this small, circa 1914 historic home classic character. The Surles rent out two suites in-season, plus a self-sufficient apartment during the summer. The two suites each have their own porch entryway, bath, and decorative (i.e., nonworking) fireplace. Original glossy pine floors and white bead-and-board are enhanced by a marble mantel in one room, the original brick mantel in another, and Virginia colonial antiques and Victorian bric-a-brac. A common area between the two suites provides a television, microwave, and minifridge. The apartment rents by the month, occupies the old carriage house, and feels like a sanctuary for the soul. Homemade continental breakfast is served around a communal table either on the screened porch (which also holds a hot tub) or in the Surles's dining room.

HOME & CONDO RENTALS

Boca Grande Real Estate (941-964-0338, 800-881-2622; www.bocagrande-realestate.com; 430 W. Fourth St., PO Box 686, Boca Grande 33921) Large selection of vacation and seasonal accommodations.

Manasota Key Realty (941-474-9536, 800-870-6432; www.englewoodfl.com; 1927 Beach Rd., Englewood 34223) Grand mansions, beachside cottages, and bayside homes.

RV RESORTS

Most of the area's RV accommodations lie east of Interstate 75.

Water's Edge RV Resort (941-637-4677, 800-637-9224; www.watersedgervresort.com; 6800 Golf Course Blvd., Punta Gorda 33982) Full hookups, fishing lake, convenience store, and rural setting.

DINING

Local cuisine smacks of midwestern influence, but in recent years Floribbean flavors have livened things up. My favorite places to eat are in Boca Grande and Englewood, where chefs get a bit more creative than in the mainland towns. Fishing crews bring just-hooked seafood to the table, but that doesn't mean some restaurants won't try to pawn off frozen products. Here I've tried to include a few that believe in freshness and fanfare at the dining table.

The following listings sample all the variety of Charlotte Coast feasting in these price categories:

Inexpensive	Up to $15
Moderate	$15 to $25
Expensive	$25 to $35
Very Expensive	$35 or more

Cost is figured on a typical meal (at dinner, unless dinner is not served) that would include an appetizer or dessert, salad (if included with the meal), entrée, and coffee.

The following abbreviations are used for credit card information and meals:

AE: American Express	B: Breakfast
D: Discover Card	L: Lunch
DC: Diners Club	D: Dinner
MC: MasterCard	SB: Sunday Brunch
V: Visa	

Boca Grande

PJ'S SEAGRILLE
239-964-0806.
321 Park Ave., Boca Grande 33921.
In the Old Theatre Building.
Price: Expensive to Very Expensive.
Cuisine: Seafood.
Children's Menu: Yes.
Liquor: Full.
Serving: L, D.
Closed: Sun. and late July–Sept.
Credit Cards: AE, DC, MC, V.
Handicap Access: Yes.
Reservations: Recommended for dinner.

PJ's is one of Boca Grande's most popular fine-dining experiences. Family-owned and operated for ten-plus years, it exudes an air of island familiarity, with regulars returning year after year. Dinners offer linen and candlelight, lunch is more casual, all in the setting of unfinished wood and aquariums. The menus change according to fish availability and Chef Jim's creative mood swings. At lunch, you'll find standard fare with sporadic flares of creativeness, such as pita chicken sandwich with pesto mayo and open-faced eggplant sandwich with buffalo mozzarella, sliced tomatoes, and pesto. Dinner features seafood and grilled meats: Asian tuna tartar and grilled prosciutto-wrapped scallops for appetizers; key-lime chicken, coconut shrimp, and grouper your way for entrées.

SOUTH BEACH
239-964-0765.
777 Gulf Blvd., Boca Grande 33921.
Price: Expensive.

This slouchy beachside restaurant seems a stitch schizophrenic to me. On the one hand, it's one of those locals' kind of places that I love, where you can hang out on the beach and at the bar. In season,

Cuisine: Seafood.
Children's Menu: No, but menu contains items kids like at full price.
Liquor: Full.
Serving: L, D.
Credit Cards: AE, MC, V.
Handicap Access: Yes.
Reservations: For dinner only.

though, it fills with Boca's wealthy vacationers, who don't mind paying inflated prices for plastic chairs on a screened porch (there's also indoor seating around the bar) and standard resort seafood fare. Unless you are one of those, I would recommend this place for lunch. Come to the beach, spread a towel, and dip into the dark coolness for a burger (there's one with jalapeños and salsa if you're in a spicy mood), Philly cheese steak, or grouper reuben. Grouper, shrimp, and crab cakes are specialties both lunch and dinner. I tried the "old favorite" Grouper Gaspar, named for a local pirate legend and swimming in garlic butter; very rich and unnecessarily salty. Other entrées: seafood baskets, stuffed shrimp, barbecue ribs. All heavy stuff but fresh and homemade. Do not miss the World Famous Boca Banana Pie. To tell you the truth, I'd never heard of it, and I live just a couple of islands down, but it deserves world fame — frozen banana, caramel, and pecan confection that it is.

Englewood Beach

BARNACLE BILL'S
941-474-9703.
1599 McCall Rd. S., Englewood 34223.
Price: Moderate to Expensive.
Children's Menu: Yes.
Cuisine: Seafood.
Liquor: Full.
Serving: L, D.
Closed: Sun. June–Nov., Mon. year-round.
Credit Cards: MC, V.
Handicap Access: Yes.
Reservations: No.
Special Features: Waterfront view and outdoor dining.

A longtime (20, the menu brags) fixture on Englewood Beach, it recently reopened, to the delight of many, on the mainland. I go there for its wonderful homemade soups, six varieties offered daily. For $1.25 extra, you get fresh cornbread. Its other endearing quality is the freshness of its seafood. Specialty of the house is the baked grouper with garlic butter, tomatoes, and cheese. This is an old-fashioned fish house, so expect things fried or buttery — but most importantly, expect them fresh. Other reputation builders at Bill's include its mammoth sandwiches at lunch, burgers nine different ways (including pizza and Mardi Gras burgers), and "pie!" (yes, with an exclamation mark). The peanut-butter-and-chocolate-chip pie is signature.

MAD SAM'S
941-475-9505.
www.gtesupersite.com/ madsamsgrill.
1375 Beach Rd., Englewood 33423.
Price: Moderate.
Children's Menu: Yes.
Cuisine: American/ Regional.
Liquor: Full.
Serving: L, D.

People all the way up in Venice told me about Mad Sam's. The name alone made me like it. They said I couldn't miss it. With a bright, grimacing, skeletal fish crashing through the entryway roof, it does defy nonchalance. The restaurant looks as though it sits upon its own cement island at the edge of the intracoastal waterway. Mad Sam's is all bright, airy, tropical, and many windowed. The food is as fresh as the setting but not too daring in this part of back-roads Florida. The

A grumpy fish crashes through the entryway ceiling at Mad Sam's, Englewood's newest culinary sensation.

Karen T. Bartlett

Closed: Mon.
Credit Cards: AE, D, MC, V.
Handicap Access: Yes.
Reservations: No.
Special Features: Waterfront view and outdoor dining.

chefs smartly add subtle touches of inspiration, such as margarita-soaked pork chops served with a side of tropical salsa and chutney-glazed duck mango tango. Other lunch and dinner offerings include 'gator bites, pasta sandwich, oyster sandwich (topped with prosciutto and provolone), grilled lamb chops with tangerine marinade, grilled key-lime grouper, and blackened tuna pesto. The desserts posed further temptation, and I yielded to the hot, homemade, and walnut-studded strawberry-rhubarb crisp à la mode. Almost as good as mom's.

Punta Gorda

AMIMOTO JAPANESE RESTAURANT
941-505-1515.
2705 S. Tamiami Trail, Punta Gorda 33950.
At Towles Plaza.
Price: Moderate to Expensive.
Cuisine: Japanese.
Serving: L, D.
Closed: Lunch Sat. and Sun.
Liquor: Beer and wine.
Credit Cards: AE, D, DC, MC, V.
Handicap Access: Yes.
Reservations: Accepted.
Special Features: Sushi bar.

Soothing and authentic, Amimoto satisfies the spirit as well as the stomach. The décor is simple, contemporary, and clean, decorated with tasteful Eastern art and arranged around the sushi bar. The server presents you with the traditional warm, damp towel and a sushi menu as you are seated to a place setting of napkin, chopsticks, and clay pots of soy sauce. The sushi menu itself presents more than 50 choices. I order the spicy *maguro* — sushi tuna and *kimchee* rolled in seaweed, sticky rice, and sesame seeds and served with pickled ginger and wasabi. Remarkable! The lunch and dinner menus list yet dozens of more options for appetizers such as ginger shrimp, squid tempura, seaweed salad, and scads of exotic combinations involving seafood, tofu, and Oriental vegetables and sauces. For entrées, the menus describe a few possible preparations of chicken, pork, and beef, then go on to list a selection of seafood. Fish can be grilled with wasabi or teriyaki sauce, or deep-fried. The scallops sautéed with lime and special sauce sounded tempting. From the lunch menu, I selected *yakisoba*, a flavorful noodle dish with sautéed shrimp and vegetables — not overly soy sauced and kicked up with a liberal application of ginger. A bowl of tofu and shiitake soup preceded, a delicate prelude to a noble feast. The restaurant does provide forks, by the way, for the chopsticks challenged like me.

FOOD PURVEYORS

BAKERIES

Belgian Bakery (941-625-1252; 4040 N. Tamiami Trail, Port Charlotte 33952) Belgian breads from Old World recipes using no sugar, preservatives, milk, or eggs; Belgian-French pastries, Belgian cookies, meringues.

Flour Bag (239-964-5818; 348 E. Railroad Ave. Boca Grande 33921) Homemade breads, creative muffins, scones, pizza, cakes, and other desserts in an inviting setting; also sandwiches and other eat-in or take-out items.

CANDY & ICE CREAM

Flamingo Yogurt (941-639-5515; www.fishville.com; 1200 W. Retta Esplanade, Punta Gorda 33950; at Fishermen's Village) Premium yogurt, granita, cold cappuccino, frozen fruit drinks, ice cream, and candy.

The Loose Caboose in Boca Grande's Railroad Plaza carries a cargo of highly acclaimed homemade ice cream.

Karen T. Bartlett

The Loose Caboose (239-964-0440; 433 W. Fourth St., Boca Grande 33921; at Park Ave.) Katharine Hepburn, among scores of others, once left her compliments on the bulletin board at this restaurant known for its homemade ice cream and smoothies in many flavors.

DELI & SPECIALTY FOODS

Gill's Grocery & Deli (239-964-2506; 5800 Gasparilla Rd., Boca Grande 33921; at The Courtyard) Freshly made sandwiches, salads, and heat-up entrées, plus grocery items, ice cream, party trays, and bakery goods. Delivery available.

GrapeVine (239-964-0614; 321 Park Ave., Boca Grande 33921; in the Old Theatre Building) Specialty wines, imported cheese, fish, prepared dishes, sandwiches, gourmet products, and baked goods Monday through Saturday.

Kalli's German Butcher Sausage Kitchen (941-627-1413; kallis@isni.net; 2420 Tamiami Trail, Port Charlotte 33952) *Wursts* of every variety, many of which you've probably never heard of; also fine cuts of meat, rouladen, cheese, hams, and gourmet European imports. This place is a lot of fun.

COFFEE

Bike 'N Beach Café (239-964-0711; 333 Park Ave., Boca Grande 33921) Espresso, cappuccino, smoothies, fresh fruit and vegetable juices.

Coffee à la Carte (941-575-4344; www.fishville.com/shops; 1200 W. Retta Esplanade, Punta Gorda 33950; at Fishermen's Village) Gourmet coffee, espresso, cappuccino, iced and frozen drinks, pastries, bagels, sandwiches, and ice cream.

The Lemon Bay Buzz (941-460-0696; 420 W. Dearborn St., Englewood 34223) Cheery little spot for hot and cold flavored coffees and teas as well as cold sandwiches and pastries.

FRUIT & VEGETABLE STANDS

De Soto Groves (941-625-2737; 1750 Tamiami Trail, Murdock 33948) Just-picked Florida citrus fruit.

PIZZA & TAKEOUT

Angelo's Pizza (941-474-2477; 2611 Placida Rd., Englewood 34223) Pizza and Italian specialties. Takeout and delivery.

Flour Bag (239-964-5818; 348 E. Railroad Ave. Boca Grande 33921) Sandwiches, homemade pizza, breads, desserts, and other take-out items.

SEAFOOD

Village Fish Market (941-639-7959; www.fishville.com/shops; 1200 W. Retta Esplanade, Punta Gorda 33950; at Fishermen's Village) A small market featuring New England and Florida seafood, with dining.

CULTURE

The Charlotte Harbor coast is small town, even in its larger, urban-sprawl-infected communities. Long considered a refuge for the retired, the region is not known for its vibrant arts scene or cultural diversity. Overall, it has a Midwestern flavor in coastal areas but is definitely Old Florida in inland rural parts. Awareness of the arts has developed slowly and on a hobby level.

ARCHITECTURE

Town citizens worked to beautify downtown Punta Gorda with historic and educational murals.

Chelle Koster Walton

In the smaller towns around Charlotte Harbor, single examples of historic character appear serendipitously in the midst of concrete-block homes. Downtown Englewood, a destination off the beaten path of Tamiami Trail, holds a few such treasures that have been reincarnated as shops, boutiques, and galleries.

Punta Gorda sprinkles its architectural prizes along Marion Avenue, Olympia Avenue, Retta Esplanade, and side streets such as Sullivan Street. On the Esplanade, look for impressive newly restored homes, the jewels of the old riverfront district. In and around the town's historic section, an eclectic array of architecture ranges from old shotgun cigar workers' homes and tin-roofed Cracker shacks to Victorian mansions and a neoclassical city hall. For a guide to Punta Gorda's treasures, pick up a copy of *Punta Gorda Historic Walking Tour* at the chamber of commerce. Watch for historic murals and street sculptures along the way.

Boca Grande's most noteworthy examples of architecture, aside from grande dame Gasparilla Inn, are four historic churches, each with its own style, located in a four-block area downtown. The Catholic church takes its inspiration from Spanish missions. The others occupy early-20th-century wood-frame buildings and serve Episcopal, Baptist, and Methodist congregations.

A few blocks away, on Tarpon Avenue, old spruced-up Cracker homes slump comfortably in a district sometimes called Whitewash Alley. For a taste of wealthy eccentricity, check out the Johann Fust Library on Gasparilla Road. It was built of native coquina, cypress, and pink stucco.

CINEMA

MOVIE THEATERS

Regal 16 Cinema (941-623-0111; 1441 Tamiami Trail, Port Charlotte 33948; in the Port Charlotte Town Center)

DANCE

Aki's Dancesport Centre (941-624-4001; 3109 Tamiami Trail, Port Charlotte 33983) Dancing socials, competitions, and lessons in swing, merengue, salsa, lindy, fox trot, and waltz.

Country Line Dance Lessons (941-639-8721; www.fishville.com; 1200 W. Retta Esplanade, Punta Gorda 33950; in Fishermen's Village) Every Wednesday night, 7 to 9, by Lone Star Country Dance Association; $3 per person for lessons.

HISTORIC HOMES & SITES

THE A. C. FREEMAN HOUSE
941-637-0077.
639 E. Hargreaves Ave., Punta Gorda 33950.
Open: Hourly winter tours Dec.–Apr., Fri. and Sat. 11–3.
Admission: Donations welcome.

Home of the Charlotte County Foundation today, it once was occupied by Punta Gorda's turn-of-the-century mayor and mortician. Narrowly escaping the wrecking ball in 1985, the lovely clapboard Queen Anne mansion was saved and restored by the people of Punta Gorda as a memento of gracious pioneer lifestyles.

PONCE DE LEÓN HISTORICAL PARK
End of Marion Ave., Punta Gorda.

A rock shrine containing a chipped-paint statue commemorates Ponce de León's supposed 1513 landing here and his subsequent death caused

The A. C. Freeman House survives from Punta Gorda's early days of prosperity.

Charlotte County Visitors Bureau

by an Indian attack. The park has a wildlife and recreational area on the harbor, with boat ramp, picnic facilities, small beach, and native trail into the mangroves.

Karen T. Bartlett

The Boca Grande Lighthouse is one of the state's most picturesque.

BOCA GRANDE LIGHTHOUSE MUSEUM
239-964-0060 (Geo Park Service), 941-964-0375.
PO Box 637, Boca Grande 33921.
Gasparilla Island State Recreation Area, Gulf Blvd., Boca Grande.

This 1890 structure was renovated in Old Florida style and put back into service in 1986 after twenty years of abandonment. It is the most photographed and painted landmark on the island. You can self-tour both it and the museum, which explores its history and Boca Grande bygones — from ancient Calusa civilizations through railroad and industrial eras to the island's modern-day rep-

Open: 10–4 Wed.–Sun.; also Tues. in-season; closed: Mon. in-season, Tues. in summer, Aug. and major holidays.
Admission: $2 for state recreation area park; donation of $1 requested.

utation as a tarpon-fishing mecca. Historic cisterns, the assistant lighthouse keeper's home, and a struggling native vegetation garden comprise the fenced-in complex. It sits within Gasparilla Island State Recreation Area.

MUSEUMS

FLORIDA ADVENTURE MUSEUM OF CHARLOTTE COUNTY
941-639-3777.
museum@sunline.net.
260 W. Retta Esplanade, Punta Gorda 33950.
Open: 10–5 Mon.-Fri.; 10–3 Sat.; closed Sun.
Admission: $2 adults, $1 children 12 and under.

The small facility features changing historical exhibits with a Florida focus and a roomful of stuffed wildcats. Kids enjoy the historical dress-up costumes.

MUSIC & NIGHTLIFE

Boca Grande

South Beach (239-964-0765; 777 Gulf Blvd., Boca Grande 33921) Live contemporary bands play weekend nights. Sunset plays (almost) every evening.

Englewood

Englewood Performing Arts Series (941-473-2787) Fine cultural entertainment from around the nation, mid-November through mid-April.
Grumpy's Hole (941-475-9505; 1375 Beach Rd., Englewood 33423; at Mad Sam's Grille & Bar) Live bands playing blues, zydeco, reggae, and jazz most weekend nights.

Port Charlotte

Charlotte County Jazz Society (941-766-9422; 282 Goiana St., Port Charlotte 33983) Sponsors 10 jazz concerts each year at the Cultural Center Theatre (see "Theater," below) , plus open jam sessions for local and visiting jazz musicians the third Sunday of every month.
Charlotte Symphony Orchestra (941-625-5996; PO Box 495831, Port Charlotte 33949) Performs at the Community Life Center on Edgewater Drive November through May.
Gatorz Bar & Grill (941-625-5000; 3816 Tamiami Trail, Port Charlotte 33952) Live music throughout the week: jazz and Top 40.

Punta Gorda

Charlotte County Memorial Auditorium (941-639-5833, 800-329-9988; 75 Taylor St., Punta Gorda 33950) Waterfront host to Broadway plays, big band and swing orchestras, and national stars.

Gilchrist Park, overlooking the mouth of the Peace River, is the site of Thursday night jam sessions.

Karen T. Bartlett

Gilchrist Park (Retta Esplanade) On Thursday nights local musicians gather for impromptu jamming at dusk, to which the public is invited.

THEATER

Lemon Bay Playhouse (941-475-6756; 96 W. Dearborn St., Englewood 34223) Home of the Lemon Bay Players community theater group. Performances Sept.–July.

Port Charlotte Cultural Center (941-625-4175; 2280 Aaron St., PO Box 3060, Port Charlotte 33949) Home of the Charlotte Players (941-255-1022) community-theater group and Charlotte County Jazz Society (see "Music and Nightlife," above).

Royal Palm Players (239-964-2670; 333 Park Ave., Suite 4, PO Box 954, Boca Grande 33921) A community-theater group sponsoring plays, guest-artist performances, children's performances, and concerts November into May.

VISUAL ART CENTERS

The local "Art Around Town" movement and Historic Mural Society have turned the streets of downtown Punta Gorda into one huge, outdoor gallery. Local artists lend their sculptures for display along the streets. The mural society has resulted in more than twenty historic and educational scenes painted on buildings mostly throughout the downtown area.

A listing for commercial galleries is included in the "Shopping" section of this chapter.

Arts & Humanities Council (941-764-8100; 2811 N. Tamiami Trail, Port Charlotte 33952; at LaPlaya Plaza) Hosts art displays and events.
Englewood Art Center (941-474-5548; 350 S. McCall Rd., Englewood 34223)
Visual Arts Center (941-639-8810; 210 Maude St., Punta Gorda 33950; near Fishermen's Village) Home of the Charlotte County Art Guild. Exhibit halls, gift shops, library, darkroom, and classes.

RECREATION

More behind-the-scenes than the touted playgrounds of its flanking neighbors, the Charlotte Harbor coast's greatest claim to recreational fame is its fishing — particularly for that king of all sports fish, tarpon.

BEACHES

You must drive way off the beaten path to find the beaches of Charlotte County. That keeps them more natural, less trodden.

BLIND PASS (MIDDLE) BEACH
941-316-1172.
Route 776, midisland on Manasota Key.
Facilities: Rest rooms, showers.

Sixty-three acres of lightly developed shoreline attract those drawn more to seclusion than to the sports and activities of Manasota Key's other beaches. Low dunes edge wide salt-and-pepper sands. Next door you'll see one of the island's first buildings, known as Hermitage House. From the parking lot you can follow a nature boardwalk trail into the mangroves.

CHADWICK PARK BEACH
941-475-6606.
2100 N. Beach Rd., Englewood 34223.
Route 776, south end of Manasota Key at Englewood Beach.
Facilities: Picnic areas, rest rooms, showers, volleyball, basketball, food and beach-rental concessions.
Parking: 25¢ per hour.

Many refer to this simply as Englewood Beach. A popular hangout for the local youth, it is nonetheless a well-maintained and policed area: No alcohol, dogs, glass, surfboards, or motor vehicles are allowed. The beach was widened in 2001 to combat severe erosion. Several resorts, shops, rental shops, and restaurants huddle around the area, which keeps activity levels high.

DON PEDRO ISLAND STATE RECREATION AREA
941-964-0375.

Secluded beach at a 129-acre island getaway. Once separated from Palm Island and Little Gasparilla, Don Pedro Island is now connected to

Barrier Islands GEOpark, PO Box 1150, Boca Grande 33921.
South of Palm Island, accessible only by boat.
Facilities: Picnic area, rest rooms, boat docks.
Admission: $2 per boat or family arriving by ferry.

LIGHTHOUSE BEACH/ GASPARILLA ISLAND STATE RECREATION AREA

239-964-0375.
Barrier Islands GEOpark, PO Box 1150, Boca Grande 33921.
Along Gulf Blvd., Boca Grande, Gasparilla Island.
Facilities: Picnic tables, rest rooms.
Parking: $2 per car.

MANASOTA BEACH

941-316-1172.
North end of Route 776, Manasota Key.
Facilities: Picnic area, rest rooms, showers, lifeguard, historical marker, boat ramps.

PORT CHARLOTTE BEACH PARK

941-627-1628.
4500 Harbor Blvd., Port Charlotte 33952.
At the southeast end of Harbor Blvd.
Facilities: Picnic areas, rest rooms, showers, concessions, volleyball, basketball, tennis courts, playground, horseshoes, boat ramps, fishing pier, swimming and kiddie pools.
Swimming Admission: $2.68 adult, $1.61 ages 3–15 (phone: 941-629-0170)
Parking: 25¢ per hour.

the two to form one long, lightly developed barrier island. Don Pedro, the most natural component, is toward the southern end.

Marked by a historic lighthouse with a museum inside, the park edges the deepwater tarpon grounds of Boca Grande Pass. Its plush, deep sands encompass 135 acres, although in some parts the beach gets quite narrow. The view of oil tanks tends to intrude upon the feeling of awayness. Swimming is not recommended because of strong currents through the pass. A historic chapel in the same park is under restoration.

A lively sunning and shelling venue connected to Venice's Caspersen Beach about 1½ miles to the north. It also has a reputation — but not as pointed as Venice's — for shark's teeth.

A highly developed recreational center that sits on Charlotte Harbor along a manmade beach, this is a good place to go if you (or the children) like to keep busy at the beach. A boardwalk runs along the beach and connects to the fishing pier. It looks across the way at Punta Gorda and feels more like a beach at a lake than the sea.

**STUMP PASS BEACH
STATE RECREATION
AREA**
South end of Gulf Blvd.,
Englewood Beach on
Manasota Key.
Facilities: Rest rooms,
nature trail.
Parking: $2 per car.

This uncrowded beach, though eroded in many places, offers lovely, unspoiled seclusion. Traditionally, the 255-acre park has been a magnet for fishermen who cast into Lemon Bay. Follow the 2-mile wooded trail to the south, and you'll find nice areas to spread a towel and dip your toes. The park spreads all the way to Stump Pass in a skinny strip of black-specked sand. It recently installed rest rooms and more parking spots, to the elation of most.

BICYCLING

The Charlotte Coast region, with its abundance of back roads and wide-open spaces, gives cyclists an opportunity to pedal in peace. Many of its favored bikeways are on-road or designated bike lanes, which are separated from motor traffic only by a painted white line. According to state law, bicyclists who share the road with other vehicles must heed all the rules of the road. Children under age 16 are required to wear a helmet.

Best Biking

Cape Haze Pioneer Trail is a developing county project that runs parallel to Route 771 along a former railbed. The first 3.5 miles opened in 1999, and another 2-mile segment was expected to be completed in 2001. The third phase will be constructed in 2005.

Babcock Wilderness Adventure (941-489-3911, 800-500-5583; www.babcockwilderness.com; 8000 State Rd. 31, Punta Gorda 33982) leads daily three-hour eco-bike tours through Telegraph Cypress Swamp and prairie land trails. It provides 21-speed off-road bikes for the experience. Cost is $35 for adults and $30 for children ages 10 to 14. Reservations are required.

About a mile after Gasparilla Island's causeway (which can be crossed by bicycle for $1), the Boca Grande bike path starts. Here you pedal along old railroad routes. Seven miles of pathway travel the island from tip to tip along Railroad Avenue and Gulf Boulevard. These paths are shared by golf carts, which one can rent and drive about the island, as long as you are age 14 or older. Many of Boca's downtown streets are also designated golf-cart trails.

Highway 776 through Englewood and Englewood Beach is shouldered with a bike lane that ends at the Sarasota County line. In Punta Gorda, Gilchrist Park's bike path runs along green space overlooking the Peace River on Retta Esplanade. Bike riding on city sidewalks is legal throughout the county.

For a map of Charlotte County bikeways, call the Charlotte County-Punta Gorda Metropolitan Planning Organization at 941-639-4676.

Rentals/Sales

The Bicycle Center (941-627-6600; 3755 Tamiami Trail, Port Charlotte 33952)

All types of bikes, including tandems, children's, and adult tricycles. Free pickup and delivery on weekly rentals within a 10-mile radius.

Bikes and Boards (941-474-2019; 966 S. McCall Rd., Englewood Beach 34223) Bike, skateboard, and skate rentals, sales, and service.

Island Bike 'N Beach (239-964-0711; 333 Park Ave., Boca Grande 33921) Rents bikes, inline skates, tennis racquets, and beach stuff.

Ralph's Bicycle Shop (941-639-3029; 258 W. Marion Ave., Punta Gorda 33950; downtown) Bikes for adults and kids, including BMX-style.

BOATS & BOATING

Intracoastal Waterway channel markers keep boaters in deep water and ospreys in nesting sites.

Karen T. Bartlett

Charlotte Harbor Coast offers many waterfronts for adventure — the gulf, the harbor, Peace River, Myakka River, and Lemon Bay Aquatic Preserve.

POWERBOAT RENTALS

Bay Breeze Boat Rentals (941-475-0733; 1450 Beach Rd., Englewood Beach 34223) Rents pontoon boats and fishing skiffs.

Holidaze Boat Rental (941-505-8888; www.fishville.com/services; 1200 W. Retta Esplanade, Punta Gorda 33950; at Fishermen's Village) Seventeen- to 20-foot boats and 20- to 24-foot pontoons rented hourly and by the half or full day. Also jet skis.

SunSplash Boat Rentals (941-964-1333; www.sunsplashrentals; 5800 Gasparilla Rd., Boca Grande 33921; at Uncle Henry's Marina) Rents powerboats, kayaks, and golf carts.

PUBLIC BOAT RAMPS

Indian Mound Park (941-474-8919; Englewood Recreaton Center, 101 Horn

St., Englewood 34223; downtown Englewood) On Lemon Bay. Access to Stump Pass, picnic pavilion, rest rooms, nature trails.

Laishley Park City Marina (Marion Ave. and Nesbit St., Punta Gorda)

Manasota Beach (Manasota Beach Rd., Manasota Key) One public boat ramp across the street from a county park.

Placida (Causeway Blvd.)

Ponce de León Park (west end of Marion Ave., Punta Gorda) One boat ramp close to the gulf.

Port Charlotte Beach (941-627-1628; 4500 Harbor Blvd., Port Charlotte 33952; southeast end of Harbor Blvd.) Beach recreational area, access to Charlotte Harbor. Two boat ramps.

SAILBOAT CHARTERS, RENTALS, AND INSTRUCTION

Captain Lynda Suzanne (941-964-2027; PO Box 1006, Boca Grande 33921; on First St.) Luncheon sails into Charlotte Harbor. Sailing instruction available.

Southwest Florida Yachts/Florida Sailing & Cruising School (941-656-1339, 800-262-SWFY; www.flsailandcruiseschool.com; 3444 Marinatown Ln. N.W., Suite 19, North Fort Myers 33903) American Sailing Association (ASA) certification courses and bareboat charters provide excellent adventures out of Burnt Store Marina (southwest of Punta Gorda) into Charlotte Harbor for live-aboard experiences.

International Sailing School (941-639-7492, 800-824-5040; www.intlsailsch .com; 1200 W. Retta Esplanade, Punta Gorda 33950; at Fishermen's Village Marina) Instruction, including couples classes and certification courses; rentals and club memberships.

SIGHTSEEING & ENTERTAINMENT CRUISES

Boca Boat Cruises & Charters (888-416-BOAT; www.bocaboat.com; 5800 Gasparilla Rd., PO Box 294, Boca Grande 33921; at Uncle Henry's Marina) Daily beach and lunch tours, and sunset cruises.

Grande Tours (239-697-8825; www.grandetours.com; 12575 Placida Rd., PO Box 281, Placida 33946) Tours: eco, shelling, sea-life, sunset, kid-fishing, pirate-treasure-hunt, wildlife, and narrated-sightseeing. Also kayak nature tours and rentals and water-taxi service.

King Fisher Cruise Lines (941-639-0969; www.kingfisherfleet.com/cruise; 1200 W. Retta Esplanade, Punta Gorda 33950; at Fishermen's Village Marina,) Excursions to Cayo Costa and Cabbage Key and along the Peace River aboard a 35-foot boat. Also sunset and sightseeing cruises.

Ko Ko Kai Charter Boat Service (941-474-2141; 5040 N. Beach Rd., Englewood Beach 34223) Takes you island hopping to Gasparilla, Palm, Cayo Costa, Cabbage Key, and Upper Captiva, and Captiva Islands as well as on fishing and shelling excursions.

FISHING

Tarpon, snook, sheepshead, and snapper tantalize the casting crowd.

Karen T. Bartlett

Tarpon reigns as the king of southwest Florida fish — the Silver King, to be exact, named for its silver-dollarlike scales. Boca Grande Pass is one of the most celebrated spots in the world for catching the feisty fighter.

Nonresidents age 16 and over who wish to fish must obtain a license unless fishing from a vessel or pier covered by its own license. You can buy inexpensive, temporary nonresident licenses at county tax collectors' offices and most Kmarts and bait shops. Check local regulations for season, size, and catch restrictions.

DEEP-SEA PARTY BOATS

King Fisher Fleet (941-639-0969; www.kingfisherfleet.com; 1200 W. Retta Esplanade, Punta Gorda 33950; at Fishermen's Village Marina,) Deep-sea fishing aboard a 35-foot boat with a 20-year-old operation.

FISHING CHARTERS/OUTFITTERS

Boca Grande Fishing Guides Association (800-667-1612; PO Box 676, Boca Grande 33921) Organization of more than 50 qualified charter guides especially knowledgeable about tarpon.

Captain Jack's Charters (941-475-4511; 1450 Beach Rd., Englewood Beach 34223; at the Englewood Bait House) Half-day, full-day, night, overnight, and weekend trips.

Fishing Unlimited (239-964-0907, 800-4-TARPON; 370 E. Railroad Ave., PO Box 1407, Boca Grande 33921) Outfitters, fly shop, guides and charters, authorized Orvis dealer.

King Fisher Fleet (941-639-0969; www.kingfisherfleet.com; 1200 W. Retta Esplanade, Punta Gorda 33950; at Fishermen's Village Marina) Back-bay fishing charters.

Tarpon Hunter Guide Services (941-743-6622; 265 Lomond Dr. #B, Port Charlotte 33953) Charters aboard the *Tarpon Hunter II* in Charlotte Harbor and backwaters. Specialties include fly and light-tackle fishing.

FISHING PIERS

Bayshore Fishing Pier (22967 Bayshore Dr., Charlotte Harbor) At the mouth of the Peace River.

Englewood Beach (Anger) Pier (along Beach Rd. east of the drawbridge)

Gasparilla Fishing Pier South (near Courtyard Plaza, north end of Gasparilla Rd., Gasparilla Island) An old railroad bridge.

Gilchrist Park (Retta Esplanade, Punta Gorda) Cast into the brackish waters where the Peace River empties into the gulf.

Port Charlotte Beach Park (941-627-1628; 4500 Harbor Blvd. Port Charlotte 33952; southeast end of Harbor Blvd.) Part of a beach and pool recreational center, it offers fishing clinics.

GOLF

PUBLIC GOLF COURSES & CENTERS

Deep Creek Golf Club (941-625-6911; 1260 San Cristobal Ave., Port Charlotte 33983) Semiprivate, 18 holes, par 70. Driving range, putting green, and snack bar.

Duffy's Golf Center (941-697-3900; 12455 S. McCall Rd., Port Charlotte 33981) Lit 18-hole executive course and practice range; PGA professionals, golf shop, and snack bar.

Lemon Bay Golf Club (941-697-4190; 9600 Eagle Preserve Dr., Englewood 34223) Semiprivate, 18 holes, restaurant.

Port Charlotte Golf Club (941-625-4109; 22400 Gleneagles Terrace, Port Charlotte 33952) 18 holes, full practice facilities, restaurant and lounge.

Punta Gorda Country Club (941-639-1494; 6100 Duncan Rd., Punta Gorda 33950) Semiprivate, 18 holes, snack bar. Affordable rates.

HEALTH & FITNESS CLUBS

Charlotte County Family YMCA (941-629-2220; 22425 Edgewater Dr., Charlotte Harbor 33980) Aerobics, trimnastics, body shaping, yoga, volleyball, basketball, golf tournaments, youth sports competition, steam room, and kiddie facilities and programs.

Charlotte Racquet & Health & Fitness (941-629-2223; 3250 Loveland Blvd., Port Charlotte 33952) Racquetball, squash, tennis, stairclimbers, bikes, treadmill, universal weights, ballet, karate.

The Punta Gorda Club (941-505-0999; 2905 Tamiami Trail, Punta Gorda 33950) Cardiovascular equipment, golf-enhancement program, free weights, yoga, tai chi, weight machines, tennis courts, baby-sitting.

HIKING

Charlotte Harbor Environmental Center (941-575-5435; 10941 Burnt Store Rd., Punta Gorda 33955) Four miles of nature trails.

Kiwanis Park (941-627-1628; 3100 Donora St. Port Charlotte 33952; at Victoria Ave.) Here's a nice place to hike or jog while the kids entertain themselves on the playground. Nature and fitness trails thread through the woods and alongside a creek where turtles swim.

HUNTING

Given southwest Florida's heightened environmental consciousness, most shooting of wildlife is done with a camera. But the Charlotte Harbor coast's wilderness does provide opportunities for hunting various species. The most popular game include wild hogs, deer, doves, snipe, quail, turkey, duck, and coot.

To hunt in Florida preserves, you must obtain a state license plus a Wildlife Management Area stamp (941-637-2150). Early-season hunters need a quota permit, which is awarded randomly in a drawing in June from applications submitted to the Game and Fresh Water Fish Commission. Special permits are also required for muzzle-loading guns, archery, and turkey, migratory bird, or waterfowl hunting. Daily use permit fees are levied.

For more information about hunting seasons and bag limits, pick up a copy of *Florida Hunting Handbook & Regulations Summary* when you buy your license.

Cypress Lodge at Babcock Wilderness Adventure (941-489-3911, 800-500-5583; adventure@babcockwilderness.com; www.babcockwilderness.com; 8000 State Rd. 31, Punta Gorda 33982) Experienced guides take you hunting for wild turkey, quail, and wild hogs.

Fred C. Babcock–Cecil M. Webb Wildlife Management Area (941-575-5768; 29200 Tucker Grade, Port Charlotte 33955) Some 65,000 acres, one of Florida's 62 designated hunting preserves. Advance permission is required. There is a public shooting range on the property, accessible from Tucker Grade via Rifle Range Rd. The range opens daily during daylight hours but closes the fourth Saturday of each month until 2pm for hunter education training.

KIDS' STUFF

Fish Cove Adventure Golf (941-627-5393; 4949 Tamiami Trail, Port Charlotte 33980) Two 18-hole putt-putt golf courses and a bounce house. Open daily 10am to 11pm. Admission for 18 holes of golf is $6.50 ages 14 and older; $4.50 ages 5 to13, $2 ages 4 and under, $5.50 for seniors.

KidSpace (Maracaibo St. and Avacado Rd., Port Charlotte) A county park created by the community expressly for kids, with a cool fortlike playground, baseball, and picnicking.

Pelican Pete's Playland (941-475-2008; 3101 McCall Rd. S., Englewood 34223) Miniature golf, kiddie train, go-carts for various age levels, batting cages, game room, and snack bar. A popular place that could use some renovating. Open daily; hours change according to season. Fees are charged per activity.

Tringali Recreational Complex Skating (941-473-1018; 3460 McCall Rd. S., Englewood 34223) Weekly skate parties for elementary and middle school kids and families.

RACQUET SPORTS

Boca Grande Community Center (239-964-2564; 131 First St. W., Boca Grande 33921) Two lit courts.

Charlotte Racquet & Health & Fitness (941-629-2223, 3250 Loveland Blvd., Port Charlotte 33980) Racquetball, squash, tennis, stairclimbers, bikes, treadmill, universal weights, ballet, karate.

McGuire Park (Elkcam Blvd., Port Charlotte) Four lit hard-surface courts.

The Punta Gorda Club (941-505-0999; 2905 Tamiami Trail, Punta Gorda 33950) Tennis courts plus other sports and fitness facilities, and baby-sitting.

Tringali Recreational Complex (941-473-1018; 3460 McCall Rd. S., Englewood 34223)

SHELLING

You'll find some shells on the beaches along the Charlotte Harbor coast, but if you're serious, you'll head south to the Island Coast.

SHELLING CHARTERS

Ko Ko Kai Charter Boat Service (941-474-2141; 5040 N. Beach Rd., Englewood Beach 34223; at Ko Ko Kai Resort) Shelling excursions on and around the islands of Gasparilla, Palm, Cayo Costa, Cabbage Key, Upper Captiva, and Captiva.

SPAS

Charles of the Village Salon & Day Spa (941-639-6300, 888-753-6115; www.

fishville.com/services; 1200 W. Retta Esplanade, Punta Gorda 33950; at Fishermen's Village) Massage, wraps, scrubs, polish, gommage, facials, and hair services. Packages available.

SPECTATOR SPORTS

RACING

Charlotte County Speedway (941-575-2422; 8655 Piper Rd., Punta Gorda 33982) Year-round weekend car racing. Admission.

WATER SPORTS

SAILBOARDING & SURFING

Bikes & Boards (941-474-2019; 966 S. McCall Rd., Englewood 34223) Rents sailboards and sells and services surfboards and skim boards.

Island Bike 'N Beach (239-964-0711; 333 Park Ave., Boca Grande 33921) Rents boogie and skim boards.

SNORKELING & SCUBA

The best underwater sightseeing lies offshore some distance, where divers find a few wrecks and other manmade structures.

DIVE SHOPS & CHARTERS

Ko Ko Kai Charter Boat Service (941-474-2141; 5040 N. Beach Rd., Englewood Beach 34223; at Ko Ko Kai Resort) Diving charters.

WILDLIFE SPOTTING

The Charlotte Harbor coast is a haven for many of Florida's threatened and endangered species, including Florida panthers (this relative of the mountain lion is yellow, not black, and is characterized by a kink in its tail), bobcats, manatees, brown pelicans, wood storks, and black skimmers. Manasota Key hosts the largest nesting sea turtle population on the Gulf Coast. White pelicans migrate to the region in winter. Look for them on sandbars and small mangrove islands in the bays and estuaries. They congregate in flocks and feed cooperatively by herding fish. The Cape Haze area between Englewood and Boca Grande is known for its nesting ospreys and bald eagles. Lemon Bay Park and Cedar Point Park afford the best opportunities to see the nests. Look for sandhill cranes on golf courses and other grasslands.

At Babcock Ranch, a massive preserve east of Punta Gorda, you can see native sandhills, reintroduced American bison, and contained Florida panthers, along with lots of alligators (which are farmed there).

The shy panther is rarely seen in the wilds of southwest Florida, where it makes its home.

Karen T. Bartlett

On Gasparilla Island you may spot an iguana in the wild — or trying to cross the road, for that matter. Though not native, they have established a colony along the bike path south of Boca Grande.

NATURE PRESERVES & ECO-ATTRACTIONS

CEDAR POINT ENVIRONMENTAL PARK
941-475-0769.
2300 Placida Rd,
  Englewood 34224.
Off Route 775.
Admission: Free.

Bald eagles, marsh rabbits, bobcats, gopher tortoises, and great horned owls are the stars of this 88-acre preserve, where free guided nature walks are offered on weekends and other days by appointment. It borders the Lemon Bay Aquatic Preserve.

CHARLOTTE HARBOR ENVIRONMENTAL CENTER
941-575-5435.
10941 Burnt Store Rd.,
  Punta Gorda 33955.
Hours: 8–3 Mon.–Fri.
  and 12–3 Sat.–Sun.
  (Oct.–May), 8–3
  Mon.–Fri. (summer);
  tours 10 Mon.–Fri.
  (Oct.–May only).
Admission: Free.

Conducts guided tours (in season) around 4 miles of nature trails through pine and palmetto flatlands, hammocks, and marshes, where alligators and bobcats live. Also, educational exhibits about local wildlife.

LEMON BAY PARK & ENVIRONMENTAL CENTER

Its 195 acres of mangrove forest, wetlands, pinelands, and scrub are home to bald eagles and other creatures of the sky, woods, and water.

941-474-3065.
570 Bay Park Blvd.,
  Englewood 34223.
Admission: Free.

Experience its nature trails, butterfly garden, indoor environmental displays, and educational programs and guided walks.

PEACE RIVER WILDLIFE CENTER
941-637-3830.
3400 W. Marion Ave.,
  Punta Gorda 33950.
At Ponce de León Park.
Hours: 11am–3pm
  Wed.–Mon.; tours
  11am–3pm. Admission:
  Donations requested.

A rescue and rehabilitation facility that conducts tours among cages of baby possums, taped-together gopher tortoises, and other rescued and recovering animals. It accepts about 1,300 orphaned, displaced, and injured creatures each year.

WILDLIFE TOURS & CHARTERS

This rustic shed was built at Babcock Wilderness Adventures for the filming of Sean Connery's Just Cause.

Karen T. Bartlett

BABCOCK WILDERNESS ADVENTURES
941-489-3911, 800-500-5583.
www.babcockwilderness.
  com.
8000 State Rd. 31, Punta
  Gorda 33982.
Hours: Tours 9am–3pm
  Nov.–May; mornings
  only June–Oct.
Admission: $17.95 adults,
  $9.95 children 3–12 (plus
  tax). Advance
  reservations required.

On a 90-minute swamp-buggy-bus ride through 90,000-acre Crescent B Ranch and Telegraph Cypress Swamp you will spot Old Florida wildlife, including white-tailed deer, relocated bison, fenced-in Florida panthers, wild turkeys, sandhill cranes, squirrels, and alligators. The driver gives an onboard demonstration with a live baby gator and leads a boardwalk hike through a cypress swamp to see the panthers. The adventure takes place on an actual ranch that dates back to the cow-hunting era. Cattle are still raised here as well as alligators. Off-road bike tours and night tours are also available. A restaurant, live snake display, gift shop, and the stage set from Sean Connery's *Just Cause* (filmed partly on-site) provide other activities and accommodations. This is one of Charlotte Harbor coast's finest attractions.

GRANDE TOURS
239-697-8825.
www.grandetours.com.
12575 Placida Rd., PO Box 281, Placida 33946.

Deck boat and kayaking tours of Myakka River and Charlotte Harbor Aquatic Preserve, led by a naturalist. The "Sea Life Excursion" features seine net pulling to collect and study marine life. The "Back Country Adventure" combines boat and kayak touring.

SHOPPING

SHOPPING CENTERS & MALLS

Downtown Punta Gorda Centered around Marion Ave. and Olympia, both one-way streets, between Nesbit St. and Tamiami Trail S., you'll find a quaint historic downtown that's undergone a renaissance. Cross street Sullivan Street features old residences under colorful new coats of paint reborn into retail outlets. The shops are simple and neighborly. Streetscaping includes nifty old-fashioned streetlamps, alley arcades, historic murals, street sculptures, and park benches.

Fishermen's Village gives a nautical spin to shopping.

Charlotte County Visitors Bureau

Fishermen's Village (941-639-8721, 800-639-0020; www.fishville.com; 1200 W. Retta Esplanade, Punta Gorda 33950) More than 40 shops and restaurants occupy a transformed crab-packing plant. This is Punta Gorda's most hyper center of activity, the site of festivals and social events. There's docking, lodging, charter boats, and fishing from the docks, besides shopping and dining, geared generally toward seniors. A preponderance of nautical clothing and gifts are reflective of the motif. Horse and buggy rides are offered at certain times of year.

Olde Englewood Village Dearborn Street, Englewood's main drag, has done some sprucing up in the past years. The old historic buildings hold fun-to-browse secondhand shops and other surprises. There's a new mini-mall called Olde Englewood Village Emporium, with a backyard courtyard, and galleries make a pleasing presence here and around the corner on Old Englewood Road.

Port Charlotte Town Center (941-624-4447; 1441 Tamiami Trail, Port Charlotte 33948) An indoor megamall with movie theaters and more than 100 commercial enterprises, including Burdines, Sears, and other chain outlets and specialty shops, such as Gap and Old Navy.

Boca Grande (Park Ave.) Despite the millionaires and power brokers who make Boca Grande their winter home, shopping here is low-key and affordable, with shades of historic quaintness. The restored railroad depot houses gift and apparel boutiques; there's more in back at Railroad Plaza. Across the street you'll find an eccentric general store and a department store that's been there forever, both of which set a somewhat funky tone.

ANTIQUES & COLLECTIBLES

Harbour Inn Antique Mall (941-625-6126; www.theharbourinn.com; 5000 Tamiami Trail, Charlotte Harbor 33980) More than 50 dealers selling antique furniture, dolls, china, books, and art. Antique fair held the second Saturday of every month. Have afternoon tea in the Tea Room.

Just Clowning Around (941-575-7009; www.fishville.com/shops; 1200 W. Retta Esplanade, Punta Gorda 33950; at Fishermen's Village) Colorful novelty clocks, carousels, and other circus collectibles, jewelry, glass water balls.

The Olde Curiosity Shoppe (941-473-0935; 447 W. Dearborn St., Englewood 34223) Large breadth of antiques, collectibles, and home accessories at reasonable prices. Definitely worth a look.

BOOKS

All Books (941-505-0345; 111 W. Marion Ave., Punta Gorda 33950; downtown) Used, rare, and hard-to-find volumes, local authors, and current books.

Ruhamas (239-964-5800; 5800 Gasparilla Rd., Boca Grande 33921; at Courtyard Plaza) Books of local interest and for beach reading, cards, and gifts.

CLOTHING

Captain's Landing (941-637-6000; www.fishvile.com/boutiques; 1200 W. Retta

Esplanade, Punta Gorda 33950; at Fishermen's Village) Men's casual clothing with a nautical and fishing flair; also formal wear.

Giuditta (941-639-8701; 1200 W. Retta Esplanade, Punta Gorda 33950; at Fishermen's Village) Exotic patterns and finely tailored styles for the sophisticated woman; mostly formal and dressy fashions.

The Island Bummer (239-964-2636; Boca Grande 33921; at Railroad Plaza) Casual, cotton, loose-fitting sportswear perfect for Florida climes.

Nichole's Collections (941-575-1911; www.fishville.com/boutiques; 1200 W. Retta Esplanade, Punta Gorda 33950; at Fishermen's Village) Fine cotton and casual women's fashions, including the Tommy Bahama brand.

CONSIGNMENT

Carly's Consignment (941-575-1191; 215 W. Olympia Ave., Punta Gorda 33950) Designer clothing, furniture, and collectibles.

Jim Birth's Consignment Shoppe (941-575-8685; 131-F E. Marion Ave., Punta Gorda 33950) Furniture, books, pottery, and other tableware.

FLEA MARKETS & BAZAARS

Rainbow Flea Market (941-629-1223; 4628 Tamiami Trail, Charlotte Harbor 33980) Browsing in air-conditioned comfort Friday through Sunday.

GALLERIES

Carroll Swayze Gallery (941-460-0014; 30 N. Elm St., Englewood 34223) A charming old cottage is painted bright and stuffed with surprisingly eclectic and talented collections of art in all media.

The James Sears Gallery (941-460-0067; www.thejamessearsgallery.com; 30 Old Englewood Rd., Englewood 34223) One of a cluster of small, outdoor galleries, this one features the bronze and wood sculptures of locally prominent artist Jim Sears.

Paradise (941-964-0774; 340 Park Ave., Boca Grande 33921) Small but containing Boca's best selection, it carries works by island artists and artisans and emerging Florida and national artists. Sculptures by Sarasota's Jack Dowd.

Sea Grape Art Gallery (941-575-1718; 117 W. Marion Ave., Punta Gorda 33950) Downtown Punta Gorda is growing a strong reputation for art, with its around-town murals and street sculptures. It grows stronger at the Sea Grape, which displays and sells the fine art and affordable paintings, pottery, and three-dimensional art of co-op members, who staff the gallery, so you have a chance to meet the artists.

Smart Studio & Art Gallery (239-964-0519; www.smart-studio-fl.com; 370 Park Ave., Boca Grande 33921) Shows and sells paintings of prolific wintering artist Wini Smart as well as other decorative arts. Closed in off-season.

GENERAL STORES

Gill's Grocery & Deli (239-964-2506; 5800 Gasparilla Rd., Boca Grande 33921; at The Courtyard) Beach needs, clothes, gifts, deli items.

GIFTS

Pirate's Ketch (941-637-0299; www.fishville.com/shops; 1200 W. Retta Esplanade, Punta Gorda 33950; at Fishermen's Village) Nautical clocks and lamps, weather vanes, seashell kitsch, framed sea charts, original art and prints.

Laff Out Loud (941-505-2067; www.fishville.com/shops; 1200 W. Retta Esplanade, Punta Gorda 33950; at Fishermen's Village) Whimsical toys for all ages: stuffed toys, dolls, lava lamps, and other nostalgic memorabilia.

Red Pelican (941-474-6564; 1350 Beach Rd., Englewood Beach 34223) You can find something unusual for everyone among this showroom of wall hangings, sea-themed gifts, handmade jewelry, stuffed toys and other kids' stuff, and creative beach wear.

JEWELRY

Kirsch Estate Jewelry (941-639-1964; www.fishville.com/shops; 1200 W. Retta Esplanade, Punta Gorda 33950; at Fishermen's Village) Fine and antique pieces in a refined, estate setting.

Paradise Jewelers (941-475-2396; 3700 S. McCall Rd., Englewood 34224) Custom designs, nautical pieces, diamonds, gems, and repair.

Fine Things Jewelry (239-964-2166; 321 Park Ave., Boca Grande 33921; at Serendipity Gallery, Olde Theater Building) Designer jewelry.

KITCHENWARE & HOME DECOR

The Caged Parrot (941-637-8949; www.fishville.com/shops; 1200 W. Retta Esplanade, Punta Gorda 33950; at Fishermen's Village) Garden accessories, wood-block models of Punta Gorda buildings, fanciful wall hangings, bird- and butterfly houses, and wind chimes.

Wish You Were Here (941-460-1829; 450 W. Dearborn St., Englewood 34223) Unusual collection of art, furniture, and household items new, used, and antique.

SPORTS STORES

Note: This listing includes general sports outlets only. For supplies and equipment for specific sports, please refer to "Recreation" in this chapter.

Champs Sports (941-627-5556; 1441 Tamiami Trail, Port Charlotte 33948; at

Port Charlotte Town Center) Clothes, shoes, and equipment for tennis, aerobics, weight training, and all ball sports.

CALENDAR OF EVENTS

APRIL

Ponce de León/Conquistador Landing (941-764-8100; Laishley Park, Punta Gorda) One day-staging of the conqueror's landing on the Gulf Coast.

Punta Gorda Block Party (Punta Gorda) Community celebration, with music, food, crafts, and a variety of events. Early in the month.

MAY

Boca Grande Chamber of Commerce Ladies' Tarpon Tournament (239-964-0568) All-woman, all-release competition early in the month.

Charlotte Harbor–Florida Fishing Tournament (941-625-0804) Thousands of dollars in prizes; includes a Kids' Day and barbecue. Entire month.

Florida Frontier Days (several locations in Charlotte County)

Miller's Marina Tarpon Tide Tournaments (239-964-2232; Miller's Marina, Boca Grande) Mid-May to early July.

JULY

Fourth of July Freedom Swim (941-637-1177; Seahorse Marina, Charlotte Harbor, and Fishermen's Village, Punta Gorda) More than 200 participants swim the half-mile stretch across the mouth of the Peace River from Charlotte Harbor to Fishermen's Village, accompanied by boaters. Entertainment and fireworks follow at Fishermen's Village.

Kids' Fishing Tournament (941-639-9721; www.fishville.com/calendar; 1200 W. Retta Esplanade, Punta Gorda; at Fishermen's Village) One weekend.

World's Richest Tarpon Tournament (239-964-0568; Boca Grande) Up to $150,000 top prize. Runs early May through July.

OCTOBER

Punta Gorda Waterfront Foods-Arts-Jazz Festival (941-639-3720; Gilchrist Park, Punta Gorda) Water activities, alligator wrestling, children's art fair, music, and crafts.

Salute to the Arts (throughout Charlotte County) Showcases the performing and visual arts. One week late in the month.

Southwest Florida Boat Show (941-639-8721; www.fishville.com/calendar; 1200 W. Retta Esplanade, Punta Gorda; at Fishermen's Village) Boats on display in the harbor and on trailers, in conjunction with a one-day seafood festival. Four days early in the month.

NOVEMBER

International Fall Festival and Yankee Peddler Fair (941-627-2568; 2500 Harbor Blvd., Port Charlotte; at Bon Secours–St. Joseph Hospital grounds) Ethnic crafts and foods, with children's carnival. One day.

DECEMBER

Christmas Peace River Lighted Boat Parade (941-639-3720) A procession of vessels in holiday attire. Sunday evening midmonth.

CHAPTER FIVE
Sand, Shells, and Serenity
SANIBEL ISLAND &
THE ISLAND COAST

A dreamy, tropical land necklaced with islands, this slab of coastline resembles, more than any of its neighboring regions, the laid-back islands of the Keys, Bahamas, and Caribbean. Tourism pundits term it the Lee Island Coast, a double entendre on the county's name and the island's reality-sheltered demeanor. More developed than its Charlotte Harbor neighbors and more relaxed than what lies to the south and at the Sarasota end of

Karen T. Bartlett

At surf's edge, Sanibel Island.

things, the Island Coast gives us the leafy greenery for the southwest Florida sandwich. It is considered one of Florida's most ecology-minded resort areas. How it balances its dual roles as wildlife preserver and tourism mecca has served as a model for state eco-tourism.

At their northern extreme, the islands are mired in an Old Florida time frame. **Cabbage Key**, **Useppa Island**, **Cayo Costa**, and **Pine Island** gave birth to the Gulf Coast's legacy of fishing lifestyles, back when the Calusa lived off the sea. On Pine Island, fishing, crabbing, and shrimping are still a way of life and survival, despite recent net-ban laws that make it less and less profitable. Many have turned to charter captaining in the wake of the new legislation. Protected from rampant resort development by its lack of beaches, Pine Island clings to an older way of life like a barnacle to a mangrove prop. Cayo Costa and **Upper Captiva,** both largely state owned, remain the uncut jewels in the Island Coast necklace. Useppa Island and Cabbage Key preserve another era of island bygones, days graced by celebrity sporting types in search of escape, adventure, and tarpon.

Sanibel sunrise.

Karen T. Bartlett

Out in San Carlos Bay, to the south, the islands of **Sanibel** and **Captiva** developed quietly but steadily through the years. At various times in the past, the islands have supported a government lighthouse reservation, citrus and tomato farms, communities of fishermen (who sometimes dealt in rum-smuggling on the side), and a coconut plantation. From 1910 through 1940, wealthy notables made their way to the islands, intent on the relative anonymity that the wilds afforded them. Teddy Roosevelt discovered Captiva Island in 1914. Charles Lindbergh and his wife, Anne Morrow Lindbergh, visited often, inspiring her to pen her well-loved seashell analogies in *Gift from the Sea*. Pulitzer Prize-winning cartoonist and conservationist Jay N. "Ding" Darling gained national attention for Captiva and Sanibel Islands by fighting for the preservation of their natural attributes during his winter visits. His efforts sparked the development of the Island Coast's environmental conscience.

Fort Myers Beach on **Estero Island** is synonymous with gulf shrimp, beach bustle, and spring breakers. Southward, the trickle of islands ending with **Bonita Beach** is reminiscent of the coast's earliest times, with primeval estuaries, intact shell mounds, whispers of buried pirate treasure, and fishing lifestyles.

On the mainland, **Cape Coral** once served as a hunting refuge for steel magnate Ogden Phipps, who vacationed in Naples. The second largest city in Florida in area, it was something of a developer's folly. The young city was cleared, canalled, and platted in 1970 and is slowly growing into itself, bordered on the east by **North Fort Myers** and on the south by the Caloosahatchee River.

Across the river from North Fort Myers and Cape Coral, **Fort Myers** has evolved from its fort status of Seminole wartime into the hub of communications and transportation for the Gulf Coast. Cattle barons gave the community its early wild temperament; Thomas Edison and his class of successful entrepreneurs elevated it above its cow-trail streets.

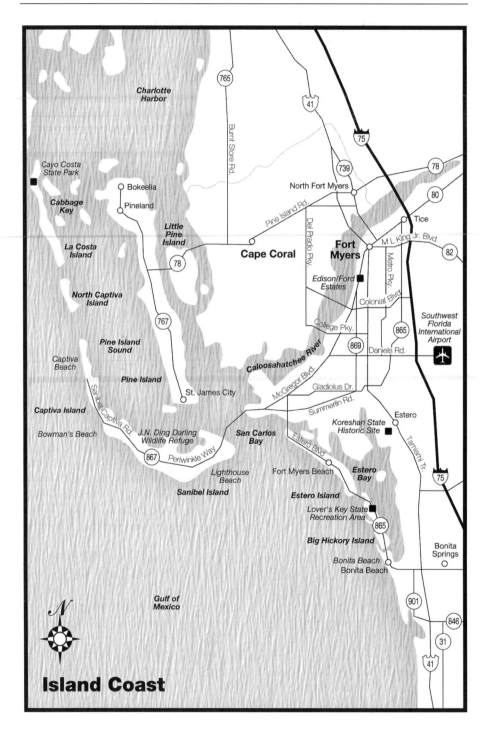

Island Coast

Most unusual circumstances created the small community along Tamiami Trail named **Estero**, south of Fort Myers. The 19th-century religious cult that called itself the Koreshan Unity first settled there, led by Cyrus Teed, or Koresh, as he called himself. The Koreshans believed that the earth clings to the inside of a hollow globe like coconut meat to its shell. Members practiced celibacy and communal living. They also experimented with tropical gardening, bringing to southwest Florida the mango and avocado. The site of their brief stay has been preserved and recreated by the state, together with their buildings and the natural Florida they discovered there.

LODGING

Maine may boast its bed-and-breakfasts, Vermont its historic inns, and Colorado its ski lodges. But when vacationers envision Florida, it's the beachside resorts that flash first through the mental slide projector. The Island Coast has perfected this image of sun-and-sand abandon. Megaresorts are designed to keep guests (and their disposable income) on property. Not only can you eat lunch, rent a bike, and get a tennis lesson, you can hire a masseur, charter a boat for a sunset sail, play golf, and enroll your child in Sandcastle Building 101. These destination resorts are in business to fulfill fantasies, and they spare no effort to achieve that goal.

Side by side with the resorts, you'll also find homey little cottages that have held their ground against buyouts and takeovers. In between the two extremes exist a wide variety of high-rise condos, funky hotels, retirement resorts, mom-and-pop motels, fishing lodges, and inns.

Privately owned second homes and condominiums provide another source of upscale accommodations along the Island Coast. For families or other groups, these can often be a better value than hotel rooms. Timeshare rental was invented on Sanibel Island, and you'll find plenty of these options around still. Vacation brokers who match visitors with such properties are listed under "Home & Condo Rentals" at the end of this section.

The highlights of Island Coast hospitality listed here — alphabetically by town — include the best and freshest in the local industry. While spanning the range of endless possibilities, this list concentrates on those properties that break out of the skyscraping, wicker-and-floral mold. Toll-free 800, 888, or 877 reservation numbers, where available, are listed after local numbers. An asterisk after the pricing designation indicates that the rate includes at least a continental breakfast in the cost of lodging, occasionally other meals as described in the listing.

Pricing codes are explained below. They are normally per person/double occupancy for hotel rooms and per unit for efficiencies, apartments, cottages, suites, and villas. The range spans low- and high-season rates. Many resorts offer off-season packages at special rates and free lodging for children. Pricing does not include the 7 percent Florida sales tax. Some large resorts add service gratuities or maid charges. Lee County imposes a 3 percent tourist tax, as well, which goes toward beach and environmental maintenance.

Rate Categories

Inexpensive	Up to $75
Moderate	$75 to $150
Expensive	$150 to $200
Very Expensive	$200 and up

The following abbreviations are used for credit card information:

AE: American Express	MC: MasterCard
D: Discover Card	V: Visa
DC: Diners Club	

Bonita Beach

THE BEACH & TENNIS CLUB
General Manager: Hank Scholz.
239-992-1121, 800-237-4934.
5700 Bonita Beach Rd. SW, Suite 3103, Bonita Springs 34134.
Price: Moderate (three-day minimum).
Credit Cards: AE, D, MC, V.

A string of five high-rise buildings and a complex of 10 Har-Tru tennis courts make up this property across the street from the bleached-blond sands of Bonita Beach. Each of the 360 one-bedroom, privately owned, individually decorated suites has a balcony with a view of either the gulf or backwaters. They are modernly equipped — though some look run-down — with full kitchens; bedrooms are not separate from living quarters in some cases (some rooms have a sliding separator between). Two heated swimming pools, a children's pool, a beauty salon, a restaurant, shuffleboard courts, a tennis pro shop, and a laundry complete the amenities. Recent new management promises changes and improvements.

Cabbage Key

CABBAGE KEY INN
Innkeepers: Rob & Phyllis Wells.
239-283-2278.
PO Box 200, Pineland 33945.
Price: Moderate to Expensive
Credit Cards: MC, V.

Cabbage Key appeals to vacationers seeking an authentic Old Florida experience. Built on an unbridged island atop an ancient shell mound, the inn and its guest accommodations are reminiscent of the 1930s, when novelist Mary Roberts Rinehart used native cypress and pine to construct a home for her son and his bride. Six unpretentious guestrooms, five historically significant cottages, and a four-bedroom home accommodate overnighters. Four of the cottages have kitchens. The restaurant

Cabbage Key harkens back to the days when the rich but rugged made their way to the Island Coast.

Karen T. Bartlett

and its currency-papered bar attract boaters and water tours for lunch, but the island shuts down to a whisper come sundown.

Cape Coral

CASA LOMA MOTEL
General Manager: Mary &
   Joseph Burun.
239-549-6000, 877-227-2566.
3608 Del Prado Blvd., Cape
   Coral 33904.
Price: Inexpensive to
   Moderate.
Credit Cards: AE, D, MC, V.

Cape Coral doesn't offer a lot in the way of resorts, but if you're looking for a place to stay while enjoying the town's family attractions or somewhere less costly than the beaches, this tidy little property does have its own charm and canal-front views and docks in the bargain. Its 49 efficiencies are each stocked with a kitchenette containing a microwave, minifridge, and stovetop. Reclining chairs and stylish motel furnishings provide comfort. Porches and balconies overlook the canal and paved sundeck. Nicely landscaped grounds complement the Spanish villa architecture, with its red roof and arched balcony openings. Waterside tables, loungers, and a tiki-covered deck offer scenic places to relax.

Captiva Island

**JENSEN'S TWIN PALM
   COTTAGES &
   MARINA**
Owners: David, John, and
   Jimmy Jensen.
239-472-5800.
www.jensen-captiva.com.
1507 Captiva Dr., PO Box
   191, Captiva Island 33924.

One of Captiva's most affordable lodging options is also one of its homier places. You get an immediate sense of neighborliness on the grounds. Perhaps it has to do with its partiality to fisherfolk — its bayside docks, fishing charters, boat rentals, and bait supplies. I expected to find the accommodations in that same vein, where what's out in the water matters more than what's

Price: Moderate to
   Expensive.
Credit Cards: AE, MC, V.

indoors. The 14 units looked plain enough from the outside: white stucco cottages with tin roofs and a splash of blue trim. Each screened-in porch holds a plain picnic table. Inside, the one- and two-bedroom cottages are entirely cheery with their immaculate white tongue-and-groove walls, perky curtains, and simple, sturdy wooden furniture. The full kitchens are modern and spotless. Nothing fishy about 'em. Just charming old-island style dressed up comfortable.

SOUTH SEAS RESORT
General Manager: Fred L.
   Hawkins.
239-472-5111, 800-572-5998.
www.south-seas-resort.
   com.
PO Box 194, Captiva Island
   33924.
Price: Expensive to Very
   Expensive.
Credit Cards: D, DC, MC,
   V.

South Seas is one of the great destination resorts of Florida, where it ranks as a standard for top-quality accommodations and service. It's one of those places where you can enter through the security gates and leave one week later without ever having gone off property. Celebrities crave its privacy and discretion. South Seas offers any type of getaway dwelling you could imagine, from tennis villas to beach cottages to harbor-side hotel rooms — nine different types of accommodations in all. Rooms are furnished with stylish, high-quality pieces and appointments. The plantation monopolizes a third of the island with 600 guest units, both privately owned and otherwise, seven eateries poolside to formal (three are closed to the public), lounges, shops, a nine-hole golf course, a fitness center, a yacht harbor, 18 swimming pools, 21 tennis courts, water-sports equipment rentals and lessons, excursion cruises, Fun Factory recreation program for children, and 2½ miles of augmented beach. A free trolley takes guests around the 330-acre property.

'TWEEN WATERS INN
General Manager: Jeff
   Shuff.
239-472-5161, 866-893-3646.
resv@tween-waters.com.
www.tween-waters.com.
15941 Captiva Rd., PO Box
   249, Captiva Island
   33924.
Price: Expensive to Very
   Expensive.
Credit Cards: AE, D, MC,
   V.

'Tween Waters spans the gap between beach cottage lodging and modern super-resort. Built early in the 1990s, when wildlife patron "Ding" Darling kept a cottage there, the property is showing its age, with glints of Old Florida architecture (some of it rather unglamorous) and easygoing attitudes. Compact but complete, it holds 149 rooms (12 of which opened in 2001), cottages, efficiencies, and apartments, as well as restaurants, a marina, tennis courts, and a swimming pool. Named for its location between two shores at Captiva's narrowest span, it lies across the road from a length of beach that is usually lightly populated because it lacks nearby public parking. Its marina, one of its best features, is the island's top water sports center, with charters, tours, boat and canoe rentals, and the Canoe & Kayak Restaurant. The Crow's Nest lounge provides the island's best nightlife.

Fort Myers

**RAMADA INN & SUITES
AT AMTEL MARINA**
Acting General Manager:
Pichai Tangnavarad.
239-337-0300, 800-833-1620,
800-2RAMADA.
www.amtelmarinahotel.
com.
2500 Edwards Dr., Fort
Myers 33901.
Price: Moderate.
Credit Cards: AE, D, DC,
MC, V.

Having undergone a recent transition that included room renovations and affiliation with Ramada, this 25-story high-rise is owned by a Thailand native, and it shows. The tropical theme that dominates the hotel's decor is touched with Thai elegance. The marble-pillared atrium lobby overlooks the city yacht basin and holds intricately carved Oriental wood tables, chairs, and benches; and two five-feet-tall carved wooden elephants. On the mezzanine you'll find a Thai restaurant, along with another serving more traditional fare, and a new popular salsa club. The 417 rooms and suites still reflect an earlier Art Deco style once prevalent throughout the hotel when it was a Sheraton, but that is gradually changing. Two swimming pools, a whirlpool, and sundecks will be embellished with fountains.

**HOLIDAY INN
SUNSPREE RESORT**
Director of Operations:
Wouter Banning.
239-334-3434, 800-664-7775.
2220 W. First St., Fort
Myers 33901.
Price: Inexpensive to
Moderate.
Credit Cards: AE, D, DC,
MC, V.

As downtown Fort Myers's future brightens, this tropical riverside gem attracts much-deserved notice. The marble-floored lobby introduces a Florida theme with coral rock block walls and jungle greenery. The 147 rooms and suites, which underwent upgrades in 2000, are lavishly furnished, some with private whirlpool baths. The hotel boasts a new special service facility designed to accommodate traveling businesswomen. The lushly landscaped courtyard holds a pool, kiddie pool, playground, spa, fitness room, and popular waterside restaurant and outdoor bar.

**SANIBEL HARBOUR
RESORT & SPA**
Managing Director: Kelly
Pastore
239-466-4000, 800-767-7777.
www.sanibel-resort.com.
17260 Harbour Pointe Dr.,
Fort Myers 33908.
Price: Expensive to Very
Expensive.
Credit Cards: AE, D, DC,
MC, V.

Stunningly beautiful for a property its size, the Sanibel Harbour capitalizes on Florida style and a spectacular location. Not actually on Sanibel Island as the name suggests, the resort's 347 rooms and suites and 70 rentable condos are located on a chin of land across San Carlos Bay from the island, on an inlet known as Sanibel Harbour. Half of the units have water views of either the bay or nearby estuaries. A new boutique inn holds 107 of the rooms decorated in European style and shiny

All that's missing from Sanibel Harbour Resort's Gatsbian setting and Old Florida demeanor is the bootleg gin.

Sanibel Harbour Resort

brass, more intimate than tower accommodations. The suites feature heavy four-poster beds and oversized bathtubs. The property encompasses three restaurants, five outdoor swimming pools, high-tech tennis courts, spa facilities, and a small beach. One of the bars has a 280-degree view of the sea, with a lovely, breezy cocktail patio. The Promenade Café, which serves spa and regular lunches, is set on a porch atop a waterside pool that brings to mind exotic Roman baths. Chez Le Bear provides a fine-dining experience. The newly renovated world-class spa and fitness center, racquetball courts, canoe/kayak trail, sun sports charters and rentals, and Sanibel Harbour *Princess II* dinner cruises provide guests a well-rounded menu of fitness and recreation options. Kids Klub takes youngsters on nature hikes and a variety of other activities.

Fort Myers Beach

THE GRAND VIEW
General Manager:
  Christopher Hearn.
239-765-4422, 800-723-4944.
www.grandviewfl.com.
8701 Estero Blvd., Fort
  Myers Beach 33931.
Price: Moderate to Very
  Expensive.
Credit Cards: AE, D, MC,
  V.

This 13-floor suite resort stands like a bookmark that separates the high-rise development of Fort Myers Beach from the natural world of Lovers Key. It overlooks the estuarine waters of Big Carlos Pass and Estero Bay, renowned for their dolphin populations. The small, unspectacular patch of sandy beach is offset by the many varieties of water-sports equipment that are available. The 104 privately owned suites (only 67 available for general-public rental) come with kitchens, balconies, and water views — the hotel's best asset. Rooms and the lobby are decorated in contemporary style, with bright colors. Modern kitchens are fully equipped. On the bay, a paved and nicely landscaped patio leads to a grill area and pool.

THE OUTRIGGER BEACH RESORT
General Manager: Dianne F. Major.
239-463-3131, 800-749-3131.
www.outriggerfmb.com.
6200 Estero Blvd., Fort Myers Beach 33931.
Price: Moderate to Very Expensive.
Credit Cards: AE, D, MC, V.

The Outrigger Beach Resort occupies the quiet south end of Fort Myers Beach, where the sand flares wide and gorgeous, protected by a sandbar where birds hang out. The 30-year-old, 144-room resort boasts a casual, unstructured vacationing style that works well for families. Activity centers around its chain-link-fenced pool and tiki bar boardwalk area, where guests can sun, mingle, or rent water-sports equipment. Rooms are compact and modern and furnished simply. Five types of accommodations range from the traditional to efficiencies with full kitchens. Prices also depend upon whether they're on the first or second floor and the quality of the view. Shuffleboard, a putting green, beach volleyball, a little café, and live weekend entertainment keep the place vivacious.

SILVER SANDS VILLAS
Owners: Tom and Andrea Groves.
239-463-2755, 800-603-0501.
www.silversands-villas.com.
1207 Estero Blvd., Fort Myers Beach 33931.
Price: Moderate to Expensive.
Credit Cards: AE, MC, V.

In the high-rise world of Fort Myers Beach, there's not much to be found that one could describe as charming. I discovered this notable exception by getting lost. Its assemblage of 20 one- and two-bedroom circa-1935 cottages caught my attention from a side street. With their pale-yellow paint jobs and tin roofs, they make a strong personality statement. Inside they are simple but in character, with white wainscoting and yellow walls, full kitchens (in all but two units), and old Florida-style porches. The compact property, within beach walking distance, holds a small pool, a fountain courtyard, a huge shady banyan tree, canal-front views, tables covered by chickee thatching, and laundry facilities all behind a picket fence right in the happening strip of Estero Boulevard, from where you hardly notice it. Very congenial and convenient while feeling deliciously hidden away.

Pine Island

BRIDGE WATER INN
Owners: Osi & Steve McCarney.
239-283-2423, 800-378-7666.
www.bridgewaterinn.com.
4331 Pine Island Rd., PO Box 457, Matlacha 33909.

In fish-frenzied Pine Island, Matlacha has its share of fishing cottages where what matters is what's biting. Fishing types will also like this tropically bright seven-unit roadside lodge because its wraparound covered deck hangs over the water. Rooms and efficiencies, decorated with distinct style and

Price: Inexpensive to Moderate.
Credit Cards: AE, MC, V.

comfort, open up onto the deck, so you can step right out the door and cast. With leather furniture and eye-catching colors (check out the hanging tropical bird planters made in Colombia from old tires), Bridge Water is a step up from other local accommodations. Restaurants, fish markets, shops, and galleries are within walking distance.

Sanibel Island

GULF BREEZE COTTAGES AND MOTEL
Owners: Sandi and Charley Hutchings.
239-472-1626, 800-388-2842.
www.gbreeze.com.
1081 Shell Basket Ln., Sanibel Island 33957.
Price: Moderate to Very Expensive (for up to 6 people).
Credit Cards: MC, V.

The address is Shell Basket Lane, and this place is just that charming and seashell-oriented. Eleven classic cottages, efficiencies, and duplexes make for the ideal barefoot beach vacation. A basket full of beach toys sits next to the sink and table where you can clean your shells and fish. The grandma and grandpa who have owned it for more than 20 years love children and treat their guests like family. Small – only 12 units – this property blends old island with new, holding its ground amid low-rise, concrete neighbors. Sea grapes, bougainvillea, Bahama shades, carved balustrades, lattice, and fish scale siding add a fairy tale quality.

ISLAND INN
General Manager: Pegge Ford-Eisea.
239-472-1561, 800-851-5088.
3111 W. Gulf Dr., PO Box 659, Sanibel Island 33957.
www.islandinnsanibel.com.
Price: Moderate to Expensive* (two-night minimum on efficiencies and weekends).
Credit Cards: AE, D, MC, V.

Sanibel's only historic lodging — over 100 years old — displays all the refinement of Florida's great old inns and hotels but without the snobbery. It has the same congenial and relaxed atmosphere that Granny Matthews, a Sanibel matriarch of renown, created at the turn of the 20th century when she entertained the whole island — including guests from other resorts — at Saturday night barbecues. She also initiated the Sanibel Shell Fair as a way to keep guests busy, and hosted it in the lobby, where white wicker, French doors, a lattice-edged dining room, and shell displays now give an immediate impression of immaculate spaciousness and island graciousness. During the winter season (November 15 to May 1) it's a Modified American Plan resort, including breakfast and dinner in its rates. Cottages and lodges house 57 units, all with a view of gentle gulf waves lapping at a shell-covered beach. Cottages have one or two bedrooms; lodges contain hotel rooms, with either full kitchens or refrigerators only. They can be combined into suites. The resort doesn't pretend to furnish extravagantly; all is done in uncontrived old island style. That does not translate into shoddiness, however. The Island Inn is owned by shareholders who reinvest profits for constant upgrading. Decor is cheerful, comfortable, and impeccably maintained. Outside each lodge room door sits a wooden table where guests display their shell finds for others to peruse and admire. It's an Island Inn tradition. The atmosphere is saturated with conviviality. Dinner, a coat-and-tie affair, is announced by the blowing of a conch shell. Outdoors, native vegetation is landscaped around tin-roofed structures. A butterfly garden frames a croquet court, a swimming pool sits squarely on the beach, and tennis and shuffleboard provide recreation.

SANIBEL'S SEASIDE INN
General Manager: Jack Reed.
www.seasideinn.com.
239-472-1400, 800-831-7384, 800-572-5998 (central reservations).
541 E. Gulf Dr., Sanibel Island 33957.
Price: Moderate to Very Expensive.*
Credit Cards: AE, D, DC, MC, V.

I recommend this place to visitors looking for intimacy on the beach without great extravagance. A measure of Key West — banana-yellow tints, tin roofs, and gingerbread-trimmed balconies — blends with Seaside Inn's old island charm. It's the kind of place where you kick off your shoes the first day and don't find them again until you're packed to leave. Kitchen facilities and video cassette players come in every studio, beach cottage, and one-, two-, and three-bedroom suite, of which there are 32 in all. A swimming pool, brick-paved deck, complimentary continental breakfast (delivered to your door if you so desire), a video and book lending library, complimentary bike use, and tropical appointments complete the picture of seaside coziness. Use of facilities and amenities at Seaside Inn's sister resorts, including Sundial Beach Resort and Sanibel Inn, is available free of charge to guests. An inter-resort trolley provides transportation.

SUNDIAL BEACH RESORT
General Manager: Pete Adania.
239-472-4151, 800-237-4184, 800-572-5998 (central reservations).
www.sundialresort.com.
1451 Middle Gulf Dr., Sanibel Island 33957.
Price: Expensive to Very Expensive.
Credit Cards: AE, D, DC, MC, V.

Sundial promises the perfection of a worry-free vacation. Sanibel's fine shelling beach is the focus of the 20-acre resort, which takes its name from a species of shell. In the stunning lobby, a sundial shell mosaic is inset on a marble floor. The resort provides extensive recreation with 12 tennis courts, five heated swimming pools, bike and beach rental concessions, a fitness center, game room, children's and family programs, and an eco-center complete with touch tank. The lavish main building houses four restaurants — two overlooking the gulf, another serving Japanese food, and one casual and poolside. Less stylish, low-rise condo buildings are camouflaged by well-maintained vegetation and hold 270 fully equipped units decorated in tropical array and natural wicker. They take advantage of gulf or garden views. Given its high level of service, the Sundial is one of the area's least pretentious, most comfortable properties, especially for families.

Useppa Island

Elegant yet sporty digs at the Collier Inn, just the way Barron himself would have liked it.

Collier Inn

COLLIER INN
General Manager: Vincent
    Formosa.
239-283-1061.
www.useppa.com.
PO Box 640, Bokeelia 33922.
Price: Very Expensive*
    (minimum stay on
    weekends and holidays).
Credit Cards: AE, MC, V.

Used to be only club members could enjoy the delicious privacy and historic elitism of Useppa Island. Once an escape for turn-of-the-century well-knowns, the island continues to remain exclusive and aloof from the world. Now, if you can afford the price, you can be admitted onto the carefully guarded island by checking into the newly opened Collier Inn. The 100-year-old building, the original circa 1900 home to Barron Collier's Izaak Walton Club, holds eleven elegant suites and cottages individually designed for classic mood and comfort. Guests have access to the Useppa Island Club's full-service marina, Har-Tru tennis courts, swimming pool, small man-made beach, croquet, outdoor chess, and fitness center. The pink paved walkway around the island takes you past historic cottages, bounteous gardens, and the 100-acre island's intriguing historical museum. Collier Inn Restaurant serves daily meals; breakfast and dinner for two are included in the rates.

HOME & CONDO RENTALS

1-800-SANIBEL (239-472-1800, 800-726-4235; www.1-800-sanibel.com; 2000 Periwinkle Way, Sanibel Island 33957) Condo, home, and cottage rentals in Sanibel and Captiva.

Hussey Company Real Estate (239-463-3178; 2450 Estero Blvd., Fort Myers Beach 33931) Condos and homes in and around Fort Myers Beach.

RV RESORTS

Fort Myers-Pine Island KOA (239-283-2415, 800-562-8505; 5120 Stringfellow Rd., St. James City 33956) 371 sites, pool, saunas, hot tub, exercise room, tennis court, shuffleboard, horseshoes, and lake fishing.

Groves Campground (239-466-5909; 16175 John Morris Rd., Fort Myers 33908) Close to Sanibel Island, with full accommodations and swimming pool.

Red Coconut RV Resort (239-463-7200 ext. 200, 888-262-6226; redcoconut @aol.com; 3001 Estero Blvd., Fort Myers Beach 33931) Right on the beach but packed in a bit tightly; 250 full hookup sites, on-site trailer rentals, laundry, shuffleboard, cable TV, and car rentals.

DINING

The Island Coast is home to two of the nation's shellfish capitals. Shrimp — that monarch of edible crustaceans — reigns in Fort Myers Beach, where a fleet of shrimp boats is headquartered and an annual festival pays homage to America's favorite seafood. The sweet, pink gulf shrimp is the trademark culinary delight of the town and its environs.

The fish markets of Pine Island, an important commercial fishing and transshipment center, sell all sorts of fresh seafood – oysters, shrimp, scallops, snapper, catfish — but the signature seafood is the blue crab and stone crab that come from local waters.

The following listings cover the variety of Island Coast feasting in these price categories:

Inexpensive	Up to $15
Moderate	$15 to $25
Expensive	$25 to $35
Very Expensive	$35 or more

Cost is figured on a typical meal (at dinner, unless dinner is not served) that would include an appetizer or dessert, salad (if included with the meal), entrée, and coffee. Many restaurants offer discounts, usually called early-bird specials. These are rarely listed on the regular menu and sometimes are not publicized by tip-conscious servers. I have noted restaurants that offer them. Certain restrictions apply, such as time constraints, a specific menu, or number of people first in the door. Call the restaurant and ask about its policy. Those restaurants listed with "Healthy Selections" usually mark such on their menu.

The following abbreviations are used for credit card information and meals:

AE: American Express	B: Breakfast
D: Discover Card	L: Lunch

DC: Diners Club
MC: MasterCard
V: Visa

D: Dinner
SB: Sunday Brunch

Sizing Up a Shrimp

Gulf shrimp are graded by size and assigned all sorts of vague measurements: jumbo, large, medium-sized, boat grade, etc. The surest way to know what size shrimp you are ordering is to ask for the count-per-pound designation. This will be something like "21–25s," meaning there are 21 to 25 shrimp per pound. "Boat grade" normally designates a mixture of sizes, usually on the small side.

Bonita Beach

DOC'S BEACH HOUSE
239-992-6444.
27980 Hickory Blvd., Bonita Beach 34134.
Price: Inexpensive to Moderate.
Cuisine: American.
Liquor: Beer and wine.
Serving: B, L, D.
Credit Cards: None.
Handicap Access: Yes.
Reservations: No.
Special Features: On the beach, with outdoor and indoor seating.

This is the kind of place where Gidget and Moondoggie would hang out. It's all about being on the beach — Bonita's colorful, action-packed beach. If you can't bear leaving the sands, you can just grab a quick burger or dog and get back to it. If you need a break from the sun, duck inside. Downstairs is open and barefoot casual. Upstairs is blessedly air-conditioned, with huge picture windows so you won't miss any of the beach action. Both levels have bars and sports TVs. The menu makes no pretense of fine dining, but the food is solid good. Other grab-and-go items include Sand Dollar Burgers, Chicago-style pizza, taco, chili, and sandwiches of all sorts. For dinner or a heartier lunch, add a choice of grilled seafood, steak sandwich, and grilled chicken breast sandwich.

RÓDES FRESH & FANCY RESTAURANT
239-992-4040, 800-786-0450.
3756 Bonita Beach Rd., Bonita Beach 34134.
Price: Moderate.
Cuisine: Florida.
Children's Menu: Yes.
Liquor: Beer and wine.
Serving: L, D.
Credit Cards: D, MC, V.
Handicap Access: Yes.
Reservations: No.

Bonita Beach's favorite seafood stand has just grown up. In fall 2000, the popular fruit and fish market's screened and casual restaurant debuted in a grand, high-ceilinged new facility up the street. Many will bemoan the loss of the old, rickety setting, but not those who were tired of waiting for a table so that they could enjoy some of the area's freshest and least expensive seafood. The menu has remained the same, and the fish and fruit market are still right outside the door, ensuring you that no freezer came in contact with your grouper. The famous real grouper sandwich still stars on both menus, along with crab cakes, stone crab, raw oysters, peel and eat shrimp, and fried and broiled seafood platters. A dessert showcase features Ródes's well-loved key lime pie, which the market sells whole. The greatly expanded dining room is furnished with a counter, sturdy tables, and silk palm trees. Signs from the old place adorn the walls.

Cape Coral

IGUANA MIA
239-945-7755.
1027 E. Cape Coral Pkwy.,
  Cape Coral 33904
Price: Inexpensive to
  Moderate.
Children's Menu: Yes.
Cuisine: Mexican-
  American.
Liquor: Full.
Serving: L, D.
Credit Cards: AE, D, MC,
  V.
Handicap Access: Yes.
Reservations: No.

This, the original Iguana Mia, spawned others in Fort Myers and Bonita Springs, but we like this one best, even if it means we have to cross the Cape Coral bridge and pay the toll to get there. It's the more down-to-earth of the three. Sure, it's just as flashy, with its electric-green exterior paint job and nicely rendered interior Mexican murals; but it still retains some of the unpretentious lunchroom ambiance it started out with. Stacked cases of Mexican beer still count as decor elements. And most importantly, the food is flat-out better. Things seem more rushed at the newer places; here it's mañana paced. My husband invariably orders the sour cream chicken chimichanga, a specialty. I — usually already half-full from shoveling in huge gobs of the salsa I can't resist with warm, crunchy tortilla chips — like their veggie burrito, nachos, or quesadilla. You're bound to find something you like on the menu — it's huge and lets you do some of your own meal engineering.

MICHEL & MICHELLE'S
239-541-1255.
1515 SE 47th Terrace, Cape
  Coral 33914.
Price: Moderate to
  Expensive.
Children's Menu: No; will
  prepare special dishes.
Cuisine: French.
Liquor: Beer and wine.
Serving: L Tues.–Fri.
  11:30am–2pm, D
  Tues.–Sun. 5:30–9:30pm.
Credit Cards: D, MC, V.
Handicap Access: Yes.
Reservations: Yes.

The food is not only fantastic here, it's a bargain to boot. It's the real thing in French cuisine, not some cheap American imitation. Lunch poses particular good value, with entrees such as grouper meuniere, chicken breast with mushrooms and Madeira glaze, and seafood casserole for less than $8. There are also sandwiches and salads. Try the Normandy sandwich — a baguette filled with ripe brie, sautéed apples, and slices of tender pork loin, served with the marvelous house salad and garnished with waffle- and rose-cut carrots. *Marveleux!* The more extensive dinner menu offers two prix fixe menus plus nouvelle continental masterpieces such as rack of lamb with Roquefort and cognac sauce, ostrich with black peppercorn sauce, and scallops in calvados and apple cider. The décor of this little strip-mall storefront is secondary to the food. Dark like a '60s coffeehouse with paper placemats atop a tablecloth (and no napkins at lunch time), it leaves the wowing to the menu and service, the latter provided by Michel himself.

Captiva Island

Captiva Island's Bubble Room effervesces fun and whimsy.

Karen T. Bartlett

THE BUBBLE ROOM
239-472-5558.
15001 Captive Dr., Captiva Island 33924.
Price: Expensive.
Children's Menu: Yes.
Cuisine: American.
Liquor: Full.
Serving: L, D.
Credit Cards: AE, CB, D, DC, MC, V.
Handicap Access: Limited.
Reservations: No.
Special Features: Museumlike displays of '30s and '40s memorabilia.

The Bubble Room is something you have to experience once. It's especially fun to take kids there. The fun begins outside, where bubbles bedeck the kitsch-cottage structure and lawn gnomes greet you. Inside, the tables are glass-topped showcases filled with jacks, Monopoly money, comic books, dominoes, and assorted toys from the past. A Christmas elves scene, circus plaques, Betty Boop, celebrity photos, a plaster hippo's mouth, and other nostalgic memorabilia fill every wall, phone booth, bathroom door, nook, and cranny. A toy train runs under the ceiling, and servers — Bubble Scouts — wear pins and badges on their uniforms and goofy stuff on their hats. So that's the atmosphere — you've gotta see it for yourself. The menu continues the frivolity. On the lunch menu, Mae's West is a charbroiled chicken breast sandwich. The Happy Tuna sandwich I ordered was charbroiled tuna, overcooked for my taste, served on foccacia, which was dry enough that the mango salsa and herb mayo couldn't help it. Dinner's Duck Ellington is a tasty rendition of roasted duck with orange and banana sauce. Other snappily titled dishes include Ponce de Paella, the Judy Garden (vegetable lasagna), and The Fleet's In (shrimp and scallops in cream sherry sauce on linguine). Service is exceptional, considering the tight quarters and volume of business. Other things for which the Bubble Room is known are its basket of bubble bread (yum! cream cheesy), its sticky buns with dinner, and its fabulous desserts. You must leave room for moist and delicious red-velvet cake, the rich almond-studded orange crunch cake, or one of the many other tempting selections.

THE PORTER HOUSE
239-472-7535.
5400 Captiva Rd., Captiva Island 33924.
At South Seas Resort.
Price: Expensive to Very Expensive.
Children's Menu: No.
Cuisine: Steak.
Liquor: Full.
Serving: D.
Credit Cards: AE, D, DC, MC, V.
Handicap Access: Yes.
Reservations: Yes.

If you're dining in a place called Porter House, what should you order? The answer seemed obvious, but which porterhouse — the beef or the veal? Tough decision, that, so we split the difference and each ordered one. Although the hefty beefsteak was outstanding, the veal was something truly unusual in our fine meat experience. As carefully aged and perfectly seasoned as the beef, it was stronger in flavor than most veal cuts, but milder than the beef and melt-in-your-mouth. Twenty ounces and at least two inches thick, it was cooked precisely to the rare side of medium rare. The strip side of the T-bone was juicy and tender; the tenderloin nugget, one of those taste experiences that can make your mouth water just thinking about it weeks later. Other menu items served in this clubby-intimate setting of red meat and cognac include escargot, lamb chop, Alaskan king crab, lobster, and all the other finer things in life. New York-style and hip to the new appeal of fine steak, it delivers your slab of meat with nothing but the pièce de résistance on a plate.

RC OTTER'S
239-395-1142.
11506 Andy Rosse Ln., Captiva Island 33924.
Price: Moderate.
Children's Menu: Yes.
Cuisine: American.
Liquor: Beer, wine, and premixed cocktails.
Serving: B, L, D.
Credit Cards: AE, D, MC, V.
Handicap Access: Yes.
Reservations: No.
Special Features: Historic setting, outdoor seating, evening entertainment.

Among Captiva's pricey, fine-dining options, RC Otter's poses a refreshing, casual, funky style like one used to find on the quirky island. The old Cracker house in Captiva's historic district has been painted and stenciled gaily. Handfuls of tables cluster on the patio, the porch, and inside the tiny shack — fewer than 20 tables in all. In the evenings, a Buffettesque crooner strums and sings on the patio. The menu — tabloid size — is practically bigger than the restaurant and gives you a lot to choose from, all cleverly described and creatively designed. Products are fresh but recipes sometimes disappointing. For instance, the crab cake is a mushy, bland result of too much breading, not enough crab. It appears in the crab-cake salad (on a marvelous bed of fresh, colorful greens and fruit with raspberry vinaigrette), as an appetizer and as an entrée. The Otter's signature quesadillas and burritos wrap up intriguing combinations such as the crab 'n black bean burrito, in a tomato-tinted burrito and oozing with sauces and stuffings. Sandwiches are the restaurant's forte, including a Cuban, lobster roll, and grouper Reuben. The menu also features an unusual variety of barbecues, from the tender and tasty BBQ steak 'n cheese sandwich to BBQ gator bites. Entrees range from a full selection of seafood dishes to meatloaf, New York strip, and Voodoo Steak (spiced and served with black beans and rice). With its nearly 20 kid choices, this is a popular place for families. The tables are covered with butcher paper to spark the creativity of budding artists.

Fort Myers

BISTRO 41
239-466-4141.
13499 S. Cleveland Ave.
 #143, Fort Myers 33907.
At Bell Tower Mall.
Price: Moderate to Very
 Expensive.
Children's Menu: No.
Cuisine: New American.
Liquor: Full.
Serving: L, D.
Credit Cards: AE, MC, V.
Handicap Access: Yes.
Reservations: Yes.
Special Features: Outdoor
 seating.

Whether you choose a sidewalk table looking out at Saks Fifth Avenue or an indoor booth between mustard-colored walls, Bistro 41 feels festive and chic. Divine "small plates" and "large plates" come out of the oak-grill kitchen, visible through a showcase window with a giant fork hanging on the wall above it. The regular lunch and dinner menus highlight grilled specialties such as Yucatan Pork as an entrée or sandwich with caramelized onions-grilled pineapple chutney, marinated rotisserie chicken, and oak-grilled salmon with Mediterranean vinaigrette. Other eclectic offerings include chicken satay appetizer, seafood paella, meat loaf and roasted-garlic mashed potatoes with veal gravy, chicken pot pie, and vegetable risotto. To further complicate decision making, a tableau of specials comprise a separate menu. We come here often, usually ordering from the specials, and we've never had one complaint about our well-crafted selections. Recently, for instance, we sampled pan-seared snapper encrusted with hazelnuts and served over caramelized plantains and stir-fried vegetable, then topped with tropical fruit relish and mocha-kahlua butter sauce; and grilled filet mignon on garlic mashed potatoes and broccolini topped with walnut pesto and gorgonzola crust on a port and sun-dried cherry demi-glace. Both were near-religious experiences.

LA CASITA
239-415-1050.
15185 McGregor Blvd.,
 Fort Myers 33908.
Price: Moderate.
Children's Menu: Yes
Cuisine: Mexican.
Liquor: Beer and wine.

Following the new trend in fresh Mex, La Casita expands beyond traditional Mexican and Tex-Mex dishes to feature the cuisine of the Guanajuato region in Mexico. Authentic dishes such as *menudo* (tripe soup, said to be a good hangover remedy), basil chicken, *camarones a la diabla* (excellent, and not too spicy hot), grilled vegetables, and shrimp ceviche intermingle with more familiar vocabulary

Serving: B, L, D; open
Mon.–Sat. 11am, Sun.
9am.
Credit Cards: AE, D, MC,
V.
Handicap Access: Yes.
Reservations: No.

— tacos, tamales, enchiladas, chimichangas, and huevos rancheros. These benefit from fresh ingredients and sauces, and creative finagling. The quesadillas, for instance, are grilled and served with green tomatillo sauce. Enchiladas are dipped in chili ancho sauce, then pan sautéed and stuffed with either beef, chicken, or potato with parmesan cheese and other standard toppings. Spicy potatoes stuff corn-husk-steamed tamales. The basil chicken — shredded in a stew of onions and tomatoes and served with tortillas — is a welcome departure from tired Mexican regulars. The setting is as fresh as the food, all served in a small, brightly decorated houselike structure with fiesta colors indoors and out. It's a popular spot for commuters from nearby Sanibel Island and for the local Hispanic population.

FIRST WATCH
941-437-0020.
13211 McGregor Blvd., Fort
Myers, FL 33919.
Price: Inexpensive.
Children's Menu: Yes
Cuisine:
American/California.
Healthy Selections: Yes.
Liquor: No.
Serving: B, L.
Credit Cards: AE, D, MC,
V.
Handicap Access: Yes.
Reservations: No.
Special Features: Breakfast
served until close
(2:30p.m.).

You'll find First Watch restaurants around Southwest Florida and in other parts of the state, where the exclusive chain has made a splash. They specialize in breakfast but also serve a well-rounded selection of sandwiches and salads such as BLTE (add an egg and cheese to BLT), chicken quesadilla, smoked turkey club with avocado and sprouts, pecan and chicken salad with honey Dijon dressing, Caesar salad, and Santa Fe Salad with Cajun chicken, avocado, and a special dressing that tastes like creamy Italian with a bite. You'll notice avocados and sprouts cropping up throughout the menu, which has a California flair. Too bad they don't use local Florida avocados in season; the California variety on my Santa Fe Salad was dried out and low on flavor. Breakfast is where First Watch shines. I was disappointed that they have removed my favorite huevos rancheros, but the variety is still extensive. Their trademark item, Crepeggs, combines two daybreak favorites. The Turkey Dill Crepegg, for instance, wraps eggs, turkey, mushrooms, fresh spinach, and jack cheese in a crepe. Crepes also figure in the Health Department selections, filled with fresh fruit and yogurt. Omelets and pancakes come in all shapes and forms, from basic to healthy to decidedly self-indulgent. Expect a wait at breakfast time, especially on weekends.

SASSE IL PIZZAIUOLO
239-278-5544.
3651 Evans Ave., Fort
Myers 33901.

Odd thing about Sasse's: If you call to make a reservation, you're told they don't take them. But if you pop in on a weekend or high-season night and ask for one of the empty tables, they'll

Price: Moderate to
  Expensive.
Cuisine: Seafood/Italian.
Liquor: Beer and wine.
Serving: L, D.
Closed: L Sat.–Mon., D
  Sun.–Tues.
Credit Cards: None.
Handicap Access: Yes.
Reservations: No.

tell you they're reserved. It's something like a private club and may leave a snobbish first impression. But waiting it out and breaking in is worth the effort. You see, unassuming Sasse's in its strip-mall location has a cultish following. Tables *are* reserved for the regulars who discovered this affordable gem a half-dozen years ago when it first opened. The food is incredibly well executed, and prices are incredibly affordable. The red-walled dining room with its modern art holds fewer than 20 butcher-paper-covered tables. Although the name sounds Italian, the restaurant's focus is more seafood than pasta. From the impeccable, bargain-priced wine list, the chef/owner chose for us an Italian Langhe Arneis 1997 with a slight sparkle that was a delightful accompaniment to our crab cakes (deviled and fried in an egg wash with a lovely Dijon cream) and seared tuna (just past rare and served with roasted garlic and red peppers and a sassy caper relish). The photocopied, hand-printed paper menu changes daily. Standard and legendary is the magnanimous Caesar salad with ricotta fritters the size of baked potatoes. It alone could be a meal for two. Sasse's bakes its own bread, with different selections nightly. Our favorites include the portobello bread and the thick red-skinned potato foccacia — as close to a pudding as it is to a bread. The menu typically offers eggplant parmigiana, spaghettini, bistecca alla chiantigiana, osso bucco and other nods to more traditional Italian cuisine. It is well-rounded with chicken, duck, veal, and lamb, presentations of which are sculptural.

UNIVERSITY GRILL
239-437-4377.
7790 Cypress Lake Dr., Fort
  Myers 33907.
Price: Moderate.
Early Dining Menu: Yes.
Children's Menu: Yes.
Cuisine: Seafood.
Liquor: Full.
Serving: L, D.
Closed: Sat. & Sun. for
  lunch.
Credit Cards: AE, MC, V.
Handicap Access: Yes.
Reservations: Yes, for
  dinner.
Special Features: Outdoor
  seating overlooking a
  fountained pond.

You feel as though you've entered a privileged men's club, surrounded as you are by dark woods, a martini bar, and library shelves. But don't feel intimidated. It's neither stuffy nor overly expensive at the University Club. The latest of a Florida-wide string of restaurants opened by Sanibel-based folks, this one, too, concentrates on seafood with a nice sampling of pasta and meat dishes besides. I invariably order the pasta Maria, penne pasta whose plum tomato sauce goes multi-dimensional with the addition of marscapone and smoked fresh mozzarella cheeses. The Absolute penne pasta is another fine choice, in a cream sauce soused with vodka. On my last visit, I decided to expand my horizons and go for the horseradish root-crusted grouper that had been tempting me. Like all the club's dishes, it arrived in over-generous portion, this one atop a mound of fresh sautéed spinach and red-skinned mashed potatoes. The pan-fried grouper was as fresh and moist as it could be, but the slivers of fresh horseradish were a bit too bitter for even a horseradish lover like myself. It, and the frizzled leeks on top, overpowered the delicate vanilla rum beurre blanc. The daily dinner menu diversifies with roast duck, crab cakes with citrus aioli, and coconut shrimp with raspberry horseradish sauce. In addition, a menu of nightly early dining and other specials offers roast ribeye crusted with boursin with mushrooms and marsala sauce, plus the night's fresh fish in various guises. At lunch, burgers, salads, deli sandwiches, and a smattering of the entrees provide a well-rounded selection.

THE VERANDA
239-332-2065.
2122 Second St., Fort Myers 33901.
Price: Expensive to Very Expensive.
Children's Menu: No.
Cuisine: Florida/Southern.
Liquor: Full.
Serving: L, D.
Closed: Sat. lunch, Sun. lunch and dinner.
Credit Cards: AE, MC, V.
Handicap Access: Yes.
Reservations: Recommended.
Special Features: Garden/courtyard dining; piano bar.

My husband and I had our first "big" dinner date at the Veranda, so it will always be one of my favorites — and not solely for sentimental reasons. Victorian trappings and southern charm create an atmosphere of romance in a historic home setting. Occupying two early-20th-century houses, the Veranda is elegantly furnished. The dining room huddles around a two-sided redbrick fireplace. A white picket fence separates the cobblestone garden courtyard from traffic. Historic Fort Myers photos and well-stocked wine cases line the dark-wood bar. Start with something unusual from the Veranda's appetizer board — perhaps escargots in puff pastry with Stilton cheese (a sublime rendition), artichoke fritters with blue crab and béarnaise sauce, or southern grit cakes with pepper jack cheese and grilled andouille sausage. The multidimensional house salad is served with fresh honey-glazed bread (worth the trip in itself), corn muffins, and the Veranda's signature southern pepper jelly. Entrées are traditional but exceed the ordinary. Medallions of filet are dressed southern style, in smoky sour-mash whiskey sauce. Rosemary merlot sauce complements the rack of New Zealand lamb. Grilled grouper is mated with blue-crab hash and caper vinaigrette. Daily specials typically include fresh seafood catches, and the menu changes to reflect the seasons. Lunches span the spectrum from creative sandwiches, such as the Carpetbagger — roast beef, turkey, bacon, and tomatoes on freshly baked bread — to Florida-accented salads, including fried green tomato salad. At a recent luncheon I sampled the highly acclaimed crab cakes, which, more like crab balls, are rolled in cracker crumbs, fried, and served with delightful sides of dilled cucumber crescents, potato salad, black bean relish, and tarragon-flavored remoulade sauce. Desserts wilt willpower with such temptations as chocolate pâté on raspberry coulis, peanut-butter-fudge pie, and pecan-praline tart.

Fort Myers Beach

Locals go to Fort Myers Beach expecting fresh seafood and reasonable prices. It's known more for fun dining and waterfront views than for culinary innovation.

**JOHNNY LEVEROCK'S
  SEAFOOD HOUSE**
239-267-2334.
18100 San Carlos Blvd., Fort Myers Beach 33931.
Price: Inexpensive to Moderate.
Cuisine: Seafood.
Children's Menu: Yes.
Early Dining Menu: Yes.
Liquor: Full.
Serving: L, D.
Credit Cards: AE, DC, MC, V.
Handicap Access: Yes.
Reservations: No.

This popular west coast Florida chain has made its way to Fort Myers Beach, a natural location for its inexpensive, volume, waterfront template. The multiroomed interior is decorated the way the chain's legendary namesake would have liked. As the story goes, Johnny, a native of the Dutch Caribbean island of Saba, won a fertile Tampa oyster bar in a poker game and opened an eatery as an outlet for all the shellfish he reaped. Spare boat motors, mounted game fish, a fishing chair, even an upside-down boat adorn the dark-wood décor. People wait in line for the seafood, priced as cheaply as it gets. In the interest of comprehensive reporting, we ordered two of the sampler plates. Of the two, the Seafood Trio won. It consists of three Leverock's specialties: onion crusted salmon with a nice horseradish sauce side, "wet batter" shrimp (is there such a thing as dry batter?), and crab cakes. The shrimp were crisply and flakily fried, the crab cakes heavily bready but nicely flavored. The most disappointing part of the Seafood Harvest is that fake melted butter accompanied the smallest lobster tail we'd ever seen (where are lobsters this paltry size legal to keep, we wondered) and tainted the flavor of the scallops in garlic "butter." The mahimahi was tough, the skewered shrimp OK. We liked the cinnamon-sweetened molasses bread. Other selections include pasta-seafood dishes, baked lobster tail, shrimp scampi, and beef tenderloin. My recommendation: Go here for value, but stick to what Leverock's built its reputation on: raw oysters, fried shrimp, and peanut-butter pie.

**SNUG HARBOR WATER-
  FRONT RESTAURANT**
239-463-4343.
www.snugharborrestaurant.com.
645 Old San Carlos Blvd., Fort Myers Beach 33931.
Price: Moderate to Expensive.
Cuisine: Seafood/American.
Children's Menu: Yes.
Early Dining Menu: Yes.

A perennial favorite, Snug Harbor has a distinct island feel — a thatched roof over part of the dining room, sculptures depicting seaside shanties on the walls, and outdoor dockside dining, where a great white egret strolls and trolls for food (it's prohibited to feed the birds, though). The main dining room is lined with windows that look out upon boat traffic, shrimpers, and an aviary island. The menu concentrates on seafood, prepared freshly and simply, with an emphasis on grouper and

Liquor: Full.
Serving: L, D.
Credit Cards: AE, D, MC, V.
Handicap Access: Yes.
Reservations: Yes, at dinner
(except early birds) for
parties of 4 or more.
Special Features: Waterside
view, open-air dining.

shrimp. Grouper Popeye is a longtime signature dish, featuring fresh steamed spinach (of course) and a light lemon-butter sauce. The mashed sweet potato accompaniment is a wise choice. Baked garlic shrimp is another Snug classic as is Buffalo shrimp, an appetizer we order every time. Fried oysters, shrimp, grouper, scallops, and lobster tails come separately or as a platter. Salmon cakes, fine cuts of beef, and pasta dishes round out the menu. A page full of changing fresh fish selections offers yet more choices on both the lunch and dinner menu. Salads, sandwiches, pasta, and seafood comprise the lunch selections.

Pine Island

LAZY FLAMINGO
239-283-5959.
16501-8 Stringfellow Rd.,
Bokeelia 33922.
Price: Inexpensive.
Children's Menu: Yes.
Cuisine: Seafood.
Liquor: Beer and wine.
Serving: L, D.
Credit Cards: AE, D, MC,
V.
Handicap Access: Yes.
Reservations: No.
Special Features:
Waterfront view.

A spin-off from a well-loved Sanibel Island establishment (see below) recently opened at Four Winds Marina. This one overlooks the harbor and its boats, and is decorated in the chain's typical old shrimp-boat wood and corrugated tin. It serves the same casual menu of prime-rib sandwich, steamed shrimp, grouper sandwich, Caesar salad, conch fritters, and other local and Caribbean-influenced specialties.

**WATERFRONT
RESTAURANT**
239-283-0592.
www.waterfrontrestaurant.
com.
2131 Oleander St., St. James
City 33956.
Price: Moderate.
Children's Menu: No, but
appropriate menu items.
Cuisine: Seafood.
Liquor: Beer and wine.
Serving: L, D.
Credit Cards: AE, D, MC, V.
Handicap Access: Limited.
Reservations: No.
Special Features: Canalside
seating.

Where schoolchildren once learned their three Rs, modern-day seafarers and islanders learn to relax and revel in fresh seafood prepared in the traditional style, with a bit of fancifying. When there's stone crab to be had, have it because this is about the most reasonably priced you'll find it in these parts. Our son automatically equates the foot-long Waterdoggie with a boat trip to Waterfront. We usually choose from the fish specials, after whetting our appetites with gator tail, spicy shrimp, or jalapeño poppers. For the hearty appetite, there's the mariner platter and seafood combo, piled with gifts from the sea, baked or fried. At lunchtime or any time, the steakburger is one great burger. The kitchen is extremely compliant, so order your seafood exactly the way you like it. Grouper comes fried, broiled, blackened, jerk, bronzed, or sautéed. Indoors, you can play hangman on the butcher paper tablecloths. Outdoors, watch boaters trying to gracefully dock their vessels under the scrutiny of an audience. The key lime pie is good, but skip the "famous" waterfront (fruit) bakes.

Sanibel Island

LAZY FLAMINGO
239-472-5353.
6520-C Pine Ave., Sanibel
  Island 33957.
At Blind Pass.
Price: Moderate.
Early Dining Menu: No.
Children's Menu: Yes.
Cuisine: Seafood/
  American.
Liquor: Beer and wine.
Serving: L, D.
Credit Cards: AE, D, MC, V.
Handicap Access: No.
Reservations: No.

This is the original Lazy Flamingo, which has spawned another on Sanibel's south end and others along the south coast. Look for a Pepto-Bismol-pink building at Blind Pass, just before the bridge to Captiva. Neighborhood and nautical are the concepts behind this first Flamingo, where you order and pick up your own food at the counter, eat off plastic plates in the shape of scallop shells, and wipe your hands with paper towels from a roll at the table. The menu and ambiance have an essence of the Florida Keys; the owners even lifted the idea of a popular ring-and-hook game from a bar down there. Conch fritters, clam pot, mesquite-grilled grouper, wings, prime rib sandwich, Caesar salad, and chocolate key-lime cheesecake are some of the most popular menu items. Avoid the Dead Parrot Wings; they are inedible to all but the most calloused. Most of the meals come with fries, but you can substitute a small Caesar salad, which is usually tasty. The place is small: about a dozen counter seats and a few booths. For the same food, but more room, shrimp-boat decor, and table service, try the one at 1036 Periwinkle Way (239-472-6939). Both are designated smoking areas in their entirety.

McT's Shrimp House serves all the shrimp you can eat in an old-island setting.

Karen T. Bartlett

McT's SHRIMP HOUSE & TAVERN
239-472-3161.

This place has been popular for years. My only problem with it is that it hasn't changed its approach to cuisine in all that time. What passed

1523 Periwinkle Way,
  Sanibel Island 33957.
Price: Moderate.
Early Dining Menu: Yes.
Children's Menu: Yes.
Cuisine: Seafood.
Liquor: Full.
Serving: D.
Credit Cards: AE, D, MC, V.
Handicap Access: Yes.
Reservations: No.

off as creative 15 years ago has become passé: huge portions, fat-laden dishes, canned products. But as they say, if it ain't broke . . . McT's made its reputation on all-you-can-eat shrimp, which is served steamed and in the shell. Fifteen other shrimp entrées range from classic fried shrimp to Cajun style shrimp. Then there are other seafood and meat dishes and nightly specials for those less than fanatical about shrimp. The specials are often more inventive and contemporary. The setting is nice — a lot of latticework and French doors, old-island style. In the bar, where you're bound to wait for seating, upside-down trees support the roof. Mud pie for dessert is a tradition.

DOLCE VITA
239-472-5555.
1244 Periwinkle Way,
  Sanibel Island 33957.
Price: Moderate to
  Expensive.
Children's Menu: No.
Cuisine: Mediterranean.
Liquor: Full.
Serving: D.
Credit Cards: AE, MC, V.
Handicap Access: Yes.
Reservations: Yes.
Special Features: Live
  piano.

Newly built and opened in 2000, this has become one of Sanibel's most glamorous and popular fine dining experiences. The large open dining room is at the same time elegant and convivial, with a live piano as centerpiece. The menu is extensive, yet each dish is well crafted with Mediterranean and New World touches, and other continental and global influences. For starters, there's everything from wok-steamed clams and mussels to antipasto and Absolut salmon gravlax. The Vietnamese spiced-duck spring rolls are excellent, filled with roasted Cornish hen, chanterrelles, brie, and pecans and served with a marvelous apricot-tamarind sauce. The cassoulet of escargot gets an injection of individual personality from mushrooms and herbs to supplement the garlic. We selected chicken quesadilla and a lobster-veal special from among the dizzying choice of entrees: Indian spiced lamb shank, Texas wild boar saddle (tamarind-honey glazed with black currant coulis), goat cheese tortelloni, shellfish linguine, and porterhouse béarnaise, to name a sampling. We were extremely pleased with our selections. The quesadilla came wrapped in an ajillo tortilla with ancho-chili prawns, spinach, and goat and jack cheeses. The black bean salsa accompaniment was superb, but the guacamole was disappointingly canned. The kitchen accommodated my son with a plate of penne marinara. Because we were eating in a place that translates as "sweet life," we all decided to have dessert, which turned out to be another highlight. Each came with a tiny scoop of homemade frozen confection: black forest cake with passionfruit sherbet, coconut flan brûlée with piña colada sherbet, and Hawaiian macadamia nut tart spiked with Kentucky bourbon and served with vanilla bean ice cream. Extremely yum!

**TRADERS STORE &
CAFÉ**
239-472-7242.
www.tradersstoreandcafe.
com..
1551 Periwinkle Way,
Sanibel Island 33957.
Price: Expensive to Very
Expensive.
Children's Menu: Yes.
Cuisine: American/Bistro.
Liquor: Beer and wine.
Serving: L, D.
Credit Cards: AE, D, MC, V.
Handicap Access: Yes.
Reservations: Yes.
Special Features: A
restaurant embedded in
the setting of a
gallerylike import store.

This is the equivalent of performance art, where you become a part of the store. You sit among wooden tribal masks on import chairs, eating terrific crusty bread out of hand-woven baskets. The café is plopped into one corner of this unusual store, owned by the founders of the Chico's clothing store dynasty (see Shopping). The food rivals the surrounding artifact-quality furnishings and objets d'art. It's become *the* place for islanders to meet for lunch, with its succinct menu of sandwiches, pastas, and small plates. The soup of the day is usually a good bet, and the seafood gumbo, fortified with rice, could be a meal. I also can recommend the grilled marinated portobello sandwich and the pan-blackened jumbo scallops on greens with lemon-caper vinaigrette. The crab cakes, served also as a dinner starter, are a bit mushy, but I loved the corn salsa bed upon which they rested, all drizzled with lime remoulade. The dinner menu describes such masterworks as prosciutto shrimp, Asian lollipop pork chops, and pan-fried red cornmeal-crusted grouper.

Nightly specials dazzle. We recently sampled three marvelous entrees from it: horseradish-crusted swordfish over a most flavorful roasted red pepper coulis, crab-stuffed mahimahi, seafood and penne tossed with Cajun cream sauce, and macadamia-crusted grouper with a wonderful Thai peanut sauce. Cutting edge aside, Traders is also known for its burgers and barbecue baby back ribs.

TWILIGHT CAFÉ
239-472-8818.
751 Tarpon Bay Rd.,
Sanibel Island 33957.
Price: Expensive.
Children's Menu: Yes.
Cuisine: New American.
Liquor: Beer and wine.
Serving: D, L in season.
Closed: Sunday
Credit Cards: AE, MC, V.
Handicap Access: Yes.
Reservations: Yes.

Twilight is our favorite special occasion dinner destination. Set back from the road, it neighbors a popular art gallery and has contracted an artistic flair by virtue of closeness. The teeny dining room is artsy in a whimsical rather than snobbish way. The ever-changing menu presents masterpieces in design-forward cuisine where oak grilling and freshness are trademark. In the open-for-view kitchen, chefs grill seafood in such dishes as Asian shrimp with Thai peanut sauce; they grill meats for the signature cowboy steak with sweet mashed potatoes and roasted green apple glaze, and rack of lamb over spinach and vegetable orzo with three-bean ratatouille. They also grill vegetables, including greens, which lends an unusual dimension to salads and beds upon which entrées come to rest. One page is devoted to vegetarian dishes starring grilled veggies. Twilight is also known for its crawfish mashed potatoes. Remember how as a kid you sometimes mashed all the food on your plate into your potatoes? This dish, chunky with corn kernels and crawfish tidbits, takes comfort food into the new age. For a starter, try one of the pizzalike flatbread crisps. We found the Cajun crawfish with tomatoes and gorgonzola divine. I also recommend the spinach and arugula salad with roasted pecans, gorgonzola, and warm pancetta vinaigrette. No matter what you order, prepare yourself for novel taste sensations.

WINDOWS ON THE WATER
239-395-6014.
1451 Middle Gulf Dr.,
　Sanibel Island 33957.
At Sundial Beach Resort.
Price: Expensive.
Children's Menu: Yes.
Cuisine: Seafood/Pacific Rim.
Liquor: Full.
Serving: B, L, D, SB.
Credit Cards: AE, D, MC, V.
Handicap Access: Yes.
Reservations: Yes.
Special Features: Gulf view.

Oddly enough, few restaurants in this town surrounded by water offer water views. Windows, on the other hand, maximizes its location overlooking Sundial Resort's main swimming pool and the beach beyond by stepping the tables. Recently the restaurant underwent a makeover in décor and menu. To match the sand and sea beyond, there's light woods and cobalt (OK, considerably more intense than the sea) accents, all very clean and contemporary. The food has swayed toward Thai and Pacific Rim while maintaining some of Windows trademarks, such as bronzed grouper, using a milder mix of spices and a lighter touch in the sauté pan than is used in traditional blackening. It comes with a garlic red wine sauce that I've found delightful in the past. New Asian creations include citrus mahimahi, salmon with peanut sauce, seafood pad Thai, and Oriental salads. I recommend the pan-seared crab croquette appetizer, an innovative twist on crab cakes in a light layer of breading with pickled ginger and decorative swirls of red pepper oil and teriyaki glaze. Entrées are often somewhat disappointing for lack of the fine execution the prices demand. Sundial excels at its lunch and Sunday brunch buffets. There's also a lunch menu with a smattering of salads, a too-gloopy and too-short-on-shrimp andouille sausage and shrimp gumbo, a few sandwiches, and some seafood and meat entrées. For dessert, try the chocolate bayou cake — a thin slice of chocolate cake wading in a pool of heavy cream sauce, topped with hot fudge — another carryover from Windows tradition.

FOOD PURVEYORS

BAKERIES

Andre's French Bakery (239-482-2011; Bridge Plaza, 12901 McGregor Blvd., Fort Myers 33919) Small but chock-full of treats *françaises*: baguettes, great olive bread, cookies, sublime tortes, and custard-filled pastries.

Bara Bread Bistro (239-334-8216; 1520 Broadway, Fort Myers 33901) A charming bistro-*boulangerie* specializing in French bread by the loaf and luscious French pastries.

CANDIES & ICE CREAM

Ben & Jerry's Ice Cream & Frozen Yogurt (239-936-4155; 12995 S. Cleveland Ave, Suite 130, Fort Myers 33907)

Big Olaf Creamery (239-590-9195; 13499 S. Cleveland Ave., Fort Myers 33907; at Bell Tower Shops) Twenty-one types of sundaes, plus homemade ice cream, smoothies, and a caboose kids can climb into to eat.

Chocolate Expressions (239-472-3837; Periwinkle Place, 2075 Periwinkle Way, Sanibel Island 33957) Candy, regular and fat-free ice cream and smoothies, coffee.

Kilwin's (239-463-4500; 50 Old San Carlos Blvd., Fort Myers Beach 33931; at Times Square) Fudge, chocolates, and ice cream in many flavors.

Pinocchio's Homemade Ice Cream (239-472-6566; 362 Periwinkle Way, Sanibel Island 33957) Homemade Italian ice cream and yogurt, cappuccino, espresso, and frozen coffee drinks.

COFFEE

The Bean (239-395-1919; 2240 Periwinkle Way, Sanibel Island 33957) Sanibel's wildly popular buzz shop, it serves the usual espresso, cappuccino, and latte selection, plus ice cream, bagels, sandwiches, and salads.

Blackhawk Fine Coffee & Provisions (239-433-7770; 13499 S. Cleveland Ave. #137, Fort Myers 33907; at Bell Tower Shops) An inviting setting of easy chairs, coffee tables, and backgammon boards where you can enjoy coffee, latte, desserts, flavored ice tea, Krispy Kreme donuts, and other goodies.

DELI & SPECIALTY FOODS

Barney's Incredible Edibles (239-472-2555; 2330 Palm Ridge Rd., Sanibel Island 33957) Bakery and deli specializing in croissants, stuffed croissants, and quiche. Also: muffins, cookies, cakes, frozen dinner entrées, coffee, and gourmet groceries.

Cheese Nook (239-472-2666; Periwinkle Place, 2075 Periwinkle Way, Sanibel Island 33957) A longtime favorite of locals for more than cheese — wine, fresh bread, and gourmet hot sauces, preserves, and soups.

Five Sisters Oriental & Thai Grocery (239-936-0916; 3258 Cleveland Ave., Fort Myers 33901) Fresh and packaged ingredients for cooking up authentic curries, soups, satays, and sauces: fresh tamarind pods, great hot sauces, coconut milk, and other Thai-specific products.

India Bazaar (239-939-0797; 5228 Bank St., Fort Myers 33907) A shop filled with exotic smells, foods, and gifts from India, Thailand, the Middle East, and Britain. Fresh, packaged, and frozen ethnic ingredients and premade meals.

Mario's Italian Meat Market & Deli (239-936-7275; 12326 Cleveland Ave., Fort Myers 33907) Fresh homemade sausage and other meats, delicious homemade Italian cheeses, sauces, pastas, soups, sandwiches, and hot and frozen prepared Italian specialties. Limited seating.

Obee's Soup Salad Subs (239-332-8802; 2117 First St., Fort Myers 33901) Deli sandwiches and three types of homemade soup daily.

FRUIT & VEGETABLE STANDS

Vitamin C the delicious Florida way.

Karen T. Bartlett

For the freshest produce, visit the plentiful roadside stands along the coast. Some feature U-Pick options, especially for tomatoes and strawberries.

Downtown Farmers Market (239-332-6813; Fort Myers, near Centennial Park under the bridge) Look for a fresh fruit, vegetables, flowers, herbs and live plants, arts, and crafts every Sunday 7–3.

Oakes Brothers Produce (239-466-4464, 800-413-6881; 16758 McGregor Blvd., Fort Myers 33908) My personal favorite place for locally grown tomatoes, citrus, and other fresh fruit, vegetables, and preserves. Also ships fruit.

Mango Street Market (Estero Blvd. at Mango St., Fort Myers Beach) Roadside stand selling fresh produce.

Ródes Fresh & Fancy (239-992-4040; 3756 Bonita Beach Rd. SW, Bonita Beach 34134) Fresh produce and local seafood market, also sells fresh breads and gourmet groceries.

Sunburst Tropical Fruit Company (239-283-1200; 7113 Howard Rd., Bokeelia 33922) One of the oldest island groves, it specializes in mangoes but also grows carambola, litchi, and other exotics, and sells fruit products.

Sun Harvest Citrus (239-768-2686, 800-743-1480; 14810 Metro Pkwy. S., Fort Myers 33912; at Six Mile Cypress) Part tourist attraction, part citrus stand, it offers free samples, tours, demonstrations, a playground, and a gift shop.

Fruitful Islands

For those in the know, Pine Island is synonymous with exotic fruit. Guavas once grew wild throughout the island, brought to this subtropical land from the tropical Caribbean. Later, mangoes flourished. The only other place in Florida where tropical fruits grow in such abundance is Homestead, on the east coast, at a latitude some 90 miles south of Pine Island.

What makes Pine Island so nearly tropical? The warm waters of Charlotte Harbor run wide at the island's north end, around Bokeelia. They insulate the land, warming cold air before it reaches fragile fruit groves. Longans, sapodillas, carambolas, lichis, and other rare treats thrive as a result of this pocket of climate. Fructose freaks from miles around make a pilgrimage to roadside stands along Pine Island and Stringfellow Roads throughout the summer and fall. To celebrate its fruity reputation, Pine Island throws Mango Mania each summer.

NATURAL FOODS

Ada's Natural Foods Market (239-939-9600; 11705 S. Cleveland Ave.., Fort Myers 33907) Extensive line of organic produce and other healthy food products. A deli/juice bar with seating in the back produces tasty meatless sandwiches, salads, and hot dishes.

Healthy Habits (239-278-4442; 11763 S. Cleveland Ave., Fort Myers 33907) Organic produce, dairy products, and other natural groceries.

Island Health Foods (239-472-3666; 1640 Periwinkle Way, Sanibel Island 33957) Complete line of food and beauty products, plus organic produce, frozen desserts, smoothies, and carrot juice.

PIZZA & TAKEOUT

Hickory Bar-B-Q (239-481-2626; 15400 McGregor Blvd., PO Box 60057, Fort Myers 33906) Hickory smoking, a secret sauce, creamy cole slaw, and fresh coconut cream pie make this my favorite barbecue around.

Johnny's Pizza (239-472-3010; 2496 Palm Ridge Rd., Sanibel Island 33957) Carryout and free delivery. Regular, gourmet (the best), and deep-dish pizza, plus Italian subs and specialties.

Tropical Beach Grill (239-454-0319; 17260 San Carlos Blvd., Fort Myers Beach 33931) Better-than-average drive-up take-out for burgers, chicken sandwiches, and more.

Mama Rosa's Pizzeria (239-472-7672; Chadwick's Square, PO Box 194, Captiva Island 33924) Subs, pizza, stromboli, calzone, and salads.

Plaka I on the Beach (239-463-4707; 1001 Estero Blvd., Fort Myers Beach 33931) Gyros, spinach pie, moussaka, and baklava in a screened-in dining room near the beach.

Taste of New York Pizzeria & Subs (239-278-3222; 2215-B Winkler Ave., Fort

Myers 33901) The best take-out or eat-in regular or gourmet pizza — white, vegetarian, tropical, garlic — and other New York-Italian specialties.

SEAFOOD

Beach Seafood (239-463-8777; 1100 Shrimp Boat Ln., PO Box 2490, Fort Myers Beach 33932; on San Carlos Island,) Fresh seafood at its source, specializing in shrimp — fresh, steamed, and dinners.

Pine Bay Seafood Market (239-283-7100; 4330 Pine Island Rd., Pine Island 33993; on Matlacha; mailing address: PO Box 6507, Fort Myers 33911) Fresh and smoked fish and shellfish from the area's major transshipment center.

Ródes Fresh & Fancy (239-992-4040; 3756 Bonita Beach Rd. SW, Bonita Springs 34134) Fresh produce and local seafood market.

CULTURE

For many years the Island Coast was considered a cultural limbo, void of strong artistic or regional identity, except for a certain retiree/Midwestern influence. Still lagging behind Sarasota and Naples in that department, the region nonetheless is making inroads toward "artsification." The population, furthermore, is diversifying in terms of ethnicity and age.

The residents of Cape Coral and North Fort Myers include many nationalities — Italian, German, Jamaican, and Hispanic — that share their customs at social clubs, restaurants, festivals, and other venues. Throughout Fort Myers, Afro-Americans, Asians, East Indians, Europeans, and other ethnic groups heighten the cosmopolitan flavor. Flashes of Southern and Cracker spirit survive in the less resortlike areas of North Fort Myers and Pine Island.

The islands along the coast have inspired their share of creativity. Singer Jimmy Buffett has frequented Cabbage Key and Captiva Island. His brand of beachy folk song is the closest thing the Gulf Coast has to homegrown music. A Sanibel musician named Danny Morgan affects that same style and has been entertaining the islands for decades.

One of the few arts that residents can truly call their own is shell art, a form that flourishes on Sanibel Island, Florida's ultimate shell island. In its highest form, shell art can be stunning and delicate; in its lowest, it can result in some pretty tacky shell animals.

Wealthy visitors to Sanibel and Captiva have exerted an influence on the fine arts through the years. The illustrious roll call began in the 1920s with Charles and Anne Morrow Lindbergh. Edna St. Vincent Millay's original manuscript for *Conversation at Midnight* burned in a hotel fire. Today Robert Rauschenberg, a maverick in the field of photographic lithography, is the Island Coast's impresario.

ARCHITECTURE

Fort Myers is home to some lovely architecture downtown and along McGregor Boulevard. Thomas Edison's home was, perhaps, Florida's first prefab structure. Because wood and materials were scarce (most newcomers made do with palmetto huts), Edison commissioned a Maine architect to draw up plans and construct sections of the home to be shipped down and pieced together on site. Downtown, the Richard Building, circa 1924, boasts an Italian influence, while the courthouse annex superbly represents Mediterranean Revival. So does the Miles Building, built in 1926 by Dr. Franklin Miles, the "Father of Alka-Seltzer," and Patio De Leon, a restored and burgeoning entertainment and shopping complex on First Street. The newer Harborside Convention Center and other recent constructions echo the motif.

Pine Island possesses the best, most concentrated collection of preserved vernacular architecture, especially in Matlacha. Pineland's mound-squatting homes are also prime examples, occasionally dressed up with latticework and vivid paint jobs. In Bokeelia, the entire Main Street is designated a historic district. Notice especially the Captain's House, a fine example of slightly upscale folk housing of the early 1900s, with French Provincial elements. Nearby Turner Mansion represents a higher standard of living and is reminiscent of New England styles. The club at Useppa Island exhibits another prime collection of Old Florida styles, both traditional and revival.

On Sanibel Island, side trips down shell-named streets such as Coquina Drive and King's Crown take you into residential areas, where styles range from renovated Cracker cottages to stately Victorian mansions. Even Art Deco dwellings are popping up, despite islanders' attempts to keep out what they call incompatible styles.

CINEMA

MOVIE THEATERS

AMC Merchants Crossing 16 (239-995-1191; 15201 N. Cleveland Ave., North Fort Myers 33903) State-of-the-art complex.

Beach Theater (239-765-9000; 6425 Estero Blvd., Fort Myers Beach 33931) A new theater with four screens, serving a full-meal (and slightly over-priced) menu, beer, and wine.

Regal Bell Tower 20 (239-590-9696; Daniels Pkwy. and U.S. 41, Fort Myers 33907) A modern megacomplex of theaters in the form of an airport hangar.

Coralwood 10 (239-590-9696; 2301 Del Prado Blvd., Cape Coral 33909; at Coralwood Mall)

Island Cinema (239-472-1701; 535 Tarpon Bay Rd., Sanibel Island 33957; at Bailey's Shopping Center) A two-screen theater showing first-run films.

Northside Drive-In (239-995-2254; 2521 N. Tamiami Trail, Fort Myers 33903)

DANCE

Salsa 2000 at Marina Lounge (239-454-8595; Ramada Inn & Suites at Amtel Marina, 2500 Edwards Dr., Fort Myers 33901; downtown) Learn salsa and merengue dancing with live Latin bands at this new hot club overlooking the city yacht basin.

Dance Ensemble of Southwest Florida (239-768-1144; Accent on Dance, 12155 Metro Pkwy. #18, Fort Myers 33907) Classes and performance of tap, jazz, ballet, lyrical, clogging, and pointe dance for children.

Dance City (239-275-3433; 1939 Park Meadows Dr., Suite 1, Fort Myers 33907) Adult ballroom instruction.

Dance Theatre Academy (239-275-3131; 2084 Beacon Manor Dr., Fort Myers 33907) Ballet, pointe, tap, jazz, and interpretative dance for adults and children.

Gulfshore Ballet (239-590-6191; 2155 Andrea Ln., Suite C 5-6, Fort Myers 33912) Ballet instruction.

Hall of Fifty States (239-338-2249; Harborside Complex, 2254 Edwards Dr., Fort Myers 33901; downtown) Hosts ballroom (no instruction) and country-and-western dancing (with instruction).

GARDENS

FRAGRANCE GARDEN OF LEE COUNTY
239-432-2000.
Lakes Regional Park, 7330 Gladiolus Rd., Fort Myers 33908.
Open: 8am–6pm daily
Parking: 75 cents per hour or $3 per day.

Located at the park's west end, the garden was designed primarily for the visually and physically impaired, although the general public also will enjoy this one-of-a-kind attraction. For the visually impaired there are pungent herbs, fragrant vines, and signs in Braille. Paved paths with vegetation planted at wheelchair height accommodate the physically handicapped. Vined arbors are built wide enough for easy wheelchair access.

HISTORIC HOMES & SITES

BURROUGHS HOME
239-332-6125.
2505 First St., Fort Myers 33901.
Downtown.
Open: Tours conducted Oct.–June every hour on the hour 11am–3pm Tues.–Fri.; the rest of the year by appointment.
Admission: $6 adults, $3 children 6–12.

Mona and Jettie Burroughs, in 1918 dress, host the living-history tour at Fort Myers's first luxury residence. Tour guides in period costume assume the playful characters of two sisters who once occupied the Georgian Revival-style home, Fort Myers's first mansion, built in 1901. They'll invite you to add a few stitches to the afghan they're knitting for the war effort, then take you back in time to when cowmen drove cattle past their home and the Henry Fords hosted square dances. Period furniture and appointments provide a charming backdrop to this improv pageant on the banks of the Caloosahatchee River.

CHAPEL-BY-THE-SEA
239-472-1646.
11580 Chapin Ln., Captiva
  Island 33924.

This quaint church is a popular spot for interdenominational Sunday services, weddings, and seaside meditation. Many of the island's early pioneers were laid to rest in its cemetery.

FISHING SHACKS
Pine Island Sound at
  Captiva Rocks, east of
  North Captiva.

The last artifacts of the region's early commercial fishing enterprises have braved weather and bureaucracy to strut the shallows along the Intracoastal Waterway. The shack at the mouth of Safety Harbor on Upper Captiva is the most noticeable. It once served as an icehouse. If you look east, you'll spot several others where fishermen and their families used to live. Privately owned and maintained as weekend fishing homes for local enthusiasts, most are listed in the National Register of Historic Places and serve as a picturesque reminder of days gone by.

**KORESHAN STATE
  HISTORIC SITE**
239-992-0311.
PO Box 7, Estero 33928.
Tamiami Trail, US 41 and
  Corkscrew Rd.
Open: 8am–sunset.
Admission: $3.25 per
  vehicle with up to 8
  passengers; $1 per
  cyclist, pedestrian, or
  extra passenger.

Contained within a state park, this site has restored the customs and ways of an early-1900s religious cult that settled on the banks of the Estero River. Under the leadership of Cyrus Teed, whose name in Hebrew is Koresh, members of Koreshan Unity were well versed in practical Christianity, speculative metaphysics, functional and aesthetic gardening, art, Koreshan Cosmogony, and occupational training. Their most unusual theory held that the earth lined the inside of a hollow globe and looked down into the solar system. Teed and his followers envisioned an academic and natural Utopia. They planted their settlement with exotic crops and vegetation. They built a theater, a communal mess hall, a store, and various workshops, all of which have been restored or reconstructed to tell the strange story of the Koreshans, who lost their momentum upon the death of their charismatic leader in 1908. Archives are kept at the Koreshan Unity Foundation and library across the road from the park (239-992-2184). Future plans call for a development named Riverplace that would integrate cabins, environmental and spiritual retreats, old-time craft shops, trails, and canoeing.

**RANDELL RESEARCH
  CENTER**
239-283-2062.
PO Box 608, Pineland
  33945.

Archaeologists from Gainesville's Florida Museum of Natural History meet here to discover the lifestyles of the lost Calusa tribes. Once an important center of Calusa culture, it encompasses 200 acres of

Pine Island.
Open: Tours at 10 on Sat., other times by appointment.
Admission: Suggested donation of $5 for adults, $3 for children.

shell mounds and old Cracker shacks on the shores of Pine Island Sound, where the ancient Indians once collected shellfish for food and tools. Tour guides reveal what they have discovered about the tall warriors on weekly walking tours and pre-arranged kayak excursions.

SANIBEL CEMETERY
Off the bike path on Middle Gulf Dr.; not accessible by car.

No signs direct you to it. Just follow the path, and you'll come across a fenced plot with wooden headstones announcing the names of early settlers — a wonderful, quiet place to ponder times past.

SANIBEL LIGHTHOUSE
Southeast end of Periwinkle Way, Sanibel Island.

Built in 1884, the lighthouse was the island's first permanent structure. Once vital to cattle transports from the mainland, it still functions as a beacon of warning and welcome. The lighthouse and Old Florida-style light keeper's cottage were renovated in 1991.

Lee Island Coast Visitor and Convention Bureau

The tropical gardens at Thomas Edison's historic winter estate in Fort Myers add color and dimension to any visit.

**THOMAS EDISON
    WINTER
    ESTATE/FORD HOME**
239-334-3614.
http://edison-ford.estate.
    com.
2350 McGregor Blvd., Fort
    Myers 33901.
Open: Continuous tours
    9am–4pm Mon.–Sat.,
    12–4 pm Sun.
Admission: $12 adults;
    $5.50 children 6–12.

Nowhere in the U.S. will you find the homes of two such important historical figures sitting side by side. This site is so much more than just a couple of preserved houses, however. It is a slice of Floridiana, Americana, and Mr. Wizard, all rolled into 17 riverside acres. The 90-minute tour begins across the street under the nation's largest banyan tree, a gift from tire mogul Harvey Firestone. The tree, 400 feet around, poses outside a museum that contains many of Edison's 1,000-plus patented inventions — the phonograph, the movie camera, the lightbulb, children's furniture — as well as the 1907 prototype Model T Ford his friend and wintertime neighbor, Henry Ford, gave him. Edison's late-1880s home hides in a jungle of tropical flora with which Edison experimented. Actually there are two homes, identically built and connected with an arcade. One contained the Edisons' living quarters; the other, guest quarters and the kitchen. His laboratory, full of dusty bottles and other ancient gizmos, sits in the backyard among reflecting pools and gardens. The Friendship Gate separates Edison's estate from Ford's. "The Mangoes," as it was called in honor of the fruit orchards the car manufacturer so loved, seems humble compared to its neighbor, with furnishings true to the era and the Fords' simple tastes. On occasion, actors portraying America's geniuses circulate around the grounds.

KIDS' STUFF

**BROADWAY PALM
    CHILDREN'S
    THEATRE**
239-278-4422
www.broadwaypalm.com.
Royal Palm Square, 1380
    Colonial Blvd., Fort
    Myers 33907.

Broadway Palm Dinner Theatre puts on three plays a year geared toward families and served up with kid's-fare lunch.

**THE CHILDREN'S
    SCIENCE CENTER**
239-997-0012.
www.cyberstreet.com/csc.
2915 NE Pine Island Rd.,
    Cape Coral 33909.
Open: 9:30–4:30 Mon.–Fri.,
    12–5 weekends.
Admission: $2 children
    3–16, $4 adults.

Encourages visitors of all ages to touch and interact with the exhibits: mind-teaser puzzles, hands-on electrical gadgets, building blocks, Calusa Indian tools, a whisper dish, and computer games. A nature trail with bug identification, plus live captured snakes, iguanas, tarantulas, and scorpions get kids excited about nature. This is a neighborhood, science-guy kind of place without all the high-tech exhibits of the genre's sophisticated high end, but we love it for its neighborliness and user-friendliness (as long as you don't let the kids try to pet the iguanas).

Waltz through a thunderstorm at Fort Myers's Imaginarium.

Lee Island Coast Visitor and Convention Bureau

IMAGINARIUM
239-337-3332.
PO Box 2217, Fort Myers 33902.
At Dr. Martin Luther King Jr. Blvd. and Cranford Ave.
Open: 10am–5pm Tues.–Sat., Sun. 12–5pm; closed Mon.
Admission: $3 children 3–12 when accompanied by an adult, $6 ages 13 and up, $5.50 seniors.

I have visited many of the new-wave interactive science museums that have hit Florida in the past decade, and I'm happy to say this is among my favorites. It is not overwhelmingly huge, like some, but is colorfully attractive and varied in its approach to teaching everything from the effects of chemical abuse to the world of finance. Emphasis is on weather and water (it occupies a former city water plant). The Hurricane Experience will, as they like to say, "blow you away." You can feel a cloud, tape yourself on location broadcasting a tornado, and walk through a thunderstorm. Aquariums, a touch tank, a swan lagoon, and alligator feedings acquaint visitors with local and reef water creatures. A new exhibit replicates the skull of a Tyrannosaurus rex dinosaur. Other displays appeal to all ages with gadgets, toys, and computers.

MUSEUMS

BAILEY-MATTHEWS SHELL MUSEUM
239-395-2233.
www.shellmuseum.org.
3075 Sanibel-Captiva Rd., PO Box 1580, Sanibel Island 33957.

The only one of its kind in the U.S., this museum reinforces Sanibel's reputation as a top shell-collecting destination. It uses nature vignettes and artistically arranged displays to demonstrate the role of shells in ecology, history, art, economics, medicine, religion, and other fields. The center-

Open: 10am–4pm
Tues.–Sun.; closed Mon.
Admission: $3 children
8–16, $5 ages 17 and up.

piece of the museum is a two-story globe surrounded by shells of the world. Outside is a memorial devoted to the late actor Raymond Burr, who helped establish the museum. The Children's Science Lab provides games and hands-on learning experiences in colorful reef-motif surroundings, but oddly with a touch tank you can't touch. The museum holds more than two million specimens in the showroom and catalogued upstairs, representing a third of the world's 100,000 species of living mollusks.

**CAPE CORAL HISTORI-
CAL MUSEUM**
239-772-7037.
544 Cultural Park Blvd.,
Cape Coral 33990.
Open: 1–4pm Wed., Thurs.,
Sun.
Admission: $1 donation per
adult.

Burrowing owls, shells, fossils, videos, and antiques comprise the headlining exhibits at this small facility. Also rotating collections on loan.

**CAPTIVA HISTORY
HOUSE**
239-472-5111.
Mail: c/o South Seas Resort,
PO Box 194,Captiva
Island 33924.
Entrance to South Seas
Resort.
Hours: 10am–4pm.
Closed: Mon., Sat.

This tiny museum occupies a 1920s cottage that originally served as a plantation worker's home back when key limes were farmed. Through photographs, memorabilia, and storyboards, the museum relates the history of Captiva Island from prehistoric man through the farming and fishing eras of the early 1900s. A docent portrays C. W. Chadwick, plantation founder and inventor of the Checkwriter machine.

**FORT MYERS
HISTORICAL
MUSEUM**
239-332-5955.
2300 Peck St. Fort Myers
33901.
At Jackson St.
Open: 9am–4pm Tues.–Sat.
Closed: Sun., Mon.
Admission: $6 adults, $5.50
seniors, $3 children 3–12;
walking tour Jan.–May:
Wed. 10am–12pm, $5.

Housed in a handsome restored railroad depot, the museum's displays take you back to the days of the Calusa Indians and through the eras of Spanish exploration, fish camps, gladiolus farming, and World War II training with well-arranged scale models, graphic depictions, and interactive historical games. A new exhibit explores the history of professional baseball in Fort Myers through artifacts, photos, and facts. (Find out about the time 80-year-old Thomas Edison knocked Ty Cobb off the pitcher's mound with a line drive.) Outdoors, tours examine a replica of a local early-1900s Cracker house and the world's last and longest Pullman private railcar, circa 1930. (Don't miss the Pullman tour; it's truly a highlight if you have a good guide.)

**MUSEUM OF THE
   ISLANDS**
239-283-1525.
5728 Sesame Dr., Pine
   Island Center 33922;
   mailing address PO Box
   305, St. James City 33956.
On Pine Island.
Open: Winter season
   (Nov.–Apr.) Tues.–Sat.
   11am–3pm, 1-4pm Sun.;
   Summer: Tues.–Sat.
   11am–3pm.
Admission: $1 per adult,
   50¢ per child.

Occupying the old Pine Island library at Phillips Park, the museum concentrates on the area's Calusa and fishing heritage. A shell mound replica is modeled after one excavated on the island. Continue on to the settlement of Pineland to see time standing still upon intact Native American mounds.

**SANIBEL HISTORICAL
   VILLAGE & MUSEUM**
239-472-4648.
950 Dunlop Rd., Sanibel
   Island 33957.
Near City Hall.
Open: 10am–4pm
   Wed.–Sat.; closed mid-
   Aug.– Nov.
Admission: $3 donation per
   adult requested.

The village began with a historical Cracker-style abode, once the home of an island pioneer. The museum focuses on Sanibel's modern history of homesteading, citrus farming, steamboating, and tourism, with photos and artifacts. It recalls the Calusa era with a dugout canoe and other relics of the times. The island's original Bailey's General Store, circa 1927, was later moved to the site in 1993 as a kickoff to establishing a pioneer village on the grounds. Since then, a 1920s post office, a teahouse, and another vintage home have been added. The latter houses a lens that outfitted the Sanibel Lighthouse in the 1960s.

USEPPA MUSEUM
239-283-1061.
Useppa Island Club,
   Useppa Island 33922.
Admission: $2.50 donation
   requested for visitors
   over age 18.

The wee island of Useppa is stuffed to the gills with history, a fact that calls for a historic museum. This one is exceptionally well presented for such a small place. (It helps that wealth outmeasures square footage on the island.) Dioramas are interpreted via taped presentations you hear from small tape recorders and headsets. They describe the island's Calusa history, its fishing and resort eras, and its role in training revolutionaries for the Cuban Bay of Pigs confrontation in 1960. Since the island is owned by a private club, visitors must be island guests or guests aboard the *Lady Chadwick* luncheon cruise to the island (see Captiva Cruises under "Sightseeing & Entertainment Cruises" in this chapter).

MUSIC AND NIGHTLIFE

Downtown Fort Myers is slowly metamorphosing into a hot entertainment district, featuring jazz bars, bistros, nightclubs, and street festivals. As for the islands, Fort Myers Beach is definitely the hoppingest. On Sanibel and Captiva, you'll find a quieter brand of partying; nightlife there is focused on theater and more highbrow forms of music. Friday's *Gulf Coasting* (www.gulf coasting.com) supplement to the *News-Press* covers the Island Coast's entertainment scene.

Cape Coral

Jimbob's (239-574-8100; 1431 SE 16th Place, Cape Coral 33904) Live music on weekends.

Waterford Ballroom (239-945-0034, 4646 SE 11th Place, Cape Coral 33904) Dinner dance every Wednesday evening and live band Thursday through Saturday.

Captiva Island

Crow's Nest Lounge (239-472-5161; 'Tween Waters Inn, 15951 Captiva Rd 33924) Live contemporary dance bands Tuesday through Sunday; entertaining crab races on Monday. The islands' hottest spot.

Fort Myers

Blackhawk Café (239-433-3333; 9101 College Pkwy., Fort Myers 33919) Fun and affordable bar/café with live music weekends.

Brick Bar (239-332-2228; 2224 Bay St., Fort Myers 33901; downtown) In a restored warehouse above a restaurant, it spotlights blues bands in a cozy setting Wednesday through Saturday.

Club Salsa at Marina Lounge (239-454-8595; 2500 Edwards Dr., Fort Myers 33901; downtown) The newest, hottest addition to downtown's night crawler's scene, featuring live salsa and merengue bands; dance lessons available.

Indigo Room (239-332-0014; 2219 Main St., Fort Myers 33901; downtown) *The* happening late-night scene, with rock and blues bands on stage.

Jazz Alliance (239-939-2787; 10091 McGregor Blvd., Fort Myers 33919; at the Lee County Alliance of the Arts headquarters) Sponsors a series of three springtime outdoor concerts featuring name artists, fine wine, and specialty foods.

Liquid Café (239-461-0444; 2236 First St., Fort Myers 33901; downtown) A sophisticated eatery with world beat and jazz musicians on stage.

Lido Café (239-461-5562; 2213 Main St., Fort Myers 33901; downtown) Upscale nightclub and restaurant ala Miami's South Beach, complete with DJs and VIP loft.

Shooters Waterfront Café (239-334-2727; 2220 W. First St., Fort Myers 33901; at the Holiday Inn Sunspree) A lively spot on the river with outdoor bar and live music. Have dinner elsewhere if you're discriminating.

Southwest Florida Jazz Society (239-945-0556; 167 S.W. 53rd St., Cape Coral 33914 or PO Box 07233, Fort Myers 33919) Sponsors a series of concerts at Cape Coral Yacht & Racquet Club (239-574-0806; 5819 Driftwood Pkwy., Cape Coral 33904) October through March and year-round Tuesday and Sunday jam sessions at local clubs.

Southwest Florida Symphony (239-418-1500; www.swflso.org ; 4560 Via Royale, Suite 2, Fort Myers 33919) Performs classical and pops series November through April at Barbara B. Mann Hall in Fort Myers and occasionally at BIG Arts on Sanibel Island.

Fort Myers Beach

Fort Myers Beach is known for its bar-hopping scene and sand castles.

Karen T. Bartlett

The Bridge Restaurant (239-765-0050; 708 Fisherman's Wharf, Fort Myers Beach 33931) A popular spot with boat-in and drive-in barflies, featuring lively dance music outdoors on the docks, including a reggae party every Sunday afternoon and evening.

Lani Kai Island Resort (239-463-3111; 1400 Estero Blvd., Fort Myers Beach 33931) The premier collegiate party spot on the beach, with live entertainment nightly and during the day on weekends, on the rooftop or on the beach.

Orpheus Café (239-463-1549; 1165 Estero Blvd., Fort Myers Beach 33931) A notch above other beach nightlife, offering jazz and world-beat entertainment.

Pine Island

Starboard Lounge and Grill (239-282-1131; 3421 Stringfellow Rd., St. James City 33956) The Banana Tree Stage hosts concerts under the stars every Friday nights, usually showcasing local talent. Pool tables provide the other source of entertainment.

Sanibel Island

BIG Arts (239-395-0900; www.bigarts.org; 900 Dunlop Rd., Sanibel Island 33957) Hosts classical musical quartets and trios, and orchestras November through April.

Jacaranda (239-472-1771; 1223 Periwinkle Way, Sanibel Island 33957) Top-40 hits, reggae, and island music performed live.

SPECIALTY LIBRARIES

For regional reference information by phone, call 239-479-INFO.

Florida Gulf Coast University Library (239-590-7610; 10501 FGCU Blvd. S, Fort Myers 33965; at Ben Hill Griffin Pkwy.) An Internet lab with 40 computer stations.

Sanibel Public Library (239-472-2483; 770 Dunlop Rd., Sanibel Island 33957) Contains an identification collection of seashells and Internet access computers by reservation.

Talking Books Library (239-995-2665; 1324 N. Cleveland Ave., N. Fort Myers 33903) Library for the blind and physically handicapped, with books on tapes or records.

THEATER

The Arcade Theatre/Florida Repertory Theatre (239-332-4488; www.floridarep.org; 2267 First St., PO Drawer 2483, Fort Myers 33902; downtown) The glory of the 1920s, this Victorian playhouse has been restored and advanced to the 21st century. Home to an energetic professional company that brings new life to old boards.

Barbara B. Mann Performing Arts Center (239-481-4849; www.bbmannpah. com; Edison Community College campus, 8099 College Pkwy. SW, Fort Myers 33919) Hosts major Broadway shows, musical performers, and dance troupes. Season runs September to late April.

Broadway Palm Dinner Theatre (239-278-4422; www.broadwaypalm.com; 1380 Colonial Blvd., Fort Myers 33907; at Royal Palm Square) Lunch and dinner musical performances starring professional actors in a made-over grocery store that seats and serves 448. Its Off-Broadway Palm Theatre presents cabaret-style shows in an adjacent, intimate ninety-seat playhouse. Lunch and dinner shows or shows only. Both closed Monday and some Tuesdays.

Clairborne & Ned Foulds Theater (239-936-3239; 10091 McGregor Blvd., Fort Myers 33919; at Lee County Alliance of the Arts headquarters) An indoor and outdoor stage for recitals, concerts, and workshops. Theatre Conspiracy, a cutting-edge, professional troupe that occasionally stages family shows performs part of its season here.

Cultural Park Theatre (239-772-5862; 528 Cultural Park Blvd., Cape Coral 33990) A 187-seat theater that hosts Cape Coral Community Theatre and Gulf Coast Opera Company.

J. Howard Wood Theatre (239-472-0006; www.thewoodtheatre.com; 2200 Periwinkle Way, Sanibel Island 33957) Formerly Pirate Playhouse. Professional actors present main-stage comedies, musicals, and drama in two seasons on a stage adaptable to proscenium, theater-in-the-round, and thrust configurations.

The J. Howard Wood Theatre, formerly the Pirate Playhouse, stages professional comedies and dramas in an intimate setting.

Karen T. Bartlett

Old Schoolhouse Theater (239-472-6862; www.oldschoolhousetheater.com; 1905 Periwinkle Way, Sanibel Island 33957) Installed in the charming setting of a historic one-room schoolhouse circa 1896, this 96-seat theater-in-the-round has served for years as the island's cultural mainstay. In its current incarnation it hosts J. T. Smith Musical Productions, a professional troupe.

TECO Arena (239-948-7825; 11000 Everblades Pkwy., Estero 33928) Home of the Everblades hockey team, it also hosts touring entertainers.

VISUAL ART CENTERS

Flocks of wildlife art and other eclectic galleries make a name for Sanibel Island in cultural circles, while smaller communities support their own off-beat galleries and art associations. On Pine Island, national artists come to hide out and renourish their souls, which has sparked a growing art colony of sorts, centered in Matlacha. The following entries introduce you to opportunities for experiencing art as either a viewer or a practicing artist. A listing of commercial galleries is included in the "Shopping" section.

Alliance of the Arts (239-939-2787; www.artinlee.org; 10091 McGregor Blvd., Fort Myers 33919) Operates a public gallery, members' gallery, 175-seat indoor theater, and outdoor stage, and conducts classes and workshops. Home to Theatre Conspiracy troupe and most local arts and cultural groups.

BIG Arts (239-395-0900; www.bigarts.org; 900 Dunlop Rd., Sanibel Island 33957) Home of Barrier Island Group for the Arts, an energetic multidisciplinary organization. Art shows and classes are scheduled regularly at the facility.

Cape Coral Arts Studio (239-574-0802; 4533 Coronado Pkwy., Cape Coral 33904) Exhibitions and sales.

Cultural Park Theatre Fine Arts Gallery (239-772-5862; 516 Cultural Park Blvd., Cape Coral 33990) Rotating exhibits of local art.

Fort Myers Beach Art Association (239-463-3909; Donora St. and Shell Mound Blvd., PO Box 2359, Fort Myers Beach 33932)

Frizzell Gallery of Fine Art (239-939-2787; Lee County Alliance of the Arts, 10091 McGregor Blvd., Fort Myers 33919) Changing exhibits in all media.

Gallery of Fine Arts (239-489-9313, Edison Community College, 8099 College Pkwy. SW, Fort Myers 33919) Exhibits works of nationally and internationally renowned artists.

RECREATION

Shelling, island-hopping, fishing, sailboarding, and warming chilled bones on hospitable beaches: These are a few of the favorite things to do along the Island Coast.

BEACHES

The Island Coast's 50 miles of local beach are known for their natural state and abundance of shells. *FamilyFun* magazine recently rated them the "#1 beach in the southeast U.S." Most charge for parking. Sanibel Island beach stickers can be purchased and allow you to park for free at most accesses. Along the Gulf Drives you will see signs at beach accesses designating resident sticker-only parking. Cyclists and walk-ins, however, can take advantage of these accesses without stickers. For more information about beach stickers, call 239-472-9075.

Bonita Beach

BAREFOOT BEACH PRESERVE
Collier County Parks & Recreation Dept.
239-353-0404,
   fax 239-353-1002.
www.co.fl.us/parks/collier countyp.
3300 Santa Barbara Blvd., Naples 34116.
Entrance at Hickory Blvd. and Bonita Beach Rd., south end of Little Hickory Island.
Facilities: Rest rooms, showers; nature learning center, aquatic butterfly garden; snack bar.
Parking: $3 per day.

Actually within neighboring Collier County but accessible from Bonita Beach, this preserve holds 342 acres that contain a coastal hammock and 8,200 feet of beach and low dunes. Sea grapes, cabbage palms, and other native vegetation landscape the grounds. Gopher tortoises often lumber across the road and footpaths. Rangers give nature walks and shell talks at the chickee learning center.

Karen T. Bartlett

Happy-go-lucky on Bonita Beach.

BONITA BEACH PARK
239-461-7400.
South end of Hickory Blvd.,
    Little Hickory Island.
Facilities: Picnic table
    shelters, rest rooms,
    lifeguard, water-sports
    and beach rentals, nearby
    restaurants.
Parking: 75¢ per hour.

The only true public park on Bonita Beach, it becomes lively during high season and on weekends. Water sports and volleyball, plus a hamburger and bar joint, create a youthful spirit. Vegetation is sparse; there's nothing hidden about this beach. Parking fills up early in season and on weekends year-round. About 10 other accesses with free but limited parking line Hickory Boulevard to the north.

Cape Coral

CAPE CORAL YACHT CLUB
239-574-0815.
5819 Driftwood Pkwy.,
    Cape Coral 33904.
Facilities: Restrooms,
    showers, picnic shelters,
    swimming pool, marina,
    shuffleboard, outdoor
    racquetball courts, fishing
    pier.
Open: Swimming pool
    (239-542-3903) open
    10am–5pm daily.
Admission: Free. Pool
    admission is $3.50 for
    ages 18 and up, $2.50 for
    10–17, and $1.50 for 9 and
    younger.

The man-made beach on the Caloosahatchee River is part of a large park that sponsors recreational and other programs and exudes a true sense of community. The groomed beach is better for sunning than swimming, for which the pool fills the void.

Captiva Island

CAPTIVA BEACH
North end Captiva Rd.,
   Captiva Island.
Parking: 75¢ per hour.

Only early arrivals get the parking spots for this prime spread of deep, shelly sand. It's a good place to watch a sunset.

Fort Myers

**LAKES REGIONAL
   PARK**
239-432-2000.
7330 Gladiolus Dr., Fort
   Myers 33908.
Facilities: Picnic areas, rest
   rooms, showers;
   playgrounds, model
   railroad ride, fitness trail,
   bike path; water-sports
   rentals; restaurant.
Parking: 75¢ per hour or $3
   per day.

This land of freshwater lakes features a small sand beach with a roped-off swimming area. The quality of the water is questionable, since the lakes — erstwhile quarries — are stagnant. A great place for the family to spend the day, it offers canoeing, paddleboating, fishing, nature and bike trails, an exercise course, an observation tower, a miniature train ride (admission), and terrific playground facilities within 277 heavily vegetated acres. The newest playground, Florida Cypress Swamp, opened May 2001, and provides wet fun with 17 squirting, spraying, and splashing frogs, snakes, and birds.

Fort Myers Beach

BOWDITCH BEACH
239-441-7400.
50 Estero Blvd., Fort Myers
   Beach 33931.
At the north end.
Facilities: Picnic shelters,
   rest rooms, showers;
   hiking paths.
Parking: 75¢ per hour.

This pretty, green, 17-acre park fronts Estero Bay and the gulf. It's a nice, quiet beach, underutilized and unspoiled. It's a favorite of boat-ins.

Aptly named Lovers Key.

Karen T. Bartlett

LOVERS KEY STATE PARK
239-463-4588.
8700 Estero Blvd., Fort Myers Beach 33931.
Route 865 between Fort Myers Beach and Bonita Beach.
Facilities: Picnic area, rest rooms, showers; boat ramps, fishing, camping, canoe and kayak rentals, bike rentals; food concession, beach shop.
Parking: $4 per vehicle with up to 8 passengers, $2 for single passengers, $1 for extra passengers, bicyclists, and pedestrians.

Ride a truck-pulled tram through the natural mangrove environment to South Beach. Or you can walk to secluded North Beach. The area between Estero and Little Hickory Island consists of natural island habitat populated by birds, dolphins, and crabs. On the barrier island of Lovers Key, Australian pines provide shaded picnicking along a narrow, natural stretch of sand that is due for renourishing in coming years. A segment of the beach, dubbed dog beach, was recently designated the couny's only off-leash dog park. A gazebo provides a picnic shelter and a popular wedding venue. Away from the beach, shaded picnic and camping grounds line estuarine inlets with a launch for canoes and kayaks, and a path accommodates hikers and cyclists. You can also kayak off the beach or across the road from the park entrance into Estero Bay.

LYNN HALL MEMORIAL PARK
239-461-7400.
Estero Blvd., Fort Myers Beach.
In the Times Square vicinity.
Facilities: Picnic areas, rest rooms, showers; playground, fishing pier, water-sports rentals; nearby restaurants and bars.
Admission: Metered parking. (*Warning:* Park only in designated areas, or your car will be towed at great expense.)

Part of the new pedestrian Times Square plaza, it attracts college students in the spring and families the rest of the year. A rocking, rollicking place, it appeals to beach bar hoppers, crowd watchers, and those interested in water sports, with volleyball, a fishing pier, beachwear stores, restaurants, ice cream shops, beachside drinks, parties, parasailing, jet skiing. For thinner crowds, hit public accesses on the south end of Estero Boulevard.

Sanibel Island

BOWMAN'S BEACH
Bowman's Beach Rd. off Sanibel-Captiva Rd., Sanibel Island.
Facilities: Picnic area, rest rooms.
Parking: 75¢ per hour.

Bowman's is Sanibel's most natural beach — long, coved, and edged by an Australian pine forest — on an island all its own. It can be reached by footbridges from the parking lot (a rather long walk, so go lightly on the beach paraphernalia). Shells are plentiful here — in some places a foot or more deep along the high-tide mark.

LIGHTHOUSE BEACH
239-472-6477 (Sanibel Parks
& Recreaton Dept.).
South end of Periwinkle
Way, Sanibel Island.
Facilities: Picnic area, rest
rooms, nature trail,
fishing pier.
Parking: 75¢ per hour.

Skirting Sanibel Island's historic lighthouse is an arc of natural beach fronting both the gulf and San Carlos Bay. One of Sanibel's most populated beaches, its highlights include a nature trail and a fishing pier. Strong currents forbid swimming off the point. The wide beach gives way to sea oats, sea grapes, and Australian pine edging. I like the neighborhood around it — historic and more laid-back than other parts of the island.

**SANIBEL CAUSEWAY
BEACH**
239-472-6477.
Sanibel Causeway Rd.
Facilities: Picnic area, rest
rooms.

Windsurfers and fishermen especially favor this packed-sand roadside beach. It's been dressed up with palms and pines, but it's still noisy and typically jammed. Beach lovers in RVs and campers often pull up here to picnic and spend the day in the sun.

TARPON BEACH
239-472-6477.
Middle Gulf Dr. at Tarpon
Bay Rd., Sanibel Island.
Facilities: Rest rooms,
mobile food concession
in season.
Parking: 75¢ per hour.

Another popular beach, this one is characterized by sugar sand and a nice spread of shells. It's a bit of a hike from the parking lot to the beach, and the area gets congested on busy days. RVs can park here. Great for swimming.

TURNER BEACH
239-472-6477.
South end Captiva Rd.,
Captiva Island.
Facilities: Rest rooms,
nearby restaurants, water
sports, and store.
Parking: 75¢ per hour.

A pretty beach with wide, powdery sand, Turner tends to get crowded, and parking is limited. The entrance is on a blind curve, which can be dangerous. More bad news: Riptides coming through the pass make this taboo for swimming. Park your beach towel far north or south of the pass for calmer, swimmable waters. We like to come here in the evening to watch the sunset and walk the beach. Surfers like the waters to the north in certain weather. It's also a hot spot for fishermen, who line bayside shores and the bridge between Sanibel and Captiva.

Upper Islands

**CAYO COSTA ISLAND
STATE PARK**
239-964-0375.
La Costa Island, accessible
only by boat.
Facilities: Picnic ground,
rest rooms, showers.

The Island Coast is blessed with some true get-away beaches, untamed by connection to the mainland. On these, one can actually realize that romantic fantasy common to beach connoisseurs — sands all your own. Cayo Costa stretches 7 miles long and is most secluded at its southern extremes.

Admission: $1 per person.

A larger population of beachers congregates at the north end, where docks and a picnic and camping ground attract those who seek creature comforts with their sun and sand. Shelling is superb in these parts, particularly at Johnson Shoals, which surfaces at the island's north end.

UPPER CAPTIVA
Across Redfish Pass from South Seas Resort and Captiva Island; accessible only by boat.

Like Cayo Costa, here's a place to go for private beaching. Though it's narrow at the south end, which is state protected, the sand is like gold dust You'll find no facilities unless you venture across the island to the bay, where restaurants and civilization inhabit the north end.

BICYCLING

Sanibel's twenty-three miles of paved bike paths take you past wildlife habitat and historic sites such as this theater, once a school for pioneer children.

Karen T. Bartlett

The bikeways of the Island Coast come in two varieties. Bicycle paths, the most common, are separated from traffic by distance and, ideally, a vegetation buffer. Bicycle lanes are a designated part of the roadway. Cyclists also take to the road in rural areas, where no bikeways exist but traffic is light. By law they must abide by the same rules as motor vehicles. Children under age 16 are required to wear a helmet.

BEST BIKING

Bike trails run through Lakes Park, where bike rentals are also available. Long stretches of bike path in Fort Myers run along Daniels Parkway, Metro Parkway, and Summerlin Road. The Summerlin path leads to the Sanibel causeway (bikers cross for $1), to connect with island paths. McGregor

Boulevard's sidewalk provides another popular and scenic circuit. Bike paths also wind through Lovers Key State Recreation Area and rentals are available there as well.

Many of Cape Coral's city streets designate bike lanes. Serious bikers favor Burnt Store Marina Road, which goes to Charlotte County from the northwest side of town.

Sanibel's 23-mile path covers most of the island and occasionally leaves the roadside to plunge you into serene backwoods scenery. Segments along busy Periwinkle Way have recently been widened and moved away from roadside. The Sanibel Historical Society (239-472-4648) distributes brochures on *Pedaling Periwinkle Way* and exploring by bike or foot Old Sanibel around the lighthouse at the east end.

A short, sporadic bike path/route travels through Bokeelia and St. James City on Pine Island.

A bike path runs the length of Bonita Beach, nearly 3 miles long, and connects to another at its south end, which leads to Vanderbilt Beach. See Chapter Six, *Naples & the South Coast*.

RENTAL/SALES

A. J. Barnes Bicycle Emporium (239-772-2453; 1109 Del Prado Blvd., Cape Coral 33990) Rentals and sales.

Billy's Rentals (239-472-5248; 1470 Periwinkle Way, Sanibel Island 33957) Bicycles, surrey bikes, and equipment for family biking. Also scooters and beach gear. Rentals by hour, day, or week.

Bonita Beach Bike (239-947-6377; 4892 Bonita Beach Rd., Bonita Beach 34134; at Bonita Harbor Plaza) A variety of bikes including kids', trailers for kids, and beach and jogging strollers.

Fun Rentals (239-463-8844; 1901 Estero Blvd., Fort Myers Beach 33931) Rentals and repairs.

Jim's Rentals (239-472-1296; www.yolo-jims.com; 11534 Andy Rosse Ln., Captiva Island 33924) Rentals by the half-day, full-day, and 24 hours. Also in-line skates.

Kayak Shack (239-765-1880; 8700 Estero Blvd., Fort Myers Beach 33931) Rent children's and adult bikes for use in Lovers Key State Recreation Area and vicinity.

BOATS & BOATING

With its procession of unbridged islands and wide bay, the Island Coast begs for outdoor types to explore her waters. Island-hopping constitutes a favorite pastime of adventurers.

Try kayaking as a form of fun — and environmentally correct — recreation.

Karen T. Bartlett

CANOEING & KAYAKING

Many resorts and parks rent canoes, in addition to those outlets listed below.

Adventure Sea Kayaking (239-437-0956; sanibelkayaking@compuserve.com; 'Tween Waters Marina, 15951 Captiva Rd., Captiva Island 33924; 1641 S. Fountainhead Rd., Fort Myers 33919) Owner Brian Houston is well-known for his kayaking enthusiasm and nationwide promotion. He is the force behind the annual Captiva Kayak Classic (see Events). From 'Tween Waters, he offers instruction in kayak operation and guided tours in local waters.

Estero River Tackle and Canoe Outfitters (239-992-4050; 20991 S. Tamiami Trail, Estero 33928; opposite Koreshan Historic Site) Rents and outfits canoes for a 4-mile adventure down the natural Estero River to Estero Bay.

G.R. Boating (239-947-4889; 4892 Bonita Beach Rd., Bonita Springs 34134; near the public beach) Rents canoes and kayaks.

Gulf Coast Kayak Company (239-283-1125; 4530 Pine Island Rd., Matlacha 33993 Pine Island) Morning nature and sunset trips in the Matlacha Aquatic Preserve and other local natural areas; full moon and manatee nature (Thanksgiving through St. Patrick's Day only) ventures.

Kayak Shack (239-765-1880; www.tarponbay.com; Lovers Key State Park, 8700 Estero Blvd., Fort Myers Beach 33931) Rents canoes, kayaks, and rudder kayaks for bay and sea ventures. Paddle tours and fishing-outfitted canoes also available.

Lakes Park (239-432-2000; 7330 Gladiolus Dr., Fort Myers 33908) Canoe rentals for paddling on freshwater lakes.

Tarpon Bay Recreation (239-472-8900; www.tarponbay.com; 900 Tarpon Bay Rd., Sanibel Island 33957) Rents canoes and kayaks for use in the bay and through "Ding" Darling Refuge's Commodore Creek Canoe Trail. Also, guided canoe/kayak tours. *Canoe & Kayak* magazine has rated Tarpon Bay among the top 10 places to paddle in the U.S. Its gift shop, incidentally, has one of the best selections of T-shirts on the island.

Tropic Star Cruises (239-283-0015; www.tropicstarcruises.com; 16499 Porto Bello St., Bokeelia 33922; on Pine Island) Rent kayaks for half- and full-day trips from Bokeelia and Cayo Costa. Singles and doubles are available.

WildSide Adventures (239-395-2925; McCarthy's Marina, 15041 Captiva Dr., Captiva Island 33924) Sea-kayaking tours focus on natural history, and sea life; sunrise, sunset, starlight, full moon, and children's adventures. Kayak and canoe rentals are available; delivery and pickup.

DINING CRUISES

Big M Casino (239-765-7529; www.bigmcasino.com; Moss Marine, 450 Harbor Ct., Fort Myers Beach 33931) Gambling cruise with live entertainment and buffet and á la carte dining.

J. C. Cruises (239-334-7474; Fort Myers Yacht Basin, PO Box 1688, Fort Myers 33902; downtown) Lunch and dinner cruises up the Caloosahatchee River aboard the *Capt. J.P.*, a three-deck paddlewheeler. Not available in summer.

Sanibel Harbour *Princess II* (239-466-2128; 17260 Harbour Pointe Dr., Fort Myers 33908; at Sanibel Harbour Resort, off Summerlin Rd. before Sanibel Island causeway) Sunset dinner buffet and hors d'oeuvre cruises aboard a sleek, elegant 100-foot luxury yacht.

PERSONAL WATERCRAFT RENTALS/TOURS

Holiday Water Sports (239-765-4386; www.ridewaves.com; Best Western Pink Shell Resort, 250 Estero Blvd. Fort Myers Beach 33931 and 239-463-6778, Best Western Beach Resort, 684 Estero Blvd., Fort Myers Beach 33931) Waverunner rentals, lessons, and dolphin-spotting/heritage tours.

POWERBOAT RENTALS

The Boat House (239-472-2531; Sanibel Marina, 634 N. Yachtsman Dr., Sanibel Island 33957) Powerboats for trips into intracoastal waters only.

Dockside Boat Rentals (239-765-4433, 275 Estero Blvd., Fort Myers Beach 33931; at Pink Shell Resort; and 239-772-4463; 2401 Andalusia Blvd., Cape Coral 33909) 18- to 22-foot bowriders, pontoons, and water-ski equipment.

Fish-Tale Marina (239-463-4448; 7225 Estero Blvd., Fort Myers Beach 33931) Grady Whites, 24-foot pontoons and center-console boats for rent.

Florida Houseboat Rentals (239-945-2628; 1227 SW 52nd Terrace, Cape Coral 33914) 41-foot air-conditioned houseboats for three- to seven-day cruises. Full galley and fishing gear included.

Four Winds Marina (239-283-0250; 16501 Stringfellow Rd., Bokeelia 33922; Pine Island) 19- to 21-foot powerboats.

G. R. Boating (239-947-4889 4892 Bonita Beach Rd., Bonita Beach 34134; near the public beach) Rents skiffs, pontoon, and deck boats.

Manatee Fun Boat Charter (239-540-9666, mobile 410-2020; 4536 SE 16th Pl., Cape Coral 33904) Skippered or nonskippered boat rentals from 16 to 45 feet, also jet skis.

Southwest Florida Yachts (239-656-1339, 800-262-SWFY; www.swfyachts.com; 3444 Marinatown Ln., Suite 19, North Fort Myers 33903) Offers power-yachting lessons and rentals in the 32- to 43-foot range. Courses include off-shore navigation, electronic navigation, overnight anchoring, advanced marlinspike, and others.

Sweet Water Boat Rentals (239-472-6336; 15951 Captiva Dr., Captiva 33924; at 'Tween Waters Inn Marina) Rents 19-foot center-console boats holding up to six passengers.

PUBLIC BOAT RAMPS

Cape Coral Yacht Club (239-574-0815; 5819 Driftwood Pkwy., Cape Coral 33904) Two free public ramps on the Caloosahatchee River, with recreational facilities.

Lovers Key State Park (8700 Estero Blvd., Fort Myers Beach 33931; at Route 865 between Fort Myers Beach and Bonita Beach) Access to Estero Bay and the gulf, with picnicking and kayak rentals.

Matlacha Park (Matlacha, Pine Island) Playground and fishing pier.

Punta Rassa (Summerlin Rd., Fort Myers, before the Sanibel causeway) Picnic facilities and rest rooms.

Sanibel (Causeway Rd.) Two ramps at the west end of the Sanibel causeway.

SAILBOAT CHARTERS

Set sail for an adventure on a chartered sailboat.

Karen T. Bartlett

Adventure Sailing Charters (239-472-5300; South Seas Resort, Captiva Island 33924) Two-hour, sunset, half- and full-day captained charters aboard a 30-foot sloop. Passengers are encouraged to participate.

New Moon (239-395-1782; www.newmoonsailing.com; 'Tween Waters Inn Marina, 15951 Captive Dr., Captiva Island 33924) Up to six passengers aboard a 35-foot sloop. Sailing classes for kids and adults and rentals available.

SAILBOAT RENTALS & INSTRUCTION

Offshore Sailing School (239-454-1700, 800-221-4326; www.offshore-sailing.com; 16731 McGregor Blvd., Fort Myers 33908; at South Seas Resort Marina on Captiva Island) Week-long certification (US SAILING) instruction offered, from beginning women's-only and mixed sailing courses to advanced racing and bareboat cruising preparation; operated by an Olympic and America's Cup veteran. Course instructors are knowledgeable, experienced, and easygoing ("no yelling" is the rule). Accommodation packages with South Seas Resort available.

Southwest Florida Yachts/Florida Sailing & Cruising School (239-656-1339, 800-262-SWFY; www.flsailandcruiseschool.com; 3444 Marinatown Ln. NW, Suite 19, N. Fort Myers 33903) American Sailing Association (ASA) certification courses and bareboat charters provide excellent adventures into Charlotte Harbor for live-aboard experiences. Also powerboat courses.

SIGHTSEEING & ENTERTAINMENT CRUISES

Captiva Cruises (239-472-5300; South Seas Resort, PO Box 194, Captiva Island 33924) A complete menu of sightseeing, upper island, and luncheon trips aboard the finely fitted 150-passenger *Lady Chadwick*, with history and lore lessons along the way. The only way, as a nonguest, to see private Useppa Island, where you can enjoy lunch at the Collier Inn restaurant.

Cookie Cutter (239-574-0806; Cape Coral Yacht Club, 5819 Driftwood Pkwy., Cape Coral 33904) Sunset and dolphin-spotting cruises, with appetizers and beverages.

J. C. Cruises (239-334-7474, 239-334-2743; PO Box 1688, Fort Myers 33902; at Fort Myers Yacht Basin) Sightseeing jungle cruises in summer.

Sun Princess (239-466-4000, ext. 2991; 17260 Harbour Pointe Dr., Fort Myers 33908; at Sanibel Harbour Resort) Beach and lunch tour that takes you to the upper islands for shelling, swimming, and lunch in a restaurant on an unbridged island. The captain who runs this tour is quite knowledgeable on local archaeology and history, making this a fascinating trip.

Tropic Star Cruises (239-283-0015; www.tropicstarcruises.com; 16499 Porto Bello St., Bokeelia 33922; on Pine Island)) Full-day nature cruises and ferry service to Cayo Costa.

FISHING

Snook and tarpon are the prized catch of local anglers. Snook, which is a game fish and cannot be sold commercially, is valued for its sweet taste
Redfish is another sought-after food fish. More common catches in back bays and waters close to shore include mangrove snapper, spotted sea trout, shark, sheepshead, pompano, and ladyfish. Deeper waters offshore yield grouper, red snapper, amberjack, mackerel, and dolphinfish. Most fish are released in these days of environmental consciousness. Check local regulations for season, size, and catch restrictions.

Nonresidents age 16 and over must obtain a license unless fishing from a vessel or pier covered by its own license. Inexpensive, temporary nonresident licenses are available at county tax collectors' offices and at most Kmarts, marinas, and bait shops.

DEEP-SEA PARTY BOATS

Getaway Deep Sea Fishing (239-466-3600; Getaway Marina, 18400 San Carlos Blvd., Fort Myers Beach 33931) Excursions are aboard a ninety-foot craft for all day or half day.

FISHING CHARTERS/OUTFITTERS

Competent fishing guides work out of the region's major marinas. If it's your first time fishing these waters, I recommend hiring someone with local knowledge.

Captain Mike Fuery (239-466-3649; PO Box 1302, Captiva Island, FL33924) Located at 'Tween Waters Inn Marina, he has a good reputation for finding fish.

Dockside Boat Rentals (239-765-4433; Pink Shell Resort, 275 Estero Blvd., Fort Myers Beach 33931) Four-hour trips aboard a 34-foot pontoon boat. Also shelling and nature tours, water-skiing, and tubing.

Estero Bay Boat Tours (239-992-2200; www.ecotours-esterobay.com; 5231 Mamie St., Bonita Springs 34134; at Weeks Fish Camp, end of Coconut Rd.) The Weeks family has been fishing these waters for generations.

Capt. Pat Hagle Charters (239-283-5991; captpathagle@aol.com; PO Box 245, Pineland 33945) Fish excursions into Pine Island Sound; also nature, history, shelling, beachcombing, and water-taxi cruises.

Lee County Professional Guides Association (239-337-1118)

Mangrove Fishing Adventures (239-395-9647; PO Box 1712, Sanibel Island 33957) Eco-fishing trips into J. N. "Ding" Darling National Wildlife Refuge and offshore.

Puddlejumper II (239-992-6752; puddlejumper2@mindspring.com; 26107 Hickory Blvd., Bonita Springs 34134; at Big Hickory Marina) Captain Bruce Clark takes you out on four-hour near shore and half- and full-day offshore excursions. Maximum six people.

Sanibel Marina (239-472-2723; 634 N. Yachtsman Dr., Sanibel Island 33957) Several experienced fishing guides operate out of the marina. Captain Dave Case (home phone 239-472-2798) has been at it a long time.

Fishing Piers

Cape Coral Yacht Club (239-574-0815; 5819 Driftwood Pkwy., Cape Coral 33904) The 620-foot lit fishing pier is part of a boating/recreational complex. Bait and tackle shop.

Centennial Park (Edwards Dr. near Yacht Basin, downtown Fort Myers) Complete park with playgrounds and other facilities.

Fort Myers Beach Pier (1000 Estero Blvd., Fort Myers Beach 33931; at Lynn Hall Memorial Park, Times Square) The pier holds a bait shop (239-765-9700), which also rents rods, and offers lots of casting room and hungry pelicans.

Manatee Park (239-432-2004, 239-694-3537; 10901 Route 80, Fort Myers 33905) On the Orange River.

Matlacha Park (Matlacha, Pine Island) Playground and boat ramps.

Sanibel Lighthouse Beach (southeast end of Periwinkle Way, Sanibel Island) A T-dock into San Carlos Bay.

GOLF

Home of such golfing greats as Patty Berg and Nolan Henke, the Island Coast keeps pace with the growing popularity of golf.

Public Golf Courses

Alden Pines (239-283-2179; 14261 Clubhouse Dr., Bokeelia 33922; on Pine Island) Semiprivate, 18 holes, par 71, with affordable rates year-round. Snack bar.

Bay Beach Golf Club (239-463-2064; 7401 Estero Blvd., Fort Myers Beach 33931) 18 holes, par 60. Affordable rates.

Cape Coral Golf and Tennis (239-542-7879; 4003 Palm Tree Blvd., Cape Coral 33909) 18 holes, par 72. Restaurant and bar.

Dunes Golf & Tennis Club (239-472-2535; 949 Sandcastle Rd., Sanibel Island 33957) Semiprivate 18-hole, par-70 course. Restaurant and bar. Lush, Audubon-preserve links. High rates, especially in season.

Eastwood Country Club (239-275-4848; 4600 Bruce Heard Ln., Fort Myers 33994) One of the region's favorites; 18 holes located away from traffic.

Fort Myers Country Club (239-936-2457; 3591 McGregor Blvd., Fort Myers 33901) Fort Myers's oldest. 18 holes, par 71. Restaurant and lounge.

Summerlin Ridge Golf Course (239-432-0000; 16660 Pine Ridge Rd., Fort Myers 33908) New, lit 18-hole executive course, popular during hot summer days. Driving range and snack bar.

HEALTH & FITNESS CLUBS

Gold's Gym (239-549-3354; 1013 Cape Coral Pkwy. E, Cape Coral 33904) Classes in spinning, step aerobics, body flex, yoga, and karate. Personal training.

Sanibel Fitness Center (239-395-2639; 975 Rabbit Rd., Sanibel Island 33957) Aerobics, free weights, cardiovascular and personal training, classes, dance, martial arts, yoga, seniors program, "mousercize" for kids. Short-term memberships (one to six days) available.

Sanibel Recreation Center (239-472-0345; 3840 Sanibel-Captiva Rd., Sanibel Island 33957; at Sanibel School) Outdoor lap pool, tennis courts, weight room, basketball courts. City owned and operated. No admission fees.

HIKING

Cayo Costa State Island Preserve (239-964-0375; PO Box 1150, Boca Grande 33921; at Barrier Islands GEO Park, LaCosta Island) Six miles of trail take you through barrier island ecology, pioneer cemetery, and remnants of a circa-1904 quarantine station.

Sanibel-Captiva Conservation Foundation (239-472-2329; www.sccf.org; 3333 Sanibel-Captiva Rd., PO Box 839, Sanibel Island 33957) Four miles through natural habitat along the Sanibel River. The majority of wildlife consists of birds, lizards, and insects.

KIDS' STUFF

BMX Park (239-458-1943; 1410 SW Sixth Place, Cape Coral 33991) A Bicycle Moto-Cross track is provided for practice and weekly races, along with picnic grounds, a playground, a softball field, and a sand volleyball court.

Fort Myers Skatium (239-461-3145; www.fortmyersskatium.com; 2250 Broadway, Fort Myers 33901) Open indoor in-line and ice skating, plus hockey and in-line leagues. The in-line rink has jumps and ramps; plus there's also a laser tag game. Hours vary. Cost is $5 for children ages 12 and under, $7 for adults, $3 for skate rental.

Greenwell's Bat-A-Ball and Family Fun Park (239-574-4386; 35 NE Pine Island Rd., Cape Coral 33909) Named after the city's favorite sports son, Red Sox player Mike Greenwell, it contains batting cages, a miniature golf course, a small playground, a maze, a video arcade, four go-cart tracks, and snack concessions. Kids really love it here, but be prepared to lay out a lot of money if you spend much time, especially in the arcade room.

Periwinkle Park (239-472-1433; 1119 Periwinkle Way, Sanibel Island 33957) The owner of this trailer park raises and breeds exotic birds and waterfowl. He daddies roughly 600 birds of 133 species, specializing in African and Asian hornbills. Flamingos, parakeets, cockatiels, cockatoos, and others occupy the park and 15 aviaries. During the off-season, visitors can drive through; in-season, biking is recommended. A few of the birds raised here can be seen more easily at **Jerry's Shopping Center** (1700 Periwinkle Way). Take the children in the evening, when the birds are most talkative.

Sanctuary Skate Park (239-337-5297; 2277 Grand Ave., Fort Myers 33901; downtown behind the Skatium) Skateboarders and in-liner skaters love this new city-owned outdoor facility with its cool ramps and half-pipes. Skate and pad rentals available. Admission: $7 for a three-hour session.

The Shell Factory (239-995-2141; www.shellfactory.com.; 888-4SHELLS; 2787 N. Tamiami Trail, N. Fort Myers 33903) A shell shop on steroids, this longtime attraction has grown into a megacomplex, still old-fashioned, with restaurants, bumper boats, a small wild animal zoo, stuffed African animal collection, aquariums, video games, and lots of souvenir shops carrying gifts from fine to tacky. Local kids can sign up for the free Kids Club, which hosts special family events. Admission to the Shell Factory is free; bumper boat rides $4 (free for child 44 inches or under riding with an adult).

Sun Splash Family Waterpark (239-574-0557; www.sunsplashwaterpark.com; 400 Santa Barbara Blvd, Cape Coral 33991) This spot offers wet fun in a dozen varieties, with pools, slides, flumes, a log roll, cable drops, a river ride, volleyball, food, lockers, and special events. Admission is $9.95 for guests 48 inches or taller, $7.95 for shorter children; $4.98 for senior citizens (plus tax). The hours here vary according to time of year; open daily May–Aug.

TECO Arena (239-948-7825; 11000 Everblades Pkwy., Estero 33928; off Interstate 75 at exit 19, at Corkscrew Rd.) The public can ice or in-line skate at one of the three indoor NHL-sized rinks daily (times vary) for $6 a one-hour and 45 minute session. Skate rental is $3. Sunday family skating is $4, with free rental for children nine and under. Learn-to-skate classes, ice-hockey league, in-line teams, and figure-skating club.

RACQUET SPORTS

Cape Coral Yacht Club Community Park (239-574-0815; 5819 Driftwood Pkwy., Cape Coral 33904) Two outdoor racquetball courts.

Fort Myers Racquet Club (239-278-7277; 4900 DeLeon St., Fort Myers 33907) Eight clay courts and two hard courts (eight lit), lessons, and tournaments. Admission.

Rutenberg Community Park (6500 S. Pointe Blvd., Fort Myers 33907)

Sanibel Recreation Complex (239-472-0345; 3840 Sanibel-Captiva Rd., Sanibel Island 33957; at Sanibel School) Four lit tennis courts.

Signal Inn Resort (239-472-4690; 1811 Olde Middle Gulf Dr., Sanibel Island 33957) Two racquetball courts. Admission.

STARS Complex (914-332-6671; 2980 Edison Ave., Fort Myers 33916; downtown Fort Myers)

SHELLING

A wealth of whelks.

Karen T. Bartlett

Welcome to shelling heaven. Sanibel Island, in particular, is known for its great pickings. Be aware that a state of Florida law prohibits the collection of live shells on Sanibel Island, to preclude the possibility of dwindling populations. Collecting live shells is also prohibited in state and national parks. Elsewhere in the county, live collecting is also discouraged. Any shell with a creature still inside is considered a live shell. Shellers who find live shells washed up on the beach — a common occurrence after storms — are urged to gently return (without flinging) the shell to deep water.

Hot Shelling Spots

Big Hickory Island (northwest of Little Hickory Island, accessible only by boat) An unhitched crook of beach favored by local boaters and shellers.

Bonita Beach (Little Hickory Island) Look north of the public beach.

La Costa Island (between Upper Captiva and Boca Grande, accessible only by boat) Because it takes a boat ride to get there, these sands hold caches of shells merely by virtue of their remoteness. North-end Johnson Shoals provides a thin strip of sandbar for good low-tide pickings.

Sanibel Island Known as the Shelling Capital of the Western Hemisphere, the island even has its own name for the peculiar, shell-bent stance of the beach collector: Sanibel Stoop. Unlike the other Gulf Coast barrier islands, Sanibel takes an east-west heading. Its perpendicular position and lack of offshore reefs allow it to intercept shells that arrive from southern seas. Its fame as a world-class shelling area has made Sanibel a prime destination for shell collectors for decades. With shell-named streets, store shelves awash in shells and shell crafts, an annual shell fair, and a shell museum, one risks suffering shell shock just by visiting there. Best gulf-side shelling spot: Bowman's Beach, midisland, away from the paths leading to the parking lot.

SHELLING CHARTERS

Adventures in Paradise (239-472-8443 , 239-437-1660; 14341 Port Comfort Rd., Fort Myers 33908; at Port Sanibel Marina, east of Sanibel toll booth) Shelling and snorkeling excursions to Cayo Costa aboard a 45-foot catamaran.

Capt. Mike Fuery's Shelling Charters (239-466-3649; PO 1302, Captiva Island 33924) A local shelling expert who authors how-to columns for the local paper takes small groups to Cayo Costa, Johnson Shoals, and other shelling hot spots.

The Playtime (239-472-5300; PO Box 194, Captiva Island 33924; at Captiva Cruises, South Seas Resort) Three-hour shelling trips to Cayo Costa and North Captiva with experienced instruction.

SPAS

Sanibel Day Spa (239-395-2220; www.sanibeldayspa.com; 2075 Periwinkle Way #27, Sanibel Island 33957; at Periwinkle Place, upstairs) Long established and well-reputed place of pampering offering à la carte and spa package services, including hair care, manicures, pedicures, men's treatments, facials, oxygen therapy, steam therapy, scrubs, and massage.

Sanibel Harbour Resort & Spa (239-466-4000, 800-767-7777; 17260 Harbour Pointe Dr., Fort Myers 33908) Directly before the Sanibel causeway, Sanibel Harbour was a spa before it became a resort (see "Lodging"). Guests, members, and day visitors can take advantage of the swimming pool, whirlpools, training room, aerobics and tai chi classes, saunas, steam rooms, and racquetball courts. Special services include herbal wraps, aromatherapy massage, Swiss shower, spa luncheon, Fitness Age evaluation, personal training, facials, and other salon treatments.

SPECTATOR SPORTS

CRAB RACES

'Tween Waters Inn Crow's Nest (239-472-5161; 15951 Captiva Dr., Captiva Island 33924) Held at 6 and 9 every Monday night. Participate or watch. The early session is geared toward families.

Pro Baseball

City of Palms Park (239-334-4700; www.redsox.com; 2201 Edison Ave., Fort Myers; 33901; downtown at Jackson St) Home of the Boston Red Sox's spring exhibition games, starting in March and played into April.

Manny Ramirez at bat. City of Palms Park hosts Red Sox spring training games.

Courtesy Boston Red Sox

Lee County Sports Complex (239-768-4270; 14100 Six Mile Cypress Rd., Fort Myers 33912) Hosts the Minnesota Twins (800-33TWINS; www.mntwins.com) for spring training in March and early April. From April through August, the Miracle Professional Baseball team (239-768-4210), member of the Florida State League, competes here.

Pro Football

Although the Island Coast claims no professional team of its own, professional and college football support runs high. Several local sports bars have designated themselves unofficial headquarters for fans from specific teams throughout the country.

Pro Hockey

Florida Everblades (239-948-7825; www.floridaeverblades.com; TECO Arena, off Interstate 75, exit 19, at Corkscrew Rd., 11000 Everblades Pkwy., Estero 33928) Southwest Florida's professional ice hockey team plays its October–April season at TECO Arena. The public can skate at the rink daily (times vary) for a fee. (See "Kids' Stuff," above.)

WATER SPORTS

Parasailing & Waterskiing

Soaring views and elevated heart rates: the thrill of parasailing.

Karen T. Bartlett

Holiday Water Sports (239-765-4FUN; 250 Estero Blvd.; at Best Western Pink Shell Resort; also 239-463-6778; 684 Estero Blvd., Fort Myers Beach 33931; at Best Western Beach Resort) Sun Cat, kayak, aquacycle, and waverunner rentals available, with lessons.

Ranalli Parasail (239-542-5511; 2000 Estero Blvd., Fort Myers Beach 33931) Rides along Fort Myers Beach and waverunner rentals.

Rebel Watersports (239-463-3351; 1028 Estero Blvd., Fort Myers Beach 33931) Parasailing, waverunner rentals, dolphin tours, banana boat rides.

YOLO Watersports (239-472-YOLO; www.yolo-jims.com; 11534 Andy Rosse Ln., Captiva Island 33924)

Sailboarding & Surfing

Summer storms bring the sort of waves surfers crave, but in general, gulf waves are too wimpy for serious wave riders. Strong winds, however, provide excellent conditions for sailboarders in several locations throughout the region. Sanibel Causeway is the most popular windsurfing spot. .

Ace Performer Windsurf, Kayak & Sailboat Shop (239-489-3513; 16842 McGregor Blvd., Fort Myers 33908) Rents and sells windsurfers, kayaks, and small sailboats. Free delivery to the Sanibel causeway.

Snorkeling & Scuba

Florida's west coast has no natural reefs, but several have been built to provide a home for marine life and make divers and fishermen happy. More than a dozen of these artificial reefs lie along the Sanibel Island area coast. The

Edison Reef, one of the largest, was created from the sinking of a former Fort Myers bridge in 42 feet of water 15 nautical miles off the Sanibel Lighthouse. The **Belton Johnson Reef**, constructed of concrete culvert, lies about 5 nautical miles off Bowman's Beach on Sanibel. Other popular sites include the **Redfish Pass Barge**, less than a nautical mile from Redfish Pass between Captiva and North Captiva, in 25 feet of water, and the **Doc Kline Reef**, a popular tarpon hole less than 8 nautical miles from the Sanibel Lighthouse. **Cayo Costa State Island Preserve** offers snorkelers nice ledges in 2 to 5 feet of water, alive with fish, sponges, and shells.

DIVE SHOPS & CHARTERS

Underwater Explorers (239-481-4733, 239-481-5005; 12600 McGregor Blvd., Fort Myers 33919) Certification courses and equipment, plus dive trips out of the region. This operation has been around for years. There are others that come and go throughout the region, but this is most dependable.

WILDERNESS CAMPING

Cayo Costa State Island Preserve (239-964-0375, PO Box 1150, Boca Grande 33921; at Barrier Islands GEO Park, LaCosta Island) You'll need boat transportation to reach this unbridged island, home to wild pigs and myriad birds. Bring your own fresh drinking water and lots of bug spray. And don't expect to plug in the camcorder. There are showers, picnic grounds, boat docks, nature trails, a tram that runs cross-island, tent sites, and some very primitive cabins. Call ahead to reserve the latter. Camping was once allowed anywhere on the 2,225-acre island, but today it's restricted to a certain area.

WILDLIFE SPOTTING

Loggerhead turtles lumber up on local beaches each summer to lay their cache of eggs. (Only vigilant night owls actually see them, but you can find their tracks and see their nests, which patrols stake off.) Brown pelicans swarm fishing piers for handouts. Black skimmers nest on uninhabited sandy islands, while hundreds of other birds visit or stay in local habitats. The Island Coast is a vital area for wildlife, and many opportunities exist to spy on them in their natural setting.

ALLIGATORS

Once endangered, the alligator population has sprung back in recent decades, thanks to organizations and laws that fought to protect the prehistoric reptiles. Sanibel Island paved the way by pioneering a no-feeding regulation that later became state law. (Hand-fed alligators lose their fear of man.)

Innate homebodies, alligators usually leave their home ponds only during spring and summer mating. Spotting them is easiest then. You will often hear the bellow of the bull gator in the night and see both males and females roaming from pond to pond in search of midsummer night's romance. They can do serious damage to a car, so be alert. And never approach one on foot.

When it's cold, alligators stay submerged to keep warm. On sunny days throughout the year you can spot them soaking up rays on banks of freshwater rivers and streams. When they're in the water, you first spot their snouts, then their prickly tire-tread profiles. Once your eye becomes trained to distinguish them from logs and background, you'll notice them more readily.

Serious searchers should try Sanibel Island's J. N. "Ding" Darling National Wildlife Refuge.

BIRDS

Roseate spoonbills are the stars of the "Ding" Darling National Wildlife Refuge, but hundreds of other species live among the sanctuary's wiry mangrove limbs and shallow estuarine waters, including ibises, brown and white pelicans, tri-color herons, red-shouldered hawks, snowy egrets, anhingas, and ospreys.

DOLPHINS

Local sightseeing tours hold the promise of sighting bottlenose dolphins, which love to play in a boat's wake.

Karen T. Bartlett

The playful bottle-nosed dolphins cruise the sea, performing impromptu acrobatic shows that are hard to believe aren't staged. When the next performance would be is anybody's guess, but if you learn their feeding schedules, you have a better chance of catching their act. They often like to leap out of the wake of large boats. Out in the gulf I've been surrounded by their antics to the point where I suffered minor whiplash from spinning around to keep track of them all. Don't expect them to get too close — take some binoculars — and forget seeing them in captivity around here. Locals once staged a protest in Pine Island Sound when collectors tried to take some of their dolphins. When a swim-with-the-dolphins facility was proposed near Sanibel Island, citizens again rose up in arms against animal exploitation.

MANATEES

In east Fort Myers, where warm waters discharged from the Florida Power & Light Company have always attracted the warm-blooded manatees in the winter months to so-called Yankee Canal, Manatee Park (see below) recently opened to provide a manatee viewing area, exhibits, and other recreational and educational assets on the wild and natural Orange River.

Pine Island's backwaters offer a good venue for manatee spotting. Check out the bay behind Island Shell & Gifts, a popular sea-watch site, just before the Matlacha Bridge. If you're around South Seas Resort on Captiva Island, watch the marina waters for surfacing manatees.

NATURE PRESERVES & ECO-ATTRACTIONS

CALUSA NATURE CENTER & PLANETARIUM
239-275-3435.
www.calusanature.com.
3450 Ortiz Ave., Fort Myers 33905.
Open: 9am–5pm Mon.–Sat., 11am–5pm Sun. Call for astronomy and laser show times.
Admission: Museum and trails, $4 adults, $2.50 children 3–12, free under 3. Planetarium shows $3 for adults, $2 for children 3–12.

Offers a free 2-mile wildlife trail with Seminole Amerindian village, caged bobcat, and native bird aviary. Indoors you can see live animal exhibits — snakes, tarantulas, alligators, and bees — and demonstrations. The newly renovated planetarium uses telescopes, laser lights, and astronomy lessons in its presentations.

CAYO COSTA STATE ISLAND PRESERVE
239-964-0375.
PO Box 1150, Boca Grande 33921.
Barrier Islands GEO Park, La Costa Island, accessible only by boat.
Admission: $1 per person.

A refuge occupies about 90 percent of this 2,225-acre island. Cayo Costa preserves the Florida that the Native Americans tried to protect against European invasion. Besides the occasional wild hog that survives on the island, egrets, white pelicans, raccoons, osprey, and black skimmers frequent the area. The path across the island's northern end features a side trip to a pioneer cemetery. Blooming cacti and other flora festoon the walk, which is sometimes a run when the weather turns warm and uncontrolled mosquito populations remind us of the hardships of eras gone by.

C.R.O.W.
239-472-3644.
3883 Sanibel-Captiva Rd.,
  Sanibel Island 33957.
Open: Tours at 11am
  Mon.–Fri., 1pm Sun.,
  Nov.–Apr. only.
Admission: $5 adults, free
  for children 12 and
  under.

C.R.O.W. is the acronym for Clinic for the Rehabilitation of Wildlife. This hospital complex duplicates natural habitats and tends to sick and injured wildlife: birds, bobcats, raccoons, rabbits, and otters. It cares for more than 2,200 patients a year. You can visit animals on the mend by tour.

FOUR MILE COVE
ECOLOGICAL
PRESERVE
239-574-0883.
At the end of SE 23rd
  Terrace, north of
  Midpoint Memorial
  Bridge in Cape Coral
  (follow the signs off Del
  Prado Blvd. north of
  Coralwood Mall at SE
  21st Ln.).
Open: 8am–5pm daily.
Admission: Free.

This urban preserve runs parallel to the bridge and allows exploration of 365 acres of wetlands along a 4,500-foot boardwalk and nature trails that take you away from the bustle of traffic. Interpretative center, restrooms, picnicking, guided nature walks, and kayak rentals on the weekends (Oct.–Apr. only).

J. N. "DING" DARLING
WILDLIFE REFUGE
239-472-1100.
1 Wildlife Dr., Sanibel
  Island 33957.
Off Sanibel-Captiva Rd.
Open: Refuge, sunrise to
  sunset. Visitors' center,
  9am–5pm, 9am–4pm
  May–Oct.. Refuge is
  closed Fri. (visitors'
  center open).
Admission: Free to visitor's
  center; $5 per car for
  refuge, $1 per cyclist or
  walk-in.

More than 6,000 acres of pristine wetlands and wildlife are protected by the federal government, thanks to the efforts of Pulitzer Prize–winning cartoonist and politically active conservationist J. N. "Ding" Darling, a regular Captiva visitor in the 1930s. A 5-mile drive takes you through the refuge, originally a satellite of the original Everglades National Wildlife Refuge. To really experience "Ding," get out of the car. At the very least follow the easy trails into mangrove, bird, and alligator territory. Look for roseate spoonbills, yellow-crowned night herons, white pelicans, painted buntings, and dozens of other life-list prizes. Narrated tram and guided canoe tours are available (239-472-8900). The new and still developing visitors center holds wildlife displays, a mangrove vignette, bird sculptures, and a peek into the world of the refuge's namesake. Naturalist programs take place throughout the week in season.

MANATEE PARK
239-432-2004, 239-694-3537.
www.lee-county.com/
  parks&rec/regionalparks
  /manateepark/default.

A 16-acre passive recreational park feeds our fascination for the loveable manatee, teddy bear of the water world. In addition to a manatee viewing area, it provides interpretative exhibits, a

Lee Island Coast Visitor and Convention Bureau

Fort Myers's new Manatee Park overlooks the sea cow's favorite winter vacation spot.

10901 Route 80, Fort Myers 33905.
Open: 8am–8pm daily Apr.–Sept.; 8am–5pm daily Oct.–Mar.
Parking: 75¢ per hour, $3 per day.

MATANZAS PASS PRESERVE
End of Bay Rd. of School St., Fort Myers Beach.
Open: Dawn to dusk.
Admission: Free.

OSTEGO BAY FOUNDATION EDUCATION CENTER
239-765-8101.
718 Fisherman Wharf, Fort Myers Beach 33931.
Open: 10am–4pm Wed.–Fri., 10am–1pm Sat.
Admission: By donation.

nature boardwalk, a canoe and kayak launch (and rentals in winter), canoe tours (call ahead), a fishing pier, wildlife habitat areas, and picnic facilities. The park also serves as a rescue and release site for injured and rehabilitated manatees. For manatee viewing updates, call 239-694-3537.

A quiet respite from vacationland action, the preserve provides a short loop trail and boardwalks through mangroves and hammocks to out-of-the-way bay waters.

Primarily a marine-science education and research facility, Ostego Bay maintains a showroom of local sealife for visitors to tour. Aquariums hold local species in various habitats, such as sea grass, estuarine, and gulf. Manatee, loggerhead, and other kiosks explain the plight of endangered species and the workings of the local shrimping industry. Interactive displays include a dry-touch table, microscopes, and a touchable shark's skin and blue marlin's bill. The

Foundation is building a boardwalk along the bay where the shrimp boats dock off of Main Street. Here you can learn yet more about shrimping, estuaries, and local maritime heritage.

SANIBEL-CAPTIVA CONSERVATION FOUNDATION CENTER
239-472-2329.
www.sccf.org.
3333 Sanibel-Captiva Rd.,
   PO Box 839, Sanibel
   Island 33957.
Open: 8:30am–3pm
   Mon.–Fri. during
   summer; 8:30am–4pm
   Mon.–Sat. mid-Oct.–mid-
   May.; Closed Sun. and
   most Sat. during summer.
Admission: $3 for visitors 12
   and older.

This research and preservation facility encompasses more than 1,800 acres. A guided or self-guided tour introduces you to indigenous flora and natural bird habitats. Indoor displays and dioramas further educate and include a touch tank. Guest lecturers, seminars, and workshops address environmental issues during the winter season. The weekly beach walk is fun and informative. Native plant nursery and butterfly house also on the premises.

WILDLIFE TOURS & CHARTERS

Adventures in Paradise (239-472-8443, 239-437-1660; 14341 Port Comfort Rd., Fort Myers 33908; at Port Sanibel Marina off Summerlin Rd. before the Sanibel causeway) Sea-life-encounter excursions led by marine biologist aboard a pontoon boat; also shelling snorkel quests.

Canoe Adventures (239-472-5218; 716 Rabbit Rd., Sanibel Island 33957) Guided tours with a noted island naturalist in "Ding" Darling National Wildlife Refuge, on the Sanibel River, and in other natural areas.

Estero Explorer (239-765-1880; 8700 Estero Blvd., Fort Myers Beach 33931; at Kayak Shack, Lovers Key State Park) Eco-minded tours of Estero Bay's wild life.

Fort Myers Manatee World (239-693-1434; 5605 Palm Beach Blvd., Fort Myers 33905; at Coastal Marine Mart, Route 80 at Interstate 75 exit 25, East Fort Myers) Specializes in two-hour tours up the Orange River to spot manatees. Educational video viewing and canoe and kayak rentals.

Sanibel-Captiva Conservation Foundation Center (239-472-2329; 3333 Sanibel-Captiva Rd., Sanibel Island 33957) Hosts guided nature-trail, beach-walk, and island-boat tours.

Tarpon Bay Recreation (239-472-8900; www.tarponbay.com; 900 Tarpon Bay Rd., Sanibel Island 33957) Naturalist-guided canoe and tram tours through "Ding" Darling National Wildlife Refuge. Also free lunchtime wildlife talks and guided trail tours.

SHOPPING

SHOPPING CENTERS & MALLS

Bell Tower Shops (239-489-1221; 13499 S. Cleveland Ave., Fort Myers 33907) Jacobson's, a small and exclusive department store, and Saks Fifth Avenue anchor this alfresco, Mediterranean-style plaza of one-of-a-kind shops, upscale chains (Victoria's Secret, Brookstone, Gap), restaurants, and movie theaters.

Captiva Island Like Captiva in general, the shopping scene here is quirky and beach-oriented. Chadwick's Square, near the entrance to the South Seas Resort, provides the best (if somewhat pricey) concentration of gifts and fashion.

Coralwood Mall (2301 Del Prado Blvd., Cape Coral 33909) An outdoor mall of restaurants and chain stores, including Bealls Department Store.

Downtown Fort Myers (First Street) Downtown is slowly looking up. More business- and government-minded than commercial, it does harbor some interesting book and cigar stores and unusual antique and what-not shops. Emphasis for urban renewal is on entertainment and dining, so most shops are utilitarian.

Edison Mall (239-939-5464; www.simon.com; 4125 Cleveland Ave., Fort Myers 33901) An entirely commercial, enclosed, and air-conditioned mall with major department stores such as Burdines, Dillards, J.C. Penney, and Sears, plus about 150 smaller clothing and gift shops and a food court.

Matlacha (Pine Island) Sagging old fish houses, cracker-box shops, quirky art galleries, and fishing motels heavily salt the flavor of this island village. Knickknack historic structures painted in candy-store colors give the town an artistic, Hansel and Gretel feel. Sea-themed gifts, art, and jewelry comprise the majority of merchandise.

McGregor Antiques District (Fort Myers) A nucleus of 17 shops spread around five small strip centers at College Parkway.

Page Field Commons (Cleveland Ave. at Fowler Ave., Fort Myers) A conglomeration of mega-marts such as Old Navy, Toys 'R Us, Best Buys, Books-A-Million, and Michael's Crafts.

Sanibel Island Periwinkle Way and Palm Ridge Road constitute the shopper's routes on Sanibel, which is known for its galleries (specializing in wildlife art), shell shops, and resort-wear stores. These are clustered in tastefully landscaped, nature-compatible outdoor centers, the largest being Periwinkle Place on Periwinkle Way. One of the most interesting, both architecturally and in terms of merchandise, is The Village on Periwinkle Way.

Times Square (at the foot and just north of Matanzas Pass Bridge, Fort Myers Beach) Shop in your bikini, if you wish, at this hub of ultracasual island activity. You'll find a profusion of swimsuit boutiques, surf shops, and food outlets. Recently, $2.3 million turned the area north of the fishing pier into a pedestrian mall, causing those shops to the south a setback resulting in empty storefronts.

ANTIQUES & COLLECTIBLES

Albert Meadow Antiques (239-472-8442; 15000 Captiva Dr., Captiva Island 33924) Turn-of-the-century decorative arts by Tiffany, Gorham, and Steuben; antique jewelry, Navajo weavings, and Art Deco and Art Nouveau.

Judy's Antiques (239-481-9600; 12710 McGregor Blvd., Fort Myers 33919) One of the oldest in the McGregor Antiques District, it is well-organized and sells quality merchandise: furniture, jewelry, clothes, and decorative items.

BOOKS

Barnes & Noble (239-437-0654; 13751 S. Tamiami Trail, Fort Myers 33912.) Complete book dealer with extensive periodicals, local and travel section, children's books and activities, and coffee bar.

Beach Book Nook (239-463-3999; 7205 Estero Blvd., Fort Myers Beach 33931; at Villa Santini Plaza) New and used paperback exchange.

The Island Book Nook (239-472-6777; 2330 Palm Ridge Rd., Sanibel Island 33957; at Palm Ridge Place) Paperback exchange, hardbacks for sale and rent, complete collection of local books.

MacIntosh Books (239-472-1447; 2365 Periwinkle Way, Sanibel Island 33957) A tiny shop packed full of books of local and general interest. A special room stocks children's books and provides toys to help out shopping parents.

Shakespeare Beethoven & Company (239-332-8300; 1520 Broadway, Suite 107, Fort Myers 33901; downtown) Moved from Royal Palm Square, it still sells its highbrow line of books, music, greeting cards, and magazines.

CLOTHING

Candace's at Frangi-pani (239-472-3777; PO Box 425, Captiva Island 33924; unit #110 at Chadwick's Square) Stylish and casual women's resort fashions; lots of swimsuits.

Chico's (239-472-3773; 2330 Palm Ridge Rd., Sanibel Island 33957; at Palm Ridge Place) I prefer this Chico's store to the original because it's more low-key, with less hustle and bustle.

Dockside (239-472-9098; 2075 Periwinkle Way, Sanibel Island 33957; at Periwinkle Place) Shirts and sportswear for men with a fishing, marine, and tropical sensibility; shoes and sandals.

H20 Outfitters (239-472-7507; PO Box 665, Captiva Island 33924; at Chadwick's Square) Men's and women's beach and marina fashions, shoes, quality souvenir T-shirts and sweatshirts.

Lads & Lassies (239-472-1180; www.ladsandlassies.com; 2075 Periwinkle Way, Sanibel Island 33957; at Periwinkle Place) Adorable kids clothes, from swimsuits to Dalmatian rain jackets.

Peach Republic (239-472-8444; 2075 Periwinkle Way, Sanibel Island 22957; at

Periwinkle Place) Stylish cotton and other tropical resort wear for women, shoes, and jewelry.

Trader Rick's (239-489-2240; 13499 US 41 #217, Fort Myers 33907; at Bell Tower Shops) Casual cotton Florida wear for women, plus unusual and handmade jewelry and other accessories.

T-Shirt Hut (239-472-1415; 1504 Periwinkle Way, Sanibel Island 33957) The best T-shirts on the island; also other clothing, gifts, and beach supplies.

CONSIGNMENT

Buying secondhand on the Island Coast is not the embarrassment it is in some places. Because of the wealthy and transient nature of its residents, the area offers the possibility of great discoveries in its consignment shops.

Classy Exchange (239-278-1123; 12791 Kenwood Ln. #B1, Fort Myers 33907) Designer women's fashions and housewares.

Designer Consigner (239-472-1266; 2460 Palm Ridge Rd., Sanibel Island 33957; at Tarpon Bay Center) Clothing, furniture, and household items.

The Encore Shop (239-936-6335; 3563 Fowler St., Fort Myers 33901; at Columbus Square) Household items and décor; men's and women's fashions.

Perenniels (239-275-8838; 7051 Crystal Dr., Fort Myers 33907) Baby furniture, toys, and children's and women's clothes.

Sarah's Consignments (239-283-3302; 5990 Mackerel Rd., Bokeelia 33922; on Pine Island) Stuffed full with housewares, decorative items, and women's clothing.

Second Hand Rose (239-574-6919; 1532 SE 14th St., Cape Coral 33990; at Del Prado Mall) Extensive selection of fashion, jewelry, household items, furniture, and collectibles.

FACTORY OUTLET CENTERS

Miromar Outlets (239-948-3766; 10801 Corkscrew Rd., Estero 33928; at exit 19 off Interstate 75) An above-average assortment of factory shops, designer outlets, and eateries, including Adidas, Nike, Reebok, Harry and David, Nautica, Calvin Klein, and Pottery Row.

Sanibel Tanger Factory Outlets (239-454-1974, 888-471-3939; www.tangeroutlet.com; 20350 Summerlin Rd., Fort Myers 33908; at McGregor Blvd.) Sitting at Sanibel's doorstep, outlets for Corning-Revere, Maidenform, Levi's, Docker's, Reebok, OshKosh, and Bass Shoes.

FLEA MARKETS & BAZAARS

Fleamasters Fleamarket (239-334-7001; www.fleamall.com; 4135 Dr. Martin

Luther King Jr. Blvd., Fort Myers 33916) Some 300,000 indoor square feet of produce, souvenirs, and novelties, open Friday through Sunday.

McGregor Boulevard Garage Sales (Fort Myers) Drive the boulevard early — the earlier you go, the better the pickings — every Friday and Saturday morning and watch for garage sale signs directing you to private sales.

Ortiz Fleamarket (239-694-5019; 1501 Ortiz Ave., Fort Myers 33905) Smaller than Fleamasters, this market convenes every Saturday and Sunday.

GALLERIES

Captiva's Jungle Drums Gallery fits right in with the historic district's whimsical idiosyncrasies.

Karen T. Bartlett

Aboriginals: Art of the First Person (239-395-2200; www.tribalworks.com; 2340 Periwinkle Way, Sanibel Island 33957; at The Village) More of a museum than a store, it focuses on the tribal art of Africa, Australia, and native Americans.

Captiva's Finest (239-472-8222; 110 Chadwick's Square #340, Captiva Island 33924) Local artists' rendition of bird and other wildlife, framed decorative prints, animal sculptures — all in an affordable price range.

Crossed Palms Gallery (239-283-2283; 8315 Main St., Bokeelia 33922; Pine Island) A delightful gallery facing the sea, it occupies two restored '50s fishermen's cottages, built around a cistern, which becomes part of the gallery. Its rooms are filled with original fine arts, glasswork, pottery, and jewelry by local and national artists.

Island Gallery (239-463-7100; 6151 Estero Blvd. #5, Fort Myers Beach 33931) Affordable framed art and prints by local artists, nice paintings by a Seminole Indian, statues, wall hangings, and other decorative items.

Jungle Drums (239-395-2266; 11532 Andy Rosse Ln., PO Box 368, Captiva Island 33924) On the outside, dolphins and birds are carved into the stair rail and floor studs. Inside, local and national artists depict wildlife themes in various media, much of it whimsical.

Matlacha Art Gallery (239-283-6453; 4637 Pine Island Rd., Matlacha 33993) Too much fun to be taken seriously as a gallery, it does sell the work of local sculptors, painters, and the owner, who specializes in colorized photographs and painted coconut postcards. Look for the trademark mannequins, dressed for the weather, outside. Stay for a cup of coffee in the waterfront Oz gallery garden in back.

Tower Gallery (239-472-4557; 751 Tarpon Bay Rd., Sanibel Island 33957) In its charming Caribbean-motif old-beach-house digs, this artist's cooperative specializes in fine tropical art by area artists: masterful black-and-white photography by Charles McCullough, Sanibel scenes, batik, pottery, and baskets.

GENERAL STORES

Bailey's General Store (239-472-1516; 2477 Periwinkle Way, Sanibel Island 33957; at Bailey's Shopping Center, corner Tarpon Bay Rd.) An island fixture for ages, it stocks mostly hardware and fishing and kitchen supplies, with an attached grocery, bakery, and deli.

Island Store (239-472-2374; 11500 Andy Rosse Ln., PO Box 907, Captiva Island 33924) Here's where you can buy those necessities you forgot, but try not to forget too much because the prices reflect the location, here at the end of the earth.

GIFTS

A Swedish Affair (239-275-8004; 1400 Colonial Blvd., Fort Myers 33907; at Royal Palm Square) Scandinavian gifts from funny to fine: Swedish joke books, lingonberry preserves, folk art, candles, glassware, Christmas ornaments, and fine pewter serving pieces.

Cheshire Cat (239-472-3545; 1999 Periwinkle Way, Sanibel Island 33957; also 239-482-8697; 13499 S. Cleveland Ave., Fort Myers 33907; at Bell Tower Shops) Old-fashioned, Brio, and learning toys.

Jerry's Bazaar (239-472-5636; 1700 Periwinkle Way, Sanibel Island 33957; at Jerry's Shopping Center) Collection of T-shirt, beach toy, shell, and candy shops all under one roof, selling affordable mementos of the island.

Pandora's Box (239-472-6263; 2075 Periwinkle Way, Sanibel Island 33957; at Periwinkle Place) A seashell motif in decorative items, creative jewelry, potpourri, specialty children's gifts, soaps, yard art, and art greeting cards.

JEWELRY

Congress Jewelers (239-472-4177; 2075 Periwinkle Way, Sanibel Island 33957; at Periwinkle Place) Dolphin, mermaid, bird, sandals, and shell gold pendants, plus other fine jewelry.

First Street Jewelers (239-337-2224; 2282 First St., Fort Myers 33901; downtown) Custom designs, unset stones, watches, fine jewelry and gifts.

Kelly's Cocoons (239-472-8383; 230 Chadwick's Square, PO Box 1174, Captiva Island 33924) Specializes in jewelry made from shells and recovered treasure coins, gold sea-life jewelry, and butterfly art.

KITCHENWARE & HOME DECOR

Cheese Nook (239-472-2666; 2075 Periwinkle Way, Sanibel Island 33957; at Periwinkle Place) Placemats, towels, and dishware fun and tropical; also gourmet food items.

Island Style (239-472-6657; www.islandstylegallery.com; 2075 Periwinkle Way, Sanibel Island 33957; at 16 Periwinkle Place; also 239-472-4343; 210 Chadwick's Square, Captiva Island 33924) Whimsical, artistic, and one-of-a-kind decorative elements with a Sun Belt motif: hand-painted chairs, carved wooden mobiles and stabiles, brightly colored dishware, Caribbean-inspired pieces.

Nancy Young (239-489-4929; www.nancyyoung.com; 13499 S. Cleveland Ave., Fort Myers 33907; at Bell Tower Shops) Looking for fun home accessories? Clocks, tableware, chairs, and other decorative items dazzle with their bright colors and happiness. If you've ever wanted a lighted pink flamingo, this is your place.

Peel 'n Pare (239-433-3300; 13499 S. Cleveland Ave. Fort Myers 33907; at Bell Tower Shops) Kitchen accents and implements.

Traders (239-395-3151; www.tradersstoreandcafe.com; 1551 Periwinkle Way, Sanibel Island 33957) This restaurant-store combo excels at both (see "Dining"). Warehouse-sized, it brims with furniture, objets d'art, candles, and gifts from distant, exotic lands.

SHELL SHOPS

Island Shells & Gifts (239-283-8080; 4204-4206 Pine Island Road, Matlacha 33993) Huge facility carrying an unusual stock of shells, shell-craft materials, jewelry, candles, and other novelties. Bonus: A good location for spotting dolphin and manatees.

Neptune's Treasures (239-472-3132; 1101 Periwinkle Way, Sanibel Island 33957; at Treetops Center) Along with the usual line of shell specimens and jewelry, this shop carries fossils and arrowheads. The couple who run the store are very knowledgeable about shell hunting.

The Shell Factory (239-995-2141, 800-282-5805; 2787 N. Tamiami Tr., North Fort Myers 33903) A palace of Florida funk and junk, the Shell Factory is built like a bazaar, with dozens of minishops within its 65,500 square feet. The main part displays specimen shells and shell-craft items of every variety. Jewelry, art, clothes, and knickknacks fill other nooks. Also at the complex (can't miss it; look for the giant conch shell on the sign) you will find restaurants, an arcade, a stuffed exotic animal collection, a small zoo, and bumper-boat rides.

Showcase Shells (239-472-1971;1614 Periwinkle Way, Sanibel Island 33957; at Heart of the Islands Center) As elegant as a jewelry store, this boutique adds a touch of class to sifting through specimen shells by putting them under glass and into artistic displays.

Tarpon Bay Shell Shop (239-454-1111; 17711 San Carlos Blvd., Fort Myers Beach 33931) Loads of shells and other souvenirs, inexpensive to fine.

SPORTS STORES

Note: This listing includes general sports outlets only. For supplies and equipment for specific sports, please refer to "Recreation."

Sports Authority (239-418-0281; 2317 Colonial Blvd., Fort Myers 33907) Full line of equipment, sportswear, and shoes.

CALENDAR OF EVENTS

JANUARY

Blizzard (239-461-7437; Fort Myers Skatium, 2250 Broadway, Fort Myers 33901) Two tons of snow brings back wintry memories: ice skating, entertainment, ice carving contest. One day in late January.

FEBRUARY

Cape Coral Winter Festival (239-549-6900; Cape Coral) Ball, antique car show, parade, music, and art exhibits. Nine days in late February to early March.

Edison Pageant of Light Festival (239-334-2999; Fort Myers) Commemorates the birthday of Thomas Edison, culminating in a spectacular lighted night parade. Two weeks early in the month.

Greek Fest (239-481-2099; Greek Orthodox Church, 8210 Cypress Lake Dr., Fort Myers 33907) Ethnic food and music. Two days late in the month.

Sanibel Music Festival (239-336-7999; Sanibel Island) Features concerts by classical artists from across the nation. Most events held at Sanibel Congregational Church, 2050 Periwinkle Way.

MARCH

Fort Myers Beach Lions Club Shrimp Festival (239-454-7500; Lynn Hall Memorial Park, Fort Myers Beach) Blessing of the fleet, 5K run, parade, and shrimp boil. Two days midmonth.

India Festival (fax 239-939-2787; Lee County Alliance of the Arts, 10091 McGregor Blvd., Fort Myers 33919) Ethnic food and entertainment.

Lee County Reading Festival (239-479-4629; Centennial Park, downtown Fort Myers) One day to celebrate literacy with prominent authors and related activities.

Sanibel Shell Fair and Show (239-472-2155; Sanibel Community House, 2173 Periwinkle Way, Sanibel Island 33957) Showcases sea life, specimen shells, and shell art. Four days in early March. Admission to show.

APRIL

Best Southwest Festival (239-574-0801; German-American Social Club, Cape Coral) Live music, western saloon, casino, dancing, and a taste fair. One day late in the month.

Taste of the Islands (239-472-3644; Sanibel Island) About 20 Captiva and Sanibel restaurants participate, with live music and competitions to benefit wildlife. One day; admission.

MAY

Fort Myers Beach Offshore Grand Prix (239-454-2772; Fort Myers Beach) High-speed boat racing off the beach. For the best view, book a room or fight the crowds at the pier. One weekend midmonth.

New Arts Festival (239-939-2787; Alliance of the Arts, 10091 McGregor Blvd., Fort Myers 33919) Headquartered at the Alliance, this three-week showcase of local performance and visual arts takes place at cultural venues throughout the county.

JUNE

Caloosa Catch & Release Fishing Tournament (239-472-5111; South Seas Resort, PO Box 194, Captiva Island 33924) Four-day event.

Fort Myers Beach Taste of the Beach (239-454-7500; Fort Myers Beach) A gathering of restaurateurs and sun-loving gourmets (and gourmands).

Juneteenth Celebration (239-461-0528; Clemente Park, Dr. Martin Luther King Blvd., Fort Myers) A celebration of African-American freedom, highlighting dance, gospel music, martial arts, African fashion, drama, and ethnic food.

JULY

MangoMania (239-283-0888; Fort Myers–Pine Island KOA, 5120 Stringfellow Rd., St. James City 33956; on Pine Island) Celebrates Pine Island's favorite fruit with music and stand selling mangos, mango trees, mango drinks, mango cookies, and other local delicacies. Good honest community fun, one day in early July. Admission.

SEPTEMBER

Blue Grass 4A Blue Planet (239-432-2004; Manatee Park, State Rd. 80, Fort Myers) Live bluegrass music, butterfly garden tours, ecological information, children's activities. One day late in the month.

Taste of the Cape (239-549-6900; German-American Club, 2101 SW Pine Island Rd., Cape Coral 33904) Tastes from local restaurants, live entertainment. One day late in the month.

OCTOBER

Calusa Nature Center Haunted Walk (239-275-3435; Calusa Nature Center, 3450 Ortiz Ave., Fort Myers 33905) The great-granddaddy (dead and molding) of all local haunted walks. Takes place nightly for a couple of weeks around Halloween.

Hispanic Heritage Festival (239-334-3190, 942-334-3942; Terry Park, downtown Fort Myers) A celebration of Hispanic culture, featuring ethnic food, music, dance, and crafts. One day early in the month.

Latin Jazz Fest (239-541-7218; Centennial Park, downtown Fort Myers) Big name salsa and Latin jazz stars perform outdoors on the river. Admission.

Jazz on the Green (239-477-4683; Gateway Golf & Country Club, 11360 Championship Dr., Fort Myers 33913) One day of soothing al fresco jazz by well-known artists. Admission.

National Wildlife Refuge Week (239-472-1100; J. N. "Ding" Darling National Wildlife Refuge, Sanibel Island) One week in October is devoted to exploring the refuge.

Octoberfest (239-540-0411; German-American Social Club, Cape Coral) Cape Coral celebrates its strong German heritage with Oktoberfest music, food, and activities. Two weekends.

NOVEMBER

American Sandsculpting Contest (239-454-7500; www.sultansofsand.com; Outrigger Beach and Holiday Inn Gulfside Resorts, Fort Myers Beach) Amateur and masters divisions. One weekend in early November.

BIG Arts Fair (239-395-0900; Sanibel Community House, Sanibel Island) Juried arts and crafts exhibits. Thanksgiving weekend.

Puerto Rican Festival (239-278-5533; Casa Cabana Restaurant, 2158 Colonial Blvd., Fort Myers 33907) A family musical and food festival. Admission.

Taste of the Town (239-277-1197; Centennial Park, downtown Fort Myers) About 50 restaurants sell their specialties; live entertainment and children's games. One Sunday early in the month. Admission.

DECEMBER

Captiva Sea Kayak Classic (239-437-0956; 'Tween Waters Inn Marina) Twelve- and six-mile races, with seminars and other related offerings; this is a respected event among Florida kayakers one early weekend in the month.

Christmas Luminary Trail (239-472-1080; Sanibel and Captiva Islands) Luminary candles light the path down Sanibel's and Captiva's commercial areas, where businesses stay open and dole out free drinks and food. One evening early in the month.

Edison/Ford Homes Holiday House (239-461-2687; Edison/Ford complex, Fort Myers) Period and seasonal exhibits and miles of light strings draw crowds to this popular attraction. Admission.

Holiday Boat-a-Long (239-574-0801; Four Freedoms Park, Cape Coral) Decorated boat parade with live entertainment, Santa, and other events.

CHAPTER SIX
Precious Commodities
NAPLES & THE SOUTH COAST

Karen T. Bartlett

The architecture of the Village on Venetian Bay shopping district contributes to the Italian flavor of America's Naples.

Perched on alabaster sands at the edge of Florida's **Everglades**, meticulous Naples transcends its wild setting like a diamond in the rough. Settled by land developers late in its life, this cultural oasis historically has appealed to the rich and the sporting. Today the state's final frontier is known for its million-dollar homes, great golfing, art galleries, posh resorts, world-class shopping, and fine dining. In the spirit of its Italian namesake, Naples has in the past decade undergone a sort of renaissance that has included a highly successive urban renewal project on Fifth Avenue South, a developing residential-shopping community nearby at Bayfront Center, and various new cultural venues, including Sugden Community Theatre, von Liebig Art Center, and the world-class Naples Museum of Art. In 2003 watch for the opening of an exciting new and progressively planned botanical garden. In its northern reaches the town spreads into the quiet, residential district of **North Naples**, seaside **Vanderbilt Beach**, and the town of **Bonita Springs**.

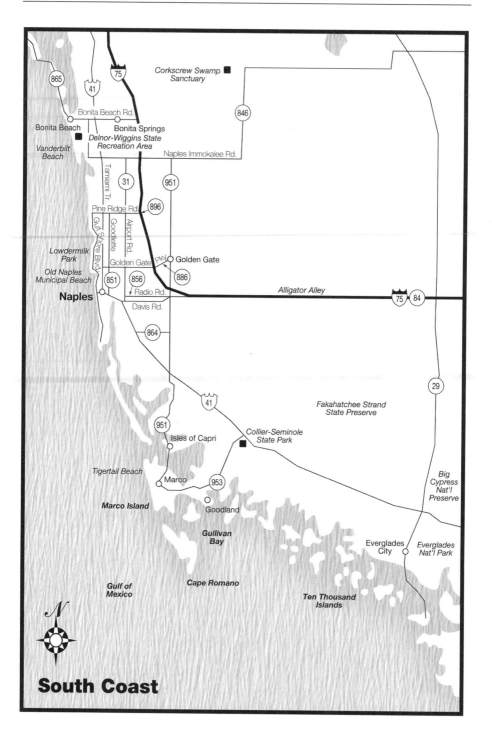

South Coast

The latter adheres to an early agricultural heritage with a reputation for tomatoes, citrus, and other cash crops. Citrus freeze outs farther north, and the town's navigable Imperial River, created the community first called Survey in 1893. Here Henry Ford maintained a hunting lodge to which he and his Fort Myers friends traveled by horseback. Today, where the tomato fields end, upscale golfing communities begin, all surrounding a neighborly little town left frozen in time by dint of Tamiami Trail's rerouting. These days Bonita Springs starts to blend in with north Naples, both physically and in its character. New residential, hotel, and shopping developments boost it upward like an overachieving tomato vine climbing above its stake.

At the south coast's southern and eastern extremes, the civility is balanced with swamp-buggy mud races, agriculture, Native-American villages, fishing lodges, vanishing Florida panthers, and the unvarnished wilderness of the Everglades.

Karen T. Bartlett

An old fishing shack in Ten Thousand Islands, remnant of a rougher, tougher era.

Neighboring **Marco Island** introduces the labyrinthine, mysterious land of **Ten Thousand Islands**. It was once an important center of the ancient Calusa culture, and the carved Key Marco Cat archaeological find (now exhibited at the Smithsonian Institution) has become an island icon. Tempered in a rough-and-tumble history, the island also boasts contemporary upscale resorts and good manners. Ancient Indian mounds, clam canneries, and pineapple plantations color the past of its three communities: **Isles of Capri**, **Marco**, and **Goodland**. First settled by the William Collier clan in 1871, Marco Island has done most of its growing in the past few decades. Between 1960, when plans for a modern bridge were being formed, and 1980, the population increased by 755 percent. Goodland, so named because its land provided fertile soil for avocado farming, has purposely kept itself behind the times, giddily stuck in a good-time, catch-fish mode.

Everglades City, county seat until Naples took over, languishes in its wilderness setting at the doorstep to Big Cypress Swamp and Ten Thousand Islands. Its settlers have always kept a step ahead of the law, doing what they must to survive, whether it was fishing, alligator poaching, or pot smuggling. Today commercial fishing restrictions have channeled the town's orientation toward tourism. Across a long, narrow causeway, **Chokoloskee Island** remains relatively untouched by change. It's a haven for RV campers and fishermen.

All contained within Collier County, this fast-growing region recently voted on a development moratorium in encroaching rural areas to preserve the sensitive Everglades environment that spreads before Naples doorstep.

LODGING

The south coast was once a place for roughing it and low-key vacationing. The old wooden Naples Hotel, built in the 1880s by town developers, was as posh as it got. In 1946 Naples became a forerunner in the golf resort game when the Naples Hotel was bought and converted. In 1985, the Ritz-Carlton came to town and set a new tone. Naples changed forever. The Registry and other smaller luxury hotels followed the Ritz. As Naples renovates its downtown, new properties continue to rise, tending toward intimacy and European style, giving Naples a well-rounded menu of options from cottages and inns to golf meccas and grandes dames. Bonita Springs, to the north, is growing into its own as a destination with fine lodging, including at Hyatt Regency to open in fall 2001. Nearby Marco Island lines up high-rise after high-rise resort and condo community along its coveted beaches. Away from the metropolitan airs of Naples and Marco, lodging options reflect the simple, primitive nature of the Florida Everglades.

Privately owned second homes and condominiums provide another source of upscale accommodations along the south coast. Vacation brokers who match visitors with such properties are listed under "Home & Condo Rentals" at the end of this section.

The highlights of south coast hospitality listed here include the best and freshest in the local industry. Toll-free 800, 877, 866, or 888 reservation numbers, where available, are listed after local numbers.

Pricing codes are explained below. They are normally per person/double occupancy for hotel rooms and per unit for efficiencies, apartments, cottages, suites, and villas. A star after the pricing designation indicates that the rate includes at least a continental breakfast in the cost of lodging. The range spans low- and high-season rates. Many resorts offer off-season packages at special rates. Prices do not include the 6 percent Florida sales tax. Some large resorts add service gratuities or maid charges. Collier County imposes a tourist bed tax, as well, proceeds from which are applied to beach and environmental maintenance.

Rate Categories

Inexpensive	Up to $75
Moderate	$75 to $150
Expensive	$150 to $200
Very Expensive	$200 and up

The following abbreviations are used for credit card information:

AE: American Express	MC: MasterCard
D: Discover Card	V: Visa
DC: Diners Club	

Bonita Springs

TRIANON BONITA BAY
General Manager: Darren
  Robertshaw.
239-948-4400, 800-859-3939.
3401 Bay Commons Dr.,
  Bonita Springs 34134.
Price: Moderate to Very
  Expensive.*
Credit Cards: AE, D, DC,
  MC, V.

The name implies "a special place," in the spirit of the Grand Trianon and Petit Trianon on the grounds of Versailles near Paris. It's heavy on European influence. The lobby displays both elegance and intimacy, with an inviting fireplace, polished marble, and high arched ceilings. The dramatic entryway segues into a cozy lounge-breakfast nook where tropical iced tea and fruit are on hand to refresh guests. Attention to detail is hallmark of Trianon, which is a spin-off of a Naples Fifth Avenue South prototype. In its 100 spacious guest rooms and suites you'll find the same refinement previewed in the lobby: dark-wood armoires, sliding French doors to the balcony, gourmet European coffee service, roomy all-white bath and space enough to dance. Continental breakfast, served in the lounge, is included in the rates. A small pool lies in the backyard of the three-story chateaulike structure. Shoppers will like its proximity to the fine stores and restaurants of walking-distance Promenade.

Everglades City

IVEY HOUSE B&B
General Manager: Sandee
  Harraden.
239-695-3299
www.iveyhouse.com.
107 Camellia St., Ever-
  glades City 34139.

For outdoor enthusiasts, family-run Ivey House B&B is tailor-made. The original lodgelike adjunct, a born-again boardinghouse from the 1920s, offers 10 simple B&B rooms. A new 17-room inn was opened in 2001, plus there's a cottage (two-night minimum stay) that has two small bedrooms.

Price: Inexpensive–
  Moderate .*
Credit Cards: MC, V.

Smoking or alcohol is not allowed in the rooms or inn courtyard. In the original B&B, men's and women's bathrooms are separate from the rooms, dorm style. The new inn rooms, which encircle the courtyard swimming pool, have private baths and offer added comfort and style, including TV and phones. Continental breakfast served in an antiques-furnished dining room is included in all room rates. Lunch and dinner, served in the inn's new dining room, are extra. Ivey's main attraction is its proximity to Everglades waterways and partnership with North American Canoe Tours. You could call this a BB&B: bed, breakfast, and back country. It leads tours into the Ten Thousand Islands by canoe, kayak, or boat, rents equipment, and provides shuttle service. Sightseeing, birding, and other excursions are available. Bike use is complimentary.

RAMADA AT PORT OF THE ISLANDS
General Manager: Charlie Bohner.
239-394-3101.
www.portoftheislands.com.
25000 Tamiami Trail E., Naples 34114.
Price: Moderate to Very Expensive.
Credit Cards: AE, D, MC, V.

Ramada has recently taken over this oasis of modest luxury in the wilderness. It reopened its 80 rooms in January 2001, with plans to grow to more than 200. For now, rooms — some privately owned — are housed within the lovely Mediterranean-style main building and in groups of eight clustered in one-story, red barrel-roofed stucco structures. A two-story building holds some of the privately owned units. Other octoplexes are being built as we speak, plus there's talk of a five- to ten-story building in the cards. Gasp! I don't know how that can happen here in the midst of the fragile Everglades. For now, it's something of water- and nature-lovers outpost, with its own marina and tour boats, bordering a residential community by the same name. The grand lobby sets a tone that speaks of creature comforts despite the remoteness, with high raftered ceiling, saltillo tiles, fetching rattan furniture, and a glazed-tile-trimmed fireplace. The prettily brick-paved pool area lies outside a deli-diner through French doors. Most of the rooms have a private screened patio. All are suitelike, with a divider between the bed and living areas, and include a pull-out couch, small refrigerator and sink, coffeemaker, stove top, and microwave.

ROD & GUN CLUB
Innkeeper: Marcella Bowen.
239-695-2101.
200 Broadway, PO Box 190, Everglades City 34139.
Price: Inexpensive to Moderate.

Steeped in both history and outdoorsmanship, this circa-1850 lodge crowns a modest town that serves as the south coast's gateway to the Everglades. The club's main building was built as luxury pioneer housing; the Old South-style mansion came under the ownership of the county's namesake, Barron Collier, who turned it into a fishermen's and hunters' haven during the 1920s. A

The lodge at Everglades City's Rod & Gun Club blends southern charm with wilderness sportsmanship.

Karen T. Bartlett

Credit Cards: No.
Handicap Access: No.

sportsman's lodge in the finest sense, its cypress walls are still decorated with mounted tarpon, a gator hide, and tools of the fishing trade. When I recently revisited, the old mansion was looking a little raggedy around the edges, in need of some attention. Seventeen rooms in tin-roofed cottages scatter around the white clapboard lodge, which has a wraparound veranda and yellow trim. The rooms are furnished for function rather than pampering — TV and air-conditioning are the extent of the luxury. The club's restaurant, which has a screened porch facing the river, specializes in local delicacies and will cook your catch for a nominal fee. The swimming pool lies off the dining room and is decorated with banana trees, lattice, and rock waterfalls.

Marco Island

THE BOAT HOUSE
General Manager: Nick Buhelof.
239-642-2400, 800-528-6345.
www.theboathousemotel.com.
1180 Eddington Place, Marco Island 34145.
Price: Inexpensive to Expensive.
Credit Cards: MC, V.

At Marco Island's north end, known as Olde Marco, things are a-changing. Once quiet and immune to the resort activity along the beach, the area now sees the completion of a large, fancy resort and spa adjunct to the historic Marco Inn. If you're seeking something less upscale and expensive than Marco's trademark resort scene, drive past the new Olde Marco Inn and turn the corner to this waterfront gem. Twenty rooms, studios, condos, and the two-bedroom gazebo house (expensive to very expensive) line boat docks and a small pool in a two-story strip among the giants. The rooms are nicely appointed and designed for easy, breezy waterfront living.

MARCO ISLAND MARRIOTT RESORT & GOLF CLUB
General Manager: Bob Dictor.
239-394-2511, 800-438-4373.
www.marcomarriottresort.com.
400 S. Collier Blvd., Marco Island 34145.
Price: Expensive to Very Expensive.
Credit Cards: AE, D, DC, MC, V.

This vacation complex sprawls along the beach — an extra-wide, shell-cluttered, sandbar-sheltered beach — to provide a fantasy playground for vacationers of all ages. For children there's an 18-hole miniature golf course, three swimming pools, a wading pool, water-sports rentals, a pizza parlor, a game room, and a remarkable kids' program. Adults can shop in the marble-floored arcade, golf at an off-campus Marriott course, dine grandly or beach style, and act like a kid when the mood strikes. A 24,000-square-foot spa is in the works for a proposed January 2002, opening. The 735 rooms and 62 suites provide a minifridge, coffee maker, hair dryer, and minibar and are decorated to suit the tropics. Colorful beach art adorns the walls; blond-wood furniture pieces are carved with palm fronds; curtains and spreads are jungle themed.

RADISSON SUITE BEACH RESORT
General Manager: Marcia Dmochowski.
239-394-4100, 800-333-3333.
www.marcobeachresort.com.
600 S. Collier Blvd., Marco Island 34145.
Price: Expensive to Very Expensive.
Credit Cards: AE, D, DC, MC, V.

Along the island's stretch of shell-strewn beach, the Radisson accommodates guests in typical Marco high-rise style, with 268 spacious suites and rooms. The 207 suites — all with private balconies and comfortable furniture — are of the one- or two-bedroom variety and offer a completely equipped kitchen. Microwaves, refrigerators, and coffee makers provide all guests with in-room dining options. Off the impressive marble lobby you'll find a game room as well as the gulf-side dining room, and both take advantage of the sea view. Active guests enjoy a heated free-form pool, tennis courts, whirlpool, exercise room, volleyball, kayaking, sailing, tubing, jet skiing, fishing, cruising, biking, and golf on three nearby courses. Families are attracted to the Radisson, where kids can enroll in a staffed recreational program or have fun in the splashy pool area or on the beach.

Naples

COVE INN
General Manager: Carol Nerone.
239-262-7161, 800-255-4365.
coveinn@compuserve.com.
900 Broad Ave. S., Naples 34102.
Price: Inexpensive to Expensive.

Back before the Ritz-Carlton and the Registry, this is what Naples was about: water, boating, and fishing. Like some of its old surviving fish houses, Cove Inn persists in the old tradition, with a focus on the harbor it edges. Accommodations range from rooms to efficiencies and one- and two-bedroom units. The 75 units are individually owned and decorated, most with a view of the harbor and

Credit Cards: AE, D, DC, MC, V.

all with a refrigerator, toaster oven, and microwave. An old-fashioned coffee house serves breakfast and lunch, and the marina-side chickee bar serves cold ones to sunbathers around the pool. Part of the Crayton Cove and city docks community, Cove Inn is close to casual waterfront restaurants, shops, and marina services.

THE EDGEWATER BEACH HOTEL
General Manager: William Doyle.
239-403-2000, 800-821-0196.
www.edgewaternaples.com.
1901 Gulf Shore Blvd. N., Naples 34102.
Price: Expensive to Very Expensive.
Credit Cards: AE, D, DC, MC, V.

The Edgewater hints at New Orleans style with lacy white-iron balustrades on two of its three buildings, all of which face the gulf-lapped beach. Its 124 one- and two-bedroom suites are spacious, convenient, and handsomely appointed with saltillo tile, rattan furnishings, and silk plants. The floor plan of each includes a full kitchen with microwave, living/dining area, and private patio or balcony. Guests can dine in the award-winning Club Dining Room or poolside under stylish market umbrellas. There's an on-site exercise room and opportunities for other recreation nearby, including golf at the hotel's new Naples Grande Golf Club.

HOTEL ESCALANTE
General Manager: Debi DeBenedetto.
239-659-3466, 877-GULF-INN.
www.hotelescalante.com.
290 Fifth Ave. S., Naples 34102.
Price: Expensive to Very Expensive.*
Credit Cards: AE, D, MC, V.

Just close enough to walk to downtown action but far enough removed for garden peace, the Hotel Escalante prides itself on its horticulture. Something is blooming and fruiting at all times in the lush gardens where 200 varieties of native and exotic species thrive. Although this gem just opened in December 2000, it has an air and a patina that communicates classic gentility and feels comfortable and elegant at the same time. Perhaps it's the old-brick pathways (imported from Chicago) or the easy but attentive service. Or perhaps it's the Mediterranean facades, bell tower, and ruffled red-tile roofs.

The 65 rooms and suites wear a tasteful attire of dark plantation-style furnishings and demure drapery. The highlight of the white-tile bath closets are lavish shower heads the size of pie tins that make you want to linger in the luxury of it all before you wrap up in the Frette bathrobes. Each room also has its own ice maker (mine was unfortunately malfunctioning), minibar, data port, and hair dryer. The compact property also holds a spa and small fitness room. Only minutes from the beach by foot, the hotel provides a delivery service that includes setting up beach chaises with towel and umbrella. Box lunch and a cooler of beverages are optional extras. Complimentary continental breakfast poolside (or at your room's private porch if you so desire) caps the whole delicious experience.

INN BY THE SEA
Innkeepers: Maas and
  Connie van den Top.
239-649-4124, 800-584-1268.
www.innbythesea-bb.com.
287 11th Ave. S., Naples
  34102.
Price: Moderate to
  Expensive.*
Credit Cards: AE, D, MC, V.

Here is a poignant taste of all that's special about Naples — its shopping, its beach, and its history. The 1937 tin-roofed bungalow is listed on the National Register of Historic Places and was one of Naples's first guesthouses. Its new owners (Maas from the Netherlands and Connie from the U.S.) have retained the charm built into the six guest rooms by former owners. Named for local islands, each exudes its own personality, with individual touches such as handmade quilts, Roman shades, a four-poster bed, and seaside motif. The three rooms downstairs claim private, attached baths. Upstairs, two suites have an adjoining room with daybed and detached baths. One also has a separate spare bedroom, making it perfect for families. Antiques adorn the downstairs sitting parlor with its fireplace, heart-pine floors, leather sofa, and the inn's only television and telephone. Maas and Connie serve fruit and fresh-baked goodies in the breakfast room each morning. Guests have complimentary use of bicycles, beach chairs, and beach towels.

INN ON FIFTH
Owner: Philip McCabe.
239-403-8777, 888-403-8778.
www.naplesinn.com.
699 Fifth Ave. S., Naples
  34102.
Price: Expensive to Very
  Expensive.
Credit Cards: AE, DC, MC,
  V.

Modeled after Europe's intimate city hotels, the Inn on Fifth marks a crescendo in the burgeoning renaissance of Naples's historic downtown main street. It turned a staid, ugly bank building into an ocher-colored eye-opener with Mediterranean archways and flourishes. Smack dab in the middle of downtown's lively dining, shopping, and entertainment scene, it fronts Fifth Avenue South and edges the new Sugden Theatre. Its greatest sensation is an Irish pub originally built near Dublin and reassembled on site here. It spills out into the plaza and serves guests and the local community alike. The inn's magnificent marble lobby foreshadows the rich European style carried out in the rooms. The 102 rooms and suites overlook the street, plaza, or hotel's courtyard. Thick-paned French doors and careful soundproofing ensure that the town's bustle does not interfere with privacy and relaxation. All rooms come with bathrobes, hair dryers, irons, and other deluxe amenities. Guests have access to a small pool located across the alley from the hotel, a small fitness room, and a spa with sauna, steam room, and massage services. This is a lovely city retreat in terms of architecture and décor, but I've heard recent complaints about bad or no service. Indeed, I experienced some of the talked-about attitude from a very rude front-desk supervisor.

LEMON TREE INN
General Manager: Steve
  Sbertomi.

Despite its lemon-pulp-yellow paint job and free lemonade in the lobby, this property is

239-262-1414.
www.lemontreeinn.com.
250 Ninth St. S., Naples
34102.
Price: Inexpensive to
Expensive.*
Credit Cards: AE, D, MC, V.

anything but a lemon. At the edge of downtown's fashionable drags, it retains a humble charm, dressed in white-tin roofs and flowering plants. The 35 rooms with porches (most of them screened) are named Periwinkle, Plumosa, Poinciana and such, after local flowers. They are spacious, simple, and clean, outfitted with a tiled kitchen containing a microwave, toaster, coffeemaker, and minifridge. Around the pool and a gazebo in the courtyard, thick foliage and stylish globe streetlamps create character. At the breakfast nook you can help yourself to continental goodies. Shopping is steps away and the beach, a short drive.

**NAPLES BEACH HOTEL
& GOLF CLUB**
Owners: The Watkins
Family.
General Manager: Jim
Gunderson.
239-261-2222, 800-237-7600.
851 Gulf Shore Blvd. N.,
Naples 34102.
Price: Expensive to Very
Expensive.
Credit Cards: AE, D, DC,
MC, V.

The doyenne of Naples resorts, this combines the best of the area — its beaches and its golf — into a three-generation tradition in the heart of the town. The 18-hole golf course hosts the Florida State PGA Seniors Open and other major golf tournaments. In 2000 the resort rolled out its new spa and clubhouse complex overlooking the greens. The spacious facility also holds meeting rooms, a fitness center, and Broadwell's, an elegant dining room. Har-Tru tennis courts, a heated pool, Beach Klub 4 Kids, and water-sports equipment rentals vie for off-the-course recreational hours. The hotel's spacious lobby and Everglades Room, where breakfast buffet is served, communicate Florida vacationing ease. Its 316 newly renovated guestrooms and suites are done in Florida decor, with some lingering classic trademarks of yesteryear. Accommodations overlook the wide palm-studded beach or the lush golf course. In-season there's a four-night minimum stay. Golf, tennis, and other packages are available.

THE REGISTRY RESORT
Resort Manager: Ron Albeit
239-597-3232, 800-247-9810.
www.registryresort.com.
475 Seagate Dr., Naples
34103.
Price: Very Expensive.
Credit Cards: AE, D, DC,
MC, V.

The Registry fits Naples like a gold lamé wetsuit. Its distinctive red-capped tower, villas, and 15 Har-Tru tennis courts dominate north Naples's pristine, mangrove-fringed estuaries. Luxury with beach casualness, the resort's style impresses from the moment you walk in the front door into a marble and crystal lobby. Outside on the second-floor level, a boardwalk leads around shops and restaurants, and downstairs the family pool has a Flintstones feel with a 100-foot on-the-rocks waterslide and private cabanas. Also for families is a fine kids' program. A long bridge leads to the beach. Tram service is available along the wooden walk that traverses tidal bays to Clam Pass Recreation Area, a 3-mile stretch of plush sands with all manner of water-sports rentals. Fifty tennis villas edge the courts; another 424 rooms and suites overlook the gulf, each furnished with a wet bar, marble vanity, spaciousness, and class. The Registry owns a nearby 18-hole golf course and provides a golf concierge. Five heated pools include Jacuzzis; the health club contains a sauna and steam baths plus a fitness room with a view of mangrove wilderness. Seven restaurants and lounges range from casual to the world-class Lafite.

An entourage of royal palms hints at the regal, Old World elegance of the Ritz-Carlton in Naples.

Karen T. Bartlett

THE RITZ-CARLTON
General Manager: Edward Staros
239-598-3300, 800-241-3333.
www.ritzcarlton.com.
280 Vanderbilt Beach Rd., Naples 34108.
Price: Very Expensive.
Credit Cards: AE, D, DC, MC, V.

The gold standard for regal accommodations, the Ritz-Carlton molds Old World elegance to Old Florida environment. The hotel's facade looms majestically classic — and the valets (sometimes in top hats) park your car. Inside, oversized vases of fresh flowers, massive chandeliers, cabinets filled with priceless china, 19th-century oil paintings, vaulted ceilings, and crystal lamps detail Ritz extravagance. Each of the 463 units in the U-shaped configuration faces the gulf. Guestrooms and suites are dressed in fine furniture, plush carpeting, and marble bath areas. Accommodations include honor bar, refrigerator, bathrobes, hypoallergenic pillows, telephones in the water closet, clothes steamers, and private balconies overlooking the hotel's backyard, where wilderness and civility meet. In the courtyard, fountains and groomed gardens exude European character. Classic arches, stone balustrades, and majestic palm-lined stairways lead to a boardwalk that takes you through mangroves, at the end of which lie golden sands, where two beach restaurants serve refreshments and water-sports rentals are available. Other amenities and services that earn the Ritz its five stars include a formal dining room, afternoon tea service, grill, café, lap pool and free-form family pool, outdoor poolside café, lounge, ballroom, tennis courts, off-property golf facilities, fitness center, beauty salon, children's programs, bicycle rental, shops, transportation services, and twice-daily maid service. A new full-service spa occupies its own separate wing at the resort's entrance, behind the rose garden.

Vanderbilt Beach

VANDERBILT INN
General Manager: Brian
  Schomacker.
239-597-3151, 800-643-8654.
www.vanderbiltinn.com.
11000 Gulf Shore Dr.,
  Naples 34108.
Price: Moderate to Very
  Expensive.
Credit Cards: AE, D, DC,
  MC, V.

Informal and beachy, this longtime Vanderbilt Beach fixture focuses on poolside and water sports along a well-populated stretch of sand. Anyone who's been around for a while knows that its chickee bar is a place of vitality and fun, day or night. Its 147 rooms and efficiencies, like its lobby, restaurant, and grounds, let you know with cool, breezy lushness that you're in the tropics.

HOME & CONDO RENTALS

Resort Quest Southwest Florida (239-597-1102, 800-237-2010; www.resort quest.com; 26201 Hickory Blvd., Bonita Springs 34134) Rentals from Fort Myers Beach to Marco Island.

Florida Vacation Accommodations (239-261-7577, 800-462-4403; www.vacationinfl.com; 3757 Tamiami Trail N., Naples 34103) Send for a vacation planner with color photos and floor plans of vacation homes, condos, and resorts for rent in the area.

RV RESORTS

Chokoloskee Island Park (239-695-2414; PO Box 430, Chokoloskee, 34138) Rustic fisherman's paradise with easy access to the Everglades and the gulf. Full-service marina, tackle shop, guide service, boat rentals, ramps, and docks. Overnight or seasonal RV sites with complete hookups.

Mar-Good Resort (239-394-6383; 321 Peartree Ave., Goodland 34140) Site on the waterfront, with a restaurant, store, small museum, boat docking, laundry, rec room, and cottages.

Outdoor Resorts of Chokoloskee Island (239-695-3788; 150 Smallwood Dr., PO Box 39, Chokoloskee 34138). Marina, boat rentals, a bait and tackle shop, and guide service for fishing and touring. Pull into one of 283 full-service sites, or stay in the motel. Either way you can take advantage of the resort's three pools, health spa, lit tennis and shuffleboard courts, and restaurant .

Rock Creek RV Resort (239-643-3100; 3100 North Rd. at Airport Rd., Naples 34104) Full hookups for 221 RVs, pool, laundry, and shade trees. No pets.

DINING

Everglades City considers itself a fishing and stone-crab capital, so figure you can expect some highly fresh seafood in these parts. Stone crab, in fact, was discovered as a food source in the Everglades — at least that's the way some of the old-timers tell it. Before a couple of locals began trapping them and selling them to a Miami restaurant, the delicate, meaty flavor of stone crabs went unappreciated. Along with stone crab, alligator, frog legs, and other local delicacies make up the substance of Everglades cookery.

Marco Island, too, is known as a good market for buying stone crab, which gets quite expensive the farther from the source. With more than 100 restaurants on the island, Marco covers every genre of cuisine. Its trademark is its Old-Florida style of no-nonsense, trend-resistant seafood preparation. German cuisine also surfaces frequently.

Naples's dining reputation is staked on hauteur and creativity. Even the old fish houses dress up their catches in the latest fashion, which ranges from redesigned home cooking and continental nouvelle to Floribbean and Pacific Rim styles. Naples is a dining-out kind of place. The renovation of downtown's Fifth Avenue South has brought restaurants out into the street and sparked the genesis of what has been termed Naples's "café society."

The following listings sample all the variety of south coast feasting in these price categories:

Inexpensive	Up to $15	Expensive	$25 to $35
Moderate	$15 to $25	Very Expensive	$35 or more

Cost is figured on a typical dinner (unless dinner is not served) that would include an appetizer or dessert, salad (if included with the meal), entrée, and coffee.

The following abbreviations are used for credit card information and meals:

AE: American Express	B: Breakfast
D: Discover Card	L: Lunch
DC: Diners Club	D: Dinner
MC: MasterCard	SB: Sunday Brunch
V: Visa	

Bonita Springs

SOUTH BAY BISTRO
239-949-6030.
26821 South Bay Dr., Ste.
  114, Bonita Springs 34134.
The Promenade at Bonita
  Bay.
Price: Expensive to Very
  Expensive.
Children's Menu: Yes.
Cuisine: American Fusion.
Liquor: Full.
Serving: L, D.
Closed: Sat. and Sun. for
  lunch.
Credit Cards: AE, D, MC, V.
Handicap Access: Yes.
Reservations: Yes.
Special Features: Courtyard
  seating.

South Bay, one of the latest sensations at the new sensational Promenade shopping-dining center, is sophisticated without sacrificing casual and space age in its retro-futuristic décor and ahead-of-its-time menu. Not afraid to be daring, it adds fire and flair where others cater to bland. Rolls arrived in a spiral funnel, and the curried sweet potato vichyssoise with Gulf shrimp and scallion oil was spunky. The pan-seared yellowfin tuna appetizer with sesame sea salad and citrus teriyaki glaze, like the vichyssoise and many of the chef's creations, benefited from a drizzle of flavored oil — in this case, chili oil for added kick to the spectrum of sensations. Other small-plate offerings include inventive novelties such as panko breaded oysters with prosciutto, garlic spinach, and smoked tomato hollandaise; and spinach salad with oven-dried tomatoes, stilton cheese, and pear vinaigrette. Entrées are equally virtuoso. Try the tuna ahi, blackened and served on a bed of marvelous orange flavored sticky rice and coconut curry sauce for a bold taste of tropical. Want something more like comfort food? The grilled pork porterhouse reminisces winter delights. Thick and juicy, it was topped with shredded sour apple and a spiced blueberry compote that brought a playfulness and burst of flavors to the meat. The chop balanced atop the most intriguing sage bread pudding, slightly sweet and cinnamony, and flecked with tidbits of vegetables. The lunch menu features equally inspired sandwiches (jerk chicken with red onion relish and boursin, for instance), focaccia pizza, and entrées. And come dessert time, the pastry chef wows with a dandy selection, ranging from baked Alaskan coconut bomba with golden pineapple sauce to Florida citrus crème brûlée. We settled on a chocolate soufflé pudding — thickened and countrified with flour — swimming in espresso cream. Flawless, fun, and defiant, like everything we relished at South Bay.

ROY'S
239-498-7697.
26831 South Bay Dr., Suite
  #100, Bonita Springs 34134.
The Promenade at Bonita
  Bay.
Price: Expensive to Very
  Expensive.
Children's Menu: Yes.
Cuisine: Hawaiian/Asian.
Liquor: Full.

When you walk through the door at Roy's, everyone greets you with "Aloha." That's where the threat of Hawaiian kitsch ends — no leis, no flowered shirts, no Don Ho. Roy's Hawaiian conception and culinary inclination convey like a South Seas breeze rather than a tropical tempest. Like the simplicity of the decor, the flavors wrought by a fascinating menu are minimalist yet elegant, with one page of regular offerings and

Born in Hawaii, Roy's has flourished into a spin-off restaurant chain in Florida.

Karen T. Bartlett

Serving: D.
Credit Cards: AE, D, MC, V.
Handicap Access: Yes.
Reservations: Yes.
Special Features: Open
    kitchen and progressive
    design.

another, more extensive, selection of daily specials, all with a Pacific Rim backbone. Our server spent time familiarizing us with ingredients — particularly intriguing fish species such as *opakapaka*, butterfish, *moi,* and *ono*. My salad, a daily special, was a pleasing, light toss of pepper-vodka salmon and greens dressed in roasted garlic citrus vinaigrette. The dressing was subtle, allowing the bite of the greens to be felt. The attractive presentation was finished with a dollop of sour cream and caviar, pleasantly crunchy. My partner's Asian BBQ Chicken Salad off the regular menu came closer to a meal. Along with tender slices of chicken, candied pecans were tucked into the greens. Crispy noodles and bean sprouts added texture, all doused in a nicely balanced orange hoisin sesame vinaigrette. Seafood dominates Roy's menu and comprises the duel selection in the Surfah Special: blackened rare ahi tuna and lemongrass-crusted *ono* — a sculptural work of art. On a molded pallet of rice and steamed vegetables, the chef had stacked the two fish fillets, then sprouts, greenery, and slivers of pickled ginger. The accompanying Thai basil peanut sauce and soy mustard butter sauce swirled yin-yang on the plate. In the meat department, there's garlic mustard short ribs, porterhouse pork chop with gorgonzola peppercorn sauce, and the like. For dessert, try the peanut butter mousse cake on a slick of sweet-tart raspberry coulis topped with feathers of fried phyllo. Or indulge in the marvelous baklavalike macadamia and honey tart.

Chokoloskee Island

JT'S ISLAND GRILL & GALLERY
239-695-3633.
238 Mamie St.,
  Chokoloskee 34138.
Price: Inxpensive.
Cuisine: Southern/Deli.
Liquor: No.
Serving: B, L.
Closed: Mon.
Credit Cards: No.
Handicap Access: No.
Reservations: No.
Special Features: Historic
  building.

Come sit awhile at JT's. That's what the locals in Chokoloskee do. They mosey on up for some good hot, homemade breakfast, Southern-style, and sit on the porch and watch the world — or what little corner of it they see — go by. Food has been served here since 1886, when pioneer C. G. McKinney opened his store. Just a smidgen of a place, it sets up almost a dozen tables on the front porch and in the back among shelves of local paintings and Venezuelan napkin holders (that's where the gallery part of the name comes in), mosquito head nets, jellies, and genuine Seminole-made traditional clothing. The simple menu consists of Southern biscuit dishes for breakfast along with the day's specials, which could include French toast, omelets, and bagel sandwiches. The biscuits and gravy, served on a paper plate, taste down-home hardy and lick-the-plate delicious. Lunchtime brings deli and other specials, best washed down with a vanilla soft drink or sweet iced tea and topped off with homemade key lime pie.

Everglades City

ROD & GUN CLUB
239-695-2101.
200 Broadway, PO Box 190,
  Everglades City 34139.
Price: Moderate to
  Expensive.
Early Dining Menu: No.
Children's Menu:
  Sometimes, dinner only.
Cuisine: Florida.
Healthy Selections: No.
Liquor: Full.
Serving: L, D.
Credit Cards: No.
Handicap Access: No.
Reservations: No.
Special Features: Historic
  waterfront setting.

Dining here on a screened porch overlooking the Barron River and the mangroves on the other side always triggers the relaxation mechanism in my body, mind, and spirit. It goes deeper than the serenity of the scene, for there's a time-reversion effect here. Paddle fans twirl from pressed-tin ceilings, and white columns, a rounded portico, a porch with wicker chairs, and yellow-and-white striped awnings at the lodge's entrance evoke plantation manors of the Old South. The inside dining room, the antithesis of the patio's lightness, is all dark pecky-cypress wood, polished wood floors, and mounted fish and fowl — remnants of the lodge's sporting past. From the 1890s to 1960 the club hosted presidents, movie stars, and other intrepid Everglades hunters and fishermen. Back then guests dined on frog legs, alligator tail, and fresh fish. They still do. Menus do offer more conventional fare — reubens, burgers, New York strip steak, and fettucine Alfredo. On a recent visit, I ordered a tomato-based seafood stew with saffron rice that marvelously demonstrated the restaurant's abilities to stretch beyond Old Florida-style fried seafood. The ultimate Everglades City experience requires sitting back, taking in the view, enjoying local hospitality, and dining on Everglades specialties. The frog legs are incredibly tasty; the onion rings, the crunchiest and lightest imaginable; the gator nuggets, well tenderized but salty and a tad greasy; and the peanut butter pie and key lime pie, simply divine.

Goodland

LITTLE BAR RESTAURANT
239-394-5663.
205 Harbor Dr., Goodland 34140.
Price: Moderate to Expensive.
Children's Menu: No.
Cuisine: Seafood/Florida.
Liquor: Full.
Serving: L, D.
Credit Cards: D, MC, V.
Handicap Access: Yes.
Reservations: Yes, for dinner.
Special Features: Waterfront dining, historic "Boat Room."

Goodland is a town where a more modest pace of tourism has allowed folks to remain hometown and proud of it. A long-ingrained fishing tradition means you'll find the freshest catches and people who know how to prepare them. A friend had recommended Little Bar to me as friendly, and that it is. And then some. The hostess treated me like a regular as she led me through a forest of beautiful wood onto a screened porch overlooking Buzzard Bay harbor. Century-old stained-glass windows, hand-carved antique pieces, and a room divider made of wooden organ pipes bespeak the owner's passion for collectibles. One entire dining room, in fact, was created from the wreck of a 1927 boat, *Star of the Everglades*, which starred in movies and carried two presidents. From the porch I watched cruising boats bobbing alongside fishing scows as the waitress presented the menu board on a metal stand. The selections reflect the village's fishing reputation, with pleasant departures from standard fish-house fare — everything from Buffalo frog legs and grouper balls to kielbasa and kraut, tournedos au poivre, and shrimp de jonghe. On my first visit I ordered the softshell crab sandwich, a certain obsession of mine. It was the best I've had. More recently I sampled the day's blackened fish on greens, in this case, mahimahi. The fish was fresh and prepared to a T, though the greens were less than crisp, and the flavorful sesame dressing too thick for my liking. Desserts are equally fresh. Try Papa Ray's chocolate peanut butter pie. The coconut crunch pie is full of coconut but dry. The wine list is surprisingly extensive, but beer — which arrived with the requisite frosty mug — seemed more appropriate here.

Isles of Capri

**NICK'S BACKWATER
CAFÉ**
239-642-5700.
231 Capri Blvd., Isles of
Capri 34113.
Price: Moderate to
Expensive.
Children's Menu: Yes.
Cuisine: Seafood/
Floribbean.
Liquor: Full.
Serving: L, D.
Credit Cards: AE, MC, V.
Handicap Access: Dining
area, yes; rest rooms, no.
Reservations: Yes, for
dinner.
Special Features:
Waterfront dining.

Tucked away in the less-traveled Isles of Capri, Nick's outlooks Johnson Bay from beneath an authentic chickee (Indian thatched roof) open structure. When it's chilly, clear plastic sheathing rolls down and space heaters ignite around the massive wood bar that dominates the scene. In any weather, many of the patrons arrive by boat and hitch up at the docks, then settle in for a grab-and-go meal served on Styrofoam and paper. The all-day menu has a tropical sway, with things like jambalaya, coconut grouper, conch fritters, and chorizo rolls. The crab cakes are a delight, served as an appetizer or a sandwich. The crab wins in this contest of shellfish versus breading. Instead of a deep fryer, it meets a light sauté pan, just enough that it's brown and falling apart at the touch of a fork. The conch chowder was obviously homemade, but though generous with potatoes it's too stingy with the conch and weak on flavor, calling for a shot of Tabasco. In the past I've sampled the chicken, black bean, and cheese quesadilla, an appetizer I can recommend as lunch. What I like best are the view and laid-back atmosphere. In short, be in a casual mood, or don't be here.

Marco Island (see also Goodland and Isles of Capri)

**OLDE MARCO ISLAND
INN AND SUITES**
239-394-3131, 877-475-3466.
www.oldmarco.com.
100 Palm St., Marco Island
34145.
Price: Expensive to Very
Expensive.
Cuisine: Florida/Eclectic
Liquor: Full.
Serving: D, SB.
Credit Cards: AE, D, MC, V.
Handicap Access: Yes.
Reservations: Yes.
Special Features: Historic
landmark.

Back in Captain Bill Collier's day, guests were instructed to bring their own meat for dinner at the inn. Today your only requirement is an appetite for finely honed dishes that harmonize classic and modern, past and present. The inn has tread through a continuum of changes since 1883 and Captain Bill. In 1999 the century-old inn was lovingly restored and renovated. They've kept the tarpon scales and Audubon prints, the cranberry glass chandelier and the 19th-century furniture pieces. They've added whimsical Florida touches such as hand-painted trellis candleholders. The menu retains the shrimp, grouper, and snapper Captain Bill's guest probably enjoyed, along with the Wiener schnitzel made signature by the former German owners. The meal begins with a warm popover welcome, and though there's a touch of the Midwest in the roasted duckling with cashew wild rice, New Florida style dominates, adding lightness and total fresh-

When the Olde Marco Inn opened in the late 1800s, diners were required to provide their own meat.

Karen T. Bartlett

ness. Choose a wine from the reasonably priced list. After that, you may want to try the flaky Apalachicola blue crab cake with black bean salsa appetizer or hearts of palm salad, a lovely collage of mache, bibb, and oak leaf lettuces garnished with red and yellow tomatoes and strips of hearts of palm — what natives call swamp cabbage. It comes dressed with a dab of gorgonzola cheese and a light-herb vinaigrette. In the entrée department, the roasted salmon comes on a bed of sautéed endive, asparagus, and wild mushrooms, juiced up with Cabernet and shallot and thyme vinaigrette — an interesting counterpoint with the salmon's smooth richness. Ribbons of crispy leeks add yet another dimension of flavor and texture. The duckling with Grand Marnier sauce is also masterful – not too sweet, tempered by the wild rice. For dessert, the key lime pie and coconut caramel flan do sweet justice to Florida tradition.

SNOOK INN
239-394-3313.
1215 Bald Eagle Dr., Marco Island 34145
Price: Moderate to Expensive.
Children's Menu: Yes (ages 5 and under).
Cuisine: Seafood.
Liquor: Full.
Serving: L, D.
Credit Cards: V, MC, AE, DC.
Handicap Access: Yes.
Reservations: No.
Special Features: Chickee bar and outdoor waterfront seating.

Marco Island is known for its many restaurants, a great number of which serve fine, expensive food. To find something casual you have to travel to Goodland, a fishing village that shares the island, or head to Snook Inn, a long-standing tradition known equally for its congenial tiki bar (called in these parts by its Amerindian name, chickee bar) and its seafood. It still tips the scale on the overpriced side, and I found it perturbing that the children's menu was limited to preschoolers, but all in all it offers a nice taste of Marco's saltier, less-exclusive side. You can sit in the fresh sea air dockside along the peaceful Marco River. If the day is hot, you may prefer the air-conditioned porch, where picture windows let you feel a little like you're alfresco. A huge aquarium is set into wood-paneled walls. Inside it's cool and dark, and there you'll find the salad bar, a strong drawing card for the restaurant. It's small, but the contents are crisp, fresh, and varied, including a big crock of fat dill pickle chunks. Salad bar is included in most lunch and dinner menu selections, which concentrate on fish with some steak, chicken, and ribs exceptions. On Thursday and Friday nights the salad bar extends into a highly acclaimed long seafood buffet. Fried grouper is the house specialty and worthy of the renown. The grouper sandwich is generous and smacks of just-caught flavor. Buttermilk shrimp, shrimp de jonghe, grouper in a bag, and softshell crab are some other favorites. Sandwiches and salads are offered for both lunch and dinner, for a more affordable option. The spicy tomato conch chowder is chock-full of conch bits, with just the right touch of fire. Warning: Don't drink the water; even the slice of lemon doesn't disguise its off taste. Order a beer instead.

Naples

ANNABELLE'S
239-261-4275.
494 Fifth Ave. S, Naples
    34102.
Price: Very Expensive.
Children's Menu: No.
Cuisine: New American.
Liquor: Full.
Serving: D.
Credit Cards: AE, D, MC, V.
Handicap Access: Yes.
Reservations: Yes.
Special Features: Balcony
    dining overlooking lively
    Fifth Avenue.

In Naples of the new millennium, the race runs relentless and grueling to see who can be declared the latest darling of innovation. For the time being, Annabelle's wins. When we first walked in the door of the two-story downtown palace, my eyes popped while my companion, a fellow New Yorker, declared, "This is *so* New York." The design-forward décor of swirl and style seemed out of sorts in Naples. (It so disturbed my sense of place, I asked to be seated on the balcony, where we could spy down on Fifth Avenue South's famous night scene.) The menu is equally brave but less intimidating, and the staff is entirely helpful. Starters take up as much of the menu as entrées, teasing the appetite with poetic creations the likes of seared sea scallop with sautéed foie gras, black currants and port wine syrup; and a casserole of hearts of palm, Maytag blue cheese, and black truffles — both exquisite. We split our main course selections between the fish and meat halves of the entrée portion. I can highly recommend the soy-lacquered snapper with crispy shrimp, stick rice cake, and citrus vinaigrette. Every nibble was a triumph of complex and harmonious tastes. We were slightly less taken with the grilled filet mignon, which tasted mushy as from overtenderizing, but we did enjoy its smoked tomato reduction treatment. Tuna tartar, monkfish osso bucco, New Zealand loin of fallow, peeky toe crab, micro arugula: Annabelle's menu, like its ambience, is as edgy as it is sophisticated.

LE CAFFE DES ARTISTES
239-261-7598.

Ensconced in a slightly eccentric setting of animal print carpeting and accents, and hot pink trim on a black wall divider, Caffe is nonetheless

210 Ninth Street North,
   Naples 34102.
Price: Expensive.
Children's Menu: No, but
   will accommodate kids.
Cuisine: French and Italian.
Liquor: Full.
Serving: L, D.
Closed: Sun. for lunch.
Credit Cards: AE, MC, V.
Handicap Access: Yes.
Reservations: Yes.

romantic and personal. Where the table settings may fail to impress (our soup spoon was dirty, and the silverware mismatched), the food more than compensates. Although it calls its cuisine French Italian, the French accent is most pronounced. Classicism underlies an understated flair of creativity. The menu writes the names of its dishes in French and Italian, depending on their persuasion. For starters, we went both ways: soupe à l'oignon, Caesar salad, and a night's special salad of homemade mozzarella with roasted red peppers. Each selection was faultless, making us anticipate our entrées with high expectations, yet disabling us from prudently pacing ourselves by not finishing our fetching appetizers. The onion soup was full-flavored with a hint of sweetness. The Caesar salad places in my Caesar Hall of Fame. Parchment slices of parmesan and harmonically balanced dressing topped full crisp leaves from the heart of the romaine. The cheese in the mozzarella salad was creamy, not chewy, and an inimitable complement to the peppers, treated simply with basil and oregano. Again, splitting our selections between the French and Italian, we ordered steak au poivre vert and veal saltimbocca. The strip steak was unusually thick and large under a blanket of brandy cream peppercorn sauce that left a nice, tingly afterglow sans burn. The veal, breaded with thin slices of prosciutto so that the two meats fused seamlessly, languished atop a bed of fresh steamed spinach and under the influence of a subtle lemon sauce. Both entrées were equally excellent. Other entrées offered a modernized departure from the classics. Lobster ravioli, for instance, comes in a pool of sherry and creamy saffarano sauce. A dozen fresh littleneck clams accompany the linguine with clam sauce. The rack of lamb is rubbed with herbs and mustard and served with tarragon port sauce. Portobello mushrooms add a fresh spin to the pollo marsala. For a finish *parfait*, don't miss the hot apple dumpling with ice cream — a counterpoise of homemade earthiness and heavenly lightness.

BHA! BHA!

239-594-5557.
847 Vanderbilt Rd., Naples
   34108.
At the Pavilion.
Price: Moderate to
   Expensive.
Children's Menu: No.
Cuisine: Middle Eastern.
Liquor: Beer and wine.
Serving: L, D, SB.
Credit Cards: AE, MC, V.

An Iranian chef and an American artist partner in this new, deliciously exotic enterprise. The merger of creativities results in a sleek, bright, and sunny setting of ocher and key-lime-green walls, ottomans, fountain, and Turkish tapestries. They call it a Persian bistro. In an Iranian dialect the name means Yum! Yum! And that's where chef Michael Mir comes in. He fuses his native background with his experience in fine American kitchens to present an intriguing menu that maintains the authenticity

Chelle Koster Walton

Bha! Bha! fuses culinary and artistic elements from old Persia and new continental.

Handicap Access: Yes.
Reservations: Yes, for
    dinner.

and boldness of Middle Eastern cuisine while employing a few tricks of classic continental and experimental new American styles. Prepare your palate for a magic carpet ride. Flavors tick, tantalize, then burst in a medley of unusual seasonings and combinations. Aash, a peasant-style bean soup, starts out simple but, as you nibble into the center garnish of pickled Persian noodles, becomes more and more complex and extraordinary. In the appetizer of eggplant and artichoke, we could discern an orchestra of flavors: distinctive Bulgarian feta, dill and a hint of sweetness in the mustard sauce, and the peanut oil in which the eggplant was sautéed. Yum, yum. The dinner menu is divided between classic and innovative Persian cuisine and *khoreshes* (specialties). Under "innovative," saffron basmati rice accompanies seafood and meat dishes. I recommend the spicy *kermani* beef, its dark saffron sauce enlivened by pepperoncini and cucumber yogurt. Classics range from kabobs to char-broiled lamb (incredibly beautiful and tasty), and specialties include garlic eggplant chicken (wonderful!), dried-plum lamb, and duck *fesenjune* — braised in orange saffron stock and served with pomegranate walnut sauce (a bit heavy-sweet). Persian coffee comes served in a delicate espresso service with an ornamental wood box full of rock candy and sugar. Try the unusual rose-flavored ice cream or gooey baklava for dessert.

**CHARDONNAY
    RESTAURANT**
239-261-1744.
2331 N. Tamiami Trail,
    Naples 34103.
Price: Expensive to Very
    Expensive.
Children's Menu: No.

For years, Chardonnay has been equated to special-occasion dining. With its heavy brocaded draperies and chair cushions, grand brass chandelier, and large multipaned windows that effectively bring in the outdoor garden and fish pond, it sets the stage for something finely Continental and out of the ordinary. (Ask for seating in the garden

Cuisine: French.
Liquor: Full.
Serving: D.
Credit Cards: AE, MC, V.
Handicap Access: Yes.
Reservations:
  Recommended.

rooms; the interior room is cleverly decorated with painted faux sea views but more cramped.) With the name Chardonnay, you have to put forward a solid wine footing, and it does so with an extensive list of primarily high-end imports and domestics. Just as the windows let a bit of Florida into the Old World room, so do certain menu items. The shrimp à la Floridienne were interspersed with orange sections and rimmed with a sassy white horseradish and citrus sauce. The lobster bisque was tinged with orange zest, although an overgenerous application of salt overshadowed its subtlety. A masterpiece among the appetizers is the apple pancake, topped with hazelnut-studded goat cheese. The menu and specials submit a selection of about 20 options each night. Many are French classics such as its signature rack of lamb with herbs, veal sweetbreads, rabbit with champagne sauce, roast duck, and lobster and scallops St. Jacques. Others, particularly the seafood dishes, are Chardonnay's own: filet mignon with Chardonnay wine sauce, blackened mahimahi, and red snapper with cream of fresh basil sauce. No richness is spared with these dishes. The mignonette de boeuf Madagascar consists of two large medallions executed to perfection both in degree of rareness and its creamy peppercorn sauce flambé with Armagnac. Desserts pose equally diet-blasting choices, including soufflés, crème brûlée, and the highly recommended apple and rhubarb tart. The crème brûlée was slightly disappointing because of an unpleasant off taste in the brittle burnt sugar crust, a by-product of a gas flame. (Paying Chardonnay's top-dollar prices, one tends to be less forgiving of small imperfections.) The custard, nonetheless, was creamy smooth and as impeccable as the service — but not nearly as stiff).

THE DOCK AT CRAYTON COVE
239-263-9940.
www.dockcraytoncove.
  com.
845 12th Ave. S., Naples
  34102.
Price: Moderate to
  Expensive.
Children's Menu: Yes.
Cuisine: Floribbean.
Liquor: Full.
Serving: L, D.
Credit Cards: AE, D, MC,
  V.
Handicap Access: Yes.
Reservations: No.
Special Features: Open-air
  view of the marina.

The Dock remembers what Naples is about — clear down to its roots — while keeping abreast of what Naples has become. The roots part reflects in the fun, casual, waterlogged atmosphere it exudes from its breeze-through set-up. Opened in 1976, the fish-house-style eatery has kept abreast of Naples's sophistication with remakes and menu upgrades. Once a purveyor of typical fried seafood fare, today it makes a serious stance among the tough culinary standards of Naples. Seafood still reigns, but the Caribbean has washed in to give us such offerings as Cuban barbecued baby-back ribs, rum and molasses BBQ duck, Jamaican jerk shrimp, and roasted plantain snapper. One page describes peppy *rhum* (the way they spell "rum" in the French Antilles) drinks. Chefs execute the creative offerings with complexity. For instance, for lunch recently I ordered the pepper grilled yellowfin tuna on a French bread crouton with goat cheese and Caribbean slaw. The slappy-fresh tuna arrived exactly rare as I ordered and incredibly juicy, the gamy taste of the goat cheese was complemented by sweet caramelized onions, and the slaw was treated lightly with vinegar and oil, then made singular by the addition of ginger. I practically licked the plate. Crafty salads, sandwiches, and luncheon specials complete the midday offerings. Something simpler? The menu offers six fresh catches prepared just with olive oil and kosher salt. And instead of jalapeño crab fritters or lobster ravioli for appetizers, choose from a select menu of oysters imported from several seasonal locations.

GORDON'S WATERFRONT GRILL
239-434-8888.
489 Bayfront Place, Naples 34102.
In the Bayfront Center.
Price: Moderate.
Children's Menu: Yes.
Cuisine: American.
Liquor: Full.
Serving: L, D.
Credit Cards: AE, D, DC, MC, V.
Handicap Access: Yes.
Reservations: No.

It was a muggy day, so the garage-door-type glass panes were not open onto the Gordon River across the street. Still the décor created a pleasant mood. Handsome on the outside, like the rest of the crowd at Bayfront Center, the interior affects a warehouse style set off by a floating V-shaped vaulted wooden ceiling, sleek wooden booths, and fanciful lighting. Arranged on stepped levels, the dining room gives everyone a water view. The setting is fresh, and the all-day menu is undemanding of the diner, allowing you to order a cheeseburger or filet mignon any time of the day. It offers a changing homemade soup du jour, and Gordon's is worth a visit just for Friday's New England Clam Chowder. Not too thick, not too thin, it was replete with clam bits, potatoes, and

flavor. Also for a starter, we ordered the crab cake appetizer, which nestled in a flounce of colorful greens sauced with a well-balanced honey mustard dressing. Chunks of crab were embedded in the cake, light on breading. Other "Forethoughts" include spinach and artichoke dip, baked brie with flat bread, and chili. On the sandwich portion of the menu, you'll find the standard burgers, grouper sandwich, French dip, and so on but with signature touches. The grilled chicken sandwich is bulked up with Smithfield ham, bacon, and cheddar. Herbed mayo brightens the tuna and shrimp salad. That sort of thing. Gordon's specialties come off the grill — Cajun mahimahi, salmon with dill sauce, grouper, and tuna. The baked stuffed chicken breast tasted like Thanksgiving, swaddling sage bread dressing and accompanied by candied cranberries. The slow-roasted prime rib was juicy but a tad overcooked. Both entrées came with marvelous mashed potatoes, the skins squashed into the chunky-creamy mound. Gordon's is a light-hearted and festive place to wind down or up, but its food is nothing close to frivolous. Just refreshingly uncomplicated.

MESON OLÉ
239-649-6616.
2212 N. Tamiami Trail,
   Naples 34103.
At the Oaks Shopping
   Center.
Price: Moderate.
Children's Menu: Yes.
Cuisine: Mexican/Spanish.
Healthy Selections: No.
Liquor: Full.
Serving: L, D.
Credit Cards: AE, D, MC,
   V.
Handicap Access: Yes.
Reservations: Yes.

Meson Olé has descended to Florida from a New York State chain, but it has no regional counterparts and stands decidedly apart from conventional chain Mexican restaurants. Its menu does carry the typical tostados and chimichangas, but I suggest you be more daring here. The menu is certainly venturous, as it enters into genuine Spanish territory. Take, for instance, *sopa de ajo Casera*, a traditional Castilian soup that floats a crouton and a poached egg. The latter added richness to the untimid garlic broth, which suffered only from too much salt. *Los mejillones en salsa verde* — mussels in green sauce — was a totally unexpected pleasure, the sauce not spicy, peppery hot as I anticipated but buttery and garlicky, with green peas wading in it. The mussels were the most tender I've tasted in a long while. Lobster tail and seafood come in the same rich bath on the entrées portion of the menu. The shrimp in chipotle sauce, on the other hand, was spicy, just as the menu promised, but also slightly sweet and wonderfully rich and complex, but without a hint of chipotle smokiness. And again, the shrimp were cooked perfectly to the brink of doneness. Other enticements: Spanish shrimp in champagne sauce; chicken in creamy whiskey sauce; mignon of veal sautéed with mushrooms, asparagus, and ham; and two varieties of paella. The atmosphere is more typical of the Mexican genre — the requisite serapes and pounded-metal plates — and tucked into a strip mall. This place was recommended to me by a Texan connoisseur who assured me the margaritas were the real thing, not all pucker inducing or sugary. They are indeed.

OLD HEIDELBERG
239-592-7900.
10711 N. Tamiami Trail,
   Naples 34108.
Price: Moderate to
   Expensive.
Early Dining Menu: Yes.
Children's Menu: No.
Cuisine:
   German/Continental.
Liquor: Full.
Serving: B, L, D.
Credit Cards: AE, MC, V.
Handicap Access: Yes.
Reservations: Yes.

Banish oompah-pah notions! The Heidelberg restaurant is German food in the 21st century, with a menu that stretches beyond Weiner schnitzel, bratwurst, and beer. Don't get me wrong: You can find traditional specialties on the menu (and imported draft beer selections you don't normally find elsewhere). Just not the same old tired ways. Elegant chandeliers, wall sconces, and window treatments, fresh flowers and classical music set the tone in a dining room where tables are nicely spaced. The breadbasket arrives filled with sliced coarse and white varieties plus a ramekin of pâté and one of butter. Don't miss the wild mushroom bisque — dark, full-flavored, and mushroom-generous rich. Between two saucer-sized potato pancakes, perfectly crispy at the edges and supple in the middle — came delicate slices of smoked salmon, large capers, and chopped onion. The side of dill sour cream made this appetizer a marvelous mixed-culture delight that could have been its own meal. The entrées are divided by three. The main section lists Old World favorites twisted with a bit of new age ingenuity. The beef *rouladen*, for example, is rolled with bacon, onion, and pickles, then topped with burgundy mustard sauce. Venison medallions, sauerbraten, calves liver, and roasted veal shank for two received similar revision. Our jaeger-schnitzel was sautéed without breading and served with a genteel mushroom-and-cognac cream sauce. The menu also lists grilled selections — the grilled bratwurst was slender but oozing juicy — plus a page of changing-nightly recommendations. I ordered from the *Fisch* portion of the dinner menu, torn between grouper Tirolienne wrapped in Tyrolese ham and served on creamed spinach, and sea bass poached in fennel broth with shrimp, asparagus, and tomatoes. I ended up with the delicately flavored and seasoned sea bass. Hearty side dishes of mashed potatoes, stuffed zucchini, carrots, summer squash, and spaetzle seasoned with a hint of nutmeg accompanied our entrées. All in all — according to true German tradition — too much to eat for an assuredly reasonable price. Heidelberg also serves an intriguing international menu at breakfast and lunch.

AU PARADIS
239-775-7667.
11412 Tamiami Trail E.,
   Naples 34113.
Price: Very Expensive.
Children's Menu: No.
Cuisine: French.
Liquor: Beer and wine.
Serving: D.
Closed: Sunday.
Credit Cards: D, MC, V.
Handicap Access: Limited.
Reservations: Yes.

Inside you'll find a cozy but light dining room of about a dozen lace-covered tables behind three picture windows framing a gazebo garden. From those gardens are plucked the edible flowers and herbs that dress Au Paradis' cuisine in loving, imaginative style, which it terms French Floridian. Uncomplicated in its honest selection of a handful of hors d'oeuvres and nine French classics, the menu nonetheless shows complexity in the way it puts French technique to work on Florida seafood, citrus, and other ingredients.

The tender Prince Edward Island mussels are baptized in wine broth flavored with garlic and shallot subtle enough to complement without strangling. Smooth puree of butternut squash comprises the bisque de courge et crab with its small island of crab cake at center. It is divine. The interlude house salad comes garnished with flowers, a wafer of shredded Parmesan, and an intricate house vinaigrette with tones of raspberry, citrus, and Dijon. Witness how the husband-wife chef team performs its Florida transplant on other standard French specialties: risotto aux fruits de mer (superb), yellowtail snapper with toasted pine nuts and white wine reduction, grouper with caviar d'aubergine, and sea bass in sauce of tomato, caper, and olive. Recommended: the veal medallions, polished and homey with shiitake mushrooms and cider brandy cream sauce. Key lime crème brûlée epitomizes the essence of Au

Paradis on the dessert menu, but the warm apple tart is hard to resist, resting on a layer of praline cream cheese and flaky pastry, and infused with the flavors of Grand Marnier, amaretto, chantilly cream, and Cointreau caramel sauce. Magnifique!

SIGN OF THE VINE
239-261-6745.
980 Solano Rd., Naples 34103.
Off Goodlette Rd.
Price: Very Expensive.
Children's Menu: No.
Cuisine: Florida Fusion.
Liquor: Beer and wine.
Serving: D.
Closed: Sunday, and some months in summer.
Credit Cards: AE.
Handicap Access: Yes.
Reservations: Strongly advised.
Special Features: Charming cottage setting.

Tucked into tangled foliage, the charming Old Florida cottage looks like something from a fairytale. The illusion of fantasy continues inside, where cozy tables decorated with long, elegant candlesticks and mismatched antique china are disbursed throughout intimate little rooms and in front of a fireplace in the main dining room. The setting charmingly mingles homey with elegant, as does the menu — a collage of comfort food and continental flair, old family recipes and cutting-edge pairings. The meal is a progression of wonderful experiences interspersed with pleasant entr'acte surprises: unexpected house hors d'oeuvres, steaming popovers with citrus butter, grilled fruit refreshers, an eclectic relish tray, tableside salad, a plate of homemade fudge and sugared walnuts. The menu — presented framed like art — changes five times a year. Three signature dishes always appear: roasted peach and bourbon duckling, tenderloin with cognac cream, and lobster hash. The tenderloin is lightly fried in a cracked pepper and Vidalia onion crust that melts in your mouth. The chefs use flash frying liberally but creatively to seal in juices and provide interesting textures. Everything is homemade and the wine list exquisite. Attention to detail and congenial service make this the ultimate in fine dining for special romantic occasions.

FOOD PURVEYORS

BAKERIES

Bakeries today are often combined with delis, grocery stores, and even wine shops.

Island Bakery (239-394-4508; 287 N. Collier Blvd., Marco Island 34145) Specializes in cakes. Also: key lime pie, tortes, croissants, Danish, breads.

Naples Cheesecake Co. (239-598-9070, 800-325-6554; 8050 Trail Blvd., Naples 34108) Eight to twelve different flavors, including key lime, amaretto, and peanut butter.

Tony's Off Third (239-262-7999; 1300 Third Ave. S., Naples 34102) European bakery featuring legendary desserts, pastries, and breads, and a well-respected selection of wine and coffee, plus deli items and sandwiches.

CANDY & ICE CREAM

The Chocolate Strawberry (239-394-5999; 135 S. Barfield Dr., Marco Island 34145; at the Shops of Marco) Hand-dipped chocolates, seahorse lollipops, ice cream, gelato, yogurt, sorbet, chocolate turtles, shells, pelicans, fish, other local critters, and coffee.

Dip n' Dolphin (239-695-2218; 531 S. Copeland, Everglades City 34139) Cheerful, bright ice cream parlor serving cones, sundaes, key lime and other shakes, and sundaes.

Olde Naples Confectionery (239-262-3975; 1305 Third St. S., Naples 34102) Small showroom for chocolates and hard candy.

Regina's Ice Cream Pavilion (239-434-8181; 824 Fifth Ave. S., Naples 34102) An old-fashioned soda fountain with modern frozen yogurts, sorbets, and sugar-free and name-brand ice cream.

COFFEE

Bar Bados (239-643-5993; 4350 Gulf Shore Blvd. N., Suite #506, Naples 34103; at the Village on Venetian Bay) Espresso, cappuccino, flavored coffee, tea, frozen yogurt, smoothies, shakes, croissants, specialty drinks, and sandwiches.

P.J.'s Coffee & Tea Co. Cafe (239-261-5757; 599 Fifth Ave. S., Naples 34102) Hot and iced coffee and tea, cappuccino, café latte, macchata, bakery goods. Seating indoors and out.

Roberto's (239-394-8388; 1031 N. Collier Blvd., Marco Island 34145; at Marco Town Center Mall) Espresso bar, fresh bagels and other bakery goods, light breakfasts, ice cream. Seating indoors and out.

DELI & SPECIALTY FOODS

Artichoke & Co. (239-263-6979; 4370 Gulf Shore Blvd. N., Naples 34103; at the Village on Venetian Bay) Gourmet takeout, soups, breads, cheeses, pastries, salads, and wines.

Crayton Cove Gourmet (239-262-4362, 800-678-4362; www.craytoncovegourmet.com; 800 12th Ave. S., Naples 34102) Old-fashioned purveyor of Florida goodies, specializing in citrus shipping, fresh orange juice, key lime pie and other citrus sweets, and orange-blossom honey.

Fantozzi's (239-262-4808; 1148 Third St. S., Naples 34102) In a historic Naples building, Fantozzi's is a popular place to grab a specialty or deli sandwich to enjoy at the tables outside. It also sells fine cheeses, wine, premade dinners such as lamb pie and beef Wellington, salmon, and herbed vinegars.

Mel's New York Deli (239-642-6206; 571 S. Collier Blvd., Marco 34145) Deli sandwiches, subs hot and cold, bagels, knishes, muffins, pastries, home-made desserts.

Naples Finest (239-649-4866; 4202 Tamiami Trail N., Naples 34103) Grew from a fruit stand to an extensive deli, with breads, cheese, produce, wine, tea, coffee, ice cream, and gourmet food items.

Tony's Off Third (239-262-7999; 1300 Third St. S., Naples 34102) Build your own sandwich, plus prepackaged deli salads.

Wynn's Family Market (239-261-0901; 745 Fifth Ave. S., Naples 34102) Since 1945 the Wynn family has operated this Fifth Avenue landmark, most famous for its fine selection of wine, fresh bakery goodies, desserts, and hot-and-cold prepared deli foods.

FRUIT & VEGETABLE STANDS

European-style market convenes Saturdays during the winter in Old Naples.

Karen T. Bartlett

Naples Farmers' Market (Parking lot at Third St. S. and 13th Ave., Old Naples) Every Saturday, November through March, 7 to 11am.

Stallings Farm (239-263-1028; 2600 Pine Ridge Rd., Naples 34109) U-Pick, We Pick, and shipping. Citrus and vegetables.

NATURAL FOODS

Martha's Natural Food Market (239-992-5838; 9118 Bonita Beach Rd. E., Bonita Springs 34135; at Sunshine Plaza) Full line of health groceries, including food for low-carb and diabetic diets; also dietary supplements.

PIZZA & TAKEOUT

Aurelio's (239-403-8882; 590 N. Tamiami Trail, Naples 34102) Since 1959, pizza, pasta, and other Italian specialties to eat in or to go.

Cracker's Grill (239-643-7400; 493 Airport Rd. N., Naples 34109) Burgers and oversized sandwiches, eat in or take out; breakfast and lunch.

JT's Island Grill & Gallery (239-695-3633; 238 Mamie St., Chokoloskee 34138) An island-style grocery store with sandwich takeout (cooler-proof upon request) and stone crabs in season.

SEAFOOD

Captain Jerry's Seafood (239-262-7337; 141 9th St. N., Naples 34102) Shrimp, stone crab, and fish.

Ernest Hamilton's Stone Crabs (239-695-2771; 100 Hamilton Ln., Chokoloskee Island 34138) A longtime wholesaler that caters to individual buyers, as well.

Kirk's Fresh Seafood Market (239-394-8616; 417 Papaya Dr., Goodland 34140) Right on the fish docks, with crab traps piled around it, selling wholesale and retail.

Everglades Fish Company(239-695-3241, 888-968-2722; 208 Camillia St., Everglades City 34139) Right next to the stone crab docks in Everglades City, it has to sell the freshest. You can also buy shrimp, Florida lobster tails, frog legs, and fish.

CULTURE

The affluent residents of Naples — many of them transplanted CEOs and captains of industry from lands to the north — share their county with impoverished migrants who work in Immokalee, the nearby agricultural center. The influences of Haitian, Puerto Rican, Jamaican, and other Caribbean cultures are finding their way into the mainstream, while flashes of southern spirit and Cracker charm surface in Goodland, Everglades City, and Chokoloskee.

The Miccosukee and Big Cypress Seminole Indians inhabit reservations in the Everglades. They celebrate their culture each year at the Green Corn Ceremony, during the first new moon in June. They contribute the south coast's only authentic, indigenous art: colorful weaving, stitching, jewelry, and other age-old handicrafts.

Highbrow art has become a trademark of Naples and its long roll of galleries and performance spaces.

ARCHITECTURE

The humble and lavish extremes of south Coast architecture.

Karen T. Bartlett

Karen T. Bartlett

In Naples, commercial architecture is marked by style and panache, not to mention the architectural beauty of homes and resorts. Banks and insurance companies seem to compete for virtuosity. It's truly a land of visual allure. Pelican Bay developments provide examples of a new residential style and provide a contrast with old-money Port Royal.

Old Naples, that neighborhood in the vicinity of the pier and Fifth Avenue South, has held on to some real treasures, including the tabby-mortar Palm Cottage, the old Mercantile, and the Old Naples building at Broad and Third. In the same neighborhood, on Gordon Drive, pay attention to the charming board-and-batten Cracker survivors.

In Everglades City and Chokoloskee Island, recreational vehicles and cement-block boxes typify the fishing-oriented community's style. The Rod & Gun Club, built in 1850, stands out and dresses the town in southern flair. The style of thatch housing, perfected by the Indians, known as chickee (pronounced chee-KEY) prevails in the Everglades and serves as a trendy beach-bar motif at the ritziest resorts throughout the coastal region.

CINEMA

MOVIE THEATERS

Bonita Springs 12 Regal Cinemas (239-949-2600; Hwy. 41 and Pelicans Nest Dr., Bonita Springs 34134)

Hollywood Cinema 20 Regal Cinemas (239-597-9494; 6006 Airport Pulling Rd., Naples 34109; at Pine Ridge Rd.)

Marco Movie Theater (239-642-1111; 599 S. Collier Blvd., Marco Island 34245; at Marco Walk) Four screens with first-run movies, food, beer, and wine service.

Naples Twin Drive-In (239-774-6661; 7700 E. Davis Blvd., Naples 34104) Show times nightly, double features on weekends.

GARDENS

**CARIBBEAN GARDENS:
THE ZOO IN NAPLES**
239-262-5409.
www.napleszoo.com.
1590 Goodlette-Frank Rd.,
Naples 34102.
Open: 9:30am–5:30pm daily
(last ticket sold at 4:30).
Admission: $14.95 adults;
$9.95 children 4–15.

These tropical gardens, today the setting for a nicely proportioned zoo (see "Kids' Stuff" in this section), were planted in 1919 by Dr. Henry Nehrling, a botanist who brought his private collection to Naples. After he died, Julius Fleischmann, a developer, restored and expanded the doctor's 3,000-plus specimens and opened the gardens to the public in 1954. Besides native vegetation, exotics such as magnificent laurel figs, monkey-puzzle trees, white birds of paradise, poincianas, orchids, and sausage trees flourish in wetlands and on hammocks.

HISTORIC HOMES & SITES

INDIAN HILL
Scott Drive, Goodland.

Though rich in natural and historic heritage, Marco Island hides it well among 20th-century trappings. Witness Indian Hill. On your own you'll have to search to find it, and when you do, only a barely noticeable plaque marks the spot. (Or take a trolley tour — Marco Island Trolley, 239-394-1600 — to get there.) Southwest Florida's highest elevation at 58 feet above sea level, built up by ancient Caloosa Indian shell mounds, it now holds a ritzy neighborhood called the Heights, which feels a little like San Francisco.

PALM COTTAGE
239-261-8164.
137 12th Ave. S., Naples
34102.
Open: 1–4pm Tues.–Fri.
and Sun.; Fri. and Sun. in
summer.
Closed: Weekends.
Admission: Donation of $6
each requested; children
ages 10 and under free.

Land was selling for $10 a lot when Naples founder Walter N. Haldeman (no relation to H. R. Haldeman of Watergate fame) built a winter home for fellow worker Henry Watterson. Haldeman, publisher of the *Louisville Courier Journal*, had discovered the exotic beaches and jungles of Naples in 1887 and proceeded to buy up land and sing its praises. His enthusiasm persuaded winter escapees from Kentucky and Ohio to visit, including Watterson, his star editorial writer. The cottage Haldeman built for his friend was made of Florida pine, tidewater cypress, and a certain type of tabby mortar made by burning seashells over a buttonwood fire. It was one of the first buildings in southwest Florida to be constructed of local materials. Before reaching its present museum status, the cottage — rather spartan by modern standards — knew many lives. If the walls could talk at Palm Cottage, as it eventually came to be known, they would tell of wild parties with the likes of Gary Cooper and Hedy Lamarr in attendance. The cottage, which recently underwent a $400,000 renovation, is now the headquarters of the Collier County Historical Society.

SMALLWOOD STORE
239-695-2989.
360 Mamie St.,
    Chokoloskee Island
    34138.
South of Everglades City.
Open: 10am–5pm
    Dec.–May; 10am–4pm
    May–Nov.
Admission: $2.50 adults, $2
    seniors, children under
    12 free.

A historic throwback to frontier days in the 'Glades, this museum preserves a Native-American trading post of the early 1900s. Splintery shelves hold ointment containers, FlyDed insect killer, livestock spray, and hordes of memorabilia. Rooms recall life in the pioneer days. The best feature is the view from the back porch. This was the site of a Jesse James-era murder immortalized in Peter Matthiessen's novel *Killing Mr. Watson*.

KIDS' STUFF

CARIBBEAN GARDENS:
    THE ZOO IN NAPLES
239-262-5409.
www.napleszoo.com.
1590 Goodlette-Frank Rd.,
    Naples 34102.
Open: 9:30am–5:30pm daily
    (last ticket sold at 4:30).
Admission: $14.95 adults,
    $9.95 children 4–15 (plus
    tax).

Big cats are the specialty of this zoo. Not just your lions and Bengal tigers but such rarities as the white tiger, golden tiger, serval, and caracal. They are the stars of "Meet the Keeper" programs and the multimedia Safari Canyon, where predators take the stage and video footage enhances live demonstrations of dingos, monitor lizards, and leaping lemurs. Different shows concentrate on alligators, other reptiles, and mammals. A free boat ride takes a close-up look at the zoo's primate population, which is sequestered on nine islands. In spring 2001, the zoo opened Young Explorers Playground Forest, with areas for toddlers and older children. Shaded, meandering, chirp-orchestrated paths take you past other fenced animals. For $2 you can purchase a zoo key, which allows you audio access at the exhibits. The 52-acre grounds are attractively maintained with the lush vegetation of the zoo's so-called Caribbean Gardens (see "Gardens" in this section).

MUSEUMS

COLLIER COUNTY
    HISTORICAL MUSEUM

The unique aspects at this village of history include typical Seminole chickee huts, a vintage

239-774-8476.
3301 Tamiami Trail E.,
  Naples 34112.
Open: 9am–5pm.
Closed: Weekends, except
  during special winter
  exhibits.
Admission: Donations
  accepted.

swamp buggy kids can climb into, the skeleton of an Ice Age giant ground sloth, a working archaeological lab, a collection of antique stuffed local animals, and a 1910 steam locomotive from the county's cypress-logging era. Exhibits of prehistoric fossils and Native-American artifacts, housed in pretty vintage structures and nicely landscaped, take you back 10,000 years. More recent historical reminders include a recreated 19th-century trading post, 1920s furnishings, period vignettes, and a native plant garden. One exhibit likens the opening of Tamiami Trail to the Panama Canal.

KEY MARCO MUSEUM
239-394-7549.
Shops at Old Marco, P.O.
  Box 2282, Naples 34146.
Open: 9am–4pm Mon.–Fri.
Closed: Weekends.
Admission: Free.

Through photographs, artifacts, replicas, and memorabilia, this fledgling museum depicts the past of Key Marco, as it was once known. It concentrates on the island's rich Calusa Indian culture, displaying shell tools, masks, wood carvings, and other artifacts unearthed in the 1896 archeological expedition that established Marco as an important center of the Calusa kingdom. Modern times are also represented by displays exploring pineapple farming, clam canning, and residential development.

**MUSEUM OF THE
EVERGLADES**
239-695-0008.
www.colliermuseum.com.
105 W. Broadway, PO Box
  8, Everglades City 34139.
Hours: 11am–4pm
  Tues.–Sat.
Closed: Sun. and Mon.
Admission: $2 suggested
  donation.

The museum takes over a renovated historic laundry started by developer Barron Collier to serve the community of road builders during the construction of the Tamiami Trail in the 1920s. The museum, still developing, concentrates on the tremendous feat of blazing a trail through the swampy, buggy Everglades, plus the region's Calusa Indian and fishing heritage.

**TEDDY BEAR MUSEUM
OF NAPLES**
239-598-2711.
www.teddymuseum.com.
2511 Pine Ridge Rd.,
  Naples 34109.
Open: 10am–5pm
  Wed.–Sat. (also Mon. in
  season), 1–5pm Sun.

Home to nearly 4,000 teddies, this cuddly museum showcases collector, antique, and limited-edition bears and includes a signed first edition of A.A. Milne's *Winnie the Pooh*. The collection began as one woman's penchant for the stuffed animals and is whimsically displayed: bears at clown school, bears on parade, etc. There are bears hanging from the rafters everywhere you look. Tots will have fun

Closed: Tues. (also Mon. during off-season).
Admission: $6 adults, $4 seniors, $2 children 4–12.

in the Three Bears House. A gift shop sells bears and fine gifts. Saturday morning story hour for kids.

MUSIC AND NIGHTLIFE

The Naples Concert Band performs Sunday afternoons at Cambier Park.

Karen T. Bartlett

The Club at The Ritz-Carlton (239-598-3300; 280 Vanderbilt Beach Rd., Naples 34108) Live contemporary music Thursday through Saturday.

Club Zanzibar (239-514-3777; 475 Seagate Dr., Naples 34108; at the Registry Resort) Music and dancing in one of Naples's most fashionable locales.

McCabe's Irish Pub (239-403-7170; 699 Fifth Ave. S., Naples 34102) Authentic Irish music, most weekends, in a Dublin-built pub.

Naples Concert Band (239-263-9521; Naples) For 29 years, it has been performing Sunday concerts once a month at Cambier Park in Old Naples and once a year at Mackle Park on Marco Island.

Naples Jazz Society (239-566-1997; PO Box 1365, Naples 34106) Hosts jazz artists January through April at Norris Community Center (755 Eighth Ave., Naples).

Naples Orchestra & Chorus (239-353-5413; PO Box 9542, Naples 34101) Works of the masters, pops, and Broadway performed December through April.

Snook Inn (239-394-3313; 1215 Bald Eagle Dr., Marco Island 34145) Live local bands, contemporary and island music.

Vanderbilt Inn (239-597-3151; 11000 Gulf Shore Dr. N., Naples 34108) Live music and karaoke indoors and at the chickee bar on the beach.

THEATER

Marco Players (239-642-7270; 1083 N. Collier Blvd., Marco Island, FL, 34145; at Marco Town Center Mall) Nonprofit community theater that produces comedies and musicals.

Naples Dinner Theatre (239-514-STAR; 877-519-STAR; www.naplesdinnertheatre.com] 1025 Piper Blvd., Naples 34110) Top Broadway hit musicals as you dine, including "Ice Cream Theatre" for families.

Philharmonic Center for the Arts (239-597-1900, 800-597-1900; www.naplesphilcenter.org; 5833 Pelican Bay Blvd., Pelican Bay, Naples 34108) "The Phil," as locals call it, is home to the 77-piece Naples Philharmonic. It hosts audiences of up to 1,222 for Broadway shows, touring orchestras, chamber music, children's productions, and the Miami City Ballet.

Sugden Community Theatre (239-263-7990; 701 Fifth Ave. S., Naples 34102) The home of the Naples Players, a community theater troupe that has been entertaining October–May for 40 years. Completed in fall 1998, the $5.3 million complex features a main stage plus a more experimental black-box theater.

VISUAL ART CENTERS & RESOURCES

Like its Italian namesake, Naples serves as the region's aesthetic trendsetter. Gallery-lined streets host artists of local, national, and international stature. The following entries introduce you to opportunities for experiencing art as either a viewer or a practicing artist. A listing for commercial galleries is included in the "Shopping" section.

Art League of Bonita Springs Center for the Arts (239-495-8989; 26100 Old 41 Rd., Bonita Springs 34135) Classes, children's programs, exhibitions, and a national art festival in January (see Events).

Art League of Marco Island (239-394-4221; www.marcoislandarat.com; 1010 Winterberry Dr., Marco Island 34145) Workshops, lectures, gallery, and gift shop.

Naples Artcrafters (239-947-9095; PO Box 10884, Naples 34101) Artisan group that sponsors arts and crafts shows.

Naples Museum of Art (239-597-1900; www.naplesphilcenter.org; Philharmonic Center for the Arts, 5833 Pelican Bay Blvd., Pelican Bay, Naples 34108) Opened in November 2000, Naples's latest cultural showpiece is as stunning as you'd expect. Permanent exhibits include a collection of modern American masters 1900–1955, including Alexander Calder, Jackson Pollock, and Stuart Davis. The museum also holds a priceless collection of Chinese artifacts, scrolls, sculptures, pottery, and other pieces dating back to the Han dynasty (206 BC–AD 220). World-renowned glass sculptor Dale Chihuly created two magnificent chandeliers for the museum: one that hangs from the its dome glass conservatory and another suspended in the three-story stair-

World-renowned glass artist Dale Chihuly created two glass chandeliers for the new Naples Museum of Art.

Chelle Koster Walton

well. The $10.6 million museum's 15 galleries elegantly showcase world-class traveling exhibitions. Open Tuesday–Saturday 10am–4pm, Sunday 12–4pm; closed Monday. Admission: $6 adults, $3 student, free for children under 5. Free docent tours Tuesday–Saturday at 11 and 2.

Philharmonic Galleries (239-597-1111; www.naplesphilcenter.org; Philharmonic Center for the Arts, 5833 Pelican Bay Blvd., Pelican Bay, Naples 34108) Exhibitions of well-known works. Open one hour before Philharmonic Center performances, postperformances, and during intermission for patrons only.

United Arts Council (239-263-8242; 1051 Fifth Ave. S., Naples 34102) A central clearinghouse for culture, music, dance, theater, and visual arts in the Naples area.

The von Liebig Art Center (239-262-6517; www.naplesartcenter.org; 585 Park St., Naples 34102) The new home of the Naples Art Association, it holds classes, workshops, and showings for children and its members and other special exhibitions. The skylit library contains arts information.

RECREATION

The Ten Thousand Islands are the meat of the south coast's recreational banquet. Here, the old-fashioned sports — fishing, canoeing, hiking — are most in style. The beaches of Naples and Marco Island serve up the newer, exhilarating side dishes, everything from parasailing to jet skiing.

BEACHES

Parking fees are levied at most beaches; county residents can purchase stickers that allow them to park free. For information on county beaches, contact **Department of Collier County Parks & Recreation** (239-353-0404; 3300 Santa Barbara Blvd., Naples 34116; www.colliergov.net).

CLAM PASS RECREATION AREA
239-353-0404.
Registry Resort of Seagate Dr., 475 Seagate Dr., Naples 34103.
Facilities: Rest rooms, showers, food and beach concessions.
Parking: $3 per day.

This beach used by guests of Registry Resort but open to the public is reached by a tram that follows a nearly 1-mile boardwalk over a tidal bay and through mangroves. Boat and cabana rentals are available at this county facility. The sand is fine, fluffy, and newly widened. You can kayak or sail into the sea, or canoe along a trail among the mangroves, which are frequented by ospreys, hawks, and a variety of other feathered creatures.

DELNOR-WIGGINS PASS STATE RECREATION AREA
239-597-6196.
11100 Gulf Shore Dr. N., Naples 34108
At Route 846, Vanderbilt Beach.
Facilities: Picnic areas, pavilion, rest rooms, showers, boat ramp, food and rental concession, lifeguard.
Admission: $4 per car, up to 8 passengers; $2 per car, single occupant; $1 walk-ins, bike-ins, or extra passengers.

This is a highly natural, low-key beach that extends for 1 mile south from the mouth of the Cocohatchee River. The lush white sands are protected during loggerhead turtle nesting season (summer) and support stands of natural maritime vegetation such as cactus, sea grapes, nickerbean, and yucca. A nature trail leads to an observation tower at the beach's north end. This is a popular park, but you can usually find parking in one of the many lots. At the first, a concession stands sells snacks, and rents kayaks, snorkel equipment, and other beach necessities. Restrict your swimming to south of the pass's fast-moving waters, which are a boon to fishermen.

LOWDERMILK PARK
239-434-4698.
Gulf Shore Blvd. at Banyan Blvd., Naples.
Facilities: Picnic area, rest rooms, showers, volleyball, playground, concessions, special handicap access, and wheeled surf chairs.
Parking: Metered, 75¢ per hour.

Beach headquarters for the south coast. Lots of special activities at this gulf-side party spot with its thousand feet of sandy beach. Across the street, a deli and restaurant fuel your beach day.

Karen T. Bartlett

Naples pier: the heart of Old Naples.

NAPLES MUNICIPAL BEACHES
Gulf Shore Blvd. south of Doctors Pass, Naples.
Facilities: Rest rooms, shower, concessions, fishing pier.
Parking: Metered, 75¢ per hour.

Stretches of natural beach are anchored by the historic pier on 12th Avenue South, where facilities and a parking lot are located.

SOUTH MARCO BEACH
S. Collier Blvd. at Swallow Ave., south end of Marco Island.
Parking: $3 per vehicle.

Parking is on the other side of Collier Blvd. a half block away. A paved brick path beneath palm trees leads to this patch of public beach between giant high-rises. No facilities.

TIGERTAIL BEACH
Hernando Dr., north end of Marco Island.
Facilities: Picnic area, rest rooms, showers, watersports rentals, restaurant, playground volleyball.
Parking: $3 per vehicle.

This county-owned beach is a good place for shelling and sunning. In season, arrive early to find a parking spot. Wooden ramps cross dunes to thirty-one acres of wide, marvelous beach. The south end fronts high-rises, but the north end stretches into wilderness. The playground is fun and divided for two different age groups. At low tide, tidal pools and a sandbar known as Sand Dollar Island attract feeding and nesting birds and shellers.

VANDERBILT BEACH
239-353-0404.
End of Vanderbilt Dr.,
  Vanderbilt Beach, north
  of Naples.
Facilities: Rest rooms,
  showers, food; water-
  sports rentals available at
  nearby resorts.
Parking: $3 per vehicle at
  nearby lot on Vanderbilt
  Dr.; metered on the
  street.

This recently refurbished stretch runs alongside resorts and is well suited to those who like sharing the beach with a lot of people as well as bar- and restaurant-hopping along the beach.

BICYCLING

City and country biking are available to those who prefer this slow, intimate mode of exploration. Sidewalks, bike paths (marked with white diamonds), and roadsides accommodate cyclists. By state law, cyclists must conduct themselves as pedestrians when using sidewalks. Avoid cycling crowded downtown walks. Where they share the road with other vehicles, cyclists must follow all the rules of the road. Children under age 16 must wear a helmet.

BEST BIKING

Naples has laid out a sporadic system of metropolitan bike paths. A favorite route of local cyclists loops through 10 miles of pathway in the north-end Pelican Bay development. Within it, a 580-acre nature preserve provides a change of scenery from upscale suburbia.

Bike paths traverse Everglades City and cross the causeway to Chokoloskee Island. Back-road bikers take to the 12-mile W. J. Janes Memorial Scenic Drive through Fakahatchee Strand State Preserve, off Highway 29 north of Everglades City. Royal palms, cypress trees, and air plants provide pristine scenery and bird habitat. Morning or sunset riders may spot wild turkeys, alligators, raccoons, snakes, otters, bobcats, and deer. A new 5 ½-mile mountain bike trail has opened at Collier-Seminole State Park through cabbage palm hammock.

RENTALS/SALES

Many resorts rent bikes or provided bike use to guests.

Ivey House B&B (239-695-3299; 107 Camellia St., Everglades City 34139) Rents bikes to the public.
Scootertown (239-394-8400; 845 Bald Eagle Dr., Marco Island 34145) Rents scooters and bikes in various sizes and styles; also skates and strollers. Rates by the day, week, month. Delivery available.

BOATS & BOATING

Setting sail through the maze of Ten Thousand Islands.

Karen T. Bartlett

Naples, Marco Island, and Everglades City are lousy with marinas. These are headquarters for boat rentals and tours and charters to serve every interest, from shelling and fishing to gaping at mansions.

CANOEING & KAYAKING

In addition to the outlets listed below, many resorts and parks rent canoes and kayaks.

Collier-Seminole State Park (239-394-3397; 20200 E. Tamiami Trail, Naples 34114; between Naples and Everglades City) Rents canoes for use on the park's 13-mile canoe trail into wilderness preserve. Guided tours available by reservation.

Delnor-Wiggins Pass State Park concession (239-597-6196; www.tarponbay.com; located at the first parking lot in the park) Rents kayaks by the hour and half day.

Everglades National Park Boat Tours (239-695-2591, 800-445-7724 in Florida; www.nps.gov/ever; Everglades Ranger Station, PO Box 119, Everglades City 34139) Canoe rentals and shuttle service for trips 99 miles long or shorter. Ranger-guided canoe trips of four to five hours duration in season.

Get Wet Sports (239-394-9557; 203 Capri Blvd., Isles of Capri 34113) Sales, rentals, free delivery to Marco, and nature tours.

North American Canoe Tours (239-695-4666; www.evergladesadventures.com; 107 Camellia St., PO Box 5038, Everglades City 34139) Rents 17- to 19-foot aluminum canoes, high-quality kayaks, and equipment. Complete outfitting and shuttle service. Three- and nine-night tours into the Everglades.

Osprey Adventures (239-642-6600, 888-213-0316; www.ospreyadventures.com;

Marco River Marina, 951 Bald Eagle Dr., Marco Island 34145) Powerboat transport to kayaking sites in the Ten Thousand Islands, Rookery Bay, and other pristine venues.

DINING CRUISES

The Naples Princess (239-649-2275; Port-O-Call Marina, 550 Port-O-Call Way, Naples 34102; across Hwy. 41 from Tin City) Excursions include a Conservancy-narrated nature cruise with continental breakfast, island buffet lunch, sunset hors d'oeuvres, sunset dinner, or Sunday brunch.

MARINE SUPPLIES

Boat/US Marine Center (239-774-3233; 3360 E. Tamiami Trail, Naples FL 34104) All boating, yachting, and fishing needs. Discounts and emergency service available with membership.

PERSONAL WATERCRAFT RENTALS/TOURS

Marco Island Jet Ski & Water Sports (239-394-6589; 400 S. Collier Blvd., Marco Island 34145; at Marriott's Marco Island Resort) Rents waverunners and conducts one-hour waverunner excursions through Ten Thousand Islands.

POWERBOAT RENTALS

Back Bay Marina of Southwest Florida (239-992-2608; 4751 Bonita Beach Rd., Bonita Springs 34134) Skiffs and pontoons by the half and full day.

Fish Finder (239-597-2063; www.fish-finder.com; Cocohatchee River Park, 13531 Vanderbilt Dr., Naples 34110; at Vanderbilt Beach) Rentals from 15-foot skiffs to 24-foot pontoon boat. Some vessels are restricted to bay use.

Goodland Bay Marina (239-394-2797; 604 E. Palm Ave., Goodland 34140) Pontoons and 20-foot center consoles with depth finders and VHF radios.

Houseboat Rentals of Southwest Florida (239-775-2003 or 430-0638; www.ivacation.com/p6950.htm; 4185 Lorraine Ave., Naples 34104) Serving Naples, Marco Island, and Everglades City. Thirty-four-foot two-bedroom pontoon sleeps six for two to six nights. Captain available.

Moran's Barge Marina (239-642-1920; at the Goodland Bridge on San Marco Rd., PO Box 1219, Marco Island 33969) Rents 17-foot consoles.

Port-O-Call Marina (239-774-0479; off Hwy. 41 E., 550 Port-O-Call Way, Naples 34102) Rents deck boats and powerboats 17 to 23 feet in length, to accommodate 6 to 12 people.

PUBLIC BOAT RAMPS

Caxambas Park (S. Collier Ct., Marco Island) Rest rooms, bait, fuel, and access to Roberts Bay.

Cocohatchee River Park (239-566-2611; 13531 Vanderbilt Dr., Naples 34110; at Vanderbilt Beach) Park with three ramps onto the river (which runs to the gulf), rest rooms, picnic tables, and boat rentals. Parking fee.

Delnor-Wiggins Pass State Recreation Area (11100 Gulf Shore Dr. N., Naples 34108) Admission.

Marco Island approach (1 mile before the bridge on Route 951)

Naples Landing (off Ninth St. S.)

SAILBOAT CHARTERS

Sail Kahuna (239-642-7704; Marco River Marina, 951 Bald Eagle Dr., Marco Island 34145) Shelling, beaching, luau, sunset, and dolphin-watch tours.

Sailboats Unlimited (239-262-0139; captalex@juno.com; 225 Cove Ln., Naples 34102; at Naples City Dock and Marco Island) Design your own cruise from two hours to full day in duration on bare boats 29 to 42 feet. Free sailing instruction included and certification available.

Sweet Liberty (239-793-3525; www.sweetliberty.com; 4620 Gail Blvd., Naples 34104; at the Boat Haven off Hwy. 41) Daily shelling, sightseeing, and sunset trips aboard a fifty-three-foot catamaran.

SIGHTSEEING & ENTERTAINMENT CRUISES

Collier-Seminole State Park Boat Tours (239-642-8898; 20200 E. Tamiami Trail, Naples 34114; at Collier-Seminole State Park, 17 miles south of Naples on Hwy. 41) One-hour tours narrate human and natural history along the Blackwater River.

Everglades Private Airboat Tours (239-695-4637, 800-368-0065; PO Box 402, Everglades City 34139; 1 mile west of Route 29 on Hwy. 41) Two-passenger vessel zips through Florida's backyard.

Wooten's Everglades Tours (239-695-2781, 800-282-2781; 32330 Tamiami Trail, Ochopee 34141; 35 miles south of Naples) Follow ancient Native-American trails through the mysterious "River of Grass" via airboat or swamp buggy, the trademark vessels of the Everglades. The loud airboat is designed for the area's shallow waters, but can be detrimental to the environment; the swamp buggy is an all-terrain bus. Touristy, but an easy, breezy introduction to this complex wilderness.

FISHING

Many visiting sports folk arrive at the south coast eager to fight the big fish and brave the deep waters of the Gulf of Mexico. They come equipped with their 50-pound test line, heavy tackle, and tall fish tales. Yet closer to home, in the back bays and shallow waters of Ten Thousand Islands, experienced fishermen find what's best about the region. Sea trout, snook, redfish, sheepshead, mangrove snapper, and pompano abound in the brackish creeks, grass flats, and channels.

Nonresidents age 16 and over must obtain a license unless fishing from a vessel or pier covered by its own license. You can buy inexpensive temporary nonresident licenses at county tax collectors' offices and most Kmarts and bait shops. Check local regulations for season, size, and catch restrictions.

FISHING CHARTERS/OUTFITTERS

Check the large marinas for fishing guides. Experienced guides can take the intimidation and guesswork out of open-water fishing.

Captain Lee Quick (239-695-0032; PO Box 804, Chokoloskee 34138) Fly and light tackle fishing in Ten Thousand Islands and Everglades.

Captain Max Miller (239-695-2420; Everglades City 34139) Specializes in light-tackle back-bay fishing.

Captain Paul (239-263-4949; 1200 Fifth Ave. S., Naples 34102; Tin City) Backcountry fishing into Ten Thousand Islands.

Chokoloskee Island Outfitters (239-695-2286; Chokoloskee Island 34138) Capt. Dave Prickett takes you out for half and full days.

Everglades Angler (239-262-8228, 800-57-FISHY; www.evergladesangler.com; 810 Twelfth Ave. S., Naples 34102) Half and full-day backcountry fishing expeditions to the Everglades and Ten Thousand Islands, Marco Island, and Estero Bay for snook, redfish, and tarpon. Fly-tying and -casting clinics.

Fish Finder (239-597-2063; www.fish-finder.com; 13531 Vanderbilt Dr., Naples 34110; Cocohatchee River Park, Vanderbilt Beach) Backwater and deep-sea trips for one to six people, four or eight hours.

Lady Brett 45 (239-263-4949; 1200 Fifth Ave. S., Naples 34102; Tin City) Half-day offshore trips aboard a 45-foot powerboat.

Mangrove Outfitters (239-793-3370; 4111 E. Tamiami Trail, Naples 34112) Guides charters and, in season, teaches classes on casting.

Peg Leg Charters (239-642-4333 or 348-7888; PO Box 171, Goodland 34140; Moran's Barge Marina at the Goodland Bridge on San Marco Rd.) Capt. Ron Kennedy takes anglers offshore for half- and full-day trips.

Sunshine Tours (239-642-5415; www.sunshinetoursmarcoisland.com; 951 Bald Eagle Dr., Marco Island 34145; at Marco River Marina) Takes small parties aboard a 32-foot boat with bathroom for offshore excursions, half to full day. Also does backcountry fishing trips.

FISHING PIERS

Naples Fishing Pier (239-434-4696; 12th Ave. S., Naples) Extends a thousand feet into the gulf, with bait shop, snack bar, rest rooms, and showers.

GOLF

Naples earns its title as Golf Capital of the World with more golf holes per capita than any other statistically tracked metropolitan area.

PUBLIC GOLF COURSES

Bonita Fairways Country Club (239-947-9100; 9751 W. Terry St., Bonita Springs 34135) 18 holes at a reasonable price. Restaurant.

Lely Resort Flamingo Island Club (239-793-2223; 8004 Lely Resort Blvd., Naples 34113; off Route 951 east of Naples) Public course designed by Robert Trent Jones Sr. Offers 18 holes, par 72, and a golf school.

The Links of Naples (239-417-1313; 16161 E. Tamiami Trail, Naples 34110) Lit 18-hole course with driving range, PGA lessons, and rentals.

Marco Shores Country Club (239-394-2581; 1450 Mainsail Dr., Naples 34114, off Route 951 east of Marco Island) Public course, 18 holes, par 72, and golf school. Restaurant and bar.

Naples Beach Golf Club (239-434-7007; 851 Gulf Shore Blvd. N., Naples 34102) An18-hole, par 72 resort course that is host to many pro and amateur tournaments. Restaurant and lounge.

Pelican's Nest Golf Club (239-947-4600, 800-952-6378; 4450 Pelican's Nest Dr., Bonita Springs 34134) A 36-hole course, par 72.

GOLF CENTERS

David Leadbetter Golf Academy (239-592-1444, 800-424-3542; www.leadbetter.com; 6303 Burnham Rd., Naples 34112) Offers golf school at Quail West Golf Club in two different formats: three half days and three full days.

Naples Golf Center (239-775-4242; 7700 E. Davis Blvd., Naples 34104) Lit driving range with putting and chipping greens and sand traps. Home to Naples Golf Academy (239-732-9944; www.learninggolf.com): video, single, series, and group lessons.

HEALTH & FITNESS CLUBS

Fitness Quest (239-643-7546; 2970 S. Horseshoe Dr., Naples 34104) Complete fitness center, aerobics, karate, heart-healthy café, nursery.

Golden Gate Fitness Center (239-353-3636; Golden Gate Community Park, 3300 Santa Barbara Blvd., Naples 34116) Full range of Cybex and Keiser equipment, cardio machines, and free weights. Personal training and assessment available.

Gold's Gym (239-498-3339; 9110 Bonita Beach Rd., Bonita Springs 34135) Thirteen-thousand square feet of weight- and cardio-training equipment.

Marco Fitness Club (239-394-3705; 871 E. Elkcam Circle, Marco Island 34145) Top-of-the-line cardiovascular and weight machines, free weights, personal trainers, massage therapist.

HIKING

Big Cypress National Preserve (239-695-4111, ext. 0; www.nps.gov/bicy; HCR 61, Box 110, Ochopee 33141) East of Rte. 29, short hiking trails lead off Rte. 839; longer trails begin about 15 miles away at the Oasis Visitor Center.

Collier-Seminole State Park (239-394-3397; 20200 E. Tamiami Trail, Naples 34114) A 6.5-mile trail winds through pine flatwoods and cypress swamp, and a self-guided boardwalk leads into a salt marsh.

Conservancy of Southwest Florida (239-262-0304; 1450 Merrihue Dr., Naples 34102) Guided and unguided nature hikes through a subtropical hammock.

CREW Marsh (239-332-7771; mailing address: 2301 McGregor Blvd., Fort Myers 33901; Corkscrew Rd., 18 miles east of Interstate 75, North Naples) Five miles of hiking trails through peri-Everglades environment: pine flatwoods, oak and palm hammock, and sawgrass marsh. Free guided tours the second Saturday of every month, Oct.–April.

Fakahatchee Strand State Preserve (239-695-4593; W. J. Janes Scenic Dr. in Copeland, off Hwy. 29 north of Hwy. 41) Two trails traverse the strand off Janes Dr. From Gate 7, the trail is 3 miles long one way; from Gate 12, it's 5 miles. Summer flooding can make your hike a slosh.

HUNTING

The Everglades provide some of Florida's best shots at hunting. You must obtain a state license and a Wildlife Management Area stamp. Permits are required for early-season hunting and special types of hunting. For information on seasons and bag limits, request a copy of *Florida Hunting Handbook & Regulations Summary* when you buy your license. Skeet shooting is available at Port of the Islands development between Naples and Everglades City.

KIDS' STUFF

Coral Cay Adventure Golf (239-793-4999; 2205 E. Tamiami Trail, Naples 34112) Two 18-hole courses with a tropical island theme. Admission.

Golden Gate Aquatic Complex (239-353-7128; Golden Gate Community Park, 3300 Santa Barbara Blvd., Naples 34116) Swimming fun for all ages, with water slides, wading pool and fountain, and competition pool with low and high dives. Admission.

Golf Safari (239-947-1377; 3775 Bonita Beach Rd., Bonita Springs 34134) Jungle-themed miniature golf.

King Richard's Family Fun Park (239-598-1666; 6780 N. Airport Rd., Naples 34109) Merlin's Moat interactive water attraction (bring your swimsuit), roller coaster, bumper boats, batting cages, a castle full of video and other electronic games, go-carts, a kiddie train, and two 18-hole miniature golf courses. No admission; you buy tickets per attraction. Age restrictions apply for some of the rides.

Naples Go-Cart Center (239-774-7776; 11402 Tamiami Trail E., Naples 34113) Video games, pinball, and a snack center. Closed Tues.

RACQUET SPORTS

Cambier Park (239-434-4694; between Eighth and Park Streets, Naples) Twelve lit tennis courts. Fee.

Collier County Racquet Center (239-394-5454; 1275 San Marco Rd., Marco Island 34145) County facility with five deco-turf courts, two racquetball courts, pro shop, and lessons.

Fleischmann Park (239-434-4692; 1600 Fleischmann Blvd., Naples 33940) Lit racquetball courts.

Golden Gate Community Park (239-353-0404; 3300 Santa Barbara Blvd., Naples 34116) Lit tennis and racquetball courts.

Naples Park Elementary (111th Ave. N., Naples) Two lit courts.

Pelican Bay Community Park (239-353-0404; 764 Vanderbilt Rd., Naples 34108) Lit tennis and racquetball courts.

Tommie Barfield Elementary (101 Kirkwood St., Goodland, Marco Island 34140) Two lit courts.

SHELLING

It is illegal to collect live shells in state and national parks. Collier County discourages the collection of live shells.

HOT SHELLING SPOTS

Coconut Island (north of Marco Island) A destination for most Marco Island shelling expeditions.

Key Island (south of Naples, accessible only by boat) A partly private, partly state-owned unbridged island, it holds a great many shell prizes that are not as picked over as on beaches that are accessible by car. Brigg's Nature Center (see "Nature Preserves"), conducts a beachcombing-shelling tour of the island by a pontoon boat in season (December through April).

Ten Thousand Islands Shell Island, Kingston Key, and Mormon Key provide lots of empty shells to collect.

SHELLING CHARTERS

Captain Paul (239-263-4949; 1200 Fifth Ave. S., Naples 34102; in Tin City) Daily trips to Keewaydin Island.

Sail Kahuna (239-642-7704; Marco River Marina, 951 Bald Eagle Dr., Marco Island 34145) Go to unbridged barrier islands for shelling by sailboat.

SPAS

Danielle (239-947-5900; www.daniellespa.com; 27160 Bay Landing Dr., Bonita Springs 34135) An elegant spa that designs wellness programs — including Pilates, personal training, and yoga — and makes you feel pampered with massage, body treatments, hydrotherapy, facials, and the works.

La Piel Spa (239-352-5554; www.la-piel.com; 6370 Pine Ridge Rd., Ste. 101, Naples 34119) A full-service day spa incorporated into a cosmetic-surgery practice. It offers facials, peels, body treatments, massages, manicures, and other services.

SeaSide Day Spa (239-393-2288, 888-393-4SPA; www.seasidedayspa.com; 651 S. Collier Blvd., Marco Island 34145) Conveniently located across the street from the Radisson resort, it administers a full line of massages, facials, and other body and skin treatments. Try the Peppermint Sea Twist Wrap, Thai massage, or therapeutic facial.

Naples Beach Hotel & Golf Club (239-261-2222, 800-237-7600; 851 Gulf Shore Blvd. N., Naples 34102) This recent addition to a landmark Naples hotel brings full-service spa facilities, from extensive massage services (aromatherapy, reiki, shiatsu, neuro-muscular, etc.) to body treatments (wraps, gommage, scrubs), and facials. A hair salon and fitness center enhance the wellness experience here.

SPECTATOR SPORTS

RACING

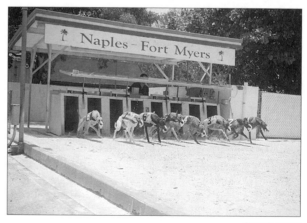

And they're off! "Going to the dogs" is a favorite pastime in Bonita Springs.

Karen T. Bartlett

Naples-Fort Myers Greyhound Track (239-992-2411; 10601 Bonita Beach Rd. SE; Bonita Springs 34135) Matinees, night races, simulcasting, and trackside dining. Free grandstand admission.

Waterskiing

Gulf Coast Skimmers (239-732-0570; gulfcoastskimmers.com ; mailing address: 4002 Cindy Ave., Naples 34112; Lake Avalon at Sugden Regional Park, Outer Drive, Naples) Gulf Coast Skimmers stage live shows every Sunday at 3pm October–April, 6:30pm May–September.

WATER SPORTS

Parasailing & Waterskiing

Marco Island Ski & Water Sports (239-394-6589; 400 S. Collier Blvd., Marco Island 34145; at Marriott's Marco Beach Resort) Parasailing; waverunner and other water-sport rentals.

Gulf Sea Adventures (239-594-2464; 11000 Gulf Shore Dr. N., Vanderbilt Beach 34108; at Vanderbilt Beach Inn) Go parasailing, kayaking, waverunning, windsurfing, sailing, sea-cycling, snorkeling, or windsurfing.

Osprey Adventures (239-642-6600; 888-213-0316; www.ospreyadventures.com; 951 Bald Eagle Dr., Marco Island 34145; at Marco River Marina) Stay dry. See dolphins, manatees, and birds.

Sky Scraper Parasailing (239-564-5686; 280 Vanderbilt Beach Rd., Naples 34108; at Ritz-Carlton Naples) Single, tandem, and triple rides; photos and videos available.

Snorkeling & Scuba

Murky waters here send most divers to Florida's east coast and the Keys, although some charters take you out into deep local waters.

Scubadventures (239-389-7889; 1141 Bald Eagle Dr., Marco Island 34145) Supplies, instruction, and diving arrangements.

WILDERNESS CAMPING

Big Cypress National Preserve (239-695-4111, ext. 0; www.nps.gov/bicy; HCR 61, Box 110, Ochopee 33141) Eight primitive campgrounds lie off loop road, about 18 miles east of Rte. 29. Some are closed in summer.

Big Cypress Trail Lakes Campground (239-695-2275; 40904 Hwy. 41 E., Ochopee 34943; Highway 41, 5 miles east of Route 29) Tent or RV camping in Big Cypress National Preserve, a 729,000-acre sanctuary adjacent to Everglades National Park.

Collier-Seminole State Park (239-642-8898; 20200 E. Tamiami Trail, Naples 34114; 17 miles south of Naples) This 6,470-acre park straddles Big Cypress Swamp and Ten Thousand Islands Mangrove Wilderness and provides the least primitive camping in Everglades Country. There are RV hookups and tent sites. The park is full of possibilities for exploring nature and history, but no swimming is allowed.

Everglades National Park (239-695-2591) Backcountry camping along the Everglades canoe trails requires a permit, available from the Everglades City Ranger Station on Route 29. Most sites provide chickee huts on pilings, with chemical toilets. Take mosquito repellent — gallons in summer.

WILDLIFE SPOTTING

Karen T. Bartlett

Pelicans gather on a "Florida snow cap" — otherwise known as a sandbar.

The Florida Everglades, Big Cypress National Preserve, and Ten Thousand Islands are home to the reclusive golden Florida panther, along with bobcats, manatees, wood storks, brown pelicans, black skimmers, roseate spoonbills, and ibises. Some creatures, such as the panther and bobcat, are rarely seen out of captivity. Others, especially the brown pelican, live side by side with residents. I've driven along Route 29 between the interstate and Tamiami Trail and spotted flocks of ibises and white-tailed deer. Deep in the 'Glades, birds flock like a blizzard. Optimum wildlife viewing is December through March, when birds migrate and dry weather concentrates them in diminished ponds and other waterways.

ALLIGATORS

The Everglades are the New York City of Florida's alligator population. They thrive in the freshwater ponds and brackish creeks of the River of Grass.

When the sun is shining along Alligator Alley (Interstate 75) and Tamiami Trail, you can see hundreds of these prehistoric reptiles on the banks, sunning themselves. Crocodiles live also in the 'Glades, but they are rare on this side.

BIRDS

The South Coast is a bird-watcher's haven — especially in winter, when migrating species add to the vast variety of the coast's residential avifauna. Rare visitors and locals include roseate spoonbills, black skimmers, yellow-crowned night herons, wood storks, white pelicans, lumpkins, and bald eagles. More commonly seen are frigates, ospreys, Louisiana herons, great blue herons, ibises, snowy egrets, brown pelicans, anhingas, cormorants, terns, seagulls, plovers, oystercatchers, pileated woodpeckers, owls, and hawks.

For the best bird-watching on the south coast, try Naples's Corkscrew Swamp, home to the largest nesting colony of wood storks in the U.S.; Rookery Bay Sanctuary near Marco Island; and Ten Thousand Islands, a haven for birds of all sorts. Marco Island is a proclaimed sanctuary for bald eagles. Barfield Bay in Goodland is one of their favorite locales. At the beach, the threatened piping plover gets support and protection from local environmentalists.

NATURE PRESERVES & ECO-ATTRACTIONS

BIG CYPRESS NATIONAL PRESERVE
239-695-4111, ext. 0.
www.nps.gov/bicy.
HCR 61, Box 110, Ochopee 33141.
Adjacent to Everglades National Park. Oasis Visitor Center about 20 miles east of Rte. 29 on Hwy. 41.

This 729,000-acre preserve abuts Everglades National Park to the north and Fakahatchee Strand to the east. From the Visitor Center you can depart on wilderness hikes to sample its Everglades environment. In summer the trails, which connect to the Florida National Scenic Trail, can be very wet. You'll see the grasslands and bald cypress stands for which Big Cypress is known as well as profuse birds and an alligator nursery. The preserve boasts the state's major population of the reclusive, endangered Florida panther. A small museum at the visitor center contains Indian artifacts and wildlife exhibits. Rangers lead swamp walks, bike and canoe trips, and campfire programs in season. A 26-mile scenic loop road is open to vehicles when road conditions allow, with several primitive campgrounds. Closer to Everglades City, Birdon Road (Rte. 841) takes a 17-mile trip through sawgrass prairie habitat. It connects to Rte. 837 and then Rte. 839, which leads to two 2.5-mile hiking trails, one to the north, the other to the south of the intersection.

NAPLES NATURE CENTER
239-262-0304.
www.conservancy.org.
1450 Merrihue Dr., Naples 34102.

This tucked-away nature complex on the Gordon River was built by the Conservancy of Southwest Florida to educate the public about the environment. Within its 13.5 acres it encompasses a

One block east of Goodlette Rd.

Open: 9am–4:30pm Mon.–Sat.

Admission: Nature Center, $7.50 adults and $2 children 3–12 (good for same-day admission to Briggs). Admission to nature trails and wildlife rehabilitation facility is free.

nature store; trail walks; free boat tours of the river; a rehabilitation center for birds, deer, turtles, and other injured animals; and a beautiful nature center with live Florida snakes, an offshore tank (where you'll often find a loggerhead turtle swimming), fascinating touch tables, interactive games, and habitat vignettes. Friendly and chattily informative guides conduct special programs throughout the day as they feed their live critters. The Conservancy also hosts interpretative nature field trips in conjunction with its Briggs Nature Center south of Naples (see "Rookery Bay Estuarine Reserve," below). Canoes and kayak rentals are available for use on the Gordon River.

CORKSCREW SWAMP SANCTUARY
239-348-9151.
375 Sanctuary Rd. Naples 34120.
Off Naples-Immokalee Rd., 21 miles east of N. Tamiami Trail.
Open: Daily 7am–5:30pm Oct.–mid-April, 7am–7:30pm mid-April–Sept.
Admission: $8 adults, $5.50 college students, $3.50 children 6–18.
Admission: $8 adults, $5.50 college students, $3.50 children 6–18.

This 11,000-acre sanctuary, operated by the National Audubon Society, protects one of the largest stands of mature bald cypress trees in the country. Some of the towering specimens date back nearly 500 years. The threatened wood stork once came to nest here in great numbers. Diminished populations still do, at which time the nesting area is roped off to protect them. A boardwalk 1.75 miles long takes you over swampland inhabited by rich plant and marine life. You can usually spot an alligator or two. In 2000 the new state-of-the-art Blair Audubon Center, a national prototype, opened at the sanctuary in a "stealth" building that blends with the pristine environment.

DELNOR-WIGGINS PASS STATE RECREATION AREA
239-597-6196.
11100 Gulf Shore Dr. N., Naples 34108.
At Vanderbilt Beach.
Admission: $4 per car, up to 8 passengers; $2 per car, single occupant; $1 bikers or walk-ins.

Prehistoric loggerhead turtles lumber ashore to lay and bury their eggs every summer, away from the lights and crowds of other area beaches. Fifty-six days later the baby turtles emerge and scurry to the sea — hopefully before birds can snatch them up. Beach turtle talks are available during the loggerhead season.

EVERGLADES NATIONAL PARK GULF COAST VISITOR CENTER

This massive wetlands — home to the endangered Florida panther and other rare animals — covers 2,200 square miles and shelters more than 600 types of fish and 347 bird species. Along

239-695-3311.
www.nps.gov/ever.
PO Box 120, Everglades
City 34139.
Tamiami Trail south of
Naples; Ranger Station
and Visitor Center on Rt.
29, before the
Chokoloskee Causeway
in Everglades City.

with Ten Thousand Islands, it also contains the largest mangrove forest in the world. So what's the best way to see this seemingly overwhelming expanse of wildlife? Take your pick. From this end, you really can't drive through it, but you can from the eastern access, two hours away. Highway 41 skirts the edge of the park and Big Cypress, which is part of the same ecosystem. Closest access to Naples is Route 29 and Everglades City. Canoe trips from 8 to 99 miles long put you in closer range of birds, manatees, dolphins, and alligators.

There's also a variety of other options. The park offers boat tours, and other sightseeing cruises exist. During the winter, ranger programs and canoe tours from the Gulf Coast Visitor Center teach about the unique environment. You can rent a pontoon boat or hire a charter captain for sightseeing and fishing. Get advice at the welcome center or visitor center, or see "Wildlife Tours & Charters," below. The visitor center holds a few wildlife and hands-on exhibits. Tables and a chickee hut accommodate picnickers.

**FAKAHATCHEE
STRAND STATE PARK
PRESERVE**
239-695-4593.
PO Box 548, Copeland
34137.
W. J. Janes Scenic Dr. in
Copeland, off Hwy. 29
north of Hwy. 41.

Rangers lead swamp walks the third Saturday each month November-February. You can also hike on your own. A 3-mile trail (one-way) begins at Gate 7 off Janes Scenic Drive, and another 5 miles long one way at Gate 12. In summer, the trails are often muddy and submerged. You can also access the strand (a linear swamp forest that snakes along ancient sloughs) via the 1-mile (round trip) Big Cypress Bend boardwalk, west of Everglades City on Hwy. 41. The eco-system is known for its orchids, particularly the rare ghost orchid, and stands of native royal palm. You may also spot white-tailed deer and bobcats.

**ROOKERY BAY
ESTUARINE RESERVE
& BRIGGS NATURE
CENTER**
239-775-8569.
401 Shell Island Road,
Naples 34133.
Off Rt. 951 on way to
Marco Island.
Open: 9am–4:30pm
Mon.–Sat., Tues. 7:30am-
4:30pm.
Closed: Sunday.

The Gulf Coast's largest and most pristine wildlife sanctuary occupies more than 12,000 acres at the gateway to Ten Thousand Islands. It's "Ding" Darling without the crowds and a favorite for fishermen and bird-watchers. Visitors can enjoy the mysteries of mangrove ecology from a half-mile boardwalk. You can stroll through the butterfly garden and walk Monument Trail around the bay. A visitor center introduces you to the estuarine world, including a touch table kids will like. I recommend taking one of the center's pontoon boat, canoe, biking, hiking, shelling, birding, or off-

Admission: $4 adults ($7.50 for joint admission to Naples Nature Center); $2 children ages 3–12.

site beach trips if you want to get close up and personal with nature in season. Birds by the score attract the binocular set. Manatees and alligators populate bay waters. Canoe and kayak rentals are available in-season.

WILDLIFE TOURS & CHARTERS

Conservancy of Southwest Florida (239-262-0304; 1450 Merrihue Dr., Naples 34102; one block east of Goodlette Rd.) Boat tours of the mangrove waterway. Hosts other interpretative hiking, beach, and canoeing nature ventures.

Double Sunshine (239-263-4949; 1200 Fifth Ave. S., Naples 34102; Tin City on Hwy. 41) Departs five times daily for 1-1/2-hour narrated nature, dolphin-sighting, mansion-ogling, and sunset cruises.

Estero Bay boat Tours (239-992-2200; www.ecotours-esterobay.com; 5231 Mamie St., Bonita Springs 34134; at Weeks Fish Camp, end of Coconut Rd.) the best sightseeing tour of Mound Key's Calusa history, Estero Bay wildlife, and Big Hickory Island's shells is conduted by a local native and his staff, who know these islands and waters like family.

Everglades National Park Boat Tours (239-695-2591, 800-445-7724; Gulf Coast Visitor Center, PO Box 119, Everglades City 34139) Naturalist-narrated tours through the maze of Ten Thousand Islands and its teeming bird and water life.

Manatee Sightseeing Adventure (239-642-8818; 25000 Tamiami Trail E., Naples 34114) Captain Barry takes you on a 90-minute sightseeing charter into manatee sanctuary by appointment. The boat departs from Port of the Islands development.

Naples Sea Kayaking Adventures (239-353-4878) Half-day, full-day, and overnight trips into local wilderness. Kayaking lessons available.

Orchids & Egrets (239-352-8586, 888-GLADES1; www.naturetour.com; 238 Silverado Dr, Naples 34119) That's what you'll see and more on these forays into Fakahatchee Strand, Cypress Swamp, Ten Thousand Islands, and other regional wilderness venues. A wide variety of tours take you into this often forbidding environment on foot or by bus, boat, kayak, and helicopter. Specialized tours focus on birding, Seminole culture, eco-psychology, dolphins, and panthers.

SHOPPING

Custom-designed jewelry, exclusive top-designer fashion lines, original masterpiece art, and the world's first street concierge make the experience of browsing, buying, and window-yearning in Naples entirely unique. Naples ranks among Florida's most chic arenas for spending, including Palm Beach's

Worth Avenue and Sarasota's St. Armands Circle. Downtown's recent renaissance concentrates the shopping frenzy in the Old Naples districts of Fifth Avenue South and Third Street Plaza, but a number of other fashionable shopping centers are found throughout town. Downtown shops are known for their individually owned, one-of-a-kind, and designer outlets.

SHOPPING CENTERS & MALLS

Art and shopping mix in Naples, here along Fifth Avenue South.

Karen T. Bartlett

Bayfront Center (Goodlette Rd. at Tamiami Trail, Naples) This new high-style apartment-shopping-dining complex does its bit to earn Naples its Italian nomenclature. At press time, only a couple of restaurants were open, but several upscale stores and galleries are expected soon.

Coastland Center (Tamiami Trail N. and Golden Gate Pkwy., Naples) Naples's largest and only enclosed, climate-controlled shopping center, its 150 stores include a full array of shopping options, from major department stores to small specialty shops. Chain names include Burdines, Sears, Old Navy, GAP, Victoria's Secret, and Bath & Body Works.

Fifth Avenue South (Naples) Once upon a time, members of the Seminole Indian tribe sold their crafts from a stand on Fifth Avenue. Today it's one of Naples's most fashionable addresses. In 1996 there was a movement to update the historic district, which had begun to look run-down. Famed Florida architect Andre Duany was hired to breathe new life into the district. Besides cosmetic improvements, he brought a new bustle to the street. Tony hotels, new shops, and twenty-some restaurants and sidewalk cafés attract Naples's new "café society." On the second Thursday of the month October through May (excluding December), the street association sponsors "Evening on Fifth," with sidewalk entertainment and shopping.

Marco Town Center Mall (Collier Blvd. and Bald Eagle Dr., Marco Island) A popular cluster of more than 10 distinctive eateries and 40 shopperies.

Mission de San Marco Plaza (599 S. Collier Blvd., Marco Island 34145) A modified strip mall, done in an interesting interpretation of Spanish style, holding specialty stores of all sorts.

Port of Marco Shopping Village (Royal Palm Dr., Marco Island) A small, comfortable, Old Florida-style center in the historical heart of Marco Island. Gifts, clothes, and souvenirs on a midrange scale.

The Promenade (239-430-1670; at Bonita Bay on Hwy. 41) Bonita's latest sprint to keep up with neighbor Naples, this new fashionable plaza even looks like Naples, with Mediterranean style, fine restaurants, galleries, and name shops. It's still developing but has already become a sensation.

Shops of Marco (San Marco Rd. and Barfield Dr., Marco Island) One-of-a-kind clothing and gift shops.

Third Street South Plaza and the Avenues (Naples) Visit this upscale shopping quarter in Old Naples, the heart of the arts scene, and view fine outdoor sculptures on loan from local galleries. This is window-shopping (on my budget, anyway) at its best: exquisite clothes, art, jewelry, and home decorations and furnishings. This shopping district is so posh it has its own street concierge, who advises shoppers, assists with package delivery, lends umbrellas, and so on.

Tin City (239-262-4200; www.tin-city.com; 1200 Fifth Ave. S., Naples 34102 Hwy. 41 at Goodlette Rd., Naples) I love the structure of this mall, which resurrected old tin-roofed docks. Comprised of two buildings, its 40 shops tend to be touristy, selling mainly nautical gifts and resort wear, but it also offers enjoyable waterfront restaurants, and it's a good place to catch a fishing or sightseeing tour.

Trade Center (Taylor Rd. and Trade Center Way) This is Naples's idea of an industrial park: a section of town off Pine Ridge Road where purveyors of home building, design, and decorating elements congregate — everything from brick layers to fine art galleries.

The Village on Venetian Bay (239-261-0030; ww.naples.com/village; 4200 Gulf Shore Blvd., Naples 34103; Gulf Shore Blvd. N. at Park Shore Dr.) Upscale, Mediterranean-style domain of fashion, jewelry, and art located on the waterfront.

Waterside Shops at Pelican Bay (239-598-1605; www.watersideshops.net; 5415 Tamiami Trail #320, Naples 34108; Seagate Dr. and Tamiami Trail N., Pelican Bay) This shopping enclave features Saks Fifth Avenue, located amidst cascading waters and lush foliage. It hosts a summer Friday concert series May through September.

ANTIQUES & COLLECTIBLES

Antiques & Collectibles (239-948-0266; 3634 Bonita Beach Rd. SW, Bonita Springs 34134) Specializes in country-cottage style; antiques and collectibles.

Glenna Moore (239-263-4121; 465 Fifth Ave. S., Naples 34102) An eclectic dis-array of religious antiques, paintings, and table and decorative items.

Jantina's Antiques Mall (941) 597-5454; www.jantinasantiques.com; 5400 Yahl St., Naples 34109) Antiques from Europe and the States, specializing in fine china and other home decorative items, including furniture.

BOOKS

The Bookstore at The Pavilion (239-598-2220; 857 Vanderbilt Beach Rd., Naples 34108; at Tamiami Trail N.) Old-fashioned bookstore that's crowded with the printed word; the antithesis of the new generation of megabookstores. Wide selection of specialty periodicals, new and used books.

Dunn & Dunn Booksellers (239-435-1911; 1300 Third St. S., Naples 34102) Smart bookstore with great local-interest section.

Sunshine Booksellers (239-393-0353; 677 S. Collier Blvd., Marco Island 34145) Large, modern store with a complete line of books, CDs, and coffee brewing.

CLOTHING

Back of the Bay (239-263-4233; www.backofthebay.com; 555 Fifth Ave. S., Naples 34102) Florida-appropriate women's fashions that express individual style.

Beth Moné Children's Shoppe (239-394-3600; Shops of Marco, 135 S. Barfield, Marco Island 34145) Florida-style and designer clothing for babies and tod-dlers.

Casablanca (239-394-2511; 400 S. Collier Blvd., Marco Island 34145; at Marco Island Marriott Resort) Fashionable women's resort apparel.

Island Woman (239-642-6116; 1 Harbor Pl., Goodland 34146) Imported batik fashions and handcrafted jewelry, tropical art, and crafts.

Kangaroo Klub (239-434-9510; 1170 Third St. S., Naples 34102) Precious chil-dren's clothes, tennis outfits, toys, and other Florida-style wear.

Kirsten's Boutique (239-598-3233; 5535 Tamiami Trail N., Naples 34108; at Waterside Shops) Subheaded "A Gallery of Fine Art to Wear," this unique shop sells Moroccan and African-inspired clothes, jewelry, and art.

Marissa Collections (239-263-4333; 1167 Third St. S., Naples 34102) Exclusive local carrier of the Donna Karan New York Collection; also Gianni Versace, Gucci, Krizia, Jill Sanders, Manolo Blahnik, and other prestige designers.

McFarland's of Marco (239-394-6464 for men's, 239-742-7277 for women's; 117 S. Barfield Dr., Marco Island 34145; at Shops of Marco) A stretch of three shops specializing in menswear — casual, golf, suits, and resort — women's dressy and bright fashions, and shoes.

Mondo Uomo (239-434-9484; 4200 Gulf Shore Blvd., Naples 34103; at the Village on Venetian Bay) Fine, tasteful fashion and European styles for men: tropical wool, German cotton, sweaters, and distinctive casual and dress wear for Gulf Coast climes.

Outback T-Shirts (239-261-7869; 1200 Fifth Ave. S., Naples 34102; Tin City, Hwy. 41 E. and Goodlette Rd.) The best in souvenir T-shirts, with wildlife and local themes.

Simply Natural (239-643-5571; 4330 Gulf Shore Blvd. N., Ste. 302, Naples 34103; at the Village on Venetian Bay) Unusual, bright, casual wear — some wild, others conservative.

CONSIGNMENT

Naples is a secondhand shopper's paradise. In many of the clothing consignment shops you can find designer fashions with the price tags still attached. Oh, the joys of hunting down the castoffs of the well-to-do!

Act II (239-495-6647; 8951 Bonita Beach Rd. #605, Bonita Springs 34135; at Springs Plaza, Hwy. 41) Women's clothing and accessories.

Encore Shop (239-775-0032; 3105 Davis Blvd., Naples 34104) Designer furniture, paintings, decorative items, and collectibles.

Kid's Consignment (239-596-1764; 5400 Taylor Rd., Naples 34109) Children's clothing, toys, furniture, and equipment; maternity and teens wear.

New to You Consignments (239-262-6869; 933 Creech Rd., Naples 34103; at Hwy. 41) Women's designer clothing, furniture, and decorative items.

OUTLET CENTERS

Prime Outlets of Naples (239-775-8083, 888-545-7196; .; www.primeoutlets.com; mailing address: 6060 Collier Blvd. #121, Naples 34114; 1920 Isle of Capri Rd., Route 951 on the way to Marco Island) Factory outlet discounts of up to 65 percent off for Coach purses, Dansk, Liz Claiborne, Geoffrey Beene, and Izod clothing, and other name brands.

FLEA MARKETS & BAZAARS

Flamingo Island Flea Market (239-948-7799; 11902 Bonita Beach Rd., Bonita Springs 34134)

Naples Drive-In Flea Market (239-774-2900; 7700 Davis Blvd., Naples 34104) Open Friday through Sunday.

GALLERIES

Naples has earned a reputation as a mecca for fine art. Gallery Row (239-513-3888; www.ongalleryrow.com), along Broad Avenue South at Third Street South, is a good place to begin in your art quest. About a dozen galleries line the street selling a wide spectrum of art. Several more lie in the immediate vicinity. Fifth Avenue South is another arena, although the galleries are more spread out, less concentrated. Trade Center, off Pine Ridge Road in north Naples is the latest to make the art scene, bringing galleries to an area known for its home décor and design outlets.

The Darvish Collection (239-261-7581; 1199 Third St. S., Naples 34102) Features the work of North American and European masters within its seven wood-lined clublike galleries. Most works in the four- to six-figure range.

Gallery One (239-263-0835; www.galleryoneand2.com; 1301 Third St. S., Naples 34102) Gallery One upholds Naples long-established reputation for glass artistry with stunning works; also raku, fountain and garden sculpture, and other decorative art.

Harmon-Meek Gallery (239-261-2637; 601 Fifth Ave. S., Naples 34102) A respected name in fine art, it hosts changing exhibitions of American master artists of the 20th century and local artists.

Kahn Galleries International (239-434-9200; www.kahn-galleries.com; 378 13th Ave. S., Naples 34102) A complex selling fine art from Southern Africa, authentic African artifacts and sculptures, and South African Cape wines.

Knox Galleries (239-263-7994; www.knoxgalleries.com; 375 Broad Ave. S., Naples 34102) One of the Gallery Row collection, it specializes in large and small realistic bronze sculptures of people and animals, showcasing the work of George Lundeen.

Koucky Gallery (239-261-8988; 4330 Gulf Shore Blvd. #306, Naples 34103; Village on Venetian Bay) I like this gallery, which recently moved from the Third Street South area, because it shows a sense of humor with a variety of whimsical carvings, painted pillows and furniture, fun sculptures and fine exhibition art.

Native Visions Gallery (239-643-3785; www.callofafrica.com; 737 Fifth Ave. S., Naples 34102) Remarkable works themed around Africa, the sea, and the environment.

PaduloArt (239-514-2773; www.paduloart.com; 1826 Trade Center Way, Naples 34109) Imminent, progressive New York and Miami artists' exhibitions.

Prospero's Gallerie Eclectic (239-435-4517; www.prosperosgallerie.com; 659 Fifth Ave. S., Naples 34102) I like this one. It's relaxed, daring, and, yes, eclectic. A refreshing find among the sobriety and self-importance of other local galleries.

Rick Moore Fine Art (239-592-5455; 5415 Tamiami Trail N., Naples 34108; at Waterside Shops; and 239-434-6464; 4200 Gulf Shore Blvd., Naples 34103; the Village on Venetian Bay) A pleasing selection of glass and wood animal sculptures, paintings, and ceramics.

Trudy Labell Fine Art (239-593-0211; 1610 Trade Center Way #2, Naples 34109) This is one of my favorite Naples galleries. Spacious and airy, its collection is extraordinary, with a subtle Florida focus. Find sculptures, fine oils, and unusual Eastern art.

GIFTS

Some of Naples's best souvenirs are found in the gift shops at nature and other attractions.

Born to Be Wild (239-261-0560; Dockside Boardwalk, 1100 Sixth Ave. S., Naples 34102) Stuffed toys, books, T-shirts, and gifts dedicated to promoting environmental awareness.

Coconuts Children's Shop (239-642-2645; 400 S. Collier Blvd., Marco Island 34245; at Marco Island Marriott Resort) Beanie babies, books, games, T-shirts, and Sesame Street and Rugrats toys.

Conch Shelf (239-394-2511; Marco Island Marriott Resort, 400 S. Collier Blvd., Marco Island 34145) Fine sea-themed gifts and art.

Holiday House Gifts (239-642-7113; Shops of Marco, Marco Island 34145) Yankee Candles, country- and tropical-style items, Christmas ornaments and decorations.

Mango's (239-434-1800; Coastland Center, 1794 Ninth St., Naples 34102) Yankee candles, stuffed toys, bright whimsical gifts, and decorative items with a tropical theme.

Regatta (239-263-4491; 1 Dockside Boardwalk, 1100 Sixth Ave. S., Naples 34102) A fun shop stuffed with unusual, funny, and tropical gifts, such as belly-button lights and a Simpson's chess game.

Things from the Sea (239-261-3820; 1200 Fifth Ave. S., Naples 34102; Tin City, Hwy. 41 E. and Goodlette Rd.) Quality souvenirs: scrimshaw, metal sculptures, brass, and other nautical gifts.

Thirsty Mouse (239-261-4148; 1200 Fifth Ave. S., Naples 34102; Tin City, Hwy. 41 E. and Goodlette Rd.) Florida food and gifts, sea-themed tableware, and other decorative items.

JEWELRY

Cleopatra's Barge (239-261-7952; 1197 Third St. S., Naples 34102) Home of "Naples Medallion" jewelry and other fine and estate pieces. Certified jewelers and diamond setters.

I'll Never Tell (239-403-9229, 877-528-2789; #D014 Third Street S., Naples 34102) Can't afford the shocking stickers at many Naples jewelry stores? Try out the carefully crafted synthetic jewelry here, inspired by leading jewelry designers.

Port Royal Jewelers (239-263-3071; 623 Fifth Ave. S., Naples 34102) 18th-century royal jewels, custom-designed, estate, Diamond Deco, and other rare jewelry. So exclusive you have to ring a doorbell to get in.

Schilling Jewelers (239-642-3001; 121 S. Barfield Dr., Marco 34145; at Shops of Marco) Custom design and manufacturing; cloisonné turtles and fish jewelry.

Thalheimer's Fine Jewelers (239-261-8422, 800-998-8423; 3200 Tamiami Trail N., Naples 34103) The most respected name in jewelers, carrying quality watches, diamond jewelry, gems, crystal, and porcelain. Watchmaker, designer, and appraiser on premises.

William Phelps, Custom Jeweler (239-434-2233; 4200 Gulf Shore Blvd., Naples 34103; at the Village on Venetian Bay) Fine-crafted pendants, rings, earrings, and pins on display, plus colored stones and diamonds for customizing.

Yamron Jewelers (239-592-7707; 5415 Tamiami Trail N., Naples 34108; at Waterside Shops) A select stock of exquisite jewelry and Swiss watches.

KITCHENWARE & HOME DECOR

Chelsea Gardens French Collection (239-643-2268; 1170 Third St. S. #B101, Naples 34102) Genteel collection of hand-painted tableware, statues, sculptures, tea towels and the likes, all tres francais.

Casa Condor (239-591-2833; 1786 Trade Center Way, Naples 34109) Rooms filled with colorful tropical imports: furniture, pottery, wall hangings, glassware, cookware, and other gifts.

Fabec-Young & Company (239-649-5501; 4360 Gulfshore Blvd., Ste. 604, Naples 34103; at the Village on Venetian Bay) Unusual table settings from napkins and candles to glassware and ceramics.

The Gallery (239-949-1181; South Bay Dr. #116, Bonita 26821; at the Promenade) Splashy, make-an-impression tableware, avant-garde furniture, vases, sculptures, and affordable framed paintings.

Gattle's (239-262-4791, 800-344-4552; 1250 Third St. S., Naples 34102) Linens for bed, bath, and table; fine home accessories and nursery items.

The Good Life (239-262-4355, 800-846-2540; 1170 Third St. S., Ste. A101, Naples 34102) Gourmet cookware, tabletops, serving pieces, imported Portmeiron and colorful beach-theme tableware, quality implements, and gourmet food products.

A Horse of a Different Color (239-261-1252; 4200 Gulf Shore Blvd., Naples 34103; at the Village on Venetian Bay) One-of-a-kind, pricey, highly contemporary gifts, lamps, clocks, and accessories, featuring imports from Scandinavia and other European regions.

Lady from Haiti (239-649-8607; 476 Fifth Ave. S., Naples 34102) Steel-drum sculptures, hand-painted wooden items, fine Haitian art. Enjoy the sand on the floor and Caribbean music while you shop.

Tribal Findings Wholesale (239-593-5811; www.tribalfindings.com; 5974 Taylor Rd. #2, Naples 34109) In Naples's Trade Center, it sells an intriguing collection of masks, carvings, pottery, fountains, and other wood and clay folk art and decorative items from West Africa, Mexico, and Haiti at reasonable prices.

SHELL SHOPS

Marco Craft & Shell Company (239-394-7020; Marco Walk, 599 S. Collier Blvd., Marco Island 34145) Craft and specimen shells, locally handcrafted gifts, craft classes.

SPORTS STORES

Note: This listing includes general sports outlets only. For supplies and equipment for specific sports, please refer to "Recreation" in this chapter.

Play It Again Sports (239-263-6679; 2204 Tamiami Trail, Naples 34103) New and used sports gear; in-line skates and exercise equipment rentals.
Sports Authority (239-598-5054; 2505 Pine Ridge Rd., Naples 34109) Complete line of sports and outdoor equipment and clothing.

CALENDAR OF EVENTS

JANUARY

Bonita Springs National Art Festival (239-495-8989; www.artinusa.com /Bonita; the Promenade, Bonita Springs) Two days midmonth featuring fine artists from around the world. Also in March.
Mullet Festival (239-394-3041; Stan's Idle Hour restaurant, Goodland) Celebrating Goodland's fishing heritage and an extravaganza of music and tomfoolery. Two days late in the month.
Naples Invitational Art Fest (239-263-1667; Fleischmann Park, Naples) One of the nation's top-rated arts festivals, with select artists and artisans, and gourmet food.

FEBRUARY

Everglades Seafood Festival (239-695-4100; Everglades City) Three days of music, arts and crafts, and fresh seafood. Early in the month.
Grecian Festival (239-591-3430; St. Katherine's Greek Orthodox Church, Airport-Pulling Rd., Naples) Greek food specialties, music, costumed dancers, and exhibits. First weekend.
Senior PGA Tour Ace Group Classic (239-403-1030; Bay Colony Golf Club, Pelican Marsh, Naples) One week early in the month.
Native American and Pioneer Heritage Days (239-394-3397; Collier-Seminole State Park) Two days midmonth honoring local heritage.

MARCH

Bonita Springs Tomato Seafood Festival (239-334-7007; Bonita Recreational Center, West Terry St. and Pine St., Bonita Springs) Honors the town's two

Seafood takes many forms at Bonita Springs's annual Tomato Seafood Festival.

Karen T. Bartlett

culinary trademarks with food and entertainment. Two days at the end of the month.

Dig the Arts Festival (239-263-8242; Lowdermilk Park, Naples) Art meets the beach in typical Naples style. United Arts Council hosts one day of free music, art, sand sculpture, and kids' games. One day late in the month.

Naples Seafood Festival (239-436-6462; Naples Airport, Naples) Local delicacies, entertainment, arts and crafts fair, and a boat raffle. Three days midmonth.

Nuveen Masters Tennis Tournament (239-435-1300; www.championstour .com; Vanderbilt Country Club, Naples) The end-of-season competition for the top eight players on the senior Nuveen professional tennis tour. One week.

Seminole Indian Day (239-695-2989; Smallwood Store & Museum, Chokolo- skee Island) Re-enactments, period clothing competition, and entertainment and food of the Seminole nation.

Swamp Buggy Races (239-774-2701, 800-897-2701; Florida Sports Park, Route 951, east Naples) Nationally televised event; the Everglades's equivalent of tractor pulls or monster truck racing.

APRIL

A Taste of Collier (Fifth Ave. S., Naples) Naples's renowned restaurants serve samples of their culinary specialties. Live music. One day.

MAY

Great Dock Canoe Race (239-263-9940; The Dock at Crayton Cove restaurant, 12th Ave. S., Naples) More than 200 teams, many in festive costumes, paddle across Naples Bay in good-spirited competition one Saturday.

SummerJazz (239-261-2222; Naples Beach Hotel & Golf Club, Naples) A series of sunset concerts under the stars on the third Saturday of every month, May through September.

Swamp Buggy Races See above, under MARCH.

JUNE

South Florida PGA Open (239-261-2222, ext. 2350; Naples Beach Hotel & Golf Club, 851 Gulf Shore Blvd. N., Naples) Golf enthusiasts can qualify to play side-by-side with PGA pros in the six-day competition.

JULY

Fourth of July (239-434-3383; Fifth Avenue South and Naples Pier, Naples) Fireworks at the pier follow a main street parade.

OCTOBER

Les Masquerades (239-598-1605; Waterside Shops, Naples) Halloweening for kids and adults, with strolling costumed characters, music, a magician, and treats.

Marco Island Film Festival (239-642-FEST; www.marcoislandfilmfestival.com; Mission Plaza, Marco Island)

A parade precedes October's Swamp Buggy Races, featuring the crowning of the year's queen — who then gets initiated with a dunk in the mud.

Karen T. Bartlett

Swamp Buggy Races See above, under MARCH.

NOVEMBER

Festival of Lights (239-435-3742; Third Street Plaza and Fifth Avenue South, Naples) Holiday street- and tree-lighting festivities. Late in the month or early December.

Old Florida Festival (239-774-8476; Collier County Museum, Naples) Living history from Stone Age to World War II, with food, crafts, games, and demonstrations.

DECEMBER

Holiday Boat Parade (239-261-0882; Naples City Dock) An annual holiday maritime event midmonth.

CHAPTER SEVEN
Practical Matters
INFORMATION

A comment on crime and humor on Anna Maria Island.

Greg Wagner

W e hope that you never need a hospital or a policeman, but in case you should, we offer that information here, as well as information on other topics:

AMBULANCE/FIRE/POLICE

A ll four southwest coast counties have adopted the 911 emergency phone number system. Dial it for ambulance, fire, sheriff, and police. Listed below are non-emergency numbers for individual communities.

Town	Ambulance	Fire	Police/Sheriff
FOR EMERGENCY Anywhere in the region	911	911	911

CHARLOTTE COUNTY

Town	Ambulance	Fire	Police/Sheriff
Boca Grande			239-964-2908
Punta Gorda			941-639-4111
Charlotte County Sheriff			941-639-2101
Florida Highway Patrol (Venice)			941-483-5911

COLLIER COUNTY

Town	Ambulance	Fire	Police/Sheriff
Everglades City			239-695-2301
Naples	239-434-4844		239-434-4853
Collier County Sheriff			239-793-9300
Florida Highway Patrol			239-354-2377

LEE COUNTY

Town	Ambulance	Fire	Police/Sheriff
Bonita Springs	239-992-3320		239-495-4500
Cape Coral	239-574-0501		239-574-3223
Captiva			239-472-9494
Fort Myers	239-334-6222		239-338-2111
Fort Myers Beach	239-463-6163		239-765-2300
Pine Island (Matlacha)	239-283-0030		
Sanibel	239-472-5525		239-472-3111
Lee County Sheriff			239-477-1200
Florida Highway Patrol			239-278-7100

SARASOTA/BRADENTON COUNTIES

Town	Ambulance	Fire	Police/Sheriff
Anna Maria		941-741-3900	941-778-4711
Bradenton		941-747-1161	941-746-4111
Bradenton Beach		941-741-3900	941-778-6311
Holmes Beach		941-741-3900	941-741-7875
Longboat (Manatee County)		941-383-5666	941-383-3738
Longboat (Sarasota County)		941-316-1944	941-316-1977
Sarasota		941-951-4211	941-366-0727
Siesta Key			941-365-1616
Venice		941-492-3196	941-488-6711

Town	Ambulance	Fire	Police/Sheriff
Manatee County			941-747-3011
Sarasota County		941-951-4211	941-366-0727
Florida Highway Patrol (Bradenton)			941-751-7647

AREA CODE/TOWN GOVERNMENT & ZIP CODES

AREA CODE

The area code for the Sarasota Bay area and the Charlotte Coast is 941, with the exception of the communities of Boca Grande and Placida, where the area code is 239. The 239 code also covers the entire Island Coast and South Coast.

GOVERNMENT

All incorporated cities within the region are self-governing, with council-men, commissioners, mayors, and city managers in various roles. The unincorporated towns and communities are county-ruled.

The incorporated cities of the Sarasota Bay coast include Bradenton, Anna Maria, Holmes Beach, Bradenton Beach, Sarasota, Longboat Key, and Venice. Bradenton is the county seat for Manatee County; Sarasota for Sarasota County. On the Charlotte Harbor coast, North Port and Punta Gorda (county seat) are incorporated.

Cape Coral, Fort Myers (county seat), Fort Myers Beach, and Sanibel make up the Island Coast's incorporated cities. Naples is Collier County's seat; Naples, Marco Island, and Everglades City are incorporated.

ZIP CODES

Town	Government Center	Zip
CHARLOTTE HARBOR COAST		
North Port	941-426-8484	34287
Punta Gorda	941-575-3369	33950
ISLAND COAST		
Cape Coral	239-574-0401	33990
Fort Myers	239-332-6700	33902
Fort Myers Beach	239-765-0202	33931
Sanibel	239-472-3700	33957

Town	Government Center	Zip
SARASOTA BAY COAST		
Anna Maria	941-708-6130	34216
Bradenton Beach	941-778-1005	34217
Holmes Beach	941-708-5800	34217
Longboat Key (Manatee)	941-383-3721	34228
Longboat Key (Sarasota)	941-316-1999	34228
Sarasota	941-365-2200	34236
Venice	941-486-2626	34285
SOUTH COAST		
Everglades City	239-695-3781	34139
Marco Island	239-389-5000	34145
Naples	239-434-4717	34102

BANKS

Several old and established banks have branches located throughout Florida's Gulf Coast. Some are listed below, with toll-free information numbers where available.

Bank	Number(s)
South Trust	
Bradenton	941-361-2350
Charlotte County	888-817-9165
Englewood	941-361-2350
Fort Myers	800-239-9987
Naples	888-817-9165
Punta Gorda	888-817-9165
Sarasota	800-208-9630
Venice	800-208-9630
SunTrust	800-732-9487

BIBLIOGRAPHY

Books about the region are available in bookstores and online outlets.

BIOGRAPHY & REMINISCENCE

Brown, Loren G. "Totch." *Totch: A Life in the Everglades*. Gainesville: University Press of Florida, 1993. 279 pp., photos. Paper. $16.05. A folksy, firsthand adventure tour of Ten Thousand Islands through the words of a former native.

Lindbergh, Anne Morrow. *Gift from the Sea.* New York: Pantheon, 1955. 142 pp., illus. Hardcover $16. New York: Vintage Books, 1955. 138 pp., illus. Paper, $7. A small book packed with sea-inspired wisdom from the wife of Charles Lindbergh, who died in 2001. Strong evidence points to Captiva as the book's inspiration.

Newton, James. *Uncommon Friends.* New York: Harcourt, Brace, Jovanovich, 1987. 368 pp. $16. Local man's memories of his friendships with Fort Myers's illustrious winterers: Thomas Edison, Henry Ford, Harvey Firestone, and Charles Lindbergh.

Orlean, Susan. *The Orchid Thief: A True Story of Beauty and Obsession.* New York: Random House, 1998. 284 pp. $25. Set in Fakahatchee Strand, Naples, and other local venues, it tells a bizarre nonfiction tale about the elusive ghost orchid and the people who sought it.

Weeks, David C. *Ringling: The Florida Years, 1911–1936.* Gainesville: University Press of Florida, 1993. 350 pp., photos, annotations, index. $24.95.

COOKBOOKS

Junior League of Fort Myers. *Gulfshore Delights.* Fort Myers, Fla., 1984. 286 pp., illus., index. $14.95.

———. *Tropical Settings.* Fort Myers, Fla., 1995. 254 pp., illus., index. $19.95.

Reynolds, Doris. *When Peacocks Were Roasted and Mullet Was Fried.* Naples, Fla.: Enterprise Publishing, 1993. 175 pp., photos. $23.95. Naples history flavored with recipes.

FICTION

Dever, Sean Michael. *Blind Pass.* Kearney, Neb.: Morris Publishing, 1996. 244 pp. $7.99. Mystery set in Sanibel and Captiva.

MacDonald, John D. Many of his Travis McGee and other mysteries take place in a Sarasota Bay coast setting, where he had a home.

Matthiessen, Peter. *Killing Mr. Watson.* New York: Random House, 1990. Hardcover, 372 pp. $14. The parents of this award-winning author live on Sanibel Island. The subject of his historical trilogy is the posse killing of a murderer who hid out in the frontier of Ten Thousand Islands.

———. *Lost Man's River.* New York: Random House, 1997. Hardcover, 539 pp. $15. Second in the trilogy.

———. Bone by Bone. New York: Random House: 1999. Hardcover, 410 pp. $14. Final book in the trilogy, told in Ed Watson's own voice.

White, Randy. *Captiva.* New York: Berkley Publishing Company, 1996. 319 pp. $5.99.

———. *The Heat Islands.* New York: St. Martin's Press, 1992. 276 pp. $4.99. Mystery by a local fishing guide/journalist in local setting.

————. *The Mangrove Coast*. New York: Berkley Prime Crime, Putnam Berkley Group, 1998. Set in Sanibel and Panama.

————. *Sanibel Flats*. New York: St. Martin's Press, 1990. 307 pp. $3.95. His first Doc Ford mystery; set on Sanibel Island.

HISTORY

Anholt, Betty. *Sanibel's Story: Voices & Images from Calusa to Incorporation*. Virginia Beach, Va.: Donning, 1998. 191 pp., illustrations, maps. Written by a long-time island resident and historian.

Beater, Jack. *Pirates & Buried Treasure*. St. Petersburg: Great Outdoors Publishing, 1959. 118 pp., illus. $2.95. Somewhat factual, ever-colorful account of José Gaspar and his cohorts, by the area's foremost legendaire.

Board, Prudy Taylor, and Esther B. Colcord. *Historic Fort Myers*. Virginia Beach, Va.: Donning, 1992. 96 pp., photos, index. $15.95. Largely photographic treatment, written by two of the area's leading historians today.

————. *Pages From the Past*. Virginia Beach, Va.: Donning, 1990. 192 pp., photos, index. $29.95. Largely photographic treatment of Fort Myers's history.

Dormer, Elinore M. *The Sea Shell Islands: A History of Sanibel and Captiva*. Tallahassee: Rose Printing, 1987. 274 pp., illus., index. $16. The definitive work on island and regional history.

Jordan, Elaine Blohm. *Pine Island, the Forgotten Island*. Pine Island, Fla.: 1982. 186 pp., photos.

————. *Tales of Pine Island*. Ellijay, Ga.: Jordan Ink Publishing, 1985. 142 pp. $12.

Matthews, Janet Snyder. *Edge of Wilderness: A Settlement History of Manatee River and Sarasota Bay*. Sarasota, Fla.: Coastal Press, 1983. 464 pp., photos, index. $21.50.

————. *Journey to Centennial Sarasota*. Sarasota: Pine Level Press, 1989. 224 pp., photos, index. $29.95.

————. *Venice: Journey to Horse and Chaise*. Sarasota: Pine Level Press, 1989. 394 pp., photos, index.

Zeiss, Betsy. *The Other Side of the River: Historical Cape Coral*. Cape Coral, Fla.: 1986. 215 pp., photos, index. $8.95.

NATURAL HISTORY

Campbell, George R. *The Nature of Things on Sanibel*. Fort Myers: Press Printing, 1978. 174 pp., illus., index. $14.95. Factual yet entertaining background on native fauna and flora.

Douglas, Marjory Stoneman. *The Everglades: River of Grass*. St. Simons, Ga.: Mockingbird Books, 1947. 308 pp., $4.95. The book that focused the nation's attention on the developing plight of the pristine Everglades.

Ripple, Jeff. *Southwest Florida's Wetland Wilderness: Big Cypress Swamp and the Ten Thousand Islands.* Gainesville: University Press of Florida. Paperback, black and white photography by Clyde Butcher, 74 pp. Stunning photography.

Toops, Connie. *The Florida Everglades.* Stillwater, Minn.: Voyageur Press, 1998. Paperback, 112 pp., color photography. Written by a former national park ranger.

PICTORAL

Butcher, Clyde. *Clyde Butcher: Portfolio I.* Fort Myers: Shade Tree Press, 1994. 64 plates. The master of natural landscape photography collects his haunting black-and-white large-format images in a coffee-table edition.

Campen, Richard N. *Images of Sanibel, Captiva, Fort Myers.* Cape Coral, Fla.: Direct Impressions, 1995. 84 pp., photos, index.

Capes, Richard. *Richard Capes' Drawings Capture Siesta Key.* Sarasota: Capes Studio of Florida, 1992. 175 pp. An artistic tour of the island in pen and ink, with handwritten descriptions.

Stone, Lynn. *Sanibel Island.* Stillwater, Minn.: Voyageur Press, Inc., 1991. 96 pp., photos. $16.95. Sanibel's natural treasures in words and striking pictures.

TRAVEL

MacPerry, I. *Indian Mounds You Can Visit.* St. Petersburg: Great Outdoors Publishing, 1993. 319 pp., photos, index. $12.95. Covers the entire west coast of Florida, arranged by county.

Marquis, Darcy Lee, and Paul Roat. *The Insiders' Guide to Sarasota & Bradenton.* Manteo, N.C.: Insiders' Guides, 1996. 369 pp., photos, index. Copublished by the Bradenton Herald. Lots of information that would be especially helpful to anyone relocating to the area.

Walton, Chelle Koster. *Adventure Guide to Tampa Bay and Florida's West Coast.* Edison, N.J.: Hunter Publishing, 1998. Paperback, 322 pp., maps, index. $16.95. Covers Tampa to the western Everglades.

CHECK IT OUT

Out of print books you can find in local libraries when you're visiting.

Bickel, Karl A. *The Mangrove Coast: The Story of the West Coast of Florida.* 4th ed. New York: Coward-McCann, 1989. 332 pp., photos, index. Vintage regional history of the area from Tampa Bay to Ten Thousand Islands, from the time of Ponce de León to 1885, spiced with romantic embellishments.

Briggs, Mildred. *Pioneers of Bonita Springs (Facts and Folklore).* Bonita Springs, Fla., 1976. 100 pp., photos. Pirates, Indian healers, outlaws, and more.

Fritz, Florence. *Unknown Florida*. Coral Gables: University of Miami Press, 1963. 213 pp., photos, index. Focuses on southernmost Gulf Coast.

Gonzales, Thomas A. *The Caloosahatchee: History of the Caloosahatchee River and the City of Fort Myers, Florida*. Fort Myers Beach: Island Press, 1982. 134 pp. Memories of a native son, descendant of city's first settler.

Grismer, Karl H. The Story of Fort Myers. Fort Myers Beach: Island Press, 1982. 348 pp., photos, index.

———. *The Story of Sarasota*. Tampa: The Florida G Press, 1946. 376 pp., photos, index.

Hann, John H., ed. *Missions to the Calusa*. Gainesville: University of Florida Press, 1991. 460 pp., historic documents, index.

Marth, Del. *Yesterday's Sarasota*. Miami: E. A. Seemann Publishing, 1977. Updated. 160 pp., photos. Primarily pictorial history.

Matthews, Kenneth, and Robert McDevitt. *The Unlikely Legacy*. Sarasota: Aaron Publishers, 1980. 64 pp., illus. The story of John Ringling, the circus, and Sarasota.

Peeples, Vernon. *Punta Gorda and the Charlotte Harbor Area*. Virginia Beach, Va.: Donning, 1986. 208 pp., photos, index. Pictorial history authored by local politician.

Romans, Bernard. *A Concise Natural History of East and West Florida*. Gainesville: University of Florida Press, 1962. 342 pp., index. A facsimile reproduction of the 1775 edition.

Schell, Rolfe F. *De Soto Didn't Land at Tampa*. Fort Myers Beach: Island Press, 1966. 96 pp., illus.

———. *History of Fort Myers Beach*. Fort Myers Beach: Island Press, 1980. 96 pp., photos, index.

Tebeau, Charlton W. *Florida's Last Frontier: The History of Collier County*. Coral Gables: University of Miami Press, 1966. 278 pp., photos, index.

Widmer, Randolph J. *The Evolution of the Calusa*. Tuscaloosa: University of Alabama Press, 1988. 334 pp., index. Very technical discussion of the "nonagricultural chiefdom on the Southwest Florida Coast."

CLIMATE, SEASONS, AND WHAT TO WEAR

The tropics brush the Mangrove Coast but do not overwhelm it.

— Karl Bickel, *The Mangrove Coast*, 1942

Florida's nickname, the Sunshine State, was once as fresh as it was apt. Although overuse has tended to cloud the once-perfect image, Florida still remains the ultimate state of sunshine through the sheer power of statistics. The sun beams down on the Gulf Coast for nearly 75 percent of all daylight hours and constitutes the one asset that locals can bank on.

Predictions call for flurries of ibises in the Everglades.

Karen T. Bartlett

To residents, the sun's smile can seem more like a sneer as they await fall's begrudging permission to turn off air conditioners and open windows. They suffer their own brand of cabin fever during the summer months, which often seem to go on as long as a Canadian winter. Although visitors revel in the warmth and sunlight, they often wonder how residents endure the monotony of seasonal sameness.

The seasons do change along the southern Gulf Coast, although more subtly than "up north." Weather patterns vary within the region. The Sarasota Bay and Charlotte Harbor areas often get more rain. However, weather can be very localized — it may rain on the southern end of 12-mile-long Sanibel Island while the north end remains dry. Islands generally stay cooler than the mainland in summer and warmer in winter, thanks to their insulating jacket of water. This is especially true where Charlotte Harbor runs wide and deep, creating a small pocket of tropical climate.

Winter is everyone's favorite time of year weatherwise, with temperatures along the coast reaching generally into the 70s during the day and dropping into the 50s at night. Visitors find green, balmy relief from snow blindness and frostbite. Floridians enjoy the relative coolness that brings with it a reprieve from sweltering days, steamy nights, and bloodthirsty insects. The fragrance of oranges, grapefruits, and key limes fill the air. It's a time for activity; one can safely schedule a tee time past noon. Resort areas fill up, and migratory houseguests from the north arrive.

Spring comes on tiptoe to the coast. No thaw-and-puddle barometer alerts us; the sense of spring giddiness affects only longtime residents. Floridians emerge from hibernation raring to leap and frolic — and perhaps do a little mischief. Gardenias, Hong Kong orchids, and jasmine bloom, and everything that already looks green and alive bursts forth with an extra reserve of color. It's a time to celebrate the end of another season and to enjoy greedily the domain that's been shared with visitors during the winter months.

Green Flash

The sun is setting, melting, golden, into the sea like a round pat of butter balanced on its edge in a sauté pan. Just as the final crescent of light disappears, it sends up on the horizon a green farewell flare.

What you've just witnessed is a tropical phenomenon called a green flash. It occurs infrequently, and most people miss it — or only realize what they've seen after the fact.

Skeptics will tell you that green flashes are just a good excuse to sit on the beach at sunset, perhaps with a celebratory glass of champagne or rum punch. The drinking part of the sunset ritual, they further theorize, may be more responsible for green flash sightings than reality.

Physics, however, backs up the notion that the sun emits a split-second green explosion as it winks below the sea's surface. It all has to do with spectrum, wavelengths, refraction, and other terms you may remember from school science experiments.

In short, it takes conditions such as those we enjoy on the Gulf Coast — sunsets over the sea and near-tropical climes — to make the green flash happen. Cloudless evening skies are also required, which occur more regularly during the cool months. Binoculars or a small telescope will help widen the band of refracted green light so that it lasts longer. Patience and persistence are crucial. Once you've seen a green flash, some say, your now-trained eye is apt to spot more. With or without rum.

Summers used to be reserved for die-hard Floridians. All but the most devoted residents boarded up their homes and businesses and headed somewhere — *anywhere* — cooler. Now there's a summer trade, composed of Floridians, Europeans, and northern families — enough to keep alive the resort communities through temperatures that snuggle up to 100 degrees. Although technically classified as subtropical, starting in June the region feels the bristles of that tropical brush. The pace of life slows, and late-afternoon rains suddenly and unpredictably revolt against the sun's constancy. Mangoes and guavas blush sweet temptation. Moonlit nights bring magic to the cereus vine, with its white starburst blooms the size of a Frisbee.

Fall appears in October, as a sharpening of vision after a blur of humidity. Residents don't exactly go out and buy wool plaids, but they do break out sweatshirts. Many build fires in hearths that have held dried floral arrangements for eight months. The leathery leaves of the sea grape tree turn as red as the northern oak, and the gumbo-limbo coaxes out rakes. The best part about a Gulf Coast fall, for those residents who once endured northern winters, is that it bodes not of rubber boots and long underwear.

Winter temperatures dip, albeit rarely, into the freezing range, so be prepared for just about any weather between December and February. Fortunately swimsuits take up little room, so pack more than one (Florida's high humidity often prevents anything from ever really drying out). Loose-fitting togs and cotton work best in any season. Long sleeves are welcome in the evenings during the winter. Summer showers require rain gear, especially if you plan on boating or playing outdoors.

Don't worry about dress codes in most restaurants. Ties and pantyhose are strictly for the office and (possibly) the theater. Worry more about comfort, especially if your skin burns easily. Pack hats and lots of sunscreen. Bring insect repellent, too, especially if you plan on venturing into the jungle — or just watching an island sunset, for that matter. Counties do spray for mosquitoes, but it has little effect on the tiny but prolific no-see-um (sand flea). Any DEET product repels mosquitoes. The best protection against both pests is sitting under a ceiling fan — practically standard equipment in homes and hotels.

On the cloudier side, Florida weather includes a high incidence of lightning, summer squalls, tornadoes, waterspouts, and the dreaded H-word. Hurricane season begins in June, but activity concentrates toward season's end in November. Watches and warnings alert you in plenty of time to head inland or north; to be safest, do so at first mention, especially if you are staying on an island.

Florida's celebrated sunshine is at its best on the Gulf Coast. Ol' Sol visits practically every day, and it's also where he slips into bed. Gulf Coast Florida boasts the most spectacular sunsets in the continental United States.

AVERAGE GULF COAST AIR TEMPERATURES

Month	Avg. Max.	Avg. Min.
Jan.	72.8°	52.8°
Feb.	73.8°	53.8°
Mar.	78.3°	57.8°
Apr.	82.5°	61.6°
May	87.7°	67.1°
June	89.7°	72.1°
July	90.5°	73.7°
Aug.	90.9°	73.8°
Sept.	89.1°	72.7°
Oct.	84.9°	66.8°
Nov.	77.9°	59.4°
Dec.	74.1°	53.8°

GULF COAST WATER TEMPERATURES

Annual average	77.5°
Fall/winter average	70.8°
Spring/summer average	84.1°
Winter low	66.0°
Summer high	87.0°

SERVICES FOR THE PHYSICALLY IMPAIRED

Regulations concerning disabled access vary, depending on locale. In general, most restaurants, parks, attractions, and resorts provide physically impaired visitors with special ramps, bathroom stalls, and hotel rooms.

HOSPITALS & CLINICS

CHARLOTTE HARBOR COAST

Englewood

Englewood Community Hospital (941-475-6571; www.englewoodcommunity hospital.com; 700 Medical Blvd., Englewood 34223) Emergency room open 24 hours.

Port Charlotte

Columbia Fawcett Memorial Hospital (941-629-1181; 21298 Olean Blvd., Port Charlotte 33949) Emergency room open 24 hours.
Bon Secours-St. Joseph Hospital (941-766-4122; 2500 Harbor Blvd., Port Charlotte 33952) Emergency room open 24 hours.

Punta Gorda

Charlotte Regional Medical Center (941-639-3131; 809 E. Marion Ave., Punta Gorda 33950) Emergency room open 24 hours.

Fort Myers's new and stylish HealthPark Medical Center.

Karen T. Bartlett

ISLAND COAST

Cape Coral

Cape Coral Hospital (239-574-2323; 636 Del Prado Blvd, Cape Coral 33990) Emergency room open 24 hours.

HealthPark Medical Center (239-433-7799; 9981 HealthPark Circle, Fort Myers 33908) Emergency room open 24 hours.Twenty-four-hour medical information HealthLine, 800-936-5321,

Lee Memorial Hospital (239-332-1111; 2776 Cleveland Ave., Fort Myers 33901) Emergency room open 24 hours.

Southwest Florida Regional Medical Center (239-939-1147; www.swrfmc.com; 2727 Winkler Ave., Fort Myers 33901) Acute care and outpatient surgery. Emergency room open 24 hours. For 24-hour Consult-a-Nurse Healthcare Referral, call 800-257-0944.

SARASOTA BAY COAST

Bradenton

HCA L.W. Blake Medical Center (941-792-6611; 2020 59th St. W., Bradenton 34209) Emergency room open 24 hours.

Manatee Memorial Hospital (941-746-5111; 206 Second St. E., Bradenton 34208) Emergency room open 24 hours.

Sarasota

Doctors Hospital of Sarasota (941-342-1100; 5731 Bee Ridge Rd., Sarasota 34233) Emergency room open 24 hours.

Sarasota Memorial Hospital (941-917-9000; 1700 S. Tamiami Trail, Sarasota 34239-3555) Emergency room open 24 hours.

Venice

Bon Secours Venice Hospital (941-485-7711; 540 The Rialto, Venice 34285) Emergency room open 24 hours.

SOUTH COAST

Bonita Springs

Bonita Bay Surgery Center/Bonita Bay Diagnostic Centre (239-498-7000; 26800 Tamiami Trail, Bonita Bay 34134) Open Monday–Friday, no ER.

Marco Island

Marco Healthcare Center (239-394-8234; www.nchhcs.org; 40 Heathwood,

Marco Island 34145) Twenty-four-hour medical care and rehab on out-patient basis.

Naples

Naples Community Hospital (239-262-3131;350 Seventh St. N., Naples 34102) Emergency room open 24 hours.
North Collier Hospital (239-597-1417; 11190 Healthpark Blvd., Naples 34101) Emergency room open 24 hours.

LATE-NIGHT FOOD AND FUEL

Certain categories of Florida liquor licensing require bars to serve food, which provides a good source for late-night eating. Many chain restaurants located along major thoroughfares stay open late or all night, such as Grandma's Kitchen, Denny's, and Perkins.

Chain convenience stores, gas stations, and fuel/food marts also are open around the clock. These include 7-Eleven, Starvin' Marvin, Mobil Mart, and Circle K.

MEDIA

Media flood the Gulf Coast like high tide. Many publications are directed toward tourists, and some are only as permanent as the shoreline during a tidal surge. Magazines come and go, and radio stations often shift formats.

Four daily newspapers stand out for their endurance and dependability: the *Bradenton Herald*, the *Sarasota Herald-Tribune*, the Fort Myers *News-Press*, and the *Naples Daily News*. Weeklies are also firmly established in their respective communities, primarily because many are owned collectively by one corporation. Specialty tabloids address seniors, shoppers, fishermen, women, and other groups.

Magazines show the most fluctuation. Traditionally they were created to appeal to the region's upscale, mature population, which is concentrated in Sarasota and Naples. *Sarasota Magazine* and *Gulfshore Life* have been the stalwarts of regional lifestyle glossies, but even they shift focus to address changing populations and economic trends.

Fort Myers carries the majority of the region's broadcast media, which reach to the Charlotte Harbor and the South Coast. Much of the Sarasota Bay coast's TV comes from Tampa.

Charlotte Harbor Coast

NEWSPAPERS

Boca Beacon (239-964-2995, 800-749-2995; PO Box 313, Boca Grande 33921)
  Weekly.

Charlotte Sun-Herald (941-629-2855; PO Box 2390, Port Charlotte 33949)

Englewood Sun Herald (941-474-5521; 167 W. Dearborn St., Englewood 34223)
  Weekly.

Gasparilla Gazette (941-964-2728; PO Box 929, 301 Park Ave., Boca Grande
  33921)

RADIO

WCCF-AM 1580. Talk.
WCVU-FM 104.9. Easy listening.
WENG-AM 1530. Talk and news.
WIKX-FM 92.9. Country.
WKII-AM 1070. Adult.
WVIJ-FM 91.7. Christian.

Island Coast

NEWSPAPERS

Cape Coral Breeze (239-574-1110; 2510 Del Prado Blvd., Cape Coral 33910)
  Daily.

Fort Myers Beach Bulletin (239-463-4421; PO Box 2867, 19260 San Carlos Blvd.,
  Fort Myers Beach 33932)

Island Reporter (239-472-1587; PO Box 809, 2340 Periwinkle Way, Sanibel
  Island 33957) Weekly.

News-Press (239-335-0200; www.news-press.com; PO Box 10, 2442 Dr. Martin
  Luther King Jr. Blvd., Fort Myers 33902) The tenth-largest newspaper in the
  state in terms of circulation, it publishes editions for Charlotte County and
  Bonita Springs.

Observer Papers (239-482-7111; 17274 San Carlos Blvd., Fort Myers Beach
  33931) Publishes weekly editions for Fort Myers Beach and other neighborhoods.

Pine Island Eagle (239-283-2022; 10700 Stringfellow Rd., Suite 60, Bokeelia
  33922) Weekly.

Sanibel-Captiva Islander (239-472-5185; PO Box 56, 395 Tarpon Bay Rd.,
  Sanibel Island 33957) Weekly; free subscription.

MAGAZINES

Florida Journal (239-481-7511; 6238 Presidential Ct., Fort Myers 33919)
   German publication.
Times of the Islands (239-472-0205; PO Box 1227, Sanibel Island 33957)

RADIO

WAVV-FM 101.1. Easy listening.
WAYJ-FM 88.7. Christian.
WBBT-FM 105.5. Urban.
WCKT-FM 107.1. Country.
WCRM-AM 1350. Spanish Christian.
WDRR-FM 98.5. Jazz.
WOST-FM 100.1. Adult contemporary.
WINK-AM 1240. News/talk.
WINK-FM 96.9. Adult contemporary.
WJBX-FM 99.3. Adult alternative.
WJST-FM 106.3. Adult.
WJYO-FM 91.5. Christian.
WOLZ-FM 95.3. Oldies.
WRXK-FM 96.1. Adult rock.
WSOR-FM 90.9. Christian.
WSRX-FM 89.5. Contemporary Christian.
WWGR-FM 101.9. Country.
WXKB-FM 103.9. Adult contemporary.
WMYR-AM 1410. Radio Disney.
WWCL-AM 1440. Spanish.
WQAM-AM 770. News/talk.
WMIB-AM 1660. Stardust.

TELEVISION

WBBH-TV Channel 20; Fort Myers. NBC.
WFTX-TV Channel 36; Cape Coral. Fox.
WINK-TV Channel 11; Fort Myers. CBS.
WZVN-TV Channel 26; Fort Myers. ABC.

Sarasota Bay Coast

NEWSPAPERS

Bradenton Herald (941-748-0411; PO Box 921, Bradenton 34206;. Daily.
Longboat Observer (941-383-5509; PO Box 8100, Longboat Key 34228;. Weekly.

Pelican Press (941-349-4949; 230 Avenida Madera, Sarasota 34242;. Weekly covering Siesta Key and Sarasota.

Herald-Tribune (941-953-7755; www.newscoast.com; 801 S. Tamiami Trail, PO Box 1719, Sarasota 33577) Florida's eighth largest daily in terms of circulation.

Venice Gondolier (941-484-2611; 200 E. Venice Ave., Venice 34285) Published semiweekly.

Weekly (941-923-2544; 3755 S. Tuttle Ave., Sarasota 34239) Heavy on entertainment.

MAGAZINES

Sarasota Arts Review (941-364-5825; 1269 First St., Suite 211, Sarasota 34236) Monthly coverage of the area's lively arts scene.

Sarasota Magazine (941-366-8225; 601 S. Osprey Ave., Sarasota 34236) Lifestyle for upscale Sarasotans.

Sarasota Scene (941-365-1119; 2015 S. Tuttle Ave., Sarasota 34239) Weekly covering the Sarasota-Bradenton area.

West Coast Woman (941-954-3300; PO Box 819, Sarasota 34230) Monthly free publication.

RADIO

WAMR-AM 1320. Oldies.
WBRD-AM 1420. News/talk.
WCTQ-FM 92.1. Country.
WDUV-FM 103.5. Easy listening.
WJIS-FM 88.1. Christian jazz.
WKZM-FM 105. Christian.
WSPB-AM 1450. Classical.
WSRZ-FM 106.3. Oldies.

TELEVISION

WBSV-TV Channel 62; Sarasota. Independent.
WEDU-TV Channel 3; Sarasota. PBS.
WSB-TV Channel 40; Sarasota. ABC.

South Coast

NEWSPAPERS

Bonita Banner (239-765-0110; 9102 Bonita Beach Rd., Bonita Springs 34135) Semiweekly.

Marco Daily News (239-394-7592; www.marconews.com; 579 E. Elkcam Circle, Marco Island 34145)

Marco Island Eagle (239-394-7592; www.marcoeagle.com; 579 E. Elkcam Circle, Marco Island 34145)

Naples Daily News (239-262-3161; www.naplesnews.com; PO Box 7009, Naples 33941.

MAGAZINES

Gulfshore Life (239-643-3933; 2975 S. Horseshoe Dr., Suite 100, Naples 34104) Longtime, slick lifestyle and news guide to the southwest coast.

Home & Condo (239-643-3933; 2975 S. Horseshoe Dr., Suite 100, Naples 34104) Specifically addresses relocators.

N, The Magazine of Naples (239-594-0100; 4500 Executive Dr., Suite 1, Naples 34119) Fashion and society oriented.

Naples Illustrated (239-434-6966; www.naplesillustrated.com; 1250 Tamiami Trail, Ste. 304, Naples 34102) Haute lifestyles glossy.

RADIO

WARO-FM 94.5. Classic rock.
WGUF-FM 98.9. News/talk.
WNOG-AM 1270. News/talk.

TELEVISION

WGCU-TV Channel 30; Naples. PBS.
WTVK-TV Channel 46; Bonita Springs. UPN.

REAL ESTATE

Real-estate prices run the gamut from reasonable to ultra expensive. In parts of Bradenton, Sarasota, and Fort Myers, planned communities cater to young families. Exclusive areas such as Longboat Key, Casey Key, Manasota Key, Sanibel Island, Captiva Island, and Naples are known for their pricey waterfront homes and golfing developments. Florida's $25,000 homestead exemption gives residents a tax break on primary home purchases.

Real-estate publications can be found on the newsstands, or check local newspapers. Otherwise, contact the agencies listed below.

Florida Association of Realtors (407-438-1400; PO Box 725025, Orlando 32872-5025)

Sarasota Association of Realtors (941-923-2315; 3590 Tuttle Ave. S., Sarasota 34239)

Fort Myers Association of Realtors, Inc. (239-936-3537; 2840 Winkler Ave., Fort Myers 33916)

Sanibel & Captiva Islands Association of Realtors, Inc. (239-472-9353; 695 Tarpon Bay Rd., Suite #10, Sanibel Island 33957)

Naples Area Board of Realtors, Inc. (239-597-1666; 1455 Pine Ridge Rd., Naples 34109)

ROAD SERVICE

AAA Auto Club
941-362-2220; www.aaa.com; 3844 Bee Ridge Rd., Sarasota
941-362-2222; 24-hour emergency road service

941-362-2500; www.aaa.com; 258 Ringling Shopping Center, Sarasota

239-939-6500; www.aaa.com; 2516 Colonial Blvd., Fort Myers
800-365-0933; 24-hour emergency road service

239-594-5006; www.aaa.com; 4910 North Tamiami Trail, Suite 120, Naples
800-365-0933; 24-hour emergency road service

TOURIST INFORMATION

Visit Florida (800-7FLA-USA; 661 E. Jefferson St., Suite 300, Tallahassee 32301)

Charlotte Harbor Coast

Boca Grande Chamber of Commerce (239-964-0568; www.bocagrande.com; PO Box 704, Boca Grande 33921) Information center located in Courtyard Plaza at the island's north end.

Charlotte County Chamber of Commerce (941-627-2222; www.charlotte-florida.com/chamber; 2702 Tamiami Trail, Port Charlotte 33952 and 326 W. Marion Ave., Ste. 112, Punta Gorda 33950)

Charlotte Harbor and the Gulf Islands–The Economic Development Office of Charlotte County (921-627-3023, 800-729-5836; www.charlottecountyfl. com; 1600 Tamiami Trail, Suite 100, Punta Gorda 33948)

Englewood Area Chamber of Commerce (941-474-5511, 800-603-7198; 601 S. Indiana Ave., Englewood 34223)

Island Coast

Cape Coral Chamber of Commerce (239-549-6900, 800-226-9609; www.capec-
oralfl.com; PO Box 747, Cape Coral 33910) Information center at 2051 Cape
Coral Pkwy. E.

Estero Chamber of Commerce (239-948-7990; PO Box 508; Estero 33928)

Greater Fort Myers Beach Chamber of Commerce (239-454-7500, 800-782-
9283; www.fmbchamber.com; 17200 San Carlos Blvd., Fort Myers Beach
33931)

Greater Fort Myers Chamber of Commerce (239-332-3624, 800-366-3622;
www.fortmyers.org; PO Box 9289, Fort Myers 33902) Welcome centers
located downtown at 2310 Edwards Dr. and near the airport at 6900 Daniels
Pkwy., Ste. A-11.

Greater Pine Island Chamber of Commerce (239-283-0888; PO Box 525,
Matlacha 33909) Information center located before the bridge to Matlacha on
Pine Island Road.

Lee Island Coast Visitor & Convention Bureau (239-338-3500, 800-237-6444;
www.leeislandcoast.com; 2180 W. First St., Suite 100, Fort Myers 33901)

North Fort Myers Chamber of Commerce (239-997-9111; 13180 N. Cleveland
Ave., North Fort Myers 33903)

Sanibel-Captiva Islands Chamber of Commerce (239-472-1080; www.sanibel-
captiva.org; 1159 Causeway Rd., Sanibel Island 33957) Information center
located shortly after the causeway approach to Sanibel.

Southwest Florida Hispanic Chamber of Commerce (239-418-1441; 10051
McGregor Blvd., Suite 201, Fort Myers 33919)

Sarasota Bay Coast

Anna Maria Island Chamber of Commerce (941-778-1541; www.annamaria
islandchamber.org; 5337 Gulf Dr., Holmes Beach 34217)

Bradenton Area Convention & Visitors Bureau (941-729-9177, 800-4-MANA-
TEE; www.flagulfislands.com; PO Box 1000, Bradenton 34206) Welcome
center located off Interstate 75, exit 43.

Downtown Association of Sarasota (941-951-2656; 1818 Main Street, Sarasota
34326)

Longboat Key Chamber of Commerce (941-383-2466; Whitney Beach Plaza,
6854 Gulf of Mexico Dr., Longboat Key 34228)

Manatee Chamber of Commerce (941-748-3411; www.manateechamber.com;
222 Tenth St. W., Bradenton 34206)

Sarasota Convention & Visitors Bureau (941-957-1877, 800-522-9799; www
.sarasotafl.org; 655 N. Tamiami Trail, Sarasota 34236) Branch office: 941-957-
1877; 5947 Clark Center Ave., Suite A in the Albritton Grove Market.

Siesta Key Chamber of Commerce (941-349-3800; www.siestakeychamber.com;
5100 Ocean Blvd., Unit B, Siesta Key 34242)

Venice Area Chamber of Commerce (941-488-2236; 257 N. Tamiami Trail,
Venice 34285-1908)

South Coast

Bonita Springs Area Chamber of Commerce (239-992-2943, 800-226-2943; www
.bonitaspringschamber.com; 25071 Chamber of Commerce Dr., Bonita
Springs 34135)

Everglades Area Chamber of Commerce (239-695-3941, 800-914-6355; chamber
@florida-everglades.com; 32016 E. Tamiami Trail, PO Box 130, Everglades
City 34139) Welcome center corner of Hwy. 41 and Rte. 29.

Marco Island Area Chamber of Commerce (239-394-7549, 800-788-MARCO;
www.marco-island-florida.com/chamber; 1102 North Collier Blvd., PO Box
913, Marco Island 34145)

Naples Chamber of Commerce (239-262-6141; www.napleschamber.org; 895
5th Ave. S., Naples 34102-6605)

Visit Naples (800-605-7878; www.naples-online.com; PO Box 10129, Naples
34101)

IF TIME IS SHORT

Not enough time to do it all on this trip to southwest Florida? Here are some highlights that I suggest to weekenders and short-term vacationers who wonder how they can best spend their precious time. Beach time, of course, is a high priority for those with only a few days to spend in the sun. I list must-see beaches as well as other attractions, adventures, restaurants, and lodgings you should not miss.

Sarasota Bay Coast

Siesta Key County Beach (239-346-3310; Midnight Pass Rd. at Beach Way Dr., Siesta Key), despite its weekend and high-season crowds, is the area's ultimate beach, with sands whiter and fluffier than a down quilt. Have dinner at **The Summerhouse** (941-349-1100; 6101 Midnight Pass Rd. Siesta Key 34242), purely Florida in atmosphere and very haute in the cuisine department.

Downtown Sarasota is a happening place. Take in a play and circle the galleries of the Theatre and Arts District. Don't miss the shops of **Palm Avenue** and the galleries of **Towles Court Artist Colony** (941-365-9146; 1945 Morrill St., Sarasota 34239).

The **John and Mable Ringling Museum of Art**, the **Ringling Estate**, and its various circus and Gilded Age attractions (941-359-5700; 5401 Bay Shore Rd., Sarasota 34243) crown in glory Sarasota's famed cultural scene. **Longboat Key** provides a drive on the coast's wealthy side. Depending on your budget, dine in high style at **Euphemia Haye** (941-383-3633; 5540 Gulf of Mexico Dr., Sarasota 34228) or in the spirit of maritime fun at **Mar-Vista Dockside Restaurant & Pub** (941-383-2391; 760 Broadway St., Sarasota 34228).

Stop at **Mote Marine Aquarium** (941-388-2451, 800-691-MOTE; www .mote.org; 1600 Ken Thompson Pkwy., Sarasota 34236) to check out the new giant squid and other fishy stuff.

Charlotte Harbor Coast

The best of Charlotte Harbor lies in its hidden-from-the-spotlight barrier islands. **Manasota Key** and **Englewood Beach** boast sunny beaches flecked with sharks' teeth. For a unique and nature-intensive lodging experience, book at **Manasota Key Club** (941-383-8821, 800-237-8821; 301 Gulf of Mexico Dr., PO Box 15000, Longboat Key 34228), a long-standing beach resort with accommodations from rustic to lavish.

On Gasparilla Island, **Boca Grande** supplies a full day of beaching, shopping, and dining. Have lunch or dinner at **PJ's Seagrille** (239-964-0806; 312 Park Ave., Boca Grande 33921) and savor something from the sea, inventive and well crafted. For a different flavor of island life, take a room at the old, gracious **Gasparilla Inn** (239-964-2201; 5th St. & Palm St., PO Box 1088,Boca Grande 33921), as the Vanderbilts and Du Ponts have since 1912.

Explore the extensive aquatic preserves of Charlotte Harbor aboard a catamaran or kayak with **Grande Tours** (239-697-8825 or 239-964-0000 from Boca Grande; 12575 Placida Rd., PO Box 281, Placida 33946). For an island wilderness adventure that returns you to the days of Florida cow-hunting, ride the bouncy swamp buggy through a modern-day cattle and alligator ranch at **Babcock Wilderness Adventures** (941-489-3911, 800-500-5583; Rte. 31, Punta Gorda 33950).

Island Coast

Fort Myers's finest attraction, the **Thomas Edison Winter Estate and Ford Home** (239-334-3614; 2350-2400 McGregor Blvd., Fort Myers 33902), peeks into the times and genius of America's greatest inventors, who lived side by side in winter months. Dine Victorian in the two historic homes that make up **The Veranda** (239-332-2065; 2122 Second St., Fort Myers 33902), which specializes in southern charm and fine cuisine.

Much of what's special about the Island Coast has to do with what's wild. Half of Sanibel Island is devoted to the **J. N. "Ding" Darling National Wildlife Refuge** (239-472-1100; 1 Wildlife Dr., Sanibel Island 33957; off Sanibel-Captiva Rd.), home to alligators, roseate spoonbills, manatees, river otters, and bobcats. The best way to see it is by canoe or kayak from **Tarpon Bay Recreation** (239-472-8900; 900 Tarpon Bay Rd., Sanibel Island 33957).

Sanibel's beaches are renowned for their bountiful shells and minimal impact on nature's birthright beauty. Most natural and secluded is **Bowman's Beach** (Bowman's Beach Rd. off Sanibel-Captiva Rd.). To find the utmost in remote beaches, rent a boat or hop a charter to unbridged **LaCosta Island** and **Upper Captiva Island**, where state parks preserve slices of Old Florida.

For lively beaching, follow **Route 865** through Estero Island's Fort Myers Beach and down along lovely, undeveloped Lover's Key en route to Bonita Beach. On the way you'll pass bustling resort scenes and quiet island vistas.

South Coast

To explore the highbrow face of Naples and its environs, stop for afternoon tea at **The Ritz-Carlton** (239-598-3300; 800-241-3333; 2 Vanderbilt Beach Rd., Naples 34108) and take in a concert and art stroll at the **Naples Philharmonic** (239-597-1900, 800-597-1900; 5833 Pelican Bay Blvd., Naples

34104) and the new **Naples Museum of Art** next door (239-597-1900; 5833 Pelican Bay Blvd., Naples 34104). Downtown's **Fifth Avenue South** has evolved into a fashionable shopping and sidewalk dining district. Try **Annabelle's** (239-261-4275; 494 Fifth Ave. S., Naples 34102) for an example of the latest in Naples's cutting-edge chic.

To really have experienced Naples, you must do sunset at the **Naples Pier** (12th. Ave. S.). It's a nightly ritual for fishermen, strollers, lovers, and pelicans. By day the pier is the center of activity along a beach that stretches for miles.

My favorite part of Marco Island is **Goodland**. A little fishing village on "pause," it serves fresh seafood and country fun in its restaurants and introduces the unruly flavor of **Ten Thousand Islands** and the **Florida Everglades.**

Everglades City is headquarters for tours that explore this labyrinthine land down under. **Everglades National Park** (239-695-2591, 800-445-7724 (in Florida) Everglades Ranger Station, Everglades City) has a base here, conducts boat tours, and rents canoes for launching into the 98-mile **Wilderness Trail.**

Gulf Coast Florida time is kept by tides and the sun.

Karen T. Bartlett

Index

LODGING BY PRICE CODE

Price Codes:
Inexpensive   Up to $75
Moderate $75 to $150
Expensive $150 to $200
Very Expensive $200 and up

CHARLOTTE HARBOR COAST

Inexpensive
Banana Bay Waterfront Motel, 124

Inexpensive–Expensive
Weston's Resort, 123

Moderate
Fishermen's Village Villas, 124
Gilchrist B&B, 125
The Innlet, 122

Expensive–Very Expensive
Gasparilla Inn, 121
Palm Island Resort, 122

Very Expensive
Manasota Beach Club, 123

NAPLES & THE SOUTH COAST

Inexpensive–Moderate
Ivey House B&B, 237
Rod & Gun Club, 238

Inexpensive–Expensive
The Boat House, 239
Cove Inn, 240
Inn by the Sea, 242
Lemon Tree Inn, 242

Moderate–Very Expensive
Inn on Fifth, 242
Ramada at Port of the Islands, 238
Trianon Bonita Bay, 237
Vanderbilt Inn, 245

Expensive–Very Expensive
The Edgewater Beach Hotel, 241
Hotel Escalante, 241

Inn on Fifth, 242
Marco Island Marriott Resort & Golf Club, 240
Naples Beach Hotel & Golf Club, 243
Radisson Suite Beach Resort, 240

Very Expensive
The Registry Resort, 243
The Ritz-Carlton, 244

SANIBEL ISLAND & THE ISLAND COAST

Inexpensive–Moderate
Bridge Water Inn, 163
Casa Loma Motel, 159
Holiday Inn Sunspree Resort, 161

Moderate
The Beach & Tennis Club, 158
Ramada Inn & Suites at Amtel Marina, 161

Moderate–Expensive
Cabbage Key Inn, 158
Island Inn, 164
Jensen's Twin Palm Cottages & Marina, 159
Silver Sands Villas, 163

Moderate–Very Expensive
The Grand View, 162
Gulf Breeze Cottages and Motel, 164
The Outrigger Beach Resort, 163
Sanibel's Seaside Inn, 165

Expensive–Very Expensive
Sanibel Harbour Resort & Spa, 161
South Seas Resort, 160
Sundial Beach Resort, 165
'Tween Waters Inn, 160

Very Expensive
Collier Inn, 166

SARASOTA BAY COAST

Inexpensive–Moderate
Rod & Reel Motel, 43

DINING BY PRICE CODE

DINING BY CUISINE

About the Author

Chelle Koster Walton came to visit a friend on Sanibel Island in 1981. She's still there. As a writer, she specializes in Florida and Caribbean travel, food, and culture. She is author of *Florida*, a Fodor Compass America guide; *Fun for the Family in Florida*; Frommer's *Best Beach Vacations: Florida*; *Adventure Guide to Florida's West Coast*; and *Florida Island Hopping: The West Coast*. Her *Caribbean Ways: A Cultural Guide* and *Hidden Florida* have both won awards in Lowell Thomas Travel Journalism competitions for Best Guidebook. She has coauthored *Florida*, Frommer's America on Wheels series guide, and Reader's Digest's *Wild Kingdoms*. A member of the Society of American Travel Writers, Walton is contributing editor for *Caribbean Travel and Life*. Her work has appeared in, among other publications, *Family.Fun*, *National Geographic Traveler*, *Endless Vacation*, and the *New York Post*.